AF696705

Accountants' Legal Responsibility

By Saul Levy

CPA and Member of the New York Bar

With a Collection of Leading Cases and Articles

1954

AMERICAN INSTITUTE OF ACCOUNTANTS

270 Madison Avenue New York 16, N. Y.

Copyright, 1954.
AMERICAN INSTITUTE OF ACCOUNTANTS, NEW YORK.

FOREWORD

This volume developed as a result of the interest shown by readers of Chapter 6 of the "CPA Handbook," on the legal responsibility and civil liability of certified public accountants. That chapter referred to various American and English court cases and included numerous quotations therefrom. This has suggested the practical value of reprinting these judicial opinions, for the most part in their entirety, so that practicing accountants might explore the subject further without the need for searching for this material in a law library.

Familiarity with the facts and the law involved in these cases will serve to give the accountant a much better understanding of the legal responsibility inherent in the practice of public accountancy. The resulting awareness of the hazards which have arisen in the past should equip the accountant to avoid such difficulties in the future.

The full text of the chapter in the "CPA Handbook" is reprinted in slightly re-arranged form as a further convenience to the reader.

I wish to extend my thanks to Alan F. McHenry, director of the Legal Department of the American Institute of Accountants, and to Irving Novick, member of the Editorial Board of the New York University Law Review, for their assistance in connection with the editing and compilation of the collection of cases.

S. L.

New York, New York
September 1954

TABLE OF CONTENTS

Part One

AN ANALYTICAL SURVEY

Part Two

CASES AND ARTICLES

TABLE OF CASES

(Boldface indicates page of full reprint or excerpt)

PART ONE

An Analytical Survey

CHAPTER 1

FUNDAMENTAL CONSIDERATIONS

There are certain fundamental considerations with which the accountant is confronted. Some of these matters apply in general to practitioners in all professional fields, and some have special importance and special emphasis only in relation to accounting activities.

This preliminary phase will be approached from the following four angles:

1. Certified public accountants are members of a skilled and learned profession and as such are subject generally to the same responsibilities as members of other skilled professions.
2. Public accountancy is a relatively new profession, the status of which has been growing steadily in importance in these recent decades of dynamic economic change.
3. The nature of accounting services has an important relation to questions of legal responsibility.
4. Numerous parties other than clients often rely upon the opinions of accountants.

Members of a Skilled Profession

The general principles affecting the responsibilities of members of learned professions, and, for that matter, the responsibility of anyone who undertakes employment because of his possession of exceptional skill, have been concisely summarized in Cooley's *Torts,* which is nearly always quoted as the primary authority on this subject. So many essential aspects of the accountant's problem are here touched upon that the quotation itself bears repetition:

> In all those employments where peculiar skill is requisite, if one offers his services, he is understood as holding himself out to the public as possessing the degree of skill commonly possessed by others in the same employment, and if his pretensions are unfounded, he commits a species of fraud upon every man who employs him in reliance on his public profession. But no man, whether skilled or unskilled, undertakes that the task he assumes shall be performed successfully, and without fault or error; he undertakes for good faith and integrity, but not for infallibility, and he is liable to his employer for negligence, bad faith, or dishonesty, but not for losses consequent upon mere errors of judgment.[1]

1. 3 COOLEY, TORTS 335 (4th ed. 1932).

The relatively recent Restatement of the Law of Torts, (1938) in discussing negligent misrepresentations, comments upon "expectable care and competence" in the following language:

> Where the information concerns a fact not known to the recipient, he is entitled to expect that the supplier will exercise that care and competence in its ascertainment which the supplier's business or profession requires and which, therefore, the supplier professes to have by engaging in it. . . . Where the information consists of an opinion upon facts supplied by the recipient or otherwise known to him, the recipient is entitled to expect a careful consideration of the facts and competence in arriving at an intelligent judgment thereon.[2]

These principles have long been applied to public accountants in jurisdictions abroad where the accounting profession has an older history and where the principles of common law govern. In the United States, as early as 1905, there was specific judicial recognition "that public accountants now constitute a skilled professional class, and are subject generally to the same rules of liability for negligence in the practice of their profession as are members of other skilled professions."[3]

Certified public accountants have always recognized their professional responsibility for care and competence in the performance of their work. However, the precise boundaries of civil liability have posed many practical problems as well as highly technical legal questions, many of which will be dealt with in this chapter. The general attitude of the profession in the relatively early years of its growth and development was set forth by J. E. Sterrett, in a paper read at the annual meeting of the American Economic Association in 1908, from which the following is quoted:

> It must be borne in mind that a balance sheet of any large corporation is not a statement of facts that can be demonstrated with mathematical accuracy so much as it is an expression of an honest and intelligent opinion. In this expression of opinion the public accountant is now being recognized as an authority, and what is being widely done through the voluntary action of corporations that desire to deal fairly with their investors will doubtless become a legal requirement, and before many years the independent audit of all corporations offering their securities to the public will be firmly established.
>
> With this, or possibly preceding it, will also come a civil liability on the part of the accountant for the faithful and diligent performance of his duties. As yet there are no decisions in this country upon the question of the liability of an auditor, but under the English law his liability both civil and criminal is pretty well established. . . .
>
> Civil liability on the part of the accountant is, I believe, certain to come in this country, and while each member of the profession may well pray that the offense shall not come by him, it is, nevertheless, true that the effect of a clearly defined civil liability will be salutary. It will give confidence

2. 3 RESTATEMENT, Torts § 552, comment c (1938).

3. Smith v. London Assurance Corp., 109 App. Div. 882, 96 N.Y. Supp. 820 (2d Dep't 1905). Reprinted at p. 71 *infra*.

> to the business public in the accountant's certificate as nothing else will do, and while the best accountants to-day recognize their moral responsibility quite as much as it will ever be necessary for them to recognize any legal responsibility, the knowledge that a civil and possibly a criminal liability attaches to them will deter the careless or the indifferent.[4]

This statement by one of the most distinguished leaders in the accounting profession is remarkable for its prophetic anticipation of the present Federal regulation of securities and the vital role of public accountancy in connection with it. It also expresses a positive and constructive acceptance of legal responsibility growing out of the work which accountants do, an attitude which is as relevant to the accounting profession today as it was when expressed. It recognizes the fact that civil liability is a normal aspect of professional status and that being subject to it is an inevitable attribute of the development of the profession. It follows that the accountant's understanding of the problem is an essential part of his educational equipment for the performance of his technical functions.

Public Accountancy, a Relatively New Profession

When speaking of public accountancy as a learned profession it must be realized that in this country, at any rate, it is a relatively new profession, one, however, which has been steadily growing in importance and usefulness in these recent decades of dynamic economic change. All of this has been so generally recognized in the business community that it hardly requires documentation.[5]

Legal precedents involving public accountants in the United States are relatively few and are closely tied up with the facts involved in each situation and with the then existing practices of the profession. Even at this date, the standards are still in a state of development and clarification. As members of a skilled profession, it is the right of every accountant to be judged by the standards of the accounting profession. Correlatively, it is the duty of the accountant to establish and clarify these standards, not only for the public but for themselves. Otherwise, standards not of their own making will be imposed upon them.[6]

Expanding opportunities to serve inevitably create broader responsibilities. This has been recognized in the continuing drive within the profession to measure up to growing obligations. Without further elaboration, the following lines of endeavor have been followed:

---

4. Sterrett, *The Present Position and Probable Development of Accountancy as a Profession*, 7 JOURNAL OF ACCOUNTANCY 272 (1909).

5. Brundage, *Milestones on the Path of Accounting*, 29 HARVARD BUSINESS REVIEW 71 (1951); Brundage, *Roadblocks in the Path of Accounting*, 29 HARVARD BUSINESS REVIEW, 110 (1951).

6. Levy, *Accountants' Liability*, WARTIME ACCOUNTING 146 (papers presented at the 55th annual meeting of the American Institute of Accountants 1942). Reprinted at p. 72 *infra*.

1. The movement for obtaining legislative recognition and control of our professional activities has already resulted in CPA laws in all forty-eight states.[7] The accountant should continue to seek improvement of these laws, based upon judgment and experience. In many states there has been a transition from the permissive type of legislation to a form of regulatory statute which places accountants in a status more closely comparable to that of the medical and legal professions.
2. The development of higher educational standards and techniques for a professional career in accountancy, and the contemporaneous lifting of educational requirements for admission to the profession.
3. The development, acceptance and enforcement of a code of ethical conduct consistent with professional ideals and essential for the protection of the public interest. While this is a usual feature in the case of the regulatory type of statute, there is a trend to provide for an enforceable code of professional conduct in permissive statutes as well. In 1952, a statute of this latter type was enacted in the State of New York.
4. The growth in size, influence and effectiveness of professional societies devoted to the clarification and codification of ethical and technical standards and the extension of the usefulness of the profession in terms of the public interest. The expanding program of the American Institute of Accountants is addressed toward these objectives. More than twenty thousand members are co-operating actively in this endeavor.

The Nature of Accounting Services

Although accountants render many other types of services, it is chiefly the auditing work which differentiates the problem of legal responsibility from that of other professions. Accountants review, examine into, and consider the factual representations of management or others, and report thereon in the form of a professional opinion (where the accountant so believes) that the statements of management fairly present financial position and results of operations.

The accountant's responsibility is for the expression of a professional opinion in accordance with generally accepted accounting principles as the result of an examination conducted in accordance with generally accepted auditing standards.[8] The accountant does *not* make factual representations as to the content of financial statements; that is the function of management. He does *not* insure, guarantee, or warrant the accuracy of management's representations, which in turn include matters of estimate, judgment and opinion. He does assume responsibility for his own opinions, and represents, that in order to place himself in a position to express such opinions, he has complied with generally accepted auditing standards,[9] which provide for:

---

7. *Accountancy Law Reporter* (Commerce Clearing House) gives full text of all legislation for states, territories and the District of Columbia.

8. Accounting Series Release No. 62, Securities and Exchange Commission, Washington, 1947.

9. Tentative Statement of Auditing Standards, American Institute of Accountants, 1947; Codification of Statements on Auditing Procedure, American Institute of Accountants, 1951.

1. *An expert opinion* — implying adequate technical training, proficiency and due care in the performance of the audit;
2. *An independent opinion* — the result of an objective, impartial, and unbiased mental attitude;
3. *An informed opinion* — the result of a proper study and evaluation of internal control as a basis for reliance thereon and for determining the extent of tests in the application of auditing procedures; and based upon competent evidential matter sufficient to supply a reasonable basis for the expression of an auditor's opinion;
4. *A technical opinion* — that the statements are presented in accordance with generally accepted principles of accounting applied on a basis consistent with that of the previous year;
5. *A candid opinion* — that the financial statements are reasonably informative as to all material facts, unless otherwise stated.

Parties Other Than Our Clients Often Rely Upon Accountant's Opinions

In many instances the opinions which are expressed and the reports which embody such opinions reach innumerable interested parties other than the clients by whom the accountant has been engaged. The occasional claims of such "third parties" against accountants have raised some difficult problems of legal responsibility. Some of the leading cases dealing with such claims will be dealt with in considerable detail later in this text.

The potential and largely undefined duty under the common law to third parties has led to statutory rules of civil liability to investors, which go far beyond the limitations of the common law in such matters as duty, proof of reliance and burden of proof as to negligence or fraud.

It is in this area particularly that the accountant must realize the growing need for informing the public as to the nature of the services rendered and the standards by which such services should be judged.

CHAPTER 2

LIABILITY TO CLIENTS

In order to obtain a better understanding of possible civil liability, both to clients and to third parties, it is helpful to draw upon decided cases which may serve as legal precedents in future situations.

With respect to clients, there is a contractual relationship which is the foundation of the accountants' responsibilities and rights. This contract may be formalized in a very explicit writing. More than likely, however, if a writing exists, it is apt to be very general in its terms, setting out little more than the period to be covered, the arrangement concerning fees, with a statement that an audit is to be made in accordance with generally accepted auditing standards. Compliance with such standards ordinarily would be implied even if not expressly included in the writing. In this regard, recent literature of the American Institute of Accountants[10], serves a most useful function in defining the nature and content of what the accountant undertakes to do in making the usual audit which is to culminate in the expression of an opinion on financial position and operating results. Not so long ago, it was often an open question as to whether a so-called cash audit, a balance sheet audit, a detailed audit or some other variety of examination was contemplated. Not only was the accountant lax in definitely confirming the scope of his work at the outset of an engagement, but there was great variety and often little clarity in the form of certificate or opinion that was issued at the end of the engagement.[11] When the public accountant became involved in litigation concerning his work, the heart of the controversy often related to what he had agreed to do. Courts were inclined to take the accountant to task if he had failed to be explicit in his engagement writing. This judicial attitude is illustrated in the following admonition by the court in the case of *Maryland Casualty Co. v. Jonathon Cook*[12], where the court said:

> I think that it is high time for accountants to know that if they want a particular contract which they enter into to be measured in the technical

10. See note 9 *supra* and the following publications of the American Institute of Accountants: *Accounting Research Bulletins; Case Studies in Auditing Procedure;* and AUDITS BY CERTIFIED PUBLIC ACCOUNTANTS, 1950.

11. Levy, *The Legal Liability of Public Accountants in its Relation to a Standard Classification of Accounting Services,* 12 CERTIFIED PUBLIC ACCOUNTANT 695 (1932). Reprinted at p. 81 *infra*.

12. 35 F. Supp. 160 (E.D. Mich. 1940). Reprinted at p. 84 *infra*.

terms of a cash audit, or a balance sheet audit, or a detailed audit, they should insist that their contract and the specifications which they agree to comply with in their contract should plainly state the facts.

So I interpret this contract with its specifications according to the plain language used.

The witnesses have all agreed that no technical terms or language has been used in either the contract or the specifications. Ordinary, everyday English has been used. It is easily understood and interpreted. *If accountants wish a contract construed in accordance with their own technical language, then they must see to it that their technical language is used in their contracts.* (Emphasis added)[13]

This case dealt with an audit of the accounts of a municipal treasurer where the engagement had been accepted subject to "specifications for audit" which had been prepared by the client, which provided, among other things, that "any other duties or procedures which ordinarily become a part of a complete audit although not specifically stated herein shall be deemed a part of these specifications." The defendant-accountant sought to construe the vague expression "complete audit" in terms of the more technical concepts of a cash audit, a balance sheet audit, or a combination of the two. Such efforts were unavailing for the reason stated above. There was a further attempt by the defendant to construe the audit contract in the light of prior conversations and instructions. The court disposed of this effort in the following manner:

The defendant, Jonathon Cook testified that on receiving these specifications and on reading the specifications, he did not know just what work was required to be performed for the City of Flint and so he went to the City of Flint and had a talk with the Director of Finance and thereafter entered into the contract in reliance upon that conversation had prior to the execution of the contract. The conversation with the Director of Finance does not mean a thing. The contract was with the City of Flint and not with the Director of Finance. It is the contract which Jonathon Cook made with the City of Flint which must be construed and not conversations or oral agreements reached with independent officers of the City prior to the execution of the contract. Those prior conversations, in order to become binding, should have been embodied in the written contract and signed pursuant to proper authority. Therefore, the court has no alternative but to hold this defendant to performance in accordance with the terms of his written contract. Restatement, Contracts, Sec. 237.[14]

This case emphasizes the need for being explicit if the accountant is to rely upon technical terms and technical concepts in defining the scope of his duty. Obviously the use of such vague terms as "complete audit" or "detailed audit" must be avoided. If technical terms such as "generally accepted auditing standards" are used the security of the accountant's position depends upon the extent to which such terms have been clarified by accountants in their own practices and in the literature of the account-

13. *Id.* at 164–165.
14. *Id.* at 165.

ing profession. While established standards of today [15] afford substantially better grounds for reliance than they did during the years 1931–1932 (which were involved in the above quoted case) it is important to realize that the situation has improved only relatively. Accountants must continue to develop and clarify their own standards so that they may be judged by professional criteria of their own making and not by the factual findings of juries of laymen.

Another fairly recent case which involved construction of a contract for audit services was that of *O'Neill v. Atlas Automobile Finance Corp.*[16] Here the firm of certified public accountants contended that their contract was for a limited examination and a financial review of the client's books without verification. The client contended that the engagement "contemplated the making of a complete and detailed audit and the furnishing of certified reports which should have uncovered the shortage" here involved. It was admitted that the original retainer had been under an oral contract. The accountants testified that it was not agreed or contemplated that "certified reports" would be issued and in support of their testimony offered the letters of transmittal of their reports which used this phraseology:

> We have prepared *from the records* of Atlas Automobile Finance Corporation and *information* submitted to us a balance sheet as of (designated month and year) and a comparative statement of profit and loss based on the month of (name of month) together with relating schedules. (Italics by Court)

When the accountants were re-engaged, the extent of their undertaking was set forth by them in a letter to the client which was accepted by it as satisfactory. The letter read, in part:

> Confirming our recent conversation we agree . . . *to make a monthly examination of the transactions and submit monthly reports in substantially the same form as heretofore. . . .* (Italics by Court)

The accountants produced an expert witness who corroborated their own testimony with respect to the difference between "an ordinary audit and report and a certified one verified from independent sources." The client offered no expert testimony to contradict that offered by the accountants. Because the contract was partly oral and partly written and its terms were disputed, the trial court submitted the question of its construction to the jury. The jury accepted the accountants' version of the terms of the audit contract and the nature of the accountants' duties under it. Incidentally, the appellate court confirmed the charge to the jury on the following points, citing Cooley's *Torts* [17] as one of the supporting authorities:

> Magee, Liebman, and O'Neill, as accountants, are not guarantors or insurers of the correctness of their accounts.

15. Smith, *Written Contract With Client Should Not Be Necessary to Define Audit Engagement,* 93 JOURNAL OF ACCOUNTANCY 210 (1952).

16. 139 Pa. Super. 346, 11 A.2d 782 (1940). Reprinted at p. 95 *infra.*

17. See note 1 *supra.*

Magee, Liebman and O'Neill as accountants, do not say to the public "Let us examine your books and vouchers, and we will with absolute certainty discover any dishonesty, every mistake, that exists in those books, and we will protect you against that." That is not what they undertook to do. They agreed to use such skill in the performance of their agreement as reasonably prudent, skillful accountants would use under the circumstances.

The result in this case, in comparison with that in the *Maryland Casualty Company* case,[18] does not support a conclusion that the accountant is likely to be better off with an oral agreement than with a detailed contract specifying particular procedures. The weakness of the accountant's position in the *Maryland Casualty Company* case was that there was an omnibus provision which used the vague term "complete audit."

Had the more technical phraseology "generally accepted auditing standards" been used, the court doubtless would have given greater weight to technical literature and expert testimony as an aid to the interpretation of the contract. Of special interest in the *O'Neill* case are the facts that there was a course of conduct in performing prior audits which was continued by specific reference in the letter of arrangements with the client, and there was further confirmation of the client's acceptance of the scope of prior audits in the letters of transmittal which were an integral part of the audit reports. All of this was persuasive corroboration of the testimony of the accountant as to the limited scope of his engagement.

In this branch of the subject, namely the accountant's possible liability to clients, the claims usually are based upon the failure of the auditor to discover defalcations or other similar irregularities. It may be the client who presses the claim. It may be a surety company that is the plaintiff, having been subrogated to the rights of the client upon payment of a loss under the terms of a fidelity bond.

Where it is claimed that the accountant was negligent in the performance of his duty, and that the loss occasioned by the dishonesty of the client's employee or agent went undiscovered and unrecovered because of that negligence, the controversy concerning the accountant's work usually raises these basic factual questions:

1. What was the scope of the audit for which the accountant was engaged and which he agreed to make?
2. Was the negligent conduct of that audit responsible for the failure to uncover the defalcations and for the resulting loss?
3. Were there circumstances present which aroused or should have aroused the suspicion of the accountant and should have resulted in a more searching inquiry than would have been obligatory in the absence of suspicious circumstances?

The responsibility of the accountant in this situation is limited necessarily to the competent performance of the audit which he has been en-

18. See note 12 *supra*.

gaged to make. This usually involves compliance with generally accepted auditing standards. The accountant does not insure or guarantee the client against loss through the dishonesty of his employees, nor does he warrant that the audit will uncover any and every irregularity. The audit is nevertheless likely to safeguard the client against dishonest manipulation of his accounts. Such protection to the client might well result from the work of the auditor in reviewing the system of internal accounting control and suggesting needed improvements therein. An audit will deter dishonest practices because, from the culprit's viewpoint, it enlarges the danger of discovery. Very often an audit results in the actual discovery and exposure of dishonest practices when they do occur. All of these advantages to the client are substantial and add measurably to the value of an audit. They should not be minimized in any of the discussions of the limitations of the accountant's responsibility. On the other hand, it should be recognized that in the usual audit the primary purpose is not the discovery of defalcations but rather the expression of a professional opinion concerning financial position and operating results. The audit program involves a judicious amount of testing and sampling. It does not contemplate an all-inclusive detailed examination of all transactions and all entries with respect thereto. Thus it is not intended or designed for the purpose of uncovering or preventing all conceivable irregularities in the accounts. It should be accepted and relied upon for what it is, an examination not unlimited in scope but adequate for the purpose of expressing an opinion concerning financial position and operating results. All this has been summarized recently by the committee on auditing procedure of the Institute, as follows:

> The well-established custom of making test checks of accounting records and related data and, beyond that, relying upon the system of internal control after investigation, through appropriate checks, of its adequacy and effective functioning, has with very few exceptions proved sufficient for the purpose of expressing an opinion.
>
> The ordinary examination incident to the issuance of an opinion respecting financial statements is not designed and *cannot be relied upon* to disclose defalcations and other similar irregularities, although their discovery frequently results. In a well-organized concern reliance for the detection of such irregularities is placed principally upon the maintenance of an adequate system of accounting records with appropriate internal control. If an auditor were to attempt to discover defalcations and similar irregularities he would have to extend his work to a point where its cost would be prohibitive. It is generally recognized that good internal control and surety bonds provide protection much more cheaply. On the basis of his examination by tests and checks, made in the light of his review and tests of the system of internal control, the auditor relies upon the integrity of the client's organization unless circumstances are such as to arouse his suspicion, in which case he must extend his procedures to determine whether or not such suspicions are justified.
>
> In no sense is the independent certified public accountant an insurer or guarantor, nor do his training and experience qualify him to act as a

> general appraiser, valuer, or expert in materials. Obviously his functions do not include matters of law which require the judgment of an attorney.[19]

The foregoing is implied in the standard short-form of accountant's report or certificate which defines the scope of the audit in the following general terms:

> Our examination was made in accordance with generally accepted auditing standards, and accordingly included such tests of the accounting records and such other auditing procedures as we considered necessary in the circumstances.

It should be noted, however, that while the report or opinion of the accountant is always evidence of what he understood the scope of his audit to be, and while it is always evidence of what was the client contract, it is not necessarily conclusive evidence. Unless confirmed by a writing signed by the client, either in the form of a letter of arrangements before the commencement of the audit or included in the letter of representations of the client at the conclusion of the audit, it would be a self-serving document which the client might dispute. Of course, it also might be confirmed by a continuous course of conduct over a series of prior years when the same type of audit had been made, reported upon in the same way, and the reports had been accepted by the client. This is what happened in the *O'Neill* case[20] mentioned previously.

There has recently been some difference of opinion among leading accountants as to whether there is adequate protection for the accountant against unfair claims for failure to discover defalcations unless the limited responsibility of the accountant in this area has been defined and confirmed in an explicit written contract signed by the client. Some accountants have gone so far as to state specifically in letters to clients outlining the conditions under which an engagement is accepted, "that their examination cannot be relied on to disclose defalcations and other irregularities of the same general nature, and they therefore do not assume responsibility for detecting such irregularities."[21]

Other accountants have felt that a disclaimer, so worded, is too broad and unqualified, and consequently it might reflect unfavorably on the value of the ordinary audit. They would contend that our position should be that such examinations cannot be relied upon to disclose *all* defalcations, and that therefore the accountant does not assume responsibility for detecting irregularities where he has complied with generally accepted auditing standards and the irregularities have nevertheless remained undiscovered. Furthermore, while it may be desirable to have a written agreement or letter of arrangements confirmed by the client, it is argued

19. CODIFICATION OF STATEMENTS ON AUDITING PROCEDURE, American Institute of Accountants, 1951, p. 12.
20. See note 16 *supra.*
21. *Independent Audits and Defalcations,* 91 JOURNAL OF ACCOUNTANCY 387 (1951).

that it should not be considered mandatory to have such a letter. In many instances, the audit engagement is renewed from year to year in a more or less informal manner. The scope of the examination is evidenced by a continuous course of conduct by the accountant and the acceptance of his work by the client on the basis of the representations concerning the scope of the audit as set forth in the standard short-form certificate or opinion. The practice with respect to formalizing the audit contract varies to such an extent that the preferences of those who consider an explicit written client contract desirable should not, by implication, leave unprotected the accountant who chooses to place his chief reliance upon our professional standards and his compliance with them. The latter viewpoint is discussed fully in a recent article which quotes many relevant statements from authoritative literature and concludes with the following:

> It should be evident to all thinking people that the work of the independent public accountant is not intended to take the place of, or duplicate the protection afforded by, a system of internal control supplemented by various types of dishonesty insurance. The fact that accountants have an understandable fear of the publicity resulting from legal action may have motivated those who have suffered losses from defalcations and similar irregularities to threaten suit against an accountant who did not assume responsibility for discovery of the losses. Such tactics should be resisted by the profession. A written contract with each client, however, does not go to the root of the problem. In any case, the problem seems to call for a uniform position on the part of the profession, and the above citations would appear to mean that the profession has taken a position which it has repeatedly and consistently promulgated in its authoritative statements of auditing procedure. If further clarification seems desirable, the place for that clarification is in our published statements defining generally accepted auditing standards. These standards are the yardstick of our professional responsibility and for this reason are specifically incorporated in our opinions. Our contractual relations with clients as well as our third party responsibility will, in any event, depend upon our adherence to our generally accepted auditing standards.[22]

It should be added, however, that in any situation where there are limitations upon the scope of the ordinary audit, such as the requested omission of the independent confirmation of receivables or the omission of the usual procedures with respect to observation and checking of inventory, it is without doubt advisable to confirm such limitations in a writing which is countersigned or acknowledged by the client. If the engagement contemplates the preparation of statements without audit, obviously it is advantageous, if not altogether necessary, to reduce such an engagement to some explicit form.

In Great Britain there is the distinction between the type of audit which the accountant is required to make to fulfill his obligations under the

22. Smith, *Written Contract With Client Should Not Be Necessary to Define Audit Engagement,* 93 JOURNAL OF ACCOUNTANCY 213 (1952).

Companies Act as against the varying types of work he may be engaged to perform for so-called private companies. There it is urged that in the latter situations an explicit client contract is essential. This warning was repeated in a recent edition of one of the leading English texts on The Principles of Auditing, where it was stated:

> In the case of a company, the auditor's responsibilities are governed by statute, and it is impossible for the auditor to limit his responsibilities. In the case of a private concern, the auditor's responsibilities are governed by the terms of the contract with his client and therefore his responsibilities can be limited by agreement, but in practice it is feared that in many cases there is no written evidence of the exact terms of the contract. This position is fraught with grave danger, and in every case the practitioner is strongly advised to see that the exact terms of the contract are clearly understood by both his client and himself, and that these terms are recorded in writing.
>
> In the event of a loss through fraud occurring and remaining undetected by the auditor he may be placed in a position of grave difficulty. It is easy to be wise after the event and to see what audit tests must have revealed the fraud. On the other hand it is so difficult to define exactly what is reasonable care and skill, which is governed by the general standard of the profession. In a case before the courts expert evidence would be called, but here again the expert would have knowledge of the exact form the fraud took, and it is therefore very easy to see what checks should have been applied in order to detect the fraud and to form the opinion that one would without question have adopted them.[23]

English Cases

Although adjudicated cases in the courts of the United States involving claims of clients against accountants are limited in number, they are of great significance. The earlier English cases supply important legal background and have usually been cited as authority in the opinions of American judges. These English cases are quite numerous and go back more than sixty years. Apparently the profession in Great Britain has directed considerable attention to these precedents. This is reflected by the fact that Dicksee's *Auditing,* the leading English text, in its seventeenth edition, published in 1951, assigns almost three hundred pages of fine print to a collection of some fifty-seven cases, reprinting most of the opinions in full. Numerous other cases are referred to and discussed elsewhere in the text. Apparently the British practitioner considers this source material an indispensable part of his technical equipment.

Those English cases which deal with claims arising out of defalcations add little, if anything, to the law established by our own leading cases. For the most part, the English cases deal with the responsibilities of accountants functioning under the authority and jurisdiction of the English Companies Act. In such situations, the accountant is held to be an officer

23. DEPAULA, THE PRINCIPLES OF AUDITING 244 (11th ed. 1951).

of the corporation and is responsible as such to its stockholders. This relationship, of course, is technically different from that assumed by the auditor of the accounts of a corporation in the United States, even of a corporation whose stock is publicly held and traded in on a stock exchange. However, since the enactment of the Federal Securities Act of 1933 and the Federal Securities Exchange Act of 1934, statutory obligations have been imposed upon the independent accountant (to be considered later in this chapter) which make some of these English cases significant in relation to our possible liability to investors. This is all the more so in view of the absence of adjudicated cases under our own statutes.

Some of the pronouncements of the English cases concerning their understanding of the responsibilities of public accountants have been cited so frequently that they have acquired the status of classic utterances. Thus, in 1895, it was said of the auditor in the famous *London and General Bank* case: [24]

> His business is to ascertain and state the true financial position of the company at the time of the audit, and his duty is confined to that. But then comes the question: How is he to ascertain such position? The answer is, by examining the books of the company. But he does not discharge his duty by doing this without inquiry and without taking any trouble to see that the books themselves shew the company's true position. He must take reasonable care to ascertain that they do. Unless he does this his audit would be worse than an idle farce . . . An auditor, however, is not bound to do more than exercise reasonable care and skill in making inquiries and investigations. He is not an insurer; he does not guarantee that the books do correctly shew the true position of the company's affairs, he does not guarantee that his balance sheet is accurate according to the books of the company. If he did, he would be responsible for error on his part, even if he were himself deceived without any want of reasonable care on his part, say, by the fraudulent concealment of a book from him. His obligation is not so onerous as this. Such I take to be the duty of the auditor; he must be honest—i.e., he must not certify what he does not believe to be true, and he must take reasonable care and skill before he believes that what he certifies is true. What is reasonable care in any particular case must depend upon the circumstances of that case. Where there is nothing to excite suspicion very little inquiry will be reasonably sufficient, and in practice I believe business men select a few cases at haphazard, see that they are right, and assume that others like them are correct also. Where suspicion is aroused more care is obviously necessary; but, still, an auditor is not bound to exercise more than reasonable care and skill, even in a case of suspicion, and he is perfectly justified in acting on the opinion of an expert where special knowledge is required. . . .
>
> . . . A person whose duty it is to convey information to others does not discharge that duty by simply giving them so much information as is calculated to induce them, or some of them, to ask for more. Information and means of information are by no means equivalent terms. . . . [A]n auditor who gives shareholders means of information instead of information respecting a com-

24. *In re* London and General Bank, [1895] 2 Ch. 673 (C.A.), 21 Acct. L. R. 173, DICKSEE'S AUDITING 584 (17th ed. 1951). Reprinted at p. 100 *infra*.

> pany's financial position does so at his peril and runs the very serious risk of being held judicially to have failed to discharge his duty.[25]

This was followed shortly thereafter by the *Kingston Cotton Mill Co.* case [26] which exonerated the accountants from responsibility concerning the independent verification of inventory and approved the accountants' acceptance of and reliance upon the management's certificate with respect thereto in the absence of circumstances which would arouse suspicion. This case is no longer an authority for American practictioners with respect to inventory verification, since it has been superseded by our own extensions of auditing procedure which impose mandatory obligations in this area. However, it will continue to be quoted as a basic authority for the reasonable limitations upon the responsibility of accountants where an audit has failed to uncover defalcations and other similar irregularities. In this connection it was there stated:

> It is the duty of an auditor to bring to bear on the work he has to perform that skill, care, and caution which a reasonably competent, careful and cautious auditor would use. What is reasonable skill, care and caution must depend on the particular circumstances of each case. An auditor is not bound to be a detective, or as was said, to approach his work with suspicion or with a foregone conclusion that there is something wrong. He is a watch-dog, but not a bloodhound. He is justified in believing tried servants of the company in whom confidence is placed by the company. He is entitled to assume that they are honest, and to rely upon their representations, provided he takes reasonable care. If there is anything calculated to excite suspicion he should probe it to the bottom; but in the absence of anything of that kind he is only bound to be reasonably cautious and careful.
>
> . . . Auditors must not be made liable for not tracking out ingenious and carefully laid schemes of fraud when there is nothing to arouse their suspicion, and when those frauds are perpetrated by tried servants of the company and are undetected for years by the directors. So to hold would make the position of an auditor intolerable.[27]

It remained for the Irish Court of Appeal in *The Irish Woollen Co. Ltd. v. Tyson* [28] to indicate how precarious it is to rely upon a figure of speech as a substitute for a more technical statement of legal principle, when it stated in discussing the foregoing quotation from the *Kingston Cotton Mill Co.* case:

> Now, time after time, this passage about the "watch-dog and the bloodhound" has been made use of, and I would wish to say a word regarding it, too. His lordship then read from Lord Justice Lindley's judgment the passages dealing with the duties of auditors, in one of which it was laid down that "an auditor was a watch-dog, but not a bloodhound." This, Lord Justice Fitz-

25. *Id.* at 682–685.

26. *In re* Kingston Cotton Mill Co., [1896] 2 Ch. 279 (C.A.), 22 Acct. L.R. 77, Dicksee's Auditing 598 (17th ed. 1951). Reprinted at p. 119 *infra*.

27. *Id.* at 288–290.

28. 26 Acct. L.R. 13 (1900) (Irish C.A.), Dicksee's Auditing 608 (17th ed. 1951). Reprinted at p. 122 *infra*.

gibbon remarked, was very unfair to the bloodhound, who was just as little likely to have his sense of suspicion aroused as the watch-dog. Applying this instance of the dogs to the present case, was not the watch-dog bound to bark? and if, when sniffing round, you hit upon a trail of something wrong, surely you must follow it up, and there is just as much obligation on the auditor, who is bound to keep his eyes open, and his nose, too. As in the case of the hound, the auditor will follow up this trail to the end, and the first things he will "root up" are those statements of account, and then the fraud is discovered.[29]

Attention will now be directed to outstanding American cases which have dealt with the responsibility of public accountants.

Craig v. Anyon [30]

The plaintiffs in this action were members of a firm of brokers in stocks and commodities operating on the New York, New Orleans and Chicago exchanges. Their accounts were audited by the defendant firm of accountants during the years 1913 to 1917, under an arrangement which provided for quarterly audits and reports. The business was apparently prosperous. In May 1917, through the confession of Moore, an employee in charge of their commodities department, following an office investigation, the plaintiffs learned that their prosperity had been an illusion. Their books had been falsified by Moore throughout a period of nearly five years during which time they had been defrauded of over one million dollars. In this action they alleged that the audits by defendants had been negligently made and that had the audits been made with reasonable care the falsification of the books would have been discovered and the losses would not have occurred.

The case was tried in May 1922 in the Supreme Court of New York County, before a jury, to whom were submitted the following two specific questions:

1. Were the defendants negligent in the performance of their agreement with Craig and Co.?
2. If so, what damages to the plaintiffs resulted directly and proximately from such negligence?

The trial judge charged that if the defendants were found to be liable, the verdict must be either for $2,000, the aggregate amount paid as compensation for the defendants' services, or for $1,177,805.26, the amount of plaintiffs' actual loss as proved. The jury found the accountants negligent and brought in a verdict for $1,177,805.26. Upon motion, the court then directed a general verdict for the plaintiffs in an amount limited to $2,000 "on the ground that as a matter of law the only loss which resulted

29. *Id.* at 17.

30. 212 App. Div. 55, 208 N.Y. Supp. 259 (1st Dep't 1925), *aff'd without opinion*, 242 N.Y. 569, 152 N.E. 431 (1926). Reprinted at p. 131 *infra*.

directly and proximately from negligence of the defendants was the sum of $2,000." Thereupon the case was carried on appeal to the Appellate Division, which affirmed the trial court. Three judges concurred in this result. The presiding justice dissented and set out his views in a short dissenting opinion, to which reference will be made later. The litigation was then carried to the Court of Appeals, the highest appellate tribunal, which in turn affirmed the judgment and the order of the Trial Court and the Appellate Division, without opinion, with a single judge again dissenting. This final decision on appeal was handed down in April, 1926.

Upon the trial the defense rested without offering evidence in its own behalf, thus limiting its own proof to the cross-examination of the witnesses produced by the plaintiffs. The chief issue in the case became the contributory negligence of the plaintiffs themselves. Did such negligence contribute predominantly or materially to the loss sustained, or were the damages the proximate result of the accountants' negligence? The accountants had been paid an annual fee of only $500 for four quarterly audits. There was no independent confirmation of customers' accounts nor was any attempt made to compute the status of the open contracts which would have been necessary in order to calculate the actual liability of customers at the time of each audit. Plaintiffs testified that many years before it had been agreed that the audit would include this work, as a member of the accounting firm himself had said: "We have to make that calculation both for straddles and open accounts before we can tell you what is the actual standing of the firm." The alleged arrangement was oral and the member of the accounting firm who made it was no longer living at the time of the trial. However, plaintiffs admitted that they were aware that these calculations had not been made by the accountants for many years nor during any part of the period when the defalcations occurred.

The losses arose in a single account in the commodities department. This was a discretionary account operated by Moore, who was in charge of the department. It had been started with a margin of only $200 with instructions that it be closed as soon as the losses exceeded that amount. These facts had not been communicated to the accountants nor did they become aware of them in the course of their audits. The accounting records relating to commodities were all kept in the commodities department and under the control of Moore. This had been done over the objections of the accountants, who protested that a certain ledger previously maintained in the general office was a check on this subsidiary commodities department and should not be transferred to it. The account involved was so active that it represented between 75% and 85% of the firm's Chicago commodities business. Between audit dates plaintiffs paid out large sums of money from day to day and executed orders from hour to hour without any investigation or examination of the account or check on the sufficiency of margin, relying implicitly upon the honesty of Moore. The Appellate Division found that the plaintiffs could have prevented the loss by the exercise of reasonable care and that "they should not have relied exclusively on the accountants." It was further stated:

> We think the damages cannot be said to flow naturally and directly from defendants' negligence or breach of contract. Plaintiffs should not be allowed to recover for losses which they could have avoided by the exercise of reasonable care. . . .
>
> The plaintiffs in effect contend that defendants are chargeable with negligence because of failure to detect Moore's wrongdoing, wholly overlooking the fact that, although they were closely affiliated with Moore, who was constantly under their supervision, they were negligent in failing properly to supervise his acts or to learn the true condition of their own business and to detect his wrongdoing.[31]

It should be noted that the Appellate Division *did* affirm the verdict of the jury that the accountants had been negligent in the performance of their audit. This was so in the face of the court's instructions to the jury that these auditors did not guarantee the correctness of their accounts; that they do not say to the public: "Let us examine your books and vouchers, and we will with absolute certainly discover any dishonesty, every mistake that exists in those books, and we will protect you against that"; that that is not what the auditors undertook to do; that they agreed to use "such skill in the performance of their agreements as reasonably prudent, skillful accountants would use under the circumstances".

In limiting the recovery of the client to the amount of the fees paid, the courts followed through on the theory that the client was damaged to that extent by the failure of the accountants to render competent services,[32] but that any additional losses were the result of the client's own negligence. However, a decision relieving the accountants from liability cannot be regarded as the inevitable result where contributory negligence is proved. The result in *Craig v. Anyon* must be confined to the extraordinary facts of this case, which nevertheless failed to impress the jury before whom the case was tried. The question as to what damage was proximately caused by the negligence of the accountants, as well as the question as to whether the contributory negligence of the plaintiffs was predominantly the cause of the damage, are ordinarily factual issues for the jury. All this was emphasized in the *National Surety Corporation* case which is about to be discussed.

31. *Id.* at 66–67, 208 N.Y. Supp. at 268–269.

32. Even in the absence of proof that the client suffered any other damage, if the audit report was one which involved defective performance on the part of the accountant, it has been held that the client was damaged to the extent of the fees paid. Board of County Comm'rs v. Baker, 152 Kan. 164, 102 P. 2d 1006 (1940). Reprinted at p. 139 *infra*.

Particularly in the light of the adverse verdict of the jury, it should be obvious how vital to the accountant it is to clearly define and evidence his own limited responsibility in situations where the client insists upon limiting the scope of the examination. Such limitations should be confirmed in writing at the outset of the audit and should be reiterated in the letter of representations signed by the client before the completion of the audit. They should again be set out explicitly in the report of the accountant on the audit. If the limitations are as material as they were in this case, there should be an express denial of an opinion on the statement as a whole.[33] Our present-day standards and practices make all of this mandatory. Had these standards been observed in the *Craig v. Anyon* case the accountants would have been in a position to put in an affirmative defense and the jury's verdict in the first instance might have been favorable to the accountants.

Before concluding the discussion of this case, it would be well to quote the dissenting opinion of Presiding Justice Clarke:

> I dissent from the affirmance of so much of the judgment as sets aside the verdict of the jury assessing the damages at $1,177,805.26. The contract of audit was not one merely to discover if inadvertent clerical errors had been made in the bookkeeping, but was one of protection of the plaintiffs' firm from their own failure to find any error in their books of account. This contract the defendants failed to perform. Admitting the neglect of the plaintiffs to discover the embezzlement and falsification of the accounts through an examination of the books on their own part, the defendants' work in pursuance of the contract, owing to the manner in which it was performed, failed to save plaintiffs from the consequences of such failure and neglect, which was the very subject of the contract.[34]

This minority viewpoint seemed to influence the court in the later *National Surety Corporation* case, which now follows.

National Surety Corporation Case [35]

The plaintiff in this action was the surety company on a fidelity bond issued by them to the stock brokerage firm of Halle & Stieglitz under the terms of which the surety had paid the losses sustained through the defalcations of the cashier in the main office of Halle & Stieglitz. The defendants were members of three different firms of certified public accountants who had at different times, during the years 1928 to 1933 audited the books of account of the stock brokerage firm. The plaintiff claimed that the losses which its assignor had incurred had resulted from the failure of the accountants to discover and report substantial cash

33. See CODIFICATION OF STATEMENTS ON AUDITING PROCEDURE, American Institute of Accountants, 1951.

34. Craig v. Anyon, 212 App. Div. 55, 67–68, 208 N.Y. Supp. 259, 269–270 (1st Dep't 1925).

35. National Surety Corp. v. Lybrand, 256 App. Div. 226, 9 N.Y.S. 2d 554 (1st Dep't 1939). Reprinted at p. 146 *infra*.

shortages, which had continued during all of these years and had finally amounted to a total of $329,300.

Four separate causes of action were stated as against each of the three firms, namely: *breach of contract* in the alleged faulty performance of the audit, *breach of warranty* in representations in their reports as to cash in bank, *negligence* in the conduct of the audit, and *fraud* in the alleged misrepresentation of material facts in their reports.[36]

The case was tried before a judge and jury in the Supreme Court, New York County, in May, 1937. At the conclusion of the case, and before its submission to the jury, the trial judge dismissed the complaint and discharged the jury, stating that "the Court is unable to discover anything in the testimony indicating a violation of the obligations of an expert accountant", and on the further ground that "the principle laid down in *Craig v. Anyon* . . . is the one to be here applied". It appeared obvious to the trial judge that "more glaring than any negligence on the part of the defendants is the contributory negligence of the plaintiff's assignor," and accordingly that the loss incurred could not "be said to flow naturally and directly from defendants' negligence or breach of contract."

An appeal was taken to the Appellate Division, where the dismissal below was reversed and a new trial was ordered. The court could not have been more closely divided; three judges voted for reversal, and two judges dissented and voted to affirm. This appeal did not dispose of the issue of negligence on its merits. It merely decided that on the whole record plaintiff had established a prima facie case which should have been submitted to the jury, and that the trial judge was in error in not so doing. It was pointed out also that it was for the jury to say whether the defendants were liable for defalcations subsequent to their audits "depending upon whether such losses could reasonably have been anticipated at the time they were engaged in the performance of the work."

36. In Dantzler Lumber & Export Co. v. Columbia Casualty Co., 115 Fla. 541, 156 So. 116 (1934) the court held that in these situations, causes of action for breach of contract, for negligence and for fraud might exist simultaneously. The action was held to be not for the mere nonperformance of the contract but was said to be based ". . . upon an alleged breach of duty to skillfully perform and truly report the condition of accounts. . . ." The court quoted from 26 R.C.L. (Ruling Case Law) 758: "Whenever a negligent breach of a contract is also a violation of a common-law duty, an action *ex delicto* will lie. Accompanying every contract is a common-law duty to perform the thing agreed to be done with care, skill, reasonable expediency, and faithfulness, and a negligent failure to observe any of these conditions is a tort, as well as a breach of the contract. If the transaction complained of had its origin in a contract which placed the parties in such a relation that in attempting to perform the promised service the tort was committed, then the breach of the contract is not the gravamen of the suit. The contract in such case is mere inducement, creating the state of things which furnishes the occasion of the tort. And in all such cases the remedy is an action on the case. Based on the principle above indicated, the firmly established rule is that for injuries resulting from unskillful or otherwise negligent performance of a thing agreed to be done, an action *ex delicto* will lie, notwithstanding the act complained of would also be ground for an action *ex contractu.*" Reprinted at p. 153 *infra*.

The court also dealt at some length with the question of contributory negligence. Not only did it hold that this defense presented a factual issue which should have been submitted to the jury, but it discussed and interpreted the rule of *Craig v. Anyon*[37] and stated views with respect thereto which would indicate that such a defense might not be effective unless the facts relating to it were extraordinary, as they were in *Craig v. Anyon*. In this connection it was said:

> The defendants assert that they are not liable, no matter how negligent they may have been, because Halle & Stieglitz were guilty of contributory negligence. If it be true that Halle & Stieglitz so conducted their business as to make possible Wallach's defalcations, it did not necessarily excuse the defendants from the consequences of their negligence in failing to discover and report the facts. The action here, it must be remembered, is not to recover for the thefts committed by Wallach as it would be if it were against Wallach or against the surety. The action is for errors of the accountants in failing to discover Wallach's defalcations, thereby making further defalcations possible and rendering more difficult recovery for defalcations of the past. The measure of damages in two such classes of actions is not the same.
>
> We are, therefore, not prepared to admit that accountants are immune from the consequences of their negligence because those who employ them have conducted their own business negligently. . . Accountants, as we know, are commonly employed for the very purpose of detecting defalcations which the employer's negligence has made possible. Accordingly, we see no reason to hold that the accountant is not liable to his employer in such cases. *Negligence of the employer is a defense only when it has contributed to the accountant's failure to perform his contract and to report the truth.* Thus, by way of illustration, if it were found that the members of the firm of Halle & Stieglitz had been negligent in connection with the transfer of funds which occurred at about the time of each audit and that such negligence contributed to the defendants' false reports it would be a defense to the action for it could then be said that defendants' failure to perform their contracts was attributable, in part at least, to the negligent conduct of the firm. That was the principle applied in *Craig v. Anyon*, . . . where the embezzler had been negligently represented to the accountants as a person to be trusted. In the present case, the loss consisted of thefts by a cashier not so represented "whose own account of his receipts and payments could not reasonably be taken by an auditor without further inquiry." (Matter of Kingston Cotton Mill Company, No. 2 [1896] L.R. 2 Ch. Div. 279). (Emphasis added)[38]

While this decision was not carried to the Court of Appeals, and therefore it cannot be said to overrule *Craig v. Anyon* which was affirmed by the higher court, nevertheless it lends support to those who have contended that the result in *Craig v. Anyon* was to be limited to its facts and was not to be construed as a holding that contributory negligence, as a matter of law, would necessarily limit the plaintiff's recovery to the amount of fees paid.

---

37. See note 30 *supra*.

38. National Surety Corp. v. Lybrand, 256 App. Div. 226, 235–236, 9 N.Y.S. 2d 554, 563 (1st Dep't 1939).

This case also is of interest to the profession because of the method employed by the embezzler in concealing his abstractions from petty cash. The shortages thus created were in the first instance covered up by temporarily placing in the petty cash box checks which should have been promptly deposited. This resulted in a series of delayed and substituted bank deposits from day to day. During the period involved, Halle & Stieglitz maintained about twenty-seven accounts, nine of which were in New York City. Wallach, the cashier, apparently knew when audits were to be made and boldly resorted to "kiting" from one bank to another at the audit date. Through the use of this system of "lapping" deposits almost from day to day, and "kiting" checks at the audit date, he succeeded in avoiding detection for a period of years, while his defalcations mounted steadily. It was contended that these fraudulent practices were well known to all accountants and that the normal audit procedures usually employed in the verification of cash to guard against such practices were negligently omitted. The court made the following reference to this phase of the case:

> The evidence in this case discloses similar conditions at the time of all the audits in question. It was for the jury to say whether the practice of "lapping" and "kiting" of checks should have put the defendants upon inquiry which would have led to discovery of the defalcations, and whether, if defendants had exercised ordinary care and used proper methods of accounting as established by the expert testimony, they would have observed checks drawn out of numerical order. If they had checked "outstandings" they would have noted that the check or checks by Wallach at the audit dates were returned with the cancelled vouchers accompanying the next bank statement. Again, if there had been any substantial compliance with the requirements for verifying cash in banks, the cash shortages would have been detected, as the jury might have found. Their representations that there had been a verification of cash was a pretense of knowledge when they did not know the condition of the bank accounts and had no reasonable basis to assume that they did. This, the jury could have found, amounted at least to a constructive fraud. (*Ultramares Corp. v. Touche,* 255 N.Y. 170, 190, 191; *State Street Trust Co. v. Ernst, supra,* page 112.)[39]

Flagg v. Seng[40]

This was an action by a trustee of a bankrupt corporation for damages for alleged fraud where the defendants, who were accountants, were employed by the corporation to make periodic audits of its books and reports to its directors. The case was tried on the issue as to whether the defendant-accountants knowingly submitted false reports which deceived the directors and which caused them to declare dividends which could not be legally declared. The trial court found in all respects in favor of

39. *Id.* at 235, 9 N.Y.S.2d at 562.

40. 16 Cal. App.2d 545, 60 P.2d 1004 (1936). Reprinted at p. 163 *infra.*

the defendants. The judgment in favor of the accountants was affirmed on appeal.

The case is of special interest because of the activity and knowledge of the directors who were alleged to have been deceived and because of the reliance of the accountants upon the opinion of the attorney for the corporation concerning matters which, upon the trial of the case, were alleged to be illegal. These aspects of the case are discussed in the following excerpts from the court's opinion:

> Appellant's main contention seems to be that stock in the corporation was exchanged for real estate in violation of the permit issued by the state corporation department and that when a parcel of real estate was exchanged for other property at a price in excess of its original cost, the difference was entered on the books as a profit before the second piece was sold. The matter last referred to represents an established policy on the part of the directors, the books were thus kept on their order, and they were in no way deceived by anything done by the respondents in this connection. With respect to the other matter it appears that stock was, in effect, exchanged for real property. This was done by putting through escrows whereby the corporation's check was given in payment for the land and the other party's check was given in payment for the stock. While there is some evidence that certain papers in the files of the corporation indicated the true situation, although the same was not indicated by the books of the corporation, there is other evidence to the effect that this could not be learned from an examination of the books and records of the corporation, that *it was unknown to the respondents except in one instance, and that in that case the respondents took the matter up with the attorney for the corporation who assured them that the matter was perfectly legal.* It further appears that whatever illegality existed and whatever harm arose therefrom was caused directly by the action of the board of directors, and that all such exchanges were made with their full knowledge and consent and in accordance with their fixed policy, and no inference could be drawn that anything done by the respondents had any casual relation to any part of this situation. (Emphasis added)
>
> Not only are the findings sustained by the evidence, but we are unable to see how the matters particularly relied upon by the appellant can justify or compel any other conclusions than those drawn by the court. Conceding that certain sales of stock were illegally made this was not only well known to the directors but was intentionally done by them. They were not only not deceived by the audits and reports but they had intentionally handled the transactions in such a manner as to make them appear on the books as a cash transaction. While the court found upon sufficient evidence that the respondents had no knowledge of those parts of these transactions which had been thus covered up and conceding, for the sake of argument, that the respondents might have found out the true situation by a more extensive investigation, it in no way appears that any discovery they might have made would have affected the result. The method pursued by the directors was followed on the advice of their attorneys and although the same has since been declared illegal, no such blame can be attached to the respondents, under the circumstances here appearing, as would justify a reversal of the judgment.[41]

41. 60 P.2d at 1007–1008.

Suits by Surety Companies

Where losses occur as the result of defalcations by an employee of the client or through similar irregularities, it often happens that the client is protected by a fidelity bond. As a result, the surety company which issued the bond will indemnify the client for such losses to the extent of the fidelity bond coverage. Upon such payment, the surety company becomes subrogated to whatever claims the client may have had against the accountant for alleged negligence or fraud in the performance of auditing services. That is to say, a surety company, to the extent that it has made good such losses, succeeds to whatever rights the client may have had against the accountant for the failure of the accountant to discover such defalcations. This equitable principle of subrogation is defined as follows in Section 141, Restatement of Security:

> Where the duty of the principal to the creditor is fully satisfied, the surety to the extent that he has contributed to this satisfaction is subrogated . . . (c) to the rights of the creditor against persons other than the principal whose negligence or wilful conduct has made them liable to the creditor for the same default. . . .

Whether the surety company asserts a claim against the accountant by way of subrogation or assignment, this gives the surety company no greater rights than the client himself would have had, had he become the party plaintiff. Accordingly, the defense of the contributory negligence of the client may be asserted against the surety company.

Furthermore, the surety company cannot be neglectful in enforcing its remedies against the primary obligor (the defaulting employee) to the detriment of the accountant. Thus, in the fairly recent case of *Fidelity & Deposit Co. v. Atherton*,[42] where the County Treasurer was primarily responsible for the defalcations of his deputy, he had made substantial payment to the surety company on account of the loss and had given his note for the balance, secured by a mortgage on property valued in excess of the amount due the surety company. The surety company had made no attempt to collect on this note, though it was long past due. The court held that the negligence of the surety to collect from the County Treasurer (the man who was primarly liable for the loss) was a sufficiently equitable ground for estopping the surety from attempting to collect the unpaid portion of its loss from the accountants.

In recent years, it has become increasingly clear to the business community and to surety companies that while an audit offers a large measure of protection as a preventive of loss resulting from defalcations, the accountant does not undertake to uncover all such irregularities. Circumstances may arise where such frauds are perpetrated and remain undetected despite the fact that the audit complied with generally accepted

42. 47 N.M. 443, 144 P.2d 157 (1943). Reprinted at p. 168 *infra*.

auditing standards. In such circumstances, the accountant does not assume the responsibility of an insurer. This is the function of the surety company and generally it is recognized as such by all parties involved.

This problem of the division of responsibility between the accounting profession and the surety companies has been widely discussed over the years. Such discussions culminated in December, 1945 in an agreement between the American Institute of Accountants and some twenty-three of the companies issuing fidelity bonds, by the terms of which, the surety companies agreed that it was not their intention to assert claims against accountants, except on the basis of affirmatively dishonest or criminal acts or gross negligence on the part of the accountants.[43] It was stipulated that prior to asserting such claim, the matter would be submitted to an impartial committee of three persons who were not accountants, who would consider the evidence relating to the audit performed. It was agreed by the surety companies that unless the committee concluded that the claim involved an affirmatively dishonest or criminal act or gross negligence on the part of the auditor, the surety company would not press any claim by way of subrogation against the accountant. Subsequent to 1945, an additional number of surety companies became parties to this arrangement. It is encouraging to note that the use of this quasi-arbitration machinery has not yet been invoked. However, it has served to clear the atmosphere in defining the respective responsibilities of the accounting profession and of surety companies in these situations. It does not relieve accountants from their responsibility to comply with generally accepted auditing standards. It does, however, recognize the fact that accountants are not insurers against loss by defalcation and that an audit, as valuable as it may be, is not the legal equivalent of a fidelity bond.

---

43. See Carey, *Defalcation in Relation to Audit, Internal Control, and Fidelity Bonds*, 83 JOURNAL OF ACCOUNTANCY 353 (1947), also in 15 THE CONTROLLER 127 (1947). Reprinted at p. 172 *infra*.

CHAPTER 3

LIABILITY TO THIRD PARTIES AT COMMON LAW

The legal responsibility of accountants and auditors to parties other than their clients (herein referred to as third parties) has been dealt with in a number of highly important American cases. These cases have defined and limited the accountant's responsibility for negligence, but they have emphasized the accountant's exposure to claims of third parties on grounds of fraud, misrepresentation or deceit. These cases have also influenced the enactment of legislation which has broadened the responsibility for negligence where the claims of investors or securities purchasers are involved. These statutory rules will be outlined at a later point in this text.

The landmark cases relating to accountant's liability to third parties now will be discussed.

The Landell Case [44]

This was an action brought against a firm of certified public accountants by a plaintiff who claimed that he had suffered loss through the purchase of shares of the Employers' Indemnity Company, in reliance upon their financial statement which had been audited and certified to by the defendant-accountants. The complaint further alleged that the financial statement was false and untrue, that the stock purchased by him turned out to be valueless, that the loss he sustained was due to the negligence of the accountants in the conduct of their audit and that they were consequently liable for the loss he had sustained. The court below entered judgment for the defendants on the ground that, as a matter of law, the complaint failed to state a cause of action. On appeal, this judgment for the defendants was affirmed, for the following stated reasons:

> There were no contractual relations between the plaintiff and defendants, and, if there is any liability from them to him, it must arise out of some breach of duty, for there is no averment that they made the report with intent to deceive him. The averment in the statement of claim is that the defendants were careless and negligent in making their report; but the plaintiff was a stranger to them and to it, and, as no duty rested upon them to him, they

44. Landell v. Lybrand, 264 Pa. 406, 107 Atl. 783 (1919). Reprinted at p. 175 *infra*.

cannot be guilty of any negligence of which he can complain: *Schiffer v. Sauer Co. et al.*, 238 Pa. 550, 86 Atl. 479. This was the correct view of the court below, and the judgment is accordingly affirmed.[45]

The Ultramares Case [46]

The *Ultramares* case is undoubtedly the leading American case dealing with the legal responsibility of accountants. Early in 1924, the defendants, a firm of certified public accountants, had audited the books of account of Fred Stern & Co., Inc., who were importers and dealers in rubber, and had certified to their balance sheet as of December 31, 1923; the said certificate of the accountants reading as follows:

> We have examined the accounts of Fred Stern & Co., Inc., for the year ending December 31, 1923, and hereby certify that the annexed balance sheet is in accordance therewith and with the information and explanations given us. We further certify that, subject to provision for federal taxes on income, the said statement, in our opinion, presents a true and correct view of the financial condition of Fred Stern & Co., Inc., as at December 31, 1923.[47]

The accountants supplied their clients with thirty-two copies of the certified balance sheet, knowing in a general way that it would be exhibited by their client to banks and other creditors. The plaintiff in this action was one of the creditors to whom the balance sheet was later submitted, who claimed that he relied upon it in making substantial advances to Fred Stern & Co., Inc. It was not known to the accountants that the balance sheet would be submitted to this specific creditor.

The balance sheet as certified, showed a net worth of approximately $1,070,000, when, as a matter of fact, the corporation was at the time insolvent and its liabilities exceeded its assets by approximately $200,000. The assets had been overstated by the inclusion of over $950,000 of fictitious and nonexisting accounts receivable. The liabilities had been understated by over $300,000 through failure to record accounts payable covering merchandise which had been purchased, received, and dealt with as assets of the business. The audit had failed to detect these fraudulent entries, and for the loss suffered by the plaintiff-creditor it brought this action against the accountants.

The action was brought in November, 1926. It was not until April, 1929 that it was tried before a judge and jury in the Supreme Court of New York County. In its inception the complaint alleged a single cause

---

45. *Ibid.*

46. Ultramares Corp. v. Touche, 229 App. Div. 581, 243 N.Y.Supp. 179 (1st Dep't 1930), *rev'd*, 255 N.Y. 170, 174 N.E. 441 (1931). Both opinions reprinted at pp. 175 and 179.

47. See Beardsley v. Ernst, 47 Ohio App. 241, 191 N.E. 808 (1934), where the certificate was specifically based upon statements received from abroad with respect to foreign constitutent companies. The case was distinguished from the *Ultramares* case on that ground. Reprinted at p. 192 *infra*.

of action based upon the alleged negligence of the accountants. Upon the trial the complaint was amended to add a second cause of action in fraud. At the conclusion of the trial the complaint was dismissed as to fraud. However, the trial judge reserved decision on the motion to dismiss the negligence action and submitted the question of negligence to the jury. The jury brought in a verdict for the plaintiff in the amount of $187,576.32. The trial judge thereupon dismissed the complaint and set aside the verdict based on negligence, stating that his decision was based on the law and not on the facts. The case was taken to the Appellate Division which unanimously affirmed the dismissal of the cause of action for fraud, but, by a divided court of three to two, reversed the dismissal of negligence and reinstated the verdict.

The case was then taken on cross appeals to the Court of Appeals, which handed down its unanimous decision in 1931, reversing the Appellate Division on both causes of action. As to the cause of action for negligence, the judgment of the trial judge was affirmed, dismissing the cause of action *as a matter of law*. As to the second cause of action, based on fraud, the judgment of dismissal was reversed and a new trial granted. The opinion for the unanimous court was written by Judge Cardozo. The court expressed the view that the evidence supported a finding that the audit was negligently made, but it reached the conclusion that even if negligence existed, it did not create liability to the plaintiff in the circumstances of this case. In this connection, the court stated:

> The defendants owed to their employer a duty imposed by law to make their certificate without fraud, and a duty growing out of contract to make it with the care and caution proper to their calling. Fraud includes the pretense of knowledge when knowledge there is none. To creditors and investors to whom the employer exhibited the certificate, the defendants owed a like duty to make it without fraud, since there was notice in the circumstances of its making that the employer did not intend to keep it to himself. . . . A different question develops when we ask whether they owed a duty to these to make it without negligence. *If liability for negligence exists, a thoughtless slip or blunder, the failure to detect a theft or forgery beneath the cover of deceptive entries, may expose accountants to a liability in an The hazards of a business conducted on these terms are so extreme as to indeterminate amount for an indeterminate time to an indeterminate class. enkindle doubt whether a flaw may not exist in the implication of a duty that exposes to these consequences.* (Emphasis added)[48]

In this connection the court distinguished the facts in this case from those in *Glanzer v. Shepard.*[49] In that case a public weigher, hired by the seller of beans, issued a false certificate of weight which was relied upon by the purchaser. The purchaser sued the weigher on the ground of negligence and was permitted to recover. This earlier case was not reversed by the Court of Appeals. It was merely distinguished

48. 255 N.Y. at 179–180, 174 N.E. at 444.

49. 233 N.Y. 236, 135 N.E. 275 (1922). Reprinted at p. 194 *infra*.

on its facts and not considered applicable to the *Ultramares* case. Accordingly, it is thought by many that if a case should arise where the third party who relies upon an accountant's statement was specifically identified and known to the accountant as one for whose primary benefit the audit was made, then there might be liability even for negligence to such a third party.[50] In comparing the facts of the *Ultramares* case, the court stated:

> In *Glanzer v. Shepard,* the seller of beans requested the defendants, public weighers, to make return of the weight and furnish the buyer with a copy. This the defendants did. Their return, which was made out in duplicate, one copy to the seller and the other to the buyer, *recites that it was made by order of the former for the use of the latter.* The buyer paid the seller on the faith of the certificate which turned out to be erroneous. We held that the weighers were liable at the suit of the buyer for the moneys overpaid. Here was something more than the rendition of a service in the expectation that the one who ordered the certificate would use it thereafter in the operations of his business as occasion might require. Here was a case where the transmission of the certificate to another was not merely one possibility among many, but the "end and aim of the transaction," as certain and immediate and deliberately willed as if a husband were to order a gown to be delivered to his wife, or a telegraph company, contracting with the sender of a message, were to telegraph it wrongly to the damage of the person expected to receive it. . . . The bond was so close as to approach that of privity, if not completely one with it. Not so in the case at hand. No one would be likely to urge that there was a contractual relation, or even one approaching it, at the root of any duty that was owing from the defendants now before us to the indeterminate class of persons who, presently or in the future, might deal with the Stern Company in reliance on the audit. In a word, *the service rendered by the defendant in Glanzer v. Shepard was primarily for the information of a third person,* in effect, if not in name, a party to the contract, and only incidentally for that of the formal promisee. *In the case at hand, the service was primarily for the benefit of the Stern Company,* a convenient instrumentality for use in the development, of the business, and *only incidentally or collaterally for the use of those to whom Stern and his associates might exhibit it thereafter.* Foresight of these possibilities may charge with liability for fraud. The conclusion does not follow that it will charge with liability for negligence. (Emphasis added)[51]

In thus limiting the liability of accountants to third parties for mere negligence, the court indicated how negligence might of itself be evidence from which an inference of fraud could be drawn. In this connection, the court stated:

> Our holding does not emancipate accountants from the consequences of fraud. It does not relieve them if their audit has been so negligent as to justify a finding that they had no genuine belief in its adequacy, for this again is fraud. It does no more than say that, if less than this is proved, if there has been neither reckless misstatement nor insincere profession of an

50. See Doyle v. Chatham & Phenix Nat'l Bank, 253 N.Y. 369, 171 N.E. 574 (1930). This case was distinguished from the situation in *Ultramares* and held to be inapplicable thereto. Reprinted at p. 197 *infra.*

51. 255 N.Y. at 182–183, 174 N.E. at 445–446.

> opinion, but only honest blunder, the ensuing liability for negligence is one that is bounded by the contract, and is to be enforced between the parties by whom the contract has been made. We doubt whether the average business man receiving a certificate without paying for it, and receiving it merely as one among a multitude of possible investors, would look for anything more.[52]

In dealing with the question of the possible liability of the accountants on the second cause of action, for fraud, the court concluded that in this case the certificate of the accountants involved both the representation of fact and the expression of opinion. Thus it found that the accountants "certified as a fact, true to their own knowledge, that the balance sheet was in accordance with the books of account." As to this, *it was held, as a matter of law, that if their statement of fact was false, they were not to be exonerated because they believed it to be true.* The court further concluded that there was ample evidence from which the jury might hold such a statement to be false. The court discussed this point further, stating:

> Correspondence between the balance sheet and the books imports something more, or so the triers of the facts might say, than correspondence between the balance sheet and the general ledger, unsupported or even contradicted by every other record. The correspondence to be of any moment may not unreasonably be held to signify a correspondence between the statement and the books of original entry, the books taken as a whole. If that is what the certificate means, a jury could find that the correspondence did not exist, and that the defendants signed the certificates without knowing it to exist and even without reasonable grounds for belief in its existence.[53]

In reviewing the facts in the record concerning the audit that was made, the court dwelt upon the grounds for suspicion which existed, as reflected in the working papers of the accountants, and felt that a jury might have held that in the circumstances the limited testing and sampling employed was entirely inadequate. The following quotation from the court's opinion indicates how *neglect to follow through with the most searching inquiry when suspicions are aroused may readily present a question for the jury as to whether there was a sincere belief in the opinion expressed:*

> How far books of account fair upon their face are to be probed by accountants, in an effort to ascertain whether the transactions back of them are in accordance with the entries, involves to some extent the exercise of judgment and discretion. Not so, however, the inquiry whether the entries certified as there, are there in very truth, there in the form and in the places where men of business training would expect them to be. The defendants were put on their guard by the circumstances touching the December accounts receivable to scrutinize with special care. A jury might find that with suspicions thus awakened, they closed their eyes to the obvious, and blindly gave assent.[54]

52. *Id.* at 189, 174 N.E. at 448.
53. *Id.* at 189–190, 174 N.E. at 448.
54. *Id.* at 192, 174 N.E. at 449.

On the whole record the Court of Appeals concluded that *a jury might find* that the accountants, in certifying to the correspondence between the balance sheet and the accounts, made a statement of fact as true to their own knowledge when they had no knowledge on the subject; also that a *jury might find* that the accountants acted "without information leading to a sincere or genuine belief when they certified to an opinion that the balance sheet faithfully reflected the condition of the business." Accordingly the dismissal of the cause of action in fraud was reversed and a new trial was granted.

The State Street Trust Company Case [55]

The principles enunciated in the *Ultramares* case were soon to be applied in two other cases now to be discussed. The action in the *State Street Trust Company* case was commented in December, 1932, subsequent to Judge Cardozo's opinion in the *Ultramares* case. Accordingly the complaint was based on allegations of fraud although the evidence from which the jury was asked to find fraud involved gross negligence for the most part.

The audit covered the operations of Pelz-Greenstein Co. for the year 1928 and their financial position as at December 31, 1928. This company was engaged in the factoring business, a form of commercial financing. They loaned money to firms who were manufacturers and merchants and made a profit from charging interest, commissions, deducting interest, discounts, et cetera, in connection with the loans which they made to others and the collection of the accounts receivable assigned to them by their customers. Pelz-Greenstein Co. in turn obtained most of their own working capital from some seventeen banks to whom they were indebted in the aggregate amount of $4,275,000 on December 31, 1928. The plaintiff in this action was one of the said bank creditors who claimed that they had made loans in reliance upon the financial statements certified to by the defendant-accountants, which were here attacked as fraudulent misrepresentations.

The basic factual issues were different from those in the *Ultramares* case. Here it was claimed that the reserves set up for bad and doubtful accounts were grossly inadequate. Furthermore, it was contended that, in a long-form report which the accountants later submitted to their client only, material facts were revealed which indicated that the accountants knew that the financial position was not fairly presented in the condensed report which they had issued for distribution to the banks. It was further claimed that the long-form report to the client was qualified by making it subject to comments which were omitted from the

55. State Street Trust Co. v. Ernst, 278 N.Y. 104, 15 N.E.2d 416 (1938). Reprinted at p. 203 *infra*.

condensed statement, whereas the condensed statement carried with it the unqualified certificate of the accountants. The certificate which was attached to the short-form report (described as "condensed statement") read as follows:

> We hereby certify that we examined the books of account and record (sic) pertaining to the assets and liabilities of Pelz-Greenstein Co., Inc., New York City, as of the close of business December 31, 1928, and, based on the records examined, information submitted to us, and subject to the foregoing notes [not here material], it is our opinion that the above condensed statement shows the financial condition of the company at the date stated and that the related income and surplus account is correct.

In comparison with the accountants' certificate involved in the *Ultramares* case, it is interesting to note (a) there was no reference to the statement being in accordance with the books, (b) the certificate embraced the "related income and surplus account," as well as the balance sheet.

The case was tried in March, 1936 before a judge and jury in the Supreme Court of New York County. At the close of plaintiff's case, defendants moved to dismiss the complaint. The trial judge reserved decision. The defendants thereupon rested without calling any witnesses, renewed their motion to dismiss and also moved for a directed verdict. The trial judge reserved decision again and submitted the case to the jury. The jury rendered a verdict for plaintiffs in the amount of $246,000. Thereupon the trial judge granted a motion to set aside the verdict and directed a verdict for defendants on the ground that the jury's verdict was not supported by the evidence. The Appellate Division unanimously affirmed (without opinion) [56] the directed verdict for defendants, making it necessary for the plaintiffs to obtain permission from the Court of Appeals to carry the case to that court. The Court of Appeals by a vote of four to two reversed the judgments below and granted a new trial.

The Court of Appeals reiterated the principles laid down in the *Ultramares* case, which it summarized as follows:

> We have held that in the absence of a contractual relationship or its equivalent, accountants cannot be held liable for ordinary negligence in preparing a certified balance sheet even though they are aware that the balance sheet will be used to obtain credit. (*Ultramares Corp. v. Touche,* 255 N.Y. 170). Accountants, however, may be liable to third parties, even where there is lacking deliberate or active fraud. A representation certified as true to the knowledge of the accountants when knowledge there is none, a reckless misstatement, or an opinion based on grounds so flimsy as to lead to the conclusion that there was no genuine belief in its truth, are all sufficient upon which to base liability. A refusal to see the obvious, a failure to investigate the doubtful, if sufficiently gross, may furnish evidence leading to an inference of fraud so as to impose liability for losses suffered by those who

56. 251 App. Div. 717, 298 N.Y.Supp. 176 (1st Dep't 1937).

rely on the balance sheet. In other words, heedlessness and reckless disregard of consequence may take the place of deliberate intention.

In *Ultramares Corp. v. Touche* (255 N.Y. 170) we said with no uncertainty that *negligence, if gross, or blindness, even though not equivalent to fraud, was sufficient to sustain an inference of fraud.* Our exact words were: "In this connection we are to bear in mind the principle already stated in the course of this opinion that negligence or blindness, even when not equivalent to fraud, is none the less evidence to sustain an inference of fraud. At least this is so if the negligence is gross." (Emphasis added) [57]

It would seem that the apparent inconsistency between the long-form report later submitted to the client and the short-form report upon which the plaintiff had relied was of itself the crucial evidence which the Court of Appeals felt supported the jury verdict of fraud. In the following discussion the court refers to this long-form report as "a letter of explanation." In the absence of an affirmative defense by the accountants the court seemed to attach sinister significance to the fact that a certified report should be supplemented by a more detailed document which went only to the client and that the detailed report was not released until after a delay of thirty days. This view is indicated in the following quotation from the opinion:

The record is, indeed, replete with evidence, both oral and documentary, to make a *prima facie* case against the defendants. In the first place, we have these accountants guilty of an act which is the equivalent of active misrepresentation. On April 2, 1929, they sent to Pelz-Greenstein the certified balance sheet, with ten additional copies, knowing that it was to be used to obtain credit. "Nothing was said as to the persons to whom these counterparts would be shown, or the extent or number of the transactions in which they would be used. . . . The range of the transactions in which a certificate of audit might be expected to play a part was as indefinite and wide as the possibilities of the business that was mirrored in the summary." (*Ultramares Corp. v. Touche,* 255 N.Y. 170, 174.) Not until thirty days later did the accountants send to Pelz-Greenstein a letter of explanation of this balance sheet, and then apparently only one copy. So important was this covering letter in the minds of defendants that, although the balance sheet attached to the covering letter was in other respects substantially identical with the original balance sheet, it contained the following notation, which did not appear at all on the original balance sheet released thirty days earlier: "This balance sheet is subject to the comments contained in the letter attached to and made a part of this report." One of the copartners, testifying before trial, said: "We wanted to try to prevent anyone using this balance sheet, without knowing the scope of the examination which we made, which is set forth in paragraph 2 of the full report. . . . We have had cases where our entire covering letter had been deleted from these reports and just the balance sheet used." Yet, in effect, these defendants themselves did just this. They held back this covering letter for thirty days and issued the balance sheet alone to the world of possible lenders. The loan by the plaintiff was made long before this important covering letter was even sent.

The above act of the accountants, in placing in circulation a certified balance

57. 278 N.Y. at 111–112, 15 N.E.2d at 418–419.

> sheet which they practically conceded should not be used without knowing the scope of the examination set forth in the covering letter, and then allowing a period of thirty days to elapse before sending the covering letter, and then only one copy, whereas there had been ten copies of the certified balance sheet issued, was itself gross negligence and an important piece of evidence raising an inference of fraud.[58]

There was considerable additional evidence before the jury indicating that the accountants accepted the assurances of their client concerning the collectibility of accounts when the records before them should have aroused their suspicion to a point where independent inquiry was mandatory. From this evidence to support the allegation of gross negligence, the jury might have inferred that the expression of opinion concerning financial position (embracing the adequacy of reserves for bad and doubtful accounts) was a mere fraudulent pretense and that the accountants did not entertain a sincere and honest belief in the opinion which they expressed. On this phase of the case the court stated:

> The defendants urge that these defendants were excused from investigation because of a letter from Leon S. Pelz, treasurer of Pelz-Greenstein, in which he stated that Pelz-Greenstein had in its possession "sufficient saleable merchandise to completely liquidate" these accounts. In other words, defendants were content to certify a balance sheet knowing it would be used to secure bank credit which contained an item of over $125,000 [59] of apparently dead accounts on the uninvestigated and unsupported statement of the party seeking the credit that these accounts were amply secured, although it appeared on the face of the books that there had been no realization upon this security for years. Where the books indicate the likelihood of a substantial loss, a failure to indicate this on the balance sheet can be justified only by an actual check-up. It does not suffice to rely instead upon the statement of an officer of the firm the books of which are being examined. If an accountant may disregard a situation which indicates substantial losses because he is informed by the person whose books are being examined that there is adequate security, the balance sheet issued by the accountant, by its failure to point this out, contains a misrepresentation. The very purpose of the bank in seeking the balance sheet prepared by the accountant is to check any possible fraud on the part of the person seeking the loan. Yet these accountants contend that they may accept as true a statement by the party whose books are being examined, make no check-up or investigation on their own part, and issue a statement omitting entirely any mention of the reason why investigation of the security was omitted.
>
> We have explicit expert testimony, uncontradicted, that under these circumstances it was improper accounting practice for defendants to accept a letter from Pelz-Greenstein, and that they should have investigated these accounts very fully to ascertain whether the companies were still in business and to ascertain definitely and independently what security, if any, Pelz-Greenstein held for the payment of these accounts.[60]

The opinion of the Court of Appeals also indicates that they were un-

58. Id. at 113–114, 15 N.E.2d at 419–420.
59. *Sic,* should clearly be $215,000.
60. 278 N.Y. at 118–119, 15 N.E.2d at 421–422.

favorably impressed with the fact that the defendants rested without calling any witness, "although there would naturally be available the men who made the audit, those who prepared or supervised the preparation of the working papers or the certified balance sheet and experts to refute the testimony offered by the experts called by plaintiff." The conclusion to reverse the judgments below and grant a new trial was thus expressed:

> The foregoing presents abundant evidence from which a jury could find that defendants knew facts which vitally affected the financial worth of Pelz-Greenstein, and which defendants totally suppressed on the certified balance sheet but disclosed to Pelz-Greenstein alone in the one copy of the covering letter sent thirty days later. The jury further could have found that the computation of reserves on the certified balance sheet was a misrepresentation which did not reflect the facts as known to defendants, and which they in good faith should have revealed. Where the record shows acts on the part of the accountants, as outlined above, we cannot say, as a matter of law, that plaintiff has failed to make out a case for the jury.[61]

There was an interesting dissenting opinion representing the views of two of the six judges who sat on this appeal. They stressed the fact that *the only representation of fact here involved was the statement by the accountants that they had examined the books of account, which was undisputed.* It also pointed out that the defendants did not warrant or certify the accuracy of the balance sheet; they represented only that the balance sheet was "in their opinion" correct. With respect to the expression of such an opinion, the minority of the court went on to state:

> The defendants are not liable for error of judgment; they are not liable even for lack of care in arriving at their opinion. They are liable only if the opinion expressed was not only erroneous, but was fraudulently expressed. Actual bad faith and intent to deceive is not always, it is true, an essential element in a cause of action for deceit. Such a cause of action may be established against the defendants without proof that they expressed an opinion which they knew was incorrect; at least, however, there must be evidence of a ruthless disregard of whether the opinion was correct or not — the expression of an opinion where "the grounds supporting it are so flimsy as to lead to the conclusion that there was no genuine belief back of it." *(Ultramares Corp. v. Touche . . .)*[62]

The discussion in this dissenting opinion of the inadequacy of reserves particularly warrants quotation:

> Judge FINCH [who wrote the majority opinion] has, in his opinion, referred to the evidence upon which he bases his conclusion that it establishes fraud. I shall try to avoid repetition of that evidence. The most important of the alleged errors in the balance sheet is the failure to provide sufficient reserves for the collection of "commission accounts receivable." The amount of reserves which should be set aside to take care of loss that may be suffered by reason of inability to collect such accounts is a matter of judgment. The

61. *Id.* at 121, 15 N.E.2d at 423.
62. *Id.* at 125, 15 N.E.2d at 424–425.

defendants knew of circumstances which it is said pointed clearly to the conclusion that a reserve of $21,000 is insufficient to take care of these accounts of over $2,043,337.81. Perhaps the defendants here showed a lack of caution. Their letter sent thirty days after the certified balance sheet was sent, shows that they knew that the reserve *might* prove insufficient. None the less, the amount of probable loss even with these circumstances known remained uncertain; the estimate of one per cent loss was doubtless over-optimistic, yet the estimate was based on facts which were not "so flimsy as to lead to the conclusion that there was no genuine belief back of it" . . .

The next error which, it is argued, shows negligence so gross as to indicate a lack of honest belief based on substantial grounds is that no allowance was made for "commission account advances." Many of these accounts were old. Again there are circumstances which perhaps should have acted as a warning signal to a cautious accountant. The defendants saw the signal — that is shown by the supplementary letter — but decided, nevertheless, to make no allowance. Again it would, doubtless, have been better if the defendants had given to those who might rely upon the balance sheet, the warning signal they had seen. They did, however, give notice on the balance sheet that accounts were "inactive and in liquidation" and they removed them from the current assets of the business and placed them "below the line." The owners of the business, men who at that time had a fine reputation, assured the defendants that they had sufficient security to liquidate these dead accounts. I can find here no justification for any argument that a balance sheet which shows that no allowance or reserve has been made for inactive accounts in liquidation may be held to be a fraudulent representation that no allowance or reserve is necessary.[63]

The minority concluded:

The jury might find that the defendants' judgment was bad, but the court pointed out in the *Ultramares* case that liability cannot be predicated upon error however great in the exercise of judgment. The error of judgment does not indicate a willful expression of a false opinion, or an expression of opinion based on grounds so flimsy that the jury might conclude that the opinion was not based on genuine belief. To permit recovery in a case where the evidence does not sustain such a conclusion is to wipe out the distinction which this court has always drawn and which it reiterated in the *Ultramares* case.[64]

When one considers the views expressed in the minority opinion together with the fact that six judges in the courts below all felt the evidence did not support the jury's verdict of fraud, it would seem that the adverse decision in this litigation may have turned upon the existence of a long-form report which made the condensed statement seem misleading by comparison, coupled with the fact that the accountants chose not to defend their own work. This thought emphasizes the inherent danger, from an evidentiary standpoint, of the coexistence of a condensed and a detailed report.

63. *Id.* at 126–127, 15 N.E.2d at 425.
64. *Id.* at 128, 15 N.E.2d at 426.

The O'Connor Case [65]

This case involved an action by a group of persons who had purchased shares of the preferred stock of G. L. Miller & Company, Inc., during 1925 and 1926, in alleged reliance upon a balance sheet dated August 31, 1925, which was stated to present the financial position after giving effect to proposed new financing, namely, the sale of thirty thousand shares of preferred stock at par, an aggregate offering to the public of $3,000,000. The balance sheet was published on the letterhead of defendant-accountants and was reprinted and incorporated in the prospectus which was used in the sale of the stock. At the bottom of the balance sheet, over the signature of the accountants, appeared the following certificate:

> Our audit of the books and accounts of the G. L. Miller & Company, Incorporated, discloses that the net earnings of the Company for the year ended December 31, 1924, were in excess of 2½ times the dividend requirements of the contemplated issue of 30,000 shares of 8% cumulative preferred stock, and that the net earnings for the eight months ended August 31, 1925, were in excess of 3 times the dividend requirements of said stock for the said eight months.

The corporation was adjudicated bankrupt in 1926. Its assets were insufficient to pay the allowed claims of creditors and therefore the plaintiff-stockholders lost their entire investment. The action against the accountants was begun in 1928; it did not come to trial until 1934. During this period of time, the final decision in the *Ultramares* case was handed down. Shortly thereafter, the complaint in this case was amended so as to state a cause of action in fraud against the accountants, instead of negligence. Owing to the diversity of citizenship of the plaintiffs, the action was brought in the Federal District Court for the Southern District of New York. After a 13-week trial before a judge and jury, the jury brought in a verdict for the defendants, in May 1934. Several of the plaintiffs carried the case on appeal to the Circuit Court of Appeals where, in August 1937, by the unanimous decision of the court of three judges, the judgment for the defendants entered upon the jury verdict in the lower court was affirmed. Plaintiffs' petition to the Supreme Court of the United States for a writ of certiorari, requesting that body to review the decision of the Circuit Court of Appeals, was denied.

The business of G. L. Miller & Company, Inc. consisted in underwriting mortgage bonds on real estate, usually on buildings to be constructed, acting as trustees under the mortgage indentures, and selling the bonds to the public. The criticism of the audit and the "certified" balance sheet involved a great many very complicated transactions and

65. O'Connor v. Ludlam, 92 F.2d 50 (2d Cir.), *cert. denied,* 302 U.S. 758 (1937). Reprinted at p. 214 *infra.*

technical legal relationships growing out of the manifold functions of the client as underwriter, trustee, and disbursing agent in connection with the business which it conducted.

The main issues which emerged were the contentions of the plaintiffs that:

1. The audit and balance sheet were claimed to be "intentionally fraudulent in not adequately disclosing the amount of cash held in trust."
2. Payments made by Miller & Company to complete the construction of mortgaged buildings were falsely shown in the balance sheet to be "Secured."
3. Miller & Company itself guaranteed to bondholders the completion of buildings under construction, and the balance sheet made no mention of such contingent liabilities.
4. The defendants made a false certificate as to the net earnings of Miller & Company.

The defendants and members of their staff who worked on the audit testified at great length as to the work done. Voluminous working papers supplied further evidence of the audit procedures followed and the accounting evidence upon the basis of which their opinion was expressed. The testimony of experts was offered both on behalf of plaintiffs and defendants. There was a sharp conflict on the basic issue as to whether the audit was so conducted that a jury might infer that the accountants did not entertain a sincere and honest belief in the opinion which they expressed.

Accordingly, the judge carefully explained the applicable law and submitted the entire case to the jury. The circuit court commented as follows upon the charge to the jury:

> The charge which Judge Patterson delivered to the jury was an exceptionally clear exposition of the applicable law. Since there was no contractual relationship between the plaintiffs and the defendants, liability could be imposed only for fraud; a mistake in the balance sheet, even if it were the result of negligence, could not be the basis of a recovery. *Ultramares Corp. v. Touche, Niven & Co.*, 255 N.Y. 170, 174 N.E. 441, 74 A.L.R. 1139. Fraud presupposes not only an untrue statement but also a fraudulent intent. On the question of falsity of the representations the jury was told that the issue was whether the defendants' representations, "in the sense to be taken by an ordinary reasonable man," were, in fact, true or untrue — whether a true or a false impression was created. On the question of intent, the jury was told that fraud may be established by showing that a false representation has been made, either knowingly, or without belief in its truth, or in reckless disregard of whether it be true or false; and that the issue was whether the defendants had an honest belief that the statements made by them were true. "If they did have that honest belief, whether reasonably or unreasonably, they are not liable. If they did not have an honest belief in the truth of their statements, then they are liable, so far as this third element [scienter] is concerned." The jury was also told that an intent to deceive may be inferred from a lack of honest representation; and that, so far as alleged concealments or omissions were concerned, the issue was whether the omission to state certain matters was deliberate and intended to conceal. It was further

> charged that, if the audit made "was so superficial as to be only a pretended audit and not a real audit, then the element of knowledge of falsity of their representations is present, and they may be held liable." Reading the charge as a whole, it seems to be in strict conformity with the established law . . .[66]

Upon this appeal the issue relating to the item "Notes and Accounts Receivable and Accrued Interest — Secured," was particularly crucial. The trial judge stated that these assets were not secured as a matter of law. The plaintiffs contended that the defendants knew they were not secured. The defense maintained that they honestly, if erroneously, believed them to be secured. With respect to this issue the trial judge charged:

> As matter of law it is my opinion, and I charge you, that these advances to complete unfinished buildings are not the kind of advances that are secured under the trust deeds. The point, however, is not so clear that persons reading such parts of the deed might not, in good faith, entertain different opinions; and the good faith of the defendants in representing these advances as secured is one of the questions of fact for you to determine under all the evidence applicable to these notes, and under the rules which I will later explain to you.[67]

The plaintiffs requested the trial judge to charge the jury that if they should find that the statement as to security was false and "that the defendants represented to the plaintiffs that this was true to their own knowledge, as distinguished from belief or opinion, they were guilty of making a false balance sheet, even if they believed it to be true." This request to charge was denied, and the denial became one of the important grounds for appeal. The circuit court supported the position of the trial judge, dealing with the question in the following language:

> Accountants profess to speak with knowledge when certifying to an agreement between the audit and the entries in books audited, but there is no suggestion in the cases relied upon that a statement by an auditor that notes are secured by the provisions of a trust deed is an assertion of knowledge rather than an expression of opinion. To suggest that a title examiner was guilty of fraud if he erroneously certified a title because he had honestly misconceived the legal significance of a provision in a deed would doubtless horrify counsel for the appellants no less than other members of the legal profession. There is no reason to hold accountants to a higher standard, when they deal with legal documents. The issue of the defendants' good faith was rightly left to the jury.[68]

As to the alleged omission of contingent liabilities, it was stated:

> The charge called attention to the conflicting testimony and instructed the jury to weigh it. The refused requests were to the effect that omission of the contingent liabilities made the balance sheet false. In view of the conflicting testimony, such a charge was properly refused. *Even if it were an abuse of good accounting practice to omit them, such an abuse was not fraud unless*

---

66. *Id.* at 53–54.

67. Quoted in circuit court opinion, *id.* at 55.

68. *Id.* at 56.

accompanied by an intent to conceal. The issue of fraudulent concealment was fairly put to the jury in the general charge. (Emphasis added) [69]

The circuit court concluded that a full and fair trial had been had; that the instructions given to the jury as to the applicable law were correct; that the factual issues had been properly submitted to the jury and that the verdict of the jury for the accountants should not be disturbed.

General Comments

A comparative study of the foregoing three leading cases dealing with accountants' legal responsibility to third parties supports the following general conclusions.

In the absence of special statutory rules (such as the Federal Securities Act soon to be discussed) there is no liability for mere negligence. However, the *Ultramares* case did not reverse such authorities as *Glanzer v. Shepard* and *Doyle v. Chatham & Phenix National Bank,* where it had been held that there would be such liability if there was a sufficiently intimate relationship between the third party and the defendant. Thus, we still have the possibility of liability for mere negligence if the particular third party, or a limited group of which he was a member, was known to the accountant with sufficient definiteness as a party for whose primary benefit the certified statement of the accountant was intended.[70]

The *Ultramares* case held that a false representation of fact as of knowledge creates liability even if believed to be true. This rule emphasizes the vital distinction between representations of fact and expressions of opinion. It was a major issue in the *Ultramares* case in relation to the alleged representation that the balance sheet was in accordance with the books, and it was one of the major issues resulting in the reversal which sent the case back for a new trial. Plaintiffs in the *O'Connor* case sought unsuccessfully to have the court submit to the jury the question of whether or not the characterization "Secured" in relation to assets in the balance sheet was a representation of fact as of knowledge. However, it was there held that the use of this term involved only the expression of opinion concerning what was essentially a legal concept.

69. *Ibid.*

70. It should be noted, however, that the Court of Appeal in England, early in 1951, dealt with just such a situation and on the authority of a line of earlier English cases held that the accountant was not liable for mere negligence to a plaintiff, other than his client, even though the accountant know definitely that his report was intended for the use of and reliance upon by that specific plaintiff. The court divided two to one on the result, but the majority felt that the English precedents dictated a result in favor of the defendant accountant. The provisions of the English Companies Act were not involved *Candler v. Crane, Christmas & Co.* [1951] 2 K.B. 164 (C.A.). For a full discussion of this case, see Seavey, *Candler v. Crane, Christmas & Co., Negligent Misrepresentation by Accountants,* 67 L.Q. Rev. 466 (1951). Reprinted at p. 221 *infra*.

The principles that there is liability for fraud to persons outside the privity of contract, that gross negligence may be evidence of fraud, that even the expression of opinion may be a fraudulent representation if there is not a sincere and honest belief in that opinion — are all long established in the law.[70a] Only the application of such principles to the accountants' situation is novel. It has shifted the strategy of third party plaintiffs from the battleground of negligence to that of fraud. However, it has not eliminated the legal distinction between fraud and negligence, nor has it eliminated that distinction as a practical matter. But for the ruling in the *Ultramares* case, the *O'Connor* case would have been fought out on the issue of negligence and the jury would not have had to rest its decision upon the basic issue of the good faith of the accountants and their sincere belief in their opinion, even if erroneously held.

These cases highlight the decisive role of the jury in determining the legal responsibility of accountants. In *Ultramares* it was held that the case on fraud should have gone to the jury. In the *State Street Trust* case it was held that the verdict of the jury for plaintiff should not have been set aside. In the *O'Connor* case it was held that the jury verdict for defendants should prevail. Not only do the questions of negligence and fraud present factual issues to be passed upon by the jury, but so does the question of the reliance of plaintiff upon the work of the accountants, as well as the question of damage to plaintiff, if any, resulting from the fault of the accountants.

In the absence of a defense of his work, the jury is likely to assume a consciousness of fault on the part of the accountant. This may have been an important factor in the *State Street Trust* case. Similarly, if the testimony of plaintiffs' experts is uncontradicted, it carries maximum weight with both court and jury.

Questions of auditing standards and accounting principles are matters of fact and not of law. If there is conflicting expert testimony, it is for the jury to decide which testimony it should follow. In this connection, where the cause of action is in fraud, the jury, in order to render a verdict for the accountants, does not have to do more than conclude that the accountant had an honest belief in his expressed opinion on these technical matters, even if such belief might have been erroneous. On the other hand, in areas where standards and principles have not been clearly defined, the lay jury may be misled and reach a conclusion disastrous to the defendants. Hindsight wisdom[71] lends plausibility to the arguments of plaintiff and is always a serious threat to the defense.

70a. For a recent application by a New York referee of the rules of the Ultramares and State Street Trust cases, see Duro Sportswear, Inc. v. Cogen, 131 N. Y. LAW JOURNAL 7 (April 29, 1954). Reprinted at p. 247 ***supra.***

71. As Justice Brewer observed in United States v. American Bell Telephone Co., 167 U.S. 224, 261, "Anybody could have discovered America after 1492."

CHAPTER 4

LIABILITY TO THIRD PARTIES BY STATUTE

The common law liability of accountants to third parties has been substantially affected by the enactment of the Federal Securities Act of 1933 [72] and the Federal Securities Exchange Act of 1934.[73] Insofar as the work of the accountant falls within the jurisdiction of the 1933 Act there can be liability for mere negligence as well as for fraud, to certain large classes of third parties, namely, the purchasers and owners of securities. As was said of the 1933 Act shortly after its enactment:

> To say the least the Act goes as far in protection of purchasers of securities as plaintiff in *Ultramares Corp. v. Touche* unsuccessfully urged the New York Court of Appeals to go in the protection of a creditor. The change which that court thought so "revolutionary" as to be "wrought by legislation" has been made. And the duty placed on experts such as accountants has not been measured by the expert's relation to his employer but by his service to investors.[74]

The Federal Securities Act of 1933 regulates the offering of securities for sale to the public through the use of the mails or in interstate commerce. It provides for the prior filing of a so-called Registration Statement with the Securities and Exchange Commission, in which there is disclosure of all material facts concerning the securities to be offered. Included in the Registration Statements are the relevant financial statements of the issuer of the securities. These statements are required to be certified by independent public accountants who are usually certified public accountants. Section 11 (a) of this statute in part provides:

> In case any part of the registration statement, when such part became effective, contained an untrue statement of a material fact or omitted to state a material fact required to be stated therein or necessary to make the statements therein not misleading, any person acquiring such security (unless it is proved that at the time of such acquisition he knew of such untruth or omission) may, either at law or in equity, in any court of competent jurisdiction, sue — . . .
>
> (4) every accountant, engineer, or appraiser, or any person whose profession gives authority to a statement made by him, who has with his consent been

72. 15 U.S.C. § 77a *et seq.* (1946).
73. 15 U.S.C. § 78a *et seq.* (1946).
74. Douglas and Bates, *The Federal Scurities Act of 1933,* 43 YALE L.J. 171, 198 (1933).

> named as having prepared or certified any part of the registration statement, or as having prepared or certified any report or valuation which is used in connection with the registration statement, with respect to the statement in such registration statement report, or valuation, which purports to have been prepared or certified by him; [75]

It is further provided that no person, other than the issuer, shall be liable who shall sustain the burden of proof that:

> as regards any part of the registration statement purporting to be made upon his authority as an expert or purporting to be a copy of or extract from a report or valuation of himself as an expert, (i) he had, after reasonable investigation, reasonable ground to believe and did believe, at the time such part of the registration statement became effective, that the statements therein were true and that there was no omission to state a material fact required to be stated therein or necessary to make the statements therein not misleading, or (ii) such part of the registration statement did not fairly represent his statement as an expert or was not a fair copy of or extract from his report or valuation as an expert; [76]

With respect to the amount of damages which the plaintiff may recover under the statute, it is stated:

> *Provided,* That if the defendant proves that any portion or all of such damages represents other than the depreciation in value of such security resulting from such part of the registration statement, with respect to which his liability is asserted, not being true or omitting to state a material fact required to be stated therein or necessary to make the statements therein not misleading, such portion of or all such damages shall not be recoverable.[77]

The effect of the statute, as indicated by the above quotations, insofar as it relates to financial statements prepared or certified to by an independent public accountant and included with his consent in the Registration Statement, may be summarized as follows:

1. Any person acquiring securities described in the Registration Statement may sue the accountant, regardless of the fact that he is not the client of the accountant.
2. His claim may be based upon an alleged false statement or misleading omission in the financial statements, which constitutes his prima facie case. The plaintiff does not have the further burden of proving that the accountants were negligent or fraudulent in certifying to the financial statements involved.
3. The plaintiff does not have to prove that he relied upon the statement or that the loss which he suffered was the proximate result of the falsity or misleading character of the financial statement.
4. The accountant has thrust upon him the burden of establishing his freedom from negligence and fraud by proving that he had, after reasonable investigation, reasonable ground to believe and did believe that the financial statements to which he certified, were

75. 15 U.S.C. § 77k (1946).
76. *Ibid.*
77. *Ibid.*

true not only as of the date of the financial statements, but beyond that, *as of the time when the Registration Statement became effective.*

5. The accountant has the burden of establishing by way of defense or in reduction of alleged damages, that the loss of the plaintiff resulted in whole or in part from causes other than the false statements or the misleading omissions in the financial statements. Under the common law it would have been part of the plaintiff's affirmative case to prove that the damages which he claims he sustained were proximately caused by the negligence or fraud of the accountant.

It should be noted that Section 13 of the 1933 Act bars any action under its provisions unless brought "within one year after the discovery of the untrue statement or the omission, or after such discovery should have been made by the exercise of reasonable diligence." [78] In no event can such an action be brought "more than three years after the security was bona fide offered to the public."

No court cases against accountants have been reported under this Act since 1933 based upon alleged falsity or misleading omission as of financial statement dates. It would seem clear, however, that proof of compliance with generally accepted auditing standards would be an adequate and effective defense insofar as the statements speak as of their purported dates. It is the vague extension of responsibility beyond the financial dates and down to the "effective date" of the Registration Statement (which may be months later) which poses a difficult and unresolved problem. What constitutes the "reasonable investigation," within the meaning of the statute, that the accountant should undertake, covering the period from the completion of his audit down to the subsequent effective date, is still relatively an open question. Whereas generally accepted auditing standards have been promulgated with reasonable clarity, such standards are not applicable to the "reasonable investigation" covering this post-audit period. There is considerable difference of opinion as to what work the accountant should perform after the completion of his audit, to assure himself that the statements which are a fair presentation upon the completion of his audit work are also a fair presentation upon the subsequent effective date of the Registration Statement. It is generally considered essential to take the following steps:

1. Inspect the minutes down to a date reasonably close to the effective date.
2. Address inquiries to the management as to whether there have been significant events down to that date.
3. Inspect available unaudited financial statements dated subsequent to the audited statement dates.

The "reasonable investigation" outlined above is far less than an audit, falls far short of compliance with generally accepted auditing standards,

78. 15 U.S.C. § 77m (1946).

and is not intended to afford a basis for the expression of an opinion as to any period or any transaction subsequent to the audited statement dates. It does serve, however, as a reasonable inquiry by the accountant, within the practical limits of the situation, to place him in a position where he feels justified in relying upon a presumption of continuance as to the fairness of presentation to which he certified as of the audited statement dates. On the other hand, if the accountant does have actual knowledge, however obtained, of material subsequent events, it is generally considered to be his responsibility to insist that such facts of which he has actual knowledge are adequately disclosed.

The only recorded court case involving a claim against accountants under the Federal Securities Acts dealt with the failure to disclose a contingent liability which had developed between the date of certification and the effective date. The case [79] was dismissed against the accountants as well as against the other defendants. The case arose in 1939 and is inconclusive for a number of reasons. The opinion of the court seemed to ignore any responsibility on the part of the accountants for events subsequent to the date when they certified the financial statements. The peculiar situation existed where the Registration Statement became effective on a given date but as of a prior date, which prior date coincided with the date on the accountants' report. Furthermore, the action was dismissed on the additional grounds of a failure by the plaintiff to prove damages. The statute of limitations was also invoked. The decision was criticized in law reviews [80] on varying grounds and contributed very little toward the clarification of accountants' responsibility under the statute. This case was recently discussed at some length in *The New York Certified Public Accountant.*[81]

The Securities Exchange Act of 1934 relates in general to the regulation of securities exchanges and the securities there traded in and listed. It provides, among other things, for the filing of annual reports with the Securities and Exchange Commission, including financial statements certified by independent public accountants. Section 18 of the 1934 Act deals with the liability for misleading statements and is applicable to accountants involved in the certification of such statements. This Section provides as follows:

> (a) Any person who shall make or cause to be made any statement in any application, report, or document filed pursuant to this title or any rule or regulation thereunder or any undertaking contained in a registration statement as provided in subsection (d) of section 78*o* of this title, which statement was at the time and in the light of the circumstances under which it was made false or misleading with respect to any material fact, shall be liable

79. Shonts v. Hirliman, 28 F. Supp. 478 (S.D. Cal. 1939). Reprinted at p. 253 *infra.*

80. 38 Mich. L. Rev. 1103 (1940); 50 Yale L.J. 98 (1940)

81. Rappaport, *Accountants' Liability Under the Securities Act,* 21 N.Y. Certified Public Accountant 763 (1951).

to any person (not knowing that such statement was false or misleading) who, in reliance upon such statement, shall have purchased or sold a security at a price which was affected by such statement, for damages caused by such reliance, unless the person sued shall prove that he acted in good faith and had no knowledge that such statement was false or misleading. A person seeking to enforce such liability may sue at law or in equity in any court of competent jurisdiction. In any such suit the court may, in its discretion, require an undertaking for the payment of the costs of such suit, and assess reasonable costs, including reasonable attorneys' fees, against either party litigant.[82]

The Statute of Limitations relating to actions under the 1934 Act[83] contains 1-year and 3-year provisions which are substantially similar to those under the 1933 Act.

It will thus be seen that the provisions of Section 18 of the 1934 Act differ in the following significant respects from the comparable provisions of Section 11 of the 1933 Act:

1. There is no provision similar to the "effective date" requirement of a Registration Statement. In contrast, it is provided in the 1934 Act that to be actionable, the statement must be false or misleading "at the time and in the light of the circumstances under which it was made." It would seem from this that the accountant is not obligated to extend his examination or inquiry beyond the completion of his audit work, even though the filing with the Securities and Exchange Commission may take place at some subsequent date. In the case of the 10-K report covering a calendar year, this is required to be filed on or before April 30th following the close of the year. It usually includes financial statements, the audit work on which may have been completed two or three months earlier. The accountant's report usually bears the date of the completion of his audit and it would seem that his responsibility would be limited to his compliance with generally accepted auditing standards applied down to the date of the completion of the audit. However, if the accountant has actual knowledge of the occurrence of subsequent events which are of material significance, it would be incumbent upon him to insist upon adequate disclosure in the report.

A similar view was expressed in a paper read at the 1951 annual meeting of the American Institute of Accountants by the present chairman of its committee on auditing procedure, from which the following is quoted:

It should be recognized as entirely proper that there are situations in connection with which we may acquire no knowledge of what has occurred after the date of our examination and, in the absence of any such knowledge, are able to release a standard form certificate within a reasonable period after the completion of our field work with no fear of responsibility for what might have happened in the interim period concerning which we had no contact with the client or his affairs. It would appear that this should apply in the case of an annual report filed with the Securities and Exchange Commission

82. 15 U.S.C. § 78r (1946).
83. *Ibid.*

or any similar body. If, for instance, the field work for a printed annual report is completed and the report is certified on February 14, and the working papers then contained necessary data for checking the company's report to be rendered in April to the Commission, the independent accountant should check such report in April and furnish his certificate to accompany it with no responsibility for events which had occurred between February 15 and April unknown to him.[84]

2. The plaintiff must prove his reliance upon the financial statement and prove damages that were caused by such reliance.

3. While the plaintiff does not have the burden of proving negligence or fraud on the part of the accountant, the accountant is given the statutory defense "that he acted in good faith and had no knowledge that such statement was false or misleading." This quoted language is consistent with freedom from fraud rather than freedom from negligence. It would seem, therefore, that the rule of the *Ultramares* case has been here enacted and that there would not be liability to third parties for mere negligence where the good faith of the accountant is established.

The civil remedies under the Federal Securities Acts apply only to purchasers and owners of securities and do not include claims of creditors who are not bondholders or the owners of similar securities. Securities transactions which are strictly intrastate matters would not be covered. Most of the states have their own so-called Blue Sky laws which regulate the issuance of securities and which do not contain specific provisions modifying the legal responsibility of the accountant under the common law. However, in the case of the State of Florida, the remedies of the Federal Securities Acts have been incorporated into their own state law by the following statutory enactment:

> The same civil remedies provided by laws of the United States now or hereafter in force, for the purchasers of securities under any such laws, in interstate commerce, shall extend also to purchasers of securities under this chapter.[85]

84. Hill, *Auditor's Responsibility for Events after Balance-Sheet Date,* FIVE NEW GUIDES TO THE AUDITOR'S RESPONSIBILITY 9 (papers presented at 64th annual meeting of the American Institute of Accountants 1951).

85. FLA. STAT. ANN. § 517.23 (West 1943).

CHAPTER 5

DISCIPLINARY PROCEEDING

Situations may occasionally arise where the work of the accountant may be subjected to serious critical attack which nevertheless does not involve legal responsibility or civil liability. Though the claim may be made that an audit was performed or reported upon fraudulently or incompetently, the claimant may be unable to prove that he sustained damages. Therefore he cannot maintain any action, either at common law or under the Federal Securities Acts. He may be a third party who cannot even sue for the recovery of a fee. In such circumstances, he may resort to the filing of a complaint seeking disciplinary action against the accountant involved. Though such a complaint may not include the threat of a judgment for money damages, it may place in jeopardy the reputation of the accountant, or even the retention of his CPA certificate. From this latter viewpoint it would seem relevant to include in this chapter some mention of disciplinary proceedings.

Disciplinary powers over accounting practitioners are vested in:

1. Professional societies such as the American Institute of Accountants and the various state societies. These organizations have established codes of professional conduct for the breach of which a member may be expelled or suspended from membership, or censured.
2. Under the authority of state statutes regulating certified public accountants there is generally provision for the revocation or suspension of the CPA certificate or the censure of the CPA where, after due notice and a proper hearing, the constituted authorities find evidence of specified professional misconduct.
3. The Securities and Exchange Commission in Rule II (e) of its Rules of Practice has provided:

(e) The Commission may disqualify, and deny, temporarily or permanently, the privilege of appearing or practicing before it in any way to any person who is found by the Commission after hearing in the matter

(1) Not to possess the requisite qualifications to represent others; or

(2) To be lacking in character or integrity or to have engaged in unethical or improper professional conduct.

It is significant to note that fraud and gross negligence in the practice of public accountancy have been included in the broad concept of professional misconduct subject to disciplinary action. By way of illustration it is pertinent to quote Rule 5 of the *Rules of Professional Conduct* of the American Institute of Accountants:

> In expressing an opinion on representations in financial statements which he has examined, a member may be held guilty of an act discreditable to the profession if
>
> (a) he fails to disclose a material fact known to him which is not disclosed in the financial statements but disclosure of which is necessary to make the financial statements not misleading; or
>
> (b) he fails to report any material misstatement known to him to appear in the financial statement; or
>
> (c) he is materially negligent in the conduct of his examination or in making his report thereon; or
>
> (d) he fails to acquire sufficient information to warrant expression of an opinion, or his exceptions are sufficiently material to negative the expression of an opinion; or
>
> (e) he fails to direct attention to any material departure from generally accepted accounting principles or to disclose any material omission of generally accepted auditing procedure applicable in the circumstances.

CHAPTER 6

WORKING PAPERS

Relevancy From an Evidentiary Viewpoint

In any case brought against an accountant on the ground that negligence or fraud was involved in his work, it is altogether likely that the working papers relating to the audit will be offered in evidence in whole or in part. The evidence may be offered by the plaintiff to support his allegations of fraud or negligence. On the other hand, it may be the accountant who will introduce his working papers to establish the adequacy of his audit and the fairness of the opinion which he expressed in his report thereon.

To be more specific, the working papers may be relevant on one or more of the following issues which may arise in the case:

1. The working papers will constitute a record of the audit work performed, both from a qualitative and quantitative standpoint. That is to say, they will constitute proof of what records were examined, what inquiries were made, what confirmations were undertaken, etc. At the same time they may constitute a record of the amount of testing and sampling that was performed, which, in the judgment of the accountant, was adequate in the circumstances.
2. The extent to which the audit work was properly planned and supervised may be evident from the working papers.
3. The nature and extent of the review of the client's system of internal control and its effective operation may appear in the working papers, and therefore the extent to which the accountant relied upon his appraisal of internal control in planning and carrying out his audit program.
4. The scope of his inquiries addressed to the client and the extent to which the accountant relied upon the client's representations may be recorded in the working papers.
5. Working papers may contain information which the plaintiff claims should have aroused the suspicion of the accountant and resulted in an extension of his audit procedures beyond the work which was done.
6. The working papers in their entirety may be offered by the accountant as evidence of his compliance with generally accepted auditing standards in support of the opinion expressed in his report.
7. The working papers may contain information which the plaintiff claims should have been disclosed and the omission of which, it is claimed, makes the report of the accountant misleading.
8. Where the genuineness of the accountant's belief in the opinion which he has expressed is put in issue, the working papers may offer persuasive evidence of the thinking of the accountant in the development and formulation of his opinion.

Even where the working papers themselves are not put in evidence, they may be used to refresh the recollection of the accountant as to significant occurrences during the course of the audit and as to the circumstances existing in connection with his work which influenced his judgment in many important ways. On the other hand, an inspection of the working papers by the plaintiff's representatives may supply leads for inquiry and material for the cross-examination of the accountant.

Ownership of Working Papers — The Ipswich Mills Case

In view of the potential importance of the accountant's working papers, many states have confirmed their ownership by the accountant through specific statutory enactment.[86] Even in the absence of such statutory provisions, however, the courts have recognized and upheld such ownership by the accountant.

The leading case on this point is *Ipswich Mills v. Dillon,*[87] decided in 1927 by the Massachusetts Supreme Judicial Court. That was a case brought by a corporation against certified public accountants, the corporation seeking to gain possession of certain documents held by the accountants, who had theretofore been employed by the corporation to make annual audits, prepare tax returns and statements for banks, and to represent the corporation in a Federal tax matter before the Bureau of Internal Revenue. There had been no special agreement between the client and the accountants as to the ownership of the documents. The papers were divided into the following categories for purposes of this litigation:

> Group A consisted of papers that originated in the client's offices or in the offices of its selling agents or of someone associated with them. The accountants conceded that the client was the owner of these papers.
>
> Group B included a copy of the amended Federal tax returns of the plaintiff for the year 1918 and certain papers (not work sheets) relating thereto.
>
> Group C included copies of the client's tentative and amended tax return for 1919 with work sheets and correspondence in connection therewith.

86. The states of California, Florida, Kentucky, Missouri, New Hampshire, Oregon, Pennsylvania, Virginia and Washington, and Puerto Rico, have included such a provision in their statutes regulating the practice of public accountancy. In some instances the provision relates only to certified public accountants. In other instances, it relates to certified public accountants and public accountants. In all other respects, these provisions are substantially identical. The Virginia statute is quoted by way of illustration: "All statements, records, schedules and memoranda made by a certified public accountant or a public accountant, or by an employee or employees of a certified public accountant, or public accountant, incident to or in the course of professional service to clients by such certified public accountant, or public accountant, except reports submitted by a certified public accountant, or public accountant, to a client shall be and remain the property of such certified public accountant, or public accountant, in the absence of a written agreement between the certified public accountant, or public accountant, and the client, to the contrary." VA. CODE ANN. § 54–101 (1950).

87. 260 Mass. 453, 157 N.E. 604 (1927). Reprinted at p. 263 *infra*.

Group D consisted of papers and work sheets of revaluation of the client's plant assets.

Group E consisted of the accountants' work sheets of their July, 1922 report.

Group F included papers, reports, returns, copies, work sheets, data, correspondence and memoranda respecting the tax case, together with some letters originating in the client's office.

The trial judge had ruled that the client was the owner of all of the above enumerated papers, except those in Group F, and entitled to their immediate possession. As to Group F, he ruled that the client and the accountants were jointly interested in those papers, with the right in the client to take them temporarily from the accountants.

On appeal, this decision was reversed and it was held that except for group A (which the accountants conceded belonged to the client) *all enumerated papers and documents belonged to the accountants.* The appellate court stressed the fact that the accountants were not mere employees of the client but were independent contractors functioning in a professional capacity. The court also was impressed with the necessity for the accountants retaining possession of all of these documents "if the accuracy of their work was questioned." The following quotations from the court's opinion further explain the decision reached:

> The carbon copies of the defendants' letters to the collector of internal revenue did not belong to the plaintiff. Whatever right it may have to examine these copies, or take copies of them, which point we are not called upon to decide, the defendants' copies did not belong to the plaintiff; they were owned by the defendants. The fact that the copies of these letters concern the plaintiff is not a sufficient reason for depriving the defendants of their property. In writing the letters the defendants were not the plaintiff's servants.
>
> In group C there are copies of Federal tax returns. These, as we understand from the record, were the defendants' office copies. The record shows that copies of all returns and schedules prepared by the defendants for the plaintiff were sent to the plaintiff. Even if the plaintiff has a right to require further copies, a question not involved in this suit, it has no right to demand of the defendants the surrender of these office copies. They were the property of the defendants.
>
> The work sheets, as defined by the trial judge, were the defendants' property. They were made by them while engaged in their own business. The paper on which the computations were made belonged to them. They were not employed to make these sheets. The sheets were merely the means by which the work for which the defendants were employed might be accomplished. The title to the work sheets remained in the defendants after the computations were made. In the absence of an agreement that these sheets were to belong to the plaintiff, or were to be held for it, they were owned by the defendants. It may be that these papers contained information confidential in its nature and of importance to the plaintiff; but the defendants did not receive this information as the plaintiff's servants. . . . The interest of the plaintiff in the information collected and copied by the defendants and the confidential nature of this information do not give title to the plaintiff of

the defendants' working papers. They were made by the defendants solely for their own assistance in preparing the tax returns.

With reference to group F, the letters addressed to the defendants, copies of letters written by the defendants, copies of returns furnished to the plaintiff, and work sheets relating to the tax case, are the sole property of the defendants, and this is true of the papers and reports collected by the defendants in the preparation of the tax case. The plaintiff is not jointly interested with the defendants in these documents. We do not understand that any of these reports, papers and returns were property of the plaintiff which had been placed in the defendants' custody by the plaintiff or merely delivered to the defendants. If there are any papers belonging to the plaintiff which were lent to the defendants, the plaintiff is entitled to them; but as we construe the record, the papers referred to in group F were gathered and collected by the defendants in the course of their business, and were not papers of the plaintiff placed by it in the defendants' possession.[88]

The New York Surrogate's Court Case[89]

A case arising in the New York Surrogate's Court in 1936 indicated that the property rights of the accountant in his working papers may be qualified or limited in certain circumstances. A certified public accountant, who had been an individual practitioner for a number of years prior to his death in 1933, in his will bequeathed to his secretary "all of my office files and records." Upon the proceeding to settle the accounts of the executrix, the Surrogate's Court was called upon to decide whether the language in the will included working papers and if it did, whether or not the testator had a legal right to dispose of them by will. The Surrogate held that no such right existed, but in so holding, it did not differ with the *Ipswich Mills* case.

The *Ipswich Mills* case did not deprive the client of the right to prevent the accountant from disclosing to other persons the confidential information in his working papers. In other words, the title of the accountant to his working papers was always subject to his obligation to deal with the information there contained in compliance with the confidential relationship of client and accountant. This legal principle was not abrogated by the *Ipswich Mills* case, nor could it have been, without doing violence to the rights of the client implied in the client-accountant relationship.

If the deceased accountant had been a member of a partnership and had bequeathed his interest in the partnership papers to any one or all of his surviving partners, the question presented in this case would not have arisen. The confidential nature of the working papers would have been safeguarded despite the transfer of ownership of the interest in them

88. *Id.* at 457–458, 157 N.E. at 606–607.

89. *Estate of* William H. Dennis, 95 N.Y. Law Journal 827 (Surr. Ct. Feb. 15, 1936). Excerpt reprinted at p. 266 *infra*.

possessed by the decedent. But this was the case of an individual practitioner who had no surviving partners. If the court had recognized an unqualified right in the testator to deal with his working papers as he would with other assets of his estate, then his legatee in turn could dispose of them to anyone else, even to a competitor of the client. Similarly, if the ownership of these working papers was to be regarded in the same category as the ownership of other assets, it would have been necessary to recognize the paramount right of creditors who might assert their claims against the working papers and dispose of them by sale for the satisfaction of the debts of the decedent.

The Surrogate wisely held that after the executrix had assured herself that there was no basis for claims against the estate which would require the retention and preservation of the working papers for the protection of the accountant's estate, she was to return to the respective clients all working papers which had originated in their offices and to destroy all working papers which the deceased accountant himself had prepared.

This important case, which bristles with undecided and unresolved implications, is not recorded in the official reports. It has been rescued from obscurity, so far as accountants are concerned, through the very comprehensive discussion of it which appeared contemporaneously in *The Journal of Accountancy*.[90] The comments on the case in this chapter are based upon that discussion.

The Frye Case [91]

This case was decided by the Supreme Court of Ohio in May, 1951. It is of special interest to practicing accountants for at least three reasons:

> 1. It is an illustration of the uncomfortable predicament of an accountant who is not a party to a litigation brought against his client, but who, nevertheless, is compelled by legal process to testify against his client's interests by divulging the contents of his working papers.
>
> 2. While reaffirming the *Ipswich Mills* case, it holds that the mere possession of legal title to his working papers does not give the accountant the legal right to refuse to disclose their contents to parties other than his client, where such disclosure is ordered by the courts incidental to litigation or for other reasons.
>
> 3. It clarifies the legal limitations affecting the confidential nature of his working papers and the qualified obligation of the accountant to refrain from disclosing the contents thereof.

The client in this case was being sued by a sales agent who had been in its employ, who claimed commissions to be computed on a percentage

90. 61 JOURNAL OF ACCOUNTANCY 246 (1936).

91. *In re* Frye, 155 Ohio St. 345, 98 N.E.2d 798 (1951). Reprinted at p. 267 *infra*.

basis. The accountant, who had audited the books of the client, was served with a subpoena *duces tecum* requiring the production by the accountant of "all records or copies of records in your possession relating to the financial condition or operation of [the client] from the date of its organization to the present day; including copies of all . . . tax returns, state or federal . . ."

The accountant appeared for examination, testified that she had been the client's auditor since its organization, and presented and identified some thirty separate exhibits consisting of audit reports, financial statements, and commission statements. At a subsequent hearing the accountant appeared with counsel who objected to the introduction in evidence of the accountant's working papers previously identified or of "photostatic replicas" thereof. To lay a foundation for such objection, she testified that she did work for the defendants as an independent contractor in the capacity of auditor; that she had no records which belonged to the defendant; that the records which she had previously identified were her own personal records; that when she made out the tax returns for the client, she gave it the originals and copies for its files and that the client did the filing of the tax returns. Upon her persistent refusal, she was cited for contempt and put under technical arrest. The legal issues thus raised finally came before the Ohio Supreme Court on appeal.

The court held against the accountant and ruled that she was lawfully obligated to produce the documents for use in evidence. It was held that the *Ipswich Mills* case did not apply to this situation, the court stating:

> In that case the papers were not under subpoena in the hands of the accountants to produce them in court. Doubtless they were subject to subpoena but this question was in no way before the court. The sole question determined was the ownership of the papers. Doubtless in a proper case a court will protect the owner of papers and documents so far as their custody is concerned by requiring the party calling for them for evidential purposes to make photostatic or other proper copies of the same so that the owner may retain the originals. Such an offer was made to Frye by the plaintiff in the instant case but the offer was rejected.[92]

The accountant also contended that the documents sought in evidence related to the income tax returns of the client and that their production by the accountant would be in violation of the United States Internal Revenue Code which provided:

> It shall be unlawful . . . for any person to print or publish in any manner whatever not provided by law any income return, or any part thereof or source of income, profits, losses, or expenditures appearing in any income return. . . .[93]

92. *Id.* at 351, 98 N.E.2d at 802.

93. 26 U.S.C. § 55f (1946).

The court disposed of this contention in the following ruling:

> Furthermore, there is no infraction of the statute involved in this proceeding. The latter part of the statute above quoted prohibits any person from printing or publishing *tax returns* or sources of income, profit, losses or expenditures *appearing in any income tax return,* in any manner "not provided by law." This statute does not and could not legally inhibit the disclosure, as evidence in a proper judicial inquiry or where required by law, of the operative financial data relating to the business of a taxpayer, even though such data comprehends the elemental facts and information from which his income tax return is necessarily made up. The law could never sanction such a sweeping prohibition of disclosure of the essential facts of the business world. It must be evident that the statute in question has no such purpose or intent.[94]

The broad question of the duty of the accountant not to disclose the information involved because of its confidential nature, was dealt with by the court in the following terms:

> In the absence of a privilege created by constitution or statute not to disclose available information, a witness may not refuse to testify to pertinent facts in a judicial proceeding merely because such testimony comprehends a communication or report from himself as agent to his principal or as independent contractor to his employer, no matter how confidential may be the character of the communication itself or the relationship between the parties thereto. See 146 A.L.R. 966. And where one possesses knowledge of facts which are pertinent to a judicial inquiry, he may be required to testify or to produce papers and documents as to such facts. In discussing this subject, 58 American Jurisprudence, 40, Section 32, states the rule as follows: "It is a general rule that a witness possessing knowledge of facts material to the vindication of the rights of another may be compelled by judicial process to appear and give evidence in behalf of that other party, notwithstanding the evidence thus coerced may uncover the witness's private business. This rule is also generally held applicable when the information sought is contained in books and papers. Accordingly, it has been held that it is no ground for the refusal of a witness to produce books and papers, when required by lawful authority, that they are private. The duty of witnesses to disclose the details of their private business for the benefit of third persons when required in the administration of justice, is one devolving on them as members of a civilized community." . . .[95]

The above quoted language of the court defines and limits not only the legal obligation but the ethical duty of the accountant concerning the confidential relationship existing between himself and his client, a relationship which has been set forth in the Institute's Rule 16 of the *Rules of Professional Conduct.* The legal position of the accountant with respect to the question of privileged communication status (which will be dealt with in the following pages) was only indirectly involved in the *Frye* case.

---

94. 155 Ohio St. at 352, 98 N.E.2d at 802.
95. *Id.* at 354, 98 N.E.2d at 803.

CHAPTER 7

PRIVILEGED COMMUNICATIONS

In the *Frye* case it was emphasized that neither the confidential nature of an accountant's working papers nor the personal ownership of them by the accountant was sufficient legal reason for a refusal by the accountant to divulge their contents in a judicial proceeding to which they were relevant. A different result might have been reached by the court had the relationship of accountant and client conferred upon these documents the status of privileged communications.

Such a status of privilege has been recognized under the common law as to confidential communications between attorney and client, and between husband and wife, and by statute generally as to confidential communications between physician and patient and between priest and penitent. Statutes have also codified and to some extent limited the common law privilege accorded to the attorney-client and the husband-wife relationship. With special reference to the accountant-client relationship, however, it has been held that no such privilege ever existed under the common law and that none will be recognized in the absence of a statute specifically creating such a status.

The leading case which so held was that of In re *Fisher*,[96] decided in 1931 in the Federal District Court of the Southern District of New York (a state which has no accountant privilege statute). The question arose during the course of bankruptcy proceedings. The witness involved was both a certified public accountant and a lawyer. He had acted as the bankrupt's accountant for a number of years and, after his later admission to the bar, also acted as the bankrupt's attorney. He refused to answer questions relating to the bankrupt's books of account or to produce working papers prepared by members of his accounting staff in the course of auditing the bankrupt's books. It would appear that he relied upon the privilege arising from the attorney-client relationship with the bankrupt, but the court, in directing the witness to testify, gave consideration as well to the fact that the evidence involved was obtained by the witness in his capacity as accountant. In support of its conclusion, the court stated:

> There is no privilege with regard to communications made to accountants. The information given to the witness and to the accountants in his employ for the purpose of making financial statements and doing other work characteristically performed by accountants is not privileged, despite the fact that

96. 51 F.2d 424 (S.D. N.Y. 1931). Reprinted at p. 273 *infra*.

> the witness may also have rendered legal advice on the basis of such data. See Matter of Robinson, 140 App. Div. 329, 125 N.Y.S. 193, where it was held that an attorney for a corporation, who was one of its directors, could not refuse to disclose information about corporate affairs by claiming his professional privilege.
>
> Furthermore, the privilege accorded to an attorney is the privilege of the client and not of the attorney. Baumann v. Steingester, 213 N.Y. 328, 107 N.E. 578, Ann. Cas. 1916C, 1071. For this reason the attorney cannot claim privilege where the client has already disclosed the substance of the communication. Baumann v. Steingester supra. Nor can he claim privilege where the communication was made with the understanding that it was to be imparted to third parties. Rosseau v. Bleau, 131 N.Y. 177, 30 N.E. 52, 27 Am. St. Rep. 578.
>
> In the case at bar it appears that the bankrupt has already testified with respect to the matters contained in his books and records. And the income tax returns and financial statements drawn up from the communications made by bankrupt to the witness were obviously intended to be communicated to others.
>
> For these reasons, the witness should be directed to testify with regard to the bankrupt's books and to produce in evidence the monthly work sheets made by the accountants.[97]

In the case of *Himmelfarb v. United States,*[98] decided in 1949 in the Federal courts of California (a state which has no accountant privilege statute) it was again held that privileged communications are not recognized as between a client and his accountant. In that case the certified public accountant had been employed by the client's attorney during the pendency of an investigation by the special agents of the Intelligence Unit of the Treasury Department. The accountant attended numerous conferences with the attorney and the client and also examined the client's records. In an effort to work out a settlement, the attorney and the accountant had supplied the Treasury agents with considerable documentary material which the accountant had assembled from the books and records. On the trial which followed, the accountant was subpoenaed and identified the documents, which were then put in evidence over the objection of the client's attorney. The court held that even if the accountant had obtained some of the information by being present at conferences between the client and the attorney, such communications were not privileged. The accountant's "presence was not indispensable in the sense that the presence of an attorney's secretary may be. It was a convenience which, unfortunately for the accused, served to remove the privileged character of whatever communications were made. Of course, communications made by the client to such a third party in the presence of the attorney are not within the privilege." [99]

97. *Id.* at 425.

98. 175 F.2d 924 (9th Cir.), *cert. denied,* 338 U.S. 860 (1949). Excerpt reprinted at p. 274 *infra.*

99. *Id.* at 939.

It was held that, from any viewpoint, the documents prepared by the accountant were properly admissible. To the extent that they were based upon information given to the accountant directly by the client or obtained from the client's records, there was no privilege growing out of the accountant-client relationship. Insofar as the documents were based upon information overheard by the accountant at conferences between the client and the attorney, which would otherwise have been privileged, the presence of the accountant destroyed the privilege.

It was similarly held in the later income tax evasion case of *Gariepy v. United States*[100] that under the common law there is no accountant-client privilege. In this instance the Michigan statute creating an accountant-client privilege was expressly inapplicable in a criminal case.

The *Himmelfarb* case was specifically cited and followed in 1951, in the Federal courts in Pennsylvania, in the case of *United States v. Stoehr*.[101]

Although all of these cases arose in the Federal courts in connection with criminal or bankruptcy matters, they consistently support the proposition that, in the absence of statutory provision, there is no status of privilege applicable to the confidential communications between client and accountant similar to that which applies to the communications between attorney and client.

Statutes which confer the status of privileged communications upon information obtained by accountants during the course of their work have now been enacted by twelve of our states and by Puerto Rico. These statutes fall roughly into three groups:

1. Arizona,[102] Iowa,[103] Maryland,[104] Michigan and Tennessee[105] specifically provide that the privilege is not applicable in situations involving criminal or bankruptcy laws. All of this group, except Tennessee, apply to certified public accountants and public accountants. The Tennessee statute mentions only certified public accountants. These are other variations within this group, but the Michigan statute may be quoted as a fair example:

> Except by written permission of the client, or person, or firm, or corporation employing him, or the heirs, successors or personal representatives of such employer, a certified public accountant, or a public accountant, or a person employed by a certified public accountant or by a public accountant shall not be required to, and shall not voluntarily, disclose or divulge information of which he or she may have become possessed relative to and in connection with any examination of, audit of, or report on, any books, records, or ac-

100. 189 F.2d 459 (6th Cir. 1951). Excerpt reprinted at p. 276 *infra*.

101. 100 F. Supp. 143 (M.D. Pa. 1951), *aff'd*, 196 F.2d 276 (3d Cir. 1952), *cert. denied*, 344 U.S. 826 (1952). Excerpts reprinted at p. 277 *infra*.

102. Ariz. Code Ann. § 67–609 (1939).

103. Iowa Code Ann. § 116.15 (West 1949).

104. Md. Ann. Code Art. 75A, § 11 (1951).

105. Tenn. Code Ann. § 7097.12 (Williams Replacement Volume 1941).

counts which he or she may be employed to make. The information derived from or as the result of such professional service shall be deemed confidential and privileged: *Provided, however,* That nothing in this paragraph shall be taken or construed as modifying, changing or affecting the criminal or bankruptcy laws of this state or of the United States.[106]

2. Florida,[107] Illinois,[108] Kentucky,[109] Louisiana, New Mexico [110] and Puerto Rico [111] do not exclude criminal or bankruptcy matters from the provisions of this statute. The Louisiana statute is quoted as an example of this group:

No certified public accountant, public accountant, or person employed by certified public accountant or public accountant, shall be required to, or voluntarily disclose or divulge, the contents of any communication made to him by any person employing him to examine, audit, or report on any books, records, or accounts, or divulge any information derived from such books, records or accounts in rendering professional services except by express permission of the person employing him or his heirs, personal representatives or successors.[112]

3. Colorado and Georgia may be considered a third group which, like the second group, does not exclude criminal and bankruptcy matters from the statutes, but mentions certified public accountants only. As these statutes create a status not recognized under the common law, they would be strictly construed and therefore would exclude from their provisions accountants who were not certified public accountants. However, there are very important differences in wording between the Colorado and Georgia statutes, and for this reason it is advisable to quote both.

The Colorado statute provides:

Who may not testify without consent. There are particular relations in which it is the policy of the law to encourage confidence and to preserve it inviolate; therefore, a person shall not be examined as a witness in the following cases: . . .

Sixth — A certified public accountant shall not, without the consent of his client, be examined as to any communication made by the client to him in person or through the media of books of account and financial records, or his advice, reports or working papers given or made thereon in the course of professional employment, nor shall a secretary, stenographer, clerk or assistant of a certified public accountant be examined without the consent of the client concerned concerning any fact, the knowledge of which he has acquired in such capacity.[113]

---

106. MICH. STAT. ANN. § 18.23 (Callaghan 1937).
107. FLA. STAT. ANN. § 473.15 (West 1952).
108. ILL. ANN. STAT. Ch. 110½, § 22 (Smith-Hurd 1935).
109. KY. REV. STAT. § 325.440 (1953).
110. NEW MEXICO STAT. ANN. § 51–1736 (Cum. Supp. 1941).
111. Laws of 1945, Act No. 293, § 19.
112. LA. REV. STAT. ANN. § 37.85 (West 1951).
113. COLO. STAT. ANN. Ch. 177, § 9 (Replacement Volume 1949)

The Georgia statute provides:

> Any communications to any practicing certified public accountant transmitted to such accountant in anticipation of, or pending, the employment of such accountant shall be treated as confidential and not disclosed nor divulged by said accountant in any proceedings of any nature whatsoever. This rule shall not exclude the accountant as a witness to any facts which may transpire in connection with his employment.[114]

It should be reiterated that there are other important variations in wording in the statutes within the other groups. This should be kept in mind in considering the legal problems which may arise in any particular engagement.

There is frequently the question as to whether the federal or the state rule will govern in any particular case. This question was raised in a proceeding before the Securities and Exchange Commission, where the Commission held that it was not inhibited by the Illinois statute from admitting in evidence a confidential communication contained in the accountant's working papers. The following is quoted from the Commission's release in that case:

> Registrant also asserts that the Kuiper memorandum was erroneously admitted in evidence because of an Illinois statute which provides that a public accountant is not required to testify as to information obtained by him in his capacity as a public accountant (2 Ill. Stat. Ann. (Jones) Sec. 1.19).
>
> It is clear that the common law never recognized any privilege in the accountant-client relationship (In re *Fisher* 51 F. (2d) 424 (S.D.N.Y. 1931)). Moreover, state legislation purporting to create such a privilege is given no effect in federal courts outside the state (*Doll v. Equitable Life Assur. Soc.*, 138 Fed. 705 (C.C.A. 3d, 1905)). While, in this case, the Kuiper memorandum was introduced during a session held in Illinois, the hearing was originally ordered to be held in Washington, D.C., and a large portion of the hearing was actually conducted in that city. Since it is clear that such a statutory privilege is not recognized outside the state and that no objection based on such a privilege could have been directed to the introduction of the Kuiper memorandum during that portion of the hearing held in Washington, D.C., it would be manifestly absurd to hold that the memorandum must be excluded because of the fortuitous circumstance that it was introduced while the hearing was being conducted in Illinois. Moreover, while the question need not be resolved here, we have some doubt whether state limitations on the admissibility of evidence which go beyond the common law rules of evidence can be binding in any case in hearings of a tribunal having no fixed situs analogous to that of the federal district courts. For the underlying basis for the conformity statutes, such as 28 U.S.C. § 631, is to achieve a uniformity of evidentiary rules in forums which are permanently fixed within a single state and has no applicability to the hearings of tribunals which have no fixed situs within that state.[115]

---

114. GA. CODE ANN. § 84–216 (Cum. Supp. 1951).

115. *In the matter of* Resources Corporation International, 7 S.E.C. 689 (1940) (footnote 47 at p. 741).

A more recent instance of an apparent conflict between the Illinois statute and Federal court decisions was disposed of in Petition of *Borden Co.*[116] where the Federal court refused to give effect to the state statute because it conflicted with the Federal Rules of Criminal Procedure. In other words, the Federal court in effect attached to the Illinois statute a proviso that it did not apply to a criminal proceeding in the Federal court. The following is quoted from the court's opinion:

> It is contended that the reports made by public accountants for The Borden Company, called for by the subpoena duces tecum in question, are privileged. Section 51, Chapter 110½, Illinois Revised Statutes 1947, provides: "A public accountant shall not be required by any court to divulge information or evidence which has been obtained by him in his confidential capacity as a public accountant."
>
> It is doubtful whether the privilege granted by this section to a public accountant extends to his written report after he has released it, but it is unnecessary for the court to decide whether the privilege created by the section does extend to the report after its release for the reason that Rule 26 of the Federal Rules of Criminal Procedure, 18 U.S.C.A. following section 687, provides: "The admissibility of evidence and the compentency and privileges of witnesses shall be governed, except when an act of Congress or these rules otherwise provide, by the principles of the common law as they may be interpreted by the courts of the United States in the light of reason and experience."
>
> At common law the reports of public accountants are not privileged. No act of Congress and no one of the Federal Rules of Criminal Procedure provides otherwise. Accordingly, the court concludes that the reports of public accountants are not privileged.[117]

In another very recent case, *Falsone v. United States,*[118] where an accountant was summoned to testify and bring records to an Internal Revenue agent investigating the accountant's client, the court held that the accountant must produce the records even though the state (Florida) statute[119] made them privileged communications, and even though the tax statute of limitations had run on some of the years for which the records were demanded. In support of its holding the court quoted from *United States v. Murdock,* "Investigations for Federal purposes may not be prevented by matters depending upon state law."[120]

There is also the interesting question (raised by the dictum in the *Borden* case) as to whether the client does not waive the privilege as to accountant's reports which he has released to third parties. It may well be argued that such reports have lost their confidential character, which is the foundation of the privilege. If the accountant's report has lost its

116. 75 F. Supp. 857 (N.D. Ill. 1948). Excerpt reprinted at p. 279 *infra.*

117. *Id.* at 859–860.

118. 205 F.2d 734 (5th Cir.), *cert. denied,* 74 Sup. Ct. 103 (1953). Reprinted at p. 280 *infra.*

119. Fla. Stat. Ann. § 473.15 (West 1952).

120. 284 U.S. 141, 149 (1931).

character as a privileged communication protected by statute, it would then seem to follow that the working papers of the accountant, which were compiled in connection with the preparation of that report, have similarly been released from the prohibition of the statute.

It has been argued that even though the "accounting statements are designed for exhibition to others generally and would not therefore constitute a communication in confidence . . ., the working papers generally contain confidential matters never revealed in the financial statements." [121] This is undoubtedly so, yet the relevancy of the working papers to the financial statements which are published is so intimate and important that it is highly doubtful that courts would draw the distinction urged above. It would seem more likely that the courts would hold that the client, by publishing his financial statement, waives his privilege not only with respect to that statement but with respect to the underlying working papers assembled by the accountant in the course of preparing or examining the financial statement in question.

Furthermore, the accountant might have to resort to the working papers to defend himself against critical attack. Certainly if the client himself attacks the work of the accountant, it is inconceivable that the client would not have waived any right he might have previously had to prevent the accountant from putting the working papers in evidence. If a waiver on the part of the client were not implied in such a situation, the result obviously would be unconscionably unjust.

For the same reason, if a third party brings an action against the accountant, based on the accountant's report published by the client, the accountant should not be prevented from offering his working papers in evidence in defense of his work merely because his client's consent thereto cannot be obtained. Under Section 22 of the Federal Securities Act of 1933,[122] state courts and Federal courts have concurrent jurisdiction in all actions brought to enforce any liability created under the statute. Such an action might be brought against an accountant in the courts of the state where there is a statutory accountant privilege. The plaintiff might be a third party security owner who brings an action against the accountant based upon prima facie proof of a false statement in the balance sheet audited and certified to by the accountant. The accountant would have the burden of proof of showing that after reasonable investigation he had reason to believe, and did believe, that the financial statement was true. Without recourse to his working papers, the accountant might not be able to sustain this burden of proof. It is most unlikely that in such a situation the state court would hold that the accountant could not put his working papers in evidence or testify concerning their contents without the consent of his client. The only reasonable and just attitude

121. Rich, Legal Responsibilities and Rights of Public Accountants 180 (1935).

122. 15 U.S.C. § 77v (1946).

which the courts could take in such a situation would be that when the client caused the financial statement (based upon these very working papers) to be made available to the public through its inclusion in the Registration Statement filed with the Securities and Exchange Commission, he waived the statutory privilege, and, by implication, consented to the accountant's use of his working papers to defend his work, if need be.

One other case should be noted which dealt with the accountant's privilege under the Colorado statute. This was the case on appeal in *Hopkins v. The People,*[123] which involved the conviction for embezzlement of the administrator of a decedent's estate. On the trial a certified public accountant, employed by the prosecution, testified to certain facts obtained through an examination of the records of the estate. The defendant objected to the testimony because of the Colorado statute providing that a certified public accountant, under certain circumstances, should not be examined as a witness without the consent of his client. The court held that the statute had no application to this situation since the defendant who invoked the statute was not the client of the certified public accountant who testified, and therefore the defendant's consent was not required.

123. 89 Colo. 296, 1 P.2d 937 (1931). Excerpt reprinted at p. 288 *infra*.

PART TWO

Cases and Articles

SECTION 1

FUNDAMENTAL CONSIDERATIONS

SMITH v. LONDON ASSURANCE CORP.*

Appellate Division of the Supreme Court of New York, Second Department, 1905.
109 App. Div. 882, 96 N. Y. Supp. 820

HOOKER, J. The action is to recover for services rendered to the defendant by the plaintiffs in their capacity as public accountants. The answer admits a small payment on account, as alleged in the complaint, avers that such payment was in full of the plaintiffs' claim, and includes a counterclaim for a large sum of money embezzled by one of the defendant's employees, which embezzlement the defendant claims would not and could not have occurred except for a breach of plaintiffs' contract of employment. The plaintiffs demurred to the counterclaim on the ground that it does not state facts sufficient to constitute a cause of action, the demurrer was overruled, and plaintiffs appeal.

The plaintiffs do not challenge the proposition of law advanced by the defendant that public accountants now constitute a skilled professional class and are subject generally to the same rules of liability for negligence in the practice of their profession as are members of other skilled professions. And such is doubtless the law. Cooley states the rule governing the measure of such liability in this language: "Every man who offers his services to another and is employed, assumes the duty to exercise in the employment such skill as he possesses with reasonable care and diligence. In all those employments where peculiar skill is requisite, if one offers his services he is understood as holding himself out to the public as possessing the degree of skill commonly possessed by others in the same employment, and if his pretensions are unfounded he commits a species of fraud upon every man who employs him in reliance on his public profession. But no man, whether skilled or unskilled, undertakes that the task he assumes shall be performed successfully and without fault or error; he undertakes for good faith and integrity but not for infallibility, and he is liable to his employer for negligence, bad faith or dishonesty, but not for losses consequent upon mere errors of judgment." (Cooley Torts [2d ed.], 777. See, also, *Carpenter* v. *Blake,* 50 N.Y. 696; S. C., 75 id. 12; *Link* v. *Sheldon,* 136 id. 1; *Pike* v. *Honsinger,* 155 id. 201.)

Although the counterclaim is inartistically drawn and deficient in logical order, we believe that it does state sufficient facts to make out a cause of action. In the 10th paragraph of the answer, near the final statements of the counterclaim, is to be found an allegation that in the

* This case is cited at p. 4 *supra.*

agreement between the parties it "was expressly stipulated that there should be a frequent checking by the plaintiffs of the cash account of the New York branch of the defendant, and a verification of the items appearing thereon." Reverting to the first words of the 9th paragraph an averment is found that the plaintiffs "have negligently and willfully failed to examine and check in particular the cash account of the New York fire office of the defendant and have failed to verify the said cash and agency accounts." Then follows the allegation that Scott, its cashier, from time to time embezzled large amounts of money paid to him as such cashier, the embezzlement being assisted by his falsifying entries in defendant's books and practically its cash books. In the 11th paragraph it is alleged that the defendant's losses from Scott's embezzlements and defalcations were due to the negligence of the plaintiffs to perform their agreement with the defendant in the manner stipulated.

These allegations, with the facts that may be implied from them by reasonable and fair intendment, sufficiently plead a valid contract, its breach and the resultant damage, and require a reply from the plaintiffs. Had an examination and checking of the New York office cash account, performed with that degree of skill and care demanded by the rule which has been noticed, resulted in preventing defendant's loss, in whole or in part, the plaintiffs should respond in damages; for it must have been within the reasonable contemplation of the parties at the time of making the contract, and so it is inferentially alleged in the counterclaim that one of the objects of the frequent checking of the defendant's cash account of the New York branch and a verification of the items thereof was to prevent, or at least arrest, just such practices as it is claimed Scott indulged in, and the loss the defendant has sustained naturally flows from the breach of the contract it has plead.

The interlocutory judgment should, therefore, be affirmed * * *.

ACCOUNTANTS' LIABILITY*

By SAUL LEVY, C.P.A. and Member of the New York Bar

The subject of accountants' liability is as broad as the scope of our professional activity and the content of the opinions which we issue in the course of our work. It involves our relations with the government, the general public, our clients, and with each other. This paper will attempt to deal with only one phase of the subject. It will discuss the question of legal liability from the standpoint of its intimate relation to the development by our profession of its own technical criteria.

During the past several years the American Institute of Accountants through its committees and its members has been dealing aggressively and effectively with accounting and auditing standards, procedures, principles and terminology. Insofar as these matters are crystallized into a form or formula which has the general approval or acceptance of the

* A paper presented at the 55th annual meeting of the American Institute of Accountants, 1942. Published in WARTIME ACCOUNTING 146 and N. Y. CERTIFIED PUBLIC ACCOUNTANT 10 (1942).

profession, we succeed in establishing technical criteria "by which facts, principles, opinions and conduct are tried in forming a correct judgment respecting them." This paper is presented from the viewpoint of those who believe it is the function of every profession worthy of the name to establish its own technical criteria. The desirability of doing so in its relation to the question of legal liability will be here considered.

In recent years, considerable attention has been focused on the dual responsibility of the client and the independent public accountant. Responsibilities arise simultaneously through the publication or issuance by the client of statements whereby the client makes certain representations concerning his financial position and operating results, to which statements is attached the certificate or opinion of the independent public accountant. In an effort to clarify the situation, members of our profession have raised the question "Whose Balance Sheet is it?" Many have strenuously insisted that it is the balance sheet of the client and that it sets forth the primary representations of the client. Others have pointed to instances where the public accountant himself prepared the statements, where the public accountant was engaged to do so, and where the credit grantor and others have regarded the resulting statement as the accountant's balance sheet.

A third viewpoint has been recently asserting itself which seems to carry us along a little further toward a clearer understanding of the respective responsibilities of client and public accountant. It is pointed out that certified financial statements are the statements both of the client and of the accountant.

Insofar as such statements set forth the financial position or the operating results of the client, they are obviously the statements of the client. The client assumes responsibility for the factual representations they contain and for the accuracy of the accounting records upon which they are based. He does not relieve himself of such responsibilities by engaging a public accountant to audit his records and to express an opinion concerning his statements.

In a different sense, the statements are at the same time those of the accountant. It is through the medium of these statements that the accountant expresses a professional opinion concerning the financial position and operating results of the client. The statement becomes an integral and inseparable part of the accountant's opinion. That opinion may serve to support and tend to corroborate the representations of the client, but it does not involve the assumption by the accountant of responsibility for the factual representations of the client. From this viewpoint, it would seem to be immaterial whether the client or the accountant prepared the financial statements in the first instance. In either case, the accountant, in expressing an opinion concerning the statements, assumes responsibility for whatever opinion he expresses. The legal liability of the accountant for the expression of a professional opinion is governed by the nature of that opinion, and a finding (by whatever tribunal has the function of making such a finding) as to whether or not that professional opinion is reasonably well-founded in terms of auditing standards and procedures and accounting principles and terminology.

While the respective responsibilities of the client and the public accountant may arise out of the same financial statements, they are separate, distinct and different types of responsibility. If we speak of the primary responsibility of the client, we are in danger of implying that public accountants have a related secondary liability. This may put us in the undesired position of assuming secondary liability for factual representations, when we have done no more than express an opinion.

Since the *Ultramares* case, which was decided in 1931, we have given a great deal of thought to the fundamental distinction in our work between representations of fact and expressions of opinion. A representation of fact by the accountant is virtually warranted to be true. As was stated by the Court in the *Ultramares* case:

> "The defendants certified as a fact, true to their own knowledge, that the balance sheet was in accordance with the books of account. If their statement was false, they are not to be exonerated because they believed it to be true * * * accountants * * * by the very nature of their calling profess to speak with knowledge when certifying to an agreement between the audit and the entries."

In certifying to the statements with respect to the client's financial position or operating results, accountants usually profess to do no more than express an opinion. This is clearly indicated in the form of certificate, report or opinion now in general use by the profession. Nevertheless, an element of fact still remains in our certificates, though it relates to the scope of review or examination made, upon which our opinion is predicated. As Mr. Spencer Gordon stated at the 1939 annual meeting of this Institute:

> "If the form of report recommended by the special committee on auditing procedure is to be used it would appear that the only statements of fact will be as to the scope of the examination made. Under the doctrine promulgated by Judge Cardozo it would seem to follow that if the accountant has not *made* the examination that he states that he has made, he may be held in an action of deceit by any third party who has relied on the report, but the proposed form of report does not appear to involve any statement of fact as to the *result* of the examination. That the balance-sheet and the related statements of income and surplus fairly present the position of the company and the result of its operations is to be stated as a matter of opinion."[1]

Any such factual representation concerning the scope of review or examination which has been made, is likely to appear in very general terms, leaving much to implication and exploration should controversy arise. The scope of the examination made is so essential a prerequisite for the expression of the opinion which is founded upon it, that from the standpoint of legal liability the examination and the opinion usually merge into each other. This becomes apparent when we consider some of the characteristics of the professional opinion of the independent public accountant.

The *Ultramares* case also drew a distinction between negligence and

(1) Spencer Gordon, Liability Arising from Accountant's Report (Papers on Auditing Procedure, etc., presented at the Fifty-second Annual Meeting of the American Institute of Accountants, 1939, page 53).

fraud. It held that whereas the negligence of the accountant might create liability to his client, it would not result in liability to a third party relying upon the accountant's opinion. At the same time, however, the Court held that there would be liability to third parties for the fraud of the accountant and that such fraud might grow out of the expression of an opinion. In this connection the Court stated:

> "Even an opinion, especially an opinion by an expert, may be found to be fraudulent if the grounds supporting it are so flimsy as to lead to the conclusion that there was no genuine belief back of it. Further than that this Court has never gone. Directors of corporations have been acquitted of liability for deceit though they had been lax in investigation and negligent in speech * * *. This has not meant, to be sure, that negligence may not be evidence from which a trier of the facts may draw an inference of fraud * * * but merely that if that inference is rejected, or, in the light of all the circumstances, is found to be unreasonable, negligence alone is not a substitute for fraud."
>
> * * * * * *
>
> "Our holding does not emancipate accountants from the consequence of fraud. It does not relieve them if their audit has been so negligent as to justify a finding that they had no genuine belief in its adequacy, for this again is fraud."
>
> * * * * * *
>
> "In this connection we are to bear in mind the principle already stated in the course of this opinion that negligence or blindness, even when not equivalent to fraud, is none the less evidence to sustain an inference of fraud. At least this is so if the negligence is gross."

The *Ultramares* opinion has been followed without modification in subsequent cases both in the New York and Federal Courts. It remains our leading authority on accountants' liability. Although it drew a distinction in principle between negligence and fraud, it also established the rule that negligence may be offered as evidence of fraud. In consequence, a jury may hold that an accountant's opinion is a fraudulent pretense, merely because, in that jury's judgment, the underlying audit or examination was grossly negligent. Whether there was such negligence, and whether such negligence was sufficient to sustain an inference of fraud, are questions of fact for the jury to decide. In four of the leading cases[2] relating to accountants' liability, beginning with the *Ultramares* case, our appellate courts have consistently recognized and upheld the right of juries to pass upon these questions. Where trial courts have ruled that there was not sufficient evidence from which a jury might find fraud and where a jury verdict adverse to the accountant has been set aside by a trial judge, the appellate courts have reversed the trial courts and have sent these cases back for new trials. On the other hand, where a jury, after listening to all of the evidence, has found the accountants free from liability, the appellate court has been unwilling to disturb

(2) Ultramares Corporation v. Touche (1931) 255 N. Y. 170; O'Connor v. Ludlum (1937) 92 F. (2d) 50; State Street Trust Co. v. Ernst (1938) 278 N.Y. 104; National Surety Corp. v. Lyndbrand (1939) 256 App. Div. 226.

that finding. The significance of this is that the question of liability in any litigated case is likely to be a question of fact to be passed upon by a jury of laymen. The jury will examine the opinion of the accountant, pass upon its meaning, determine whether the opinion was properly based upon adequate examination or whether it was so negligently conceived that its expression amounted to fraud.

Some of the characteristics of the professional opinion of the public accountant which may become issues of fact for a jury to pass upon are the following. It will be seen that each of these characteristics involves an evaluation of difficult technical matters concerning which most laymen have had no previous knowledge or experience.

Without attempting a definitive description or analysis thereof, it may be pointed out that the accountant's opinion is (1) a technical opinion, (2) an informed opinion, (3) an expert opinion, (4) a candid opinion and (5) an independent opinion.

1. It is a *technical* opinion. The conclusions of the accountant are presented in the technical form of the balance sheet, income or operating statement, surplus account and supporting schedules. The opinion relates to financial position in the accounting sense and does not purport to appraise the enterprise in its entirety or evaluate any of the fixed assets. It does not guaranty the accuracy of the client's representations of fact.

This technical aspect of the accountant's opinion is further indicated in the following comments:

> "Some important elements of financial position are altogether beyond measurement and statement in terms of money values. Other elements frequently involve judgments and approximations which may be formulated or made within comparatively wide areas of reasonableness. This is particularly true, as the committee pointed out, of income statements prepared to cover the short period of a single year where, in a going concern, many items of unfinished business exist at the close of the year and where the direction of long-term trends is not fully apparent.
>
> * * * * * *
>
> "As for the balance-sheet, the committee has a full realization of the wide-spread misconception of the document as a measure of value or present worth and has repeatedly pointed out that its basic function is to measure investment rather than value. The current studies on the use of the term 'surplus' seem to indicate an unfortunate association, in the minds of many, of surplus and value."[(3)]

2. It is an *informed* opinion. It is predicated upon an examination of the books of account, supporting records, system of internal control, tests of inventory, independent confirmation of facts recorded and such other examinations or tests as the accepted and established practices of the profession require. Such procedures and practices prescribe the minimum of examination to be followed. In many important respects, the amount of detail to be reviewed, as well as the choice of method, are matters of expert judgment within the discretion of the accountant.

---

(3) James L. Dohr, Reflections on the Development of Accounting Procedures, Journal of Accountancy, July, 1942, pages 43 and 44.

3. It is an *expert* opinion. It is the work of one well-trained for the particular task, who performs the prerequisite examination of accounts and the interpretation thereof in a competent manner.

The most frequently quoted statement of the general rule of law applicable to the rendition of expert services is the following:

> "Every man who offers his services to another and is employed assumes the duty to exercise in the employment such skill as he possesses with reasonable care and diligence. In all those employments where peculiar skill is requisite, if one offers his services, he is understood as holding himself out to the public as possessing the degree of skill commonly possessed by others in the same employment, and, if his pretentions are unfounded, he commits a species of fraud upon every man who employs him in reliance on his public profession. But no man, whether skilled or unskilled, undertakes that the task he assumes shall be performed successfully, and without fault or error. He undertakes for good faith and integrity, but not for infallibility, and he is liable to his employer for negligence, bad faith, or dishonesty, but not for losses consequent upon mere errors of judgment."[4]

The Chief Accountant of the Securities and Exchange Commission recently discussed this matter and stated:

> "The new rules ask for a positive representation as to whether the audit made was in accordance with generally accepted auditing standards applicable in the circumstances. The propriety of such a requirement, as opposed to a requirement merely for a statement of the accountant's opinion on the point, was the subject of a good deal of debate and was adopted only after full consideration of opposing views. As I see it, an unqualified certificate contains an implied representation that the accountant has lived up to the standards which are generally approved by his colleagues. Such a representation, indeed, is implicit, I think, to all professions—that one who holds himself out as a professional man represents that he has and has exercised that skill and knowledge common to his calling. The new rule merely makes explicit what was before implicit."[5]

4. It is a *candid* opinion. It sets forth its conclusions in such form that material factors are not concealed or suppressed. If the opinion is subject to any important mental reservation or if facts have come to the notice of the accountant which have an adverse bearing upon the conclusion reached, such negative factors are either set forth explicitly as qualifications, reservations or exceptions, or (in the judgment of the accountant) are so material that he refrains from expressing any opinion. In this connection, the following is quoted from the bulletin of the Institute on Extensions of Auditing Procedure (Statements on Auditing Procedure—No. 1, issued October, 1939):

> "In explanation of the general principles governing the auditor's

(4) Cooley on Torts, 2nd Edition, page 277.

(5) William W. Werntz, Some Current Deficiencies in Financial Statements, Journal of Accountancy, January, 1942, page 27.

opinion, with particular regard to explanations and exceptions, it is pertinent to state that the auditor satisfies himself as to the fairness of the statements 'by methods and to the extent he deems appropriate' in general conformity with the auditing procedures recommended in the Institute's bulletin EXAMINATION OF FINANCIAL STATEMENTS. Ordinarily, if he has so satisfied himself, he is in a position to express an unqualified opinion. However, if he considers it in the interest of clear disclosure of material fact to include explanations of procedures followed, he is free to do so. If, on the other hand, such disclosures are made by reason of any reservation or desire to qualify the opinion, they become exceptions and should be expressly stated as such in the opinion paragraph of the auditor's report. As previously stated, if such exceptions are sufficiently material to negative the expression of an opinion, the auditor should refrain from giving any opinion at all, although he may render an informative report in which he states that the limitations or exceptions relating to the examination are such as to make it impossible for him to express an opinion as to the fairness of the financial statements as a whole.

"It is desirable as a general rule that exceptions by the independent certified public accountant be included in a paragraph separate from all others in the report and be referred to specifically in the final paragraph in which the opinion is stated. Any exception should be expressed clearly and unequivocally as to whether it affects the scope of the work, any particular item of the financial statements, the soundness of the company's procedures (as regards either the books or the financial statements), or the consistency of accounting practices where lack of consistency calls for exception."

5. It is an *independent* opinion. It is an unbiased and disinterested opinion. The accountant impliedly represents that he has no conflicting interest which may raise a doubt as to his independence of judgment. This vital question of independence was recently discussed at some length by a former president of the Institute, who stated, among other things:

> "Evidently it has always been considered an attribute so indispensable to the public practice of accounting that it was taken for granted, and it never occurred to anyone to attempt to define it or to create rules requiring it."
>
> * * * * * *
>
> "Independence is the certified public accountant's stock in trade. He invites public criticism which may result in his professional disaster if he permits circumstances to arise which cast doubt on his independence, even though he may be sure that his state of mind is as independent as it could be. In this case the appearance of impropriety is only slightly less dangerous than the impropriety itself."[6]

Limitations of space and time prevent a more amplified discussion of the foregoing elements and characteristics of accountant's opinion. It

[6] Frederick H. Hurdman, Independence of Auditors, Journal of Accountancy, January, 1942, page 55 and page 60.

must be obvious, however, that any one of these elements may become a crucial issue which cannot be resolved intelligently without passing judgment upon one or more technical questions of accounting and auditing principles, procedures, practices, standards, conventions, precedents, rules, forms, definitions and the like. The conclusions and findings of juries will be based upon the evidence presented of what the accountant did and what he should have done. If our profession itself has failed to agree upon these matters, there is most likely to be a confusing conflict of expert testimony, raising controverted issues concerning which juries will have the final word. On the other hand, to the extent that these technical matters are sufficiently clarified and established by the profession itself, it is likely that juries will accept the criteria of the profession and not impose upon us their own inexpert conclusions as to the accountant's duty in any given case.

There has already been reference to the fact that in four leading cases the appellate courts have indicated a consistent disinclination to disturb the findings of juries in cases involving the alleged negligence and fraud of accountants. Certainly that policy of the appellate courts will persist in situations where the existence or the content of professional criteria is seriously disputed. We have reason to expect, however, that if these matters are sufficiently clarified and established by the profession itself, courts of law will be placed in a position to set aside adverse jury verdicts as contrary to the weight of evidence when such verdicts are in conflict with recognized and accepted professional standards and criteria as testified to by experienced and reputable members of the profession.

Such clear-cut professional standards may be exacting in the matter of minimum requirements and in that way to some extent may restrict the free use of judgment on the part of the accountant. This fear has been picturesquely pointed up by one of our distinguished members in warning us that "it is easier to get into a straitjacket than to get out of it." Others have taken what is urged in this paper to be the more far-sighted view. An eminent expression of this latter viewpoint is the following quotation from a recently published article on Accounting Standards by Mr. Victor H. Stempf:

> "It follows that objective standards narrow the sphere of individual judgment and personal opinion as to what the standards are, but it does not follow that they restrict reasonably free judgment and individual opinion as to the propriety of applications of such standards. In respect of these the accountant's work must still be judged by what other competent accountants would have done under the same circumstances in conformity with the standards set by the profession. The immediate need is for the accelerated formulation of these objective standards."[7]

We owe it to our profession to guide and instruct its members in the performance of their important functions. We also have a duty to the public and to ourselves to enlighten all interested parties as to what is the technical nature of the services we render and what is the scope of the responsibility we assume in performing such services. These are

---

(7) Victor H. Stempf, Accounting Standards, Journal of Accountancy, January, 1942, page 67.

paramount considerations. Furthermore, any standards or criteria which we establish are likely always to permit wide latitude for the exercise of expert judgment. Even if such latitude is not to be unlimited, any apparent disadvantage to us will be far outweighed by the sound protection afforded accountants in the face of threatened liability. Only through well-established professional standards and criteria can accountants assure themselves of judgment by their peers. The legal liability of accountants should be confined within the framework of *professional* standards and criteria. If that framework is not constructed by the profession itself, it will be rudely fashioned for us by juries of laymen out of the unfortunate material presented to them in the extreme situations which are occasionally litigated.

SECTION 2

LIABILITY TO CLIENTS

THE LEGAL LIABILITY OF PUBLIC ACCOUNTANTS IN ITS RELATION TO A STANDARD CLASSIFICATION OF ACCOUNTING SERVICES *

By SAUL LEVY, C.P.A. and Member of the New York Bar

The movement now well under way throughout the profession of accountancy to adopt and establish a standard Classification of Accounting Services and Appropriate Certificates may well be discussed from the standpoint of the legal relationships and the legal hazards involved in the practice of accountancy. The general subject of the legal responsibility of accountants to clients and to others has received considerable attention in recent months, particularly in connection with an attempt to interpret and apply the opinion of Judge Cardozo in the well-known *Ultramares* case.

It would seem that a very close connection exists between the accountant's liability arising out of services rendered and the need for a Classification of Accounting Services and Appropriate Certificates. Perhaps it will serve to emphasize that close connection if the subject is presented from the hybrid viewpoint of the accountant-lawyer.

Accountants, like practitioners in other skilled professions, undertake to render personal services to members of the public. The nature of the services to be rendered as well as the terms and conditions under which the accountant undertakes his retainer should be found in a contract or agreement with the client. This agreement may be written or oral. Its terms may be expressed in great detail or left largely to inference and implication. Whatever be its form, however explicit or implicit its terms, a contract must always exist in legal contemplation whenever an accountant undertakes a professional engagement. Whatever questions may later arise concerning the work performed by the accountant, the interested parties and the court or jury to which their controversy ultimately may be submitted, must look to that contract for a definition of the rights and duties of the parties involved.

Curiously enough, the controversy relating to this accountant-client agreement may involve complaining parties who are not parties to the original agreement. The accountant-client relationship has always been a somewhat unique one from a legal standpoint and has never occupied quite the same status as the client relationship in other professions. Neither the common law of England nor that of the United States has seen fit to confer upon the communications between accountant and client the

---

* **Published in 12 CERTIFIED PUBLIC ACCOUNTANT 695 (1932).**

protection of privilege accorded to similar communications between lawyer and client, physician and patient, priest and penitent. An accountant must regard information obtained by him during the course of the professional engagement as a sacred trust of confidence, and it would be a serious breach of professional duty for him on his own initiative and of his own volition to violate that confidence. Nevertheless, when that confidential information becomes relevant in a legal proceeding, the accountant may be subpœnaed to court and, on penalty of contempt of court, compelled to testify and divulge that information. Under similar circumstances a lawyer, physician or priest may remain silent, claiming that the information came to him as a confidential communication in his professional capacity and that it is his privilege under the law to deem himself incompetent to testify concerning it. Not so the accountant. From this it becomes at once apparent that the accountant may become involved in litigation to which he is not a party. The work that he has performed and the conditions surrounding its performance may be indirectly in issue. The accountant, however reluctantly, may be drawn into someone else's controversy, yet find himself in the position of vindicating his own work. His reputation may be as much at stake as it would be in a litigation to which he is directly a party.

Accountants themselves have frequently pointed out a fundamental distinction between their professional function and that of the attorney. The attorney is an advocate, a partisan, a special pleader. By contrast, the accountant (at least in the performance of audit work) is primarily concerned in ascertaining facts and in expressing an impartial opinion with respect thereto. Our profession has always recognized its ethical responsibility to the general public. How far that ethical responsibility goes beyond the limits of legal responsibility has been a much mooted question.

The *Ultramares* case dealt directly with this very question of the legal responsibility of accountants to others than clients. The decision in the New York Court of Appeals has restricted liability for ordinary negligence. It would seem, however, that in practical effect the court has broadened the liability for fraud. It has held that where there is gross negligence a jury may find such negligence so flagrant that a representation of fact could not have been made in good faith because there was no knowledge of the fact and that an expression of opinion under the circumstances was a fraudulent pretense. As the court there stated:

> "Even an opinion, especially an opinion by an expert, may be found to be fraudulent if the grounds supporting it are so flimsy as to lead to the conclusion that there was no genuine belief back of it."

Thus it would seem that while the court has held that for their negligence there is no liability on the part of accountants to the general public, it has at the same time held that there is such liability for fraud. And going further, it has held that there is a type of fraud which may be inferred from negligence. To quote again from the opinion of Judge Cardozo:

> "Our holding does not emancipate accountants from the consequences of fraud. It does not relieve them if their audit has been so negligent as to justify a finding that they had no genuine belief in its adequacy, for this again is fraud. It does no more than say that if less than this is proved, if there has been neither reckless misstatement nor

insincere profession of an opinion, but only honest blunder, the ensuing liability for negligence is one that is bounded by the contract, and is to be enforced between the parties by whom the contract has been made."

Thus we must be brought to the realization that when we undertake a professional engagement we may become answerable therefor not only to our client, not only to the authorities who govern the practice of our profession, but also to some member of the general public who claims to have been injured because of the manner in which we have performed our work. The very heart of the controversy is likely to be left for decision to a jury of laymen involving findings of fact by them concerning the following basic propositions:

1. What audit work did the accountant undertake to perform?
2. Did he perform that work adequately and competently, i.e. without negligence?
3. If not, was he so grossly negligent that he could not have issued his certificate in good faith? That is to say, did his gross negligence amount to fraud within the meaning of the opinion in the *Ultramares* case?

The jury system is a condition that confronts us and not a theory. With all its imperfections and obvious limitations it has somehow withstood the criticism of centuries and is still with us. As it operates in this day and age with reference to the accountancy profession, it comes to this. The professional standing and financial fate of the ablest and best qualified accountant in the land may hang in the balance while twelve men in the jury box sit in judgment upon technical questions of accounting procedure. The likelihood is that not one of those twelve jurors is a competent accountant. The lawyers on both sides of the litigation may manage between them to excuse from service on the jury any individual whose background suggests that he may be technically qualified. The jurors who are impanelled will probably represent a cross section of the commercial community and may include amongst its number salesmen and sales executives, retired business men whose active experience dates back a long time, shipping clerks, architects, real estate brokers, installment house bill collectors, theatrical press agents, insurance agents, advertising experts, manufacturing executives and many other types, each intelligent enough in his own restricted field, but most, if not all of them, utterly uninformed with respect to accounting and auditing practice. What this oddly assorted jury is likely to have in common is a firm conviction that certified public accountants are a breed of infallible supermen whose work should not be judged by ordinary mortal standards. The existence of error is almost sufficient of itself to create a presumption of fault on the part of the accountant.

The predicament in which we find ourselves is clearly unsatisfactory. What is there to be done about it? One obvious line of attack would be to attempt to change the jury system so that accountants might be judged by those understanding accountancy. Ultimately some such reform may come to pass. But that avenue of solution seems to promise results far too remote and far too uncertain to warrant our further consideration at this time.

Another and more promising field of reform is equally obvious. Since all questions of fact to be found by the jury relate in a basic way to the original contract giving rise to the work of the accountant and to the certificate or report of the accountant covering his work, why not make that contract so explicit in its terms and make the work of the accountant and the certificate based thereon so obviously and strictly a compliance with that contract that technical questions are removed, as far as possible, from the consideration of the jury. The largest part of the difficulty has been that most of the essential terms of the accountant's contract have been left to inference and implication. The accountant's certificate has likewise shed little light upon the scope of the underlying audit work. In making a fetish of the short unqualified certificate accountants have borrowed a great deal of trouble for themselves. As a consequence, it is too often left for the jury to discover through the evidence just what it was the accountant did and what his agreement and the standards of his profession required him to do.

Accountants should be judged by the recognized and accepted standards of their own profession and not by the purely adventitious standards of a jury of laymen, whose mental processes are being manipulated by adroit and persuasive trial counsel. In order to obtain adequate consideration for such authentic standards accountants must first put their own professional house in order.

From the vantage point of legal liability, which has been my approach, the problem may be outlined in the following terms:

1. To standardize accounting and auditing technique and terminology, so far as such matters will submit to standardization without impairing their essential usefulness.

2. To make the client contract as explicit as may be feasible in terms of standardized procedure.

3. To express the accountant's conclusions and/or findings, whether of opinion or fact, in a certificate which clearly predicates such conclusions and findings upon the standardized procedure involved.

Important pioneer work along these specific lines has already been accomplished by the technical committees of accountancy societies throughout the country. Opinion may differ as to how far the classifications and standard forms thus far promulgated serve the practical requirements of the situation. Many difficult problems begin to emerge only as the discussion proceeds. The desired progress in the right direction cannot be made without the active interest and coöperation of the profession at large. Perhaps when accountants better realize *why* they should be concerned with the subject of a standard classification of accounting services and appropriate certificates, they will then more readily apply themselves toward the solution of the many technical problems involved.

MARYLAND CASUALTY CO. v. COOK *

District Court of the United States, E. D. Michigan, 1940.
35 F. Supp. 160.

TUTTLE, District Judge. Dexter G. Conklin was appointed city treasurer by the City of Flint, Michigan. This appointment was confirmed by the

* This case is discussed at p. 9 ff. *supra*.

City Commission. The period of employment was continuous, beginning April 5, 1928, and ending October 24, 1935. The employment was discontinued by resignation. The resignation was given by reason of and immediately following the discovery of misappropriations and embezzlements by said Dexter G. Conklin.

In this suit the United States Fidelity & Guaranty Company of Baltimore, Maryland, a Maryland Corporation, is designated as defendant. While it is designated as defendant, actually it appears in these proceedings presenting a statement of a cause of action as against Jonathon Cook, d/b/a Jonathon Cook & Company of Chicago, Illinois, and the Commercial Casualty Insurance Company of Newark, New Jersey, analogous to the statement of the cause of action of the Maryland Casualty Company of Baltimore, Maryland. Both the Maryland Casualty Company and the United States Fidelity & Guaranty Company present claims which are identical, excepting as to amounts, and both are therefore plaintiffs.

The City of Flint carried fidelity bond insurance for its protection, said fidelity bonds providing that if Dexter G. Conklin should embezzle, misappropriate or misapply funds belonging to the City of Flint then the surety on such fidelity contracts was to be chargeable for such loss.

During the period of time involved in this case the surety companies protected the city of Flint against embezzlement by Dexter G. Conklin as city treasurer. The dates of coverage and the amount of coverage were as follows:

Maryland Casualty Company,	6/1/31 to 6/1/32	$200,000.00
" " "	6/1/32 to 6/1/33	200,000.00
" " "	6/1/33 to 7/30/34	200,000.00
United States Fidelity & Guaranty Co.,	7/30/34 to 8/19/35	200,000.00
Maryland Casualty Company,	8/19/35 to 10/24/35	200,000.00

By reason of its contracts of fidelity insurance, the Maryland Casualty Company, a Maryland Corporation, was required to pay, and did pay, to the City of Flint on account of losses incurred by the City of Flint by reason of fraud, misappropriation and embezzlements of Dexter G. Conklin, City Treasurer, the amount of $12,969.15.

By reason of its contract of fidelity insurance the United States Fidelity & Guaranty Company, a Maryland Corporation, was required to pay, and did pay, to the City of Flint on account of losses incurred by the City of Flint by reason of fraud, misappropriation and embezzlements of Dexter G. Conklin, City Treasurer, the amount of $3,148.21.

On effecting such payments, the Maryland Casualty Company and the United States Fidelity & Guaranty Company became subrogated to and were assigned all of the rights of the City of Flint to the extent of the payments as by them effected.

The City of Flint had prepared "specifications for audit" for the year period beginning July 1, 1931, ending June 30, 1932. These specifications for audit were submitted to any certified public accountant who cared to make a bid for the doing of the work as required thereby. The specifications provided in part as follows:

"The City of Flint, Michigan, is requesting bids for a complete audit of the transactions of its various boards, departments and offices on a monthly basis for the fiscal year beginning July 1, 1931, and ending June 30, 1932, subject to the following conditions which will become a part of any contract entered into:

"1. The examination shall be a complete monthly audit. Cash balances shall be verified at the beginning of the fiscal period. Cash counts shall be made each month at irregular periods. All cash receipts shall be verified by a deposit in one of the depositories of the City. Disbursements shall be verified for the legality of same. Purchase orders shall be verified for charter provision in regards thereto, as well as, ordinance governing purchasing. Commission proceedings shall be checked for compliance with the various authorizations, agreements, allowances, contracts or other procedures contained therein. Cash balances shall be verified at the close of the fiscal period. Any other duties or procedures which ordinarily become a part of a complete audit although not specifically stated herein, shall be deemed a part of these specifications.

"2. It will not be considered the duty of the contracting auditors to bring into balance any ledger or other book of record during this engagement. It shall be their privilege to request the Director of Finance to have brought into balance any book of record which should have been in balance for their convenience.

* * * * * *

"5. * * * No payments will be made by the city before the completion and acceptance of the work for the fiscal year unless a surety bond for faithful performance of contract has been filed, and then only after the approval by resolution of the City Commission.

"6. A letter of certification shall be filed with the City Clerk monthly as a matter of record that the monthly audit has been made. The report of the contracting auditors for the fiscal year shall be a certified report stating briefly but clearly what their examination consisted of, with the necessary exhibits and schedules in support thereof. It should show particularly the exact financial condition of the various funds of the City, a proper accounting for the cash receipts and disbursements for the year, a verification of deposits, and a reconciliation of bank balances.

* * * * * *

"8. The contracting auditor's report for the fiscal year shall be made for all departments, boards and offices of the City as of June 30, 1932. The report shall be made with bound imitation leather covers, and delivered as follows: one copy containing a complete report of all departments, boards and offices, to the City Clerk, one copy containing a complete report of all departments, boards and offices, to the Director of Finance, one copy containing the board report only, to the Recreation and Park Board, one copy containing the board report only, to the Board of Hospital Managers, two copies bound separately to contain departmental reports only, to the Justice Courts and the Water Department respectively. The reports shall be submitted not later than July 30, 1932.

* * * * * *

"10. The following departments, offices and boards are to be included in this audit engagement:

"1. Director of Finance

"2. City Treasurer."

Defendant Jonathon Cook, of Chicago, Illinois, an individual, doing business as Jonathon Cook & Company, submitted his bid to the City of Flint in accordance with these specifications. This provided in part:

"We are submitting herewith our sealed bid on the audit of the books and records of the various departments of the City of Flint, Michigan, for the period from July 1, 1931 to June 30, 1932, in accordance with specifications issued by you, for a total sum not to exceed ($2,975.00) Two Thousand Nine Hundred Seventy-Five Dollars including all expenses.

* * * * * *

"Jonathon Cook & Company have been bonded at numerous times in similar cases and shall be pleased to furnish same as requested."

* * * * * *

Subsequently a contract was entered into by and between defendant Jonathon Cook and the City of Flint, which contract provided in part as follows:

"This Agreement, made this 20th day of August, A. D., 1931, by and between Jonathon Cook & Company of Muskegon, Michigan, hereinafter called The Company, and the City of Flint, a municipal corporation, in the County of Genesee, State of Michigan, hereinafter called the City.

"* * * No payments will be made by the City before the completion and acceptance of the work for the fiscal year unless a surety bond for faithful performance of contract has been filed before any monies are paid, and then only after the approval by resolution of the City Commission.

"Witnesseth: The Company hereby agrees to audit the books and accounts of the various boards, departments and offices of the City of Flint on the monthly basis for the fiscal year beginning July 1, 1931 and ending June 30, 1932 subject to the conditions and in accordance with the specifications hereto attached, which specifications are made a part hereof as fully as if written herein."

In accordance with such specifications, the Commercial Casualty Insurance Company, a New Jersey corporation, a hired surety for profit, executed bond on behalf of Jonathon Cook & Company to the benefit of the City of Flint in the sum of $2,975, the condition of their said bond being as follows:

"Whereas, said Principal has been awarded a contract under specifications for audit of the official records of the City of Flint, Michigan, for a period beginning July 1st, 1931 and ending June 30th, 1932.

"Now, Therefore, if the said Principal shall make audits of the official records of the various departments of the City of Flint, Michigan, in accordance with the specifications of audit for the period beginning July 1st, 1931, and ending June 30th, 1932, then this obligation to be void; otherwise to remain in full force and effect."

This bond was typed on the letterhead stationery of the Commercial Casualty Insurance Company; was executed in Chicago by the agent of the Commercial Casualty Insurance Company, and was sent to the City of Flint and countersigned by a Michigan agent of the Commercial Casualty Insurance Company. It was approved by the City Attorney, and I find as a fact that the bond and the language thereof were prepared by the Commercial Casualty Insurance Company.

I now proceed to discuss the various issues of fact and law as are presented as to the obligations of the several defendants.

First, as to Dexter G. Conklin, defendant herein. He was dishonest and embezzled moneys belonging to the City of Flint during each and all of the years in question. He had different ways of embezzling and misappropriating the money. Principally, such moneys collected by him and misappropriated by him were delinquent personal property taxes owing to the City of Flint. For one example, he collected delinquent taxes voluntarily paid by the taxpayer and then issued what has been termed a temporary receipt and no record was made of the tax payment in his office whatever. For another example, he issued the official receipt of the City of Flint, but duplicate copies of such receipt supposed to be recorded in his office were destroyed and no record of the taxpayer having paid such item was made. For another example, he, as permitted by the statutes of the State of Michigan, seized personal property of the taxpayers and by authorization of law sold these assets of the taxpayers who were delinquent for the purpose of satisfying the tax indebtedness. Having done this, he issued the so-called temporary receipt and no record of payment of the taxes appeared in his office.

For another example, he altered the delinquent tax rolls by increasing the amount shown to be owing in an amount sufficient so that his books balanced by reason of his collection of the tax money which he had embezzled.

Dexter G. Conklin embezzled money for a large and substantial amount. He undoubtedly embezzled money to an extent greater than the City of Flint was able to prove. I say this because of the lapse of years and the impossibility of locating certain of the taxpayers shown by the books as delinquent, many of whom undoubtedly had paid their taxes.

The embezzlements and misappropriations resulted in a loss to the Maryland Casualty Company of $12,917.30. That is the amount of their payment to the City of Flint. In addition thereto, expenses have been incurred by the Maryland Casualty Company investigation of $51.85, making a total loss to this company of $12,969.15.

The embezzlements and misappropriations resulted in a loss to the United States Fidelity & Guaranty Company of $3,148.21. That is the amount of their payment to the City of Flint. In addition thereto, expenses have been incurred by the United States Fidelity & Guaranty Company in investigation of $11.35 making a total loss to this company of $3,159.56.

These losses to the Maryland Casualty Company and to the United States Fidelity & Guaranty Company resulted entirely by reason of the fraud and embezzlements of Dexter G. Conklin, in an official capacity and while acting as fiduciary for the City of Flint. Hence, although this a chancery action it sounds in wilful, malicious and intentional tort and not in assumpsit, and if the proceedings were on the law side of the court the finding as against Dexter G. Conklin would be in wilful, malicious and intentional tort to the amount and extent as before mentioned. This fact is particularly mentioned and found as a fact for the benefit of the Maryland Casualty Company and United States Fidelity & Guaranty Company, and in order to prevent a discharge of these debts in the event that Dexter G. Conklin should attempt to secure a discharge of these obligations in bankruptcy.

As to Jonathon Cook, d/b/a Jonathon Cook & Company.

Subrogation of the Sureties to the Right of Action of the City of Flint as Against Public Accountants.

The Maryland Casualty Company, and the United States Fidelity & Guaranty Company, sureties on fidelity bonds on behalf of Dexter G. Conklin, City Treasurer, on the making good of his defalcations, are subrogated pro tanto to the City of Flint's right of action as against Jonathon Cook, d/b/a Jonathon Cook & Company, Public Accountants, for his negligence in the auditing of the books of the City of Flint, in consequence of which negligence the earlier defalcations of Dexter G. Conklin as City Treasurer were not discovered, and the City Treasurer, Dexter G. Conklin, was left in a position to commit subsequent defalcations. *Dantzler Lumber & Export Co. v. Columbia Casualty Co.,* 115 Fla. 541, 156 So. 116, 95 A.L.R. 258. Annotation 95 A.L.R. 269.

Construction of the Contract and Specifications.

I have quoted at length hereinbefore from the specifications for the audit and the contract for the audit. The contract made the specifications a part of the audit and required that the audit engagement be performed in accordance with the specifications.

What is the meaning to be given to this contract and specifications? Am I to interpret them by the usual literal meaning of the words, or am I to place an interpretation upon this contract and the specifications as requested by this defendant on the basis of accounting terms? These technical accounting terms have been referred to as a cash audit, as a balance sheet audit, and as a detailed audit. Some of the accountants here testifying have said that this contract and specifications required a cash audit. Some have said it required a balance sheet audit. Some have said it required a combination of a cash and balance sheet audit, and some others have said that it required a detailed audit.

In the first place, the Director of Finance for the City of Flint in drawing these specifications and drawing this contract had no knowledge of technical auditing terms. Neither did the City Commission, which had the authority to make the contract with the specifications, have any such knowledge. They did not know what a cash audit meant or what a detailed audit meant or what a balance sheet audit meant. They did not have these technical terms in mind. They knew they wanted a complete audit. They knew of some things that they wanted done for the City by these accountants, so they put those things down first. Then when they mentioned the specific details that they knew they wanted covered, they went on and used general language to include everything else that was ordinarily required to be done in the making of a complete audit.

Accordingly, I reach the determination, and it is my opinion, that this contract and these specifications should be interpreted according to their literal and usual meaning. There is nothing to indicate that a partial or limited audit was intended. The language calls for a complete audit. Why should I attempt to call this audit engagement by some technical term as the defendant accountant urges me to do? Neither the contract nor the specifications use any such technical terms. There is nothing to guide me in an effort to classify it as a cash audit, a balance sheet audit, or a detailed audit. If I so classified this audit contract, I would necessarily then have to reach a conclusion as to exactly what work that classification called for. The net result of such reasoning would lead me to an interpretation contrary to the plain, ordinary, everyday meaning which this contract and these specifications disclose for themselves.

Therefore, I reach the conclusion that this audit engagement is not limited; that it should be interpreted according to its literal meaning, its actual meaning, its plain everyday, common-sense meaning. Restatement, Contracts, Secs. 230 to 235 (a).

I think that it is high time for accountants to know that if they want a particular contract which they enter into to be measured in the technical terms of a cash audit, or a balance sheet audit, or a detailed audit, they should insist that their contract and the specifications which they agree to comply with in their contract should plainly state the facts.

So I interpret this contract with its specifications according to the plain language used.

The witnesses have all agreed that no technical terms or language has been used in either the contract or the specifications. Ordinary, everyday English has been used. It is easily understood and interpreted. If accountants wish a contract construed in accordance with their own technical language, then they must see to it that their technical language is used in their contracts.

The defendant, Jonathon Cook, testified that on receiving these specifications and on reading the specifications, he did not know just what work was required to be performed for the City of Flint and so he went to the City of Flint and had a talk with the Director of Finance and thereafter entered into the contract in reliance upon that conversation had prior to the execution of the contract. That conversation with the Director of Finance does not mean a thing. The contract was with the City of Flint and not with the Director of Finance. It is the contract which Jonathon Cook made with the City of Flint which must be construed and not conversations or oral agreements reached with independent officers of the City prior to the execution of the contracts. Those prior conversations, in order to become binding, should have been embodied in the written contract and signed pursuant to proper authority. Therefore, the court has no alternative but to hold this defendant to performance in accordance with the terms of his written contract. Restatement, Contracts, Sec. 237.

On this point there is an additional thing that should be mentioned. Once that contract was executed and signed by the parties, no individual officer, agent or employee of the City of Flint was authorized to alter or vary the terms of that written instrument. That cannot be done by any individual unless the City has lawfully delegated the authority to a particular individual. In this case, the City Commission of the City of Flint, the law-making body of the City of Flint, established the requirements of this audit engagement, and unless they agreed to a change or an alteration of the terms of that audit engagement and authorized an alteration, the audit engagement is to be performed in accordance with the terms of the contract. No such change was made or authorized. Restatements, Contracts, Sec. 408 (a).

Negligence of Accountants or Auditors.

While I have reached the conclusion and interpreted this contract for the audit to require a complete audit within the broad aspects of the meaning of that word, it does not make any difference in deciding as to negligence or non-negligence whether I interpret it as a complete audit within the broad aspects of this contract or whether I say it is a combination cash and balance sheet audit. I say that because if I follow the testimony in this case of all of the certified public accountants who have testified they all agree that reasonable care should be used in test checking or in some other way to see that the figures in the controls are in balance with the detailed ledgers. There was not a reasonable careful audit performed by the defendant auditor on either basis, whether it be on the basis of the complete audit or on the basis of the combination cash and balance sheet audit. I reach that conclusion for several reasons as follows:

1. The auditor made no attempt to circularize the delinquent accounts outstanding. If there had been any attempt made, the probabilities are that the discrepancies would have been discovered. Certainly there should have been some attempt made at circularization. It would not necessarily have been a 100 per cent. circularization, but there should at least have been a test circularization. The delinquent accounts should have been canvassed and selected persons contracted either by personal call, by telephone, or by a form letter.

2. Alteration of the tax rolls. There were many items of alterations of the tax rolls. The alterations were very crude. He did not even use the same kind of ink. There are many ways in which these alterations could have been discovered by this defendant auditor. The particular rolls could have been totalled and then compared with the rolls in the assessor's office, which were not altered, and the discrepancies would have immediately come to light. This auditor paid no attention to the original assessor's rolls. Those rolls are a part of the books and records of the City of Flint, and hence were required to be audited and examined.

3. When this defendant auditor or his representatives started to make his monthly audits and his annual audits it was incumbent upon him to audit various delinquent tax rolls including the current tax roll. He should have carefully examined the 1926, 1927, 1928, 1929 and 1930 delinquent tax rolls as well as the 1931 tax rolls. He should have determined whether or not the delinquent balance outstanding on each and every one of those tax rolls balanced with the controls. It is my belief and finding that this was not done. The auditor was unable to produce work sheets. The auditor said he thought that the delinquent tax rolls for several years were totalled in their entirety, and that then the totals taken from the controls for the corresponding years added and the two then compared. Even if done, this, in my judgment, is not reasonably prudent or careful auditing work.

4. This defendant auditor found the delinquent balances outstanding from these tax rolls on the basis of the total obtained over the period of years to be out of balance on the basis of the total obtained from the controls over the period of years. He says that the only thing that he did was to mention it verbally to the Director of Finance, and then he proceeded in the annual report to certify the exact balance to be a stated figure on the delinquent taxes, when actually it was not true, and he had no knowledge whatsoever of what the delinquent balance outstanding was. The auditor did not balance these books or require the City to do so. He should have required the City of Flint to bring these books into balance. It was not done.

5. When this auditor ran tapes, he used figures superimposed upon the tax roll in lead pencil. By that I mean this City Treasurer's office for their convenience had placed out at the extreme edge of the page in lead pencil what they claimed represented the delinquent balances outstanding, and when this auditor ran his tapes he used those pencil figures without checking those figures with the figures in ink to determine whether or not the pencil figures were accurate. Many of them were not accurate and a careful check would have so disclosed.

6. This auditor failed to audit the control as maintained in the City Treasurer's office, either with the control in the Director of Finance's office

or with the tax rolls themselves. Had he audited such book in comparison with either the controls or the rolls, he would have found the records decidedly out of balance. It is the failure to do these things that forces me to the conclusion that this auditor failed to faithfully perform his audit engagement. With a reasonable degree of care the many defalcations would have been discovered. It is the failure upon the part of the auditor to do these things which makes it clear that he did not make the audit he had contracted to make, and he did not do what a reasonably prudent auditor would and should have done under the circumstances. He was negligent.

For the failure to perform this audit engagement in accordance with the terms of this contract as a reasonably prudent and careful auditor would and because of such negligence, this defendant auditor, Jonathan Cook, must respond in damages, *Fox & Sons v. Moorish Grant & Co.*, 1918, 35 Times Law Report, 126; *Leeds Estate Building & Investment Co. v. Shepherd*, 36 L. R. Chancery Div. 787; *Smith, et al. v. London Assurance Corp.*, 109 App. Div. 882, 96 N. Y. S. 820; *National Surety Corp. v. Lybrand et al*, 256 App. Div. 226, 9 N. Y. S. 2d 554; *Dantzler Lumber & Export Co. v. Columbia Casualty Co.*, 115 Fla. 541, 156 So. 116, 95 A. L. R. 258; *Ultramares Corp. v. George A. Touche et al.*, 225 N. Y. 170, 174 N. E. 441, 74 A. L. R. 1139.

Is the negligence of the defendant auditor the proximate cause of the damage for which this suit against Jonathan Cook is brought?

The evidence as to all of the shortages and peculations which appear upon the books and records of the City of Flint during the yearly audit engagement of the defendant auditor must be considered. Those marks of irregularity were there in the record.

An auditor performing an audit on the basis of this contract and these specifications and doing his work as a reasonably prudent, careful auditor would have done his work, would have, and should have, discovered some of these many, many irregularities; and, having discovered some of them, all of the others would have been found.

One of the purposes of the audit was to determine whether or not any of the employees of the City of Flint, including the City Treasurer, were embezzling or misappropriating or defrauding the City of Flint of its money. These irregular items were apparent from the books. If they had been brought to the attention of the City of Flint by the auditor, the Treasurer's services would have been terminated and the City would then not have been put to the further loss suffered by it by reason of the subsequent misappropriations and peculations by this City Treasurer occurring after the negligent performance of the contract by the auditor. Restatement, Contracts, Sec. 330.

It was fairly within the contemplation of the parties to this contract that this work should be properly done. It was negligently done and thus the defaulting City Treasurer was permitted to continue on in his work. The auditor is obligated to respond in damages for the amount of the shortages accruing after the negligent performance of the audit engagement. *Hadley v. Baxendale*, 156 Eng. Rep. 145; *Fox & Son v. Moorish Grant & Co., supra; Leeds Estate Building & Investment Co. v. Shepherd, supra; Smith, et al. v. London Assurance Corp., supra; National Surety Corp. v. Lybrand, supra; Dantzler Lumber & Export Co. v. Columbia Casualty Co., supra; Ultramares Corp. v. George A. Touche et al., supra.*

The Maryland Casualty Company and the United States Fidelity & Guaranty Company having reimbursed the City of Flint for such loss and damage are subrogated to the rights of said City as against Jonathon Cook.

Of the particular loss as sustained by the Maryland Casualty Company on its payment to the City of Flint, the amount of $11,169.09 occurred subsequent to the negligent performance of the contract by the defendant Jonathon Cook.

Of the particular loss as sustained by the United States Fidelity & Guaranty Company on its payment to the City of Flint, the amount of $2,809.61 occurred subsequent to the negligent performance of the contract by the defendant Jonathan Cook.

As to the Commercial Casualty Insurance Company.

What is the obligation of the bond of the defendant Commercial Casualty Insurance Company? The obligation clause of that bond provides:

"Whereas, said Principal has been awarded a contract under specifications for audit of the official records of the City of Flint, Michigan, for a period beginning July 1st, 1931, and ending June 30th, 1932.

"Now, Therefore, if the said principal shall make audits of the official records of the various departments of the City of Flint, Michigan, in accordance with the specifications of audit for the period beginning July 1st 1931 and ending June 30th, 1932, then this obligation to be void; otherwise to remain in full force and effect."

Therefore, in determining the obligation of the Commercial Casualty Insurance Company there must be determined the obligation of the defendant Jonathon Cook & Company as per the contract and the specifications, and the requirements as set forth and enumerated by the contract and the specifications as to the obligation of the surety bond.

The specifications say, in part: "No payments will be made by the City before the completion and acceptance of the work for the fiscal year unless a surety bond for faithful performance of contract has been filed."

The contract says, in part: "No payments will be made by the City before the completion and acceptance of the work for the fiscal year unless a surety bond for faithful performance of contract has been filed."

This bond cannot be read by itself separately without reading and construing the specifications and the contract, and there is no question but that the specifications and the contract require the principal on the bond to faithfully perform his audit engagement, and if he does not faithfully perform the audit engagement then the bond has been breached. In fact, the specifications and contract specifically and definitely define the auditor's bond to be given as a "bond for faithful performance." Restatement, Contracts, Sec. 238 (a).

The defendant auditor, the principal on this bond, did not faithfully perform his audit engagement. Therefore, the bond has been breached. Therefore, the Commercial Casualty Insurance Company is holden on their bond.

It is argued by the Commercial Casualty Insurance Company that its bond is a completion bond only; that it was not required to be conditioned upon anything other than that the principal, this defendant auditor, should be there twelve times a year and make an audit, irrespective of how made, and then give a report at the end of the year irrespective of what was contained in the report.

The position which the Commercial Casualty Insurance Company would like this court to take in construing this bond cannot be taken because it is apparent that if that were all that was required by the bond, then the words "faithful performance of the contract" would not have been written in the specifications and would not have been written in the contract.

Further, both the specifications and the contract use the language, "before the completion and acceptance of the work." If this were merely a completion bond, on the basis of the argument of the Commercial Casualty Insurance Company the words "and acceptance" would not have been inserted in either contract or specifications.

There is nothing in the bond, there is nothing in the specifications, and nothing in the contract which would justify the conclusion that this is a completion bond without any regard for faithful performance of the work which was to be completed. The specifications and the contract definitely describe the bond to be given as "a surety bond for faithful performance of contract."

Counsel for the Commercial Casualty Insurance Company predicates his argument upon verbal testimony given by a former Director of Finance of the City of Flint and the City Clerk of the City of Flint. Obviously, their testimony does not alter the terms or conditions of this bond or of the contract or of the specifications, because no authority was ever conferred upon the Director of Finance or the City Clerk to decide what the obligation of the bond should be. The obligation of that bond was set by the law-making body of the City of Flint, the City Commission. No officer, agent, or employee had authority to alter or amend in any way or manner the mandate of the City Commission as to the requirements of this bond.

Further, we have the very definite proposition that, this defendant surety being a hired surety for profit and having drawn its own form of bond, any ambiguity in the bond would be construed as against it. I do not think this bond, the contract, or the specifications are ambiguous. They are as clear as the English language is capable of making them. Therefore, there is nothing to construe; but if we were to take the argument of this surety as to ambiguity, we must of necessity construe that ambiguity against it. Restatement, Contracts, Sec. 236 (d).

Lastly, we have this fact for consideration, and it cannot be refuted. If this is only a completion bond; if it only required the defendant auditor to be there twelve times annually and to submit a report at the end of the year without any regard for what work was to be done, or how the work was to be done, or the accuracy of the report when given at the end of the year, the bond would be worthless.

The Commercial Casualty Insurance Company is accordingly obligated on its bond to the Maryland Casualty Company and United States Fidelity & Guaranty Company.

Decree may enter finding for the Maryland Casualty Company and against Dexter G. Conklin as follows:

Payment to the City of Flint	$12,917.30
Cost of investigating claim	51.85
Cost of investigation—witness fees—payments to expert witnesses incidental to this suit	1,187.45
	$14,156.60

Interest may also be computed at the rate of 5 per cent per annum from December 15, 1936, as to the first and second items only.

Decree may enter finding for the United States Fidelity & Guaranty Company and against Dexter G. Conklin as follows:

Payment to the City of Flint	$3,148.21
Cost of investigating claim	11.35
	$3,159.56

Interest may also be computed at the rate of 5 per cent per annum from September 29, 1936.

Decree may enter finding for the Maryland Casualty Company as against Jonathon Cook in the sum of $11,169.09. Interest may be computed on this sum at the rate of 5 per cent from December 15, 1936.

Decree may enter finding for the United States Fidelity & Guaranty Company as against Jonathon Cook in the sum of $2,809.61. Interest may be computed on this sum at the rate of 5 per cent from December 15, 1936.

Decree may enter finding as against the Commercial Casualty Insurance Company in the amount of $2,975.00 together with interest at the rate of 5 per cent per annum from June 28, 1937, to date of entry of decree, said decree to provide that the Maryland Casualty Company and the United States Fidelity & Guaranty Company recover from the Commercial Casualty Insurance Company as follows: Maryland Casualty Company, $2,377.76, together with interest thereon at the rate of 5 per cent per annum from June 28, 1937; The United States Fidelity & Guaranty Company, $597.24, together with interest thereon at the rate of 5 per cent per annum from June 28, 1937.

The decree shall provide that on satisfaction by the Commercial Casualty Insurance Company the obligation of Jonathon Cook to the Maryland Casualty Company and the United States Fidelity & Guaranty Company shall be reduced in proportion. The decree shall further provide that on satisfaction of decree by Jonathon Cook the obligation of Dexter G. Conklin to the Maryland Casualty Company and United States Fidelity & Guaranty Company shall be reduced in proportion.

The decree shall further provide that the Maryland Casualty Company and United States Fidelity & Guaranty Company be permitted their costs as against Dexter G. Conklin, Jonathon Cook and the Commercial Casualty Insurance Company.

This opinion shall stand as findings of fact and conclusions of law. Proposals for additional findings of fact and conclusions of law may be filed at any time prior to final decree.

O'NEILL v. ATLAS AUTOMOBILE FINANCE CORP.*

Superior Court of Pennsylvania, 1940. 139 Pa. Super. 346, 11 A.2d 782.

CUNNINGHAM, Judge. The proceeding below was assumpsit by a firm of certified public accountants against the defendant finance corporation to recover $677.50, alleged to be due for professional services.

* This case is discussed at p. 11 ff. *supra*.

Plaintiffs' statement of claim included three separate items, each founded upon an alleged oral contract with defendant—$75 for an examination of defendant's transactions and a report thereon for the month of June, 1936; $456.25 for a detailed examination to determine the extent of certain embezzlements by a bookkeeper; and $146.25 for selecting and training a new bookkeeper. These services were alleged to have been rendered during July and August, 1936.

The defendant, in its pleadings, not only denied liability for any of the items set out in plaintiffs' statement, but also set up a counterclaim for damages in the net amount of $927.30 alleged to have been suffered by it by reason of the asserted negligence of plaintiffs in failing to discover that defendant's bookkeeper had been misappropriating various sums of money over a period of three years prior to July, 1936. During the trial, defendant conceded that plaintiffs were entitled to recover the first item of $75. The jury rendered a verdict in favor of plaintiffs in the amount of $487.03; the court below denied defendant's motions for judgment n. o. v., or a new trial, and entered judgment upon the verdict; this appeal by the defendant followed.

The defendant having admitted liability for the first item sued upon, and the second and third items being based upon contested oral contracts, alleged to have been made subsequent to the discovery of the shortage, these issues of fact arose: (a) Did defendant make these contracts, and if so what were their terms? (b) Did plaintiffs perform the work called for by them? (c) Were the charges for the services performed reasonable? Each issue was necessarily one of fact to be determined by the jury.

As to the second item it was not disputed that the examination was carefully and properly made, but it was contended plaintiffs volunteered these services because of their failure to discover the shortages of the bookkeeper while making prior examinations, hereinafter discussed. On behalf of plaintiffs, O'Neill testified defendant's president employed them to investigate the circumstances and amount of the shortage and agreed to pay for the work, although no specific sum was mentioned.

With respect to the third item, it was denied by defendant that it had ever agreed to pay plaintiffs for any services of that character.

An examination of the record discloses a number of conflicts in the evidence bearing upon these issues, but it also discloses that plaintiffs adduced sufficient competent evidence to take each issue to the jury. They were submitted in a manner concerning which no complaint is made in the assignments. The verdict was evidently a compromise over the inclusion or rejection of certain items claimed by plaintiffs and the reasonableness of some of their charges, but the matters at issue were exclusively for determination by the jury. We find no error upon this record which would justify the granting of a new trial with respect to these items.

We turn, therefore, to the consideration of defendant's counterclaim. It was not contended by defendant that plaintiffs had been guilty of any negligence in the performance of the contracts upon which they sued; the counterclaim was founded upon the charge that plaintiffs had negligently failed, while rendering prior accounting services to defendant, to discover that the totals upon the tapes submitted by the bookkeeper were false.

Except for a period from January to May, 1935, during which another firm of accountants was employed by defendant, plaintiffs rendered accounting services from December of 1929 up to May 31, 1936. About the middle of July, 1936, it was discovered the bookkeeper had been embezzling funds of the defendant and had concealed her thefts in the following manner; Defendant's business involved the keeping of accounts with a large number of lessees of automobiles who had obligated themselves to pay it monthly rentals. The greater part of its "accounts receivable" consisted of such rentals. A card was prepared for each lessee and payments entered thereon as made. The total of these accounts appeared in the general ledger. On the occasion of each of defendant's monthly audits, the bookkeeper ostensibly totaled the accounts receivable from the cards on the adding machine, so that the total might be compared by the plaintiffs with the ledger entry. The bookkeeper's peculations began in 1933 and her method of concealing them was by "plugging the tapes" of the adding machine. When about to run a tape, she first tabulated the amount she was short without making any figures on the tape and then proceeded to run the tape in the usual way. The result was that the totals on the tapes included not only the sum of the figures appearing thereon but also the amounts she had embezzled.

The dispute between plaintiffs and defendant is with regard to the extent of the undertaking on the part of plaintiffs, under the terms of their employment, during the years they had been examining defendant's books and making reports thereon. Plaintiff's contention is that their contract was for a limited examination, and a financial review of defendant's books, without verification. Defendant's contention is that the terms of plaintiffs' employment contemplated the making of a complete and detailed audit and the furnishing of certified reports which should have uncovered the shortage.

One of the plaintiffs, O'Neill, testified his original employment was under an oral contract (a fact conceded by defendant) and that "the nature of the work was to review [defendant's] transactions, guide the bookkeeper, preparation of Federal and State Tax Returns, advise with the management of the concern in financial affairs," and that it was not agreed or contemplated that "certified reports" would be issued. In describing the services rendered he said: "Monthly we would visit the office of the Atlas, make a revision of the transactions, not verifying the data considered, we would instruct the bookkeeper in the handling of technical transactions, we would prepare from the trial balance submitted by the bookkeeper a statement of the condition and a profit and loss statement. We would review that statement with the management, upon the submission of the typewritten report."

The letters of transmittal of the reports used this phraseology: "We have prepared *from the records* of Atlas Automobile Finance Corporation and *information* submitted to us balance sheet as of (designated month and year) and a comparative statement of profit and loss based on the month of (name of month) together with relating schedules." (Italics supplied.)

The services shown by the testimony to have been rendered were accurately described by the learned trial judge, Brown, Jr., J., in his opinion supporting the judgment, as having "consisted of making a review of defendant's transactions, guiding the bookkeeper in handling of technical transactions, preparing a statement of condition and a profit and loss statement from the trial balance submitted by defendant's bookkeeper, preparing Federal and State Tax Returns, and advising defendant in financial matters. The monthly reports submitted to defendant were uncertified and unverified. * * * The accountants' practice was to accept the totals set forth in defendant's general ledger, without checking the individual items that made up the totals. It was stated in letters accompanying the accountants' reports that they were 'prepared from the records of Atlas Automobile Finance Corporation and information submitted to us.' "

When plaintiffs were reengaged in July, 1935, the extent of their undertaking was set forth by them in a letter addressed to the president of the defendant company and accepted by it as satisfactory. The letter read:

"Confirming our recent conversation we agree, with respect to the Atlas Automobile Finance Corp. and the Universal Auto Loan Co., *to make a monthly examination of the transactions and submit monthly reports in substantially the same form as heretofore* and to prepare annually the Federal Income Tax Return, Pennsylvania State Income Tax Returns, and the Pennsylvania Capital Stock and Corporate Loans Report. In addition to the above, we will also prepare your personal Federal Income Tax Return and your Pennsylvania State Income Tax Return. This work is to commence with the transactions on June 1, 1935, and continue until May 31, 1936, for the total sum of $1,050.00, payable in twelve equal monthly amounts as reports are submitted. Please indicate your agreement to this arrangement by signing the duplicate of this letter in the space provided below and return to us." (Italics supplied.)

It was agreed that the share of the total compensation chargeable to the defendant company would be $75 a month. This contract by its terms expired May 31, 1936. The compensation therein provided for was paid up to and including the report for May, 1936. The reference in the letter to the submission of "monthly reports in substantially the same form as heretofore," is not without significance in view of the rejection by the jury of the entire counterclaim. The subsequent verbal contract made in July, 1936, and involving the first item in plaintiffs' claim of $75 for an examination of defendant's transactions and a report thereon for the month of June, 1936, was, as plaintiffs contend, for an examination and report similar to those theretofore rendered. The report was made in the usual form and defendant's concession at the trial of liability for that item may have been considered by the jury as some confirmation of plaintiff's contention relative to the extent of their duties.

In support of plaintiff's version of their responsibilities under the contract, they called, as an expert witness, Henry S. McCaffrey; no objection was made to his competency. His testimony corroborated that of O'Neill with respect to the difference between an ordinary audit and report and a certified one, verified from independent sources. Defendant offered no expert testimony to contradict that introduced by plaintiffs.

It is apparent from what has been said that the services rendered up to May 31, 1936, were rendered under a contract partly oral and partly written. It is well settled that the terms and construction of such a contract are for the jury where, as here, its terms are disputed. *Philadelphia* v. *Stewart,* 201 Pa. 526, 530, 51 A. 348; *Bastian* v. *Marienville Glass Co.,* 281 Pa. 313, 316, 126 A. 798; and *Dougherty et al.* v. *Proctor & Schwartz, Inc.,* 317 Pa. 363, 366, 176 A. 439. The jury evidently accepted plaintiffs' version of the terms of their contract and the nature of their duties under it.

The conflicting evidence relative to the counterclaim was necessarily for the jury and the twelfth assignment, based upon the refusal of the trial judge to give binding instructions for the defendant, is without merit. The court below, therefore, did not err in subsequently denying defendant's motion for judgment, n. o. v.

Defendant's other assignments of error are directed to the refusal of a new trial. The first five allege errors in the admission of the above mentioned expert testimony and evidence of a similar nature.

We adopt the following excerpts from the opinion of the trial judge as justifying the admission of that evidence:

"The qualifications of these witnesses (O'Neill and McCaffrey) were not challenged. The fact that O'Neill was a party did not, of course, disqualify him as an expert witness in his own behalf. *Beck* v. *Philadelphia Automobile Trade Ass'n,* 59 Pa. Super. 145, 147. Nor was any objection made to the form of the questions put to them. It was contended, however, that in testifying as they did they were interpreting the legal effect of the contract and were thereby usurping the function of the court. With this we were unable to agree. * * * The witnesses, moreover, did not testify as to the legal effect of the contract between the parties. They were called to explain the significance of the type of reports which plaintiffs submitted, over an extended period of time, in *performance* of the contract. It has frequently been decided that the construction placed upon a disputed contract by the parties thereto, as shown by their acts or declarations, will ordinarily be adopted, and will certainly be referred to in determining the true nature of the agreement. *Philadelphia, Trustee* v. *Lehigh Valley Coal Co.,* 290 Pa. 87, 94, 138 A. 94; *Armstrong* v. *Standard Ice Co.,* 129 Pa. Super. 207, 213, 195 A. 171. Aside from this, however, in explaining the nature of plaintiffs' performance of their obligations under the contract, the testimony aided the jury in determining whether such performance complied with the terms of the contract. For this purpose it was clearly admissible."

Complaint is made in the eighth, ninth, tenth and eleventh assignments of the disposition made by the trial judge of certain points for charge. The eighth and ninth alleged error in affirming plaintiffs' second and third points, reading:

"2. Magee, Liebman & O'Neill, as accountants, are not guarantors or insurers of the correctness of their accounts.

"3. Magee, Liebman & O'Neill, as accountants, do not say to the public 'Let us examine your books and vouchers, and we will with absolute certainty discover any dishonesty, every mistake, that exists in those books, and we will protect you against that.' That is not what they undertook to do. They agreed to use such skill in the performance of their agreement as reasonably prudent, skillful accountants would use under the circumstances."

In our opinion, these points were properly affirmed. The language of the third was taken from *Craig* v. *Anyon,* 212 App. Div. 55, 208 N.Y.S. 259, affirmed, 242 N. Y. 569, 152 N.E. 431. Reference may also be made to In re *London and General Bank,* 2 Ch.Div. (Eng) 673; Cooley, Law of Torts (2d Ed.) 277.

The tenth and eleventh assignments complain of the refusal of defendant's second and third points:

"2. If you believe from the evidence that the plaintiffs were employed to make a detailed monthly examination and audit of defendant's business transactions and books, and by reason of the plaintiffs' failure so to do a loss or losses resulted, which might otherwise have been prevented, the plaintiffs are liable to the defendant for such losses.

"3. If the work for which the plaintiffs are suing was made necessary because the plaintiffs failed to comply with their contract of employment, then the plaintiffs cannot recover for those services in default of an agreement by defendant to pay."

These points were refused, and we think properly, upon the ground that they were too comprehensive and would require extensive qualification "to present the matters referred to adequately to the jury." It must also be noted that the trial judge affirmed the following points submitted by the defendant:

"1. If you believe from the evidence that the plaintiffs were employed to make a detailed monthly examination and audit of defendant's business transactions and books, then it was the duty of the plaintiffs to ascertain the accuracy of the Accounts Receivable of the defendant and to ascertain whether the books balanced and to make a true and accurate statement of the same to the defendant.

"4. If you find that the plaintiffs broke their contract and if you find that the loss could have been prevented by the plaintiffs' careful and efficient work under their contract, the defendant is entitled to a verdict for the amount of the loss occurring after the date upon which a discovery of embezzlements and thefts should have been made."

The substance of the points refused was covered in those affirmed. Moreover, in the concluding portion of the charge the trial judge, after instructing the jury to determine whether plaintiffs had been "careless, negligent and inefficient," added: "If they were, that is if they were so neglectful in the performance of their work of examination and audit that the embezzlements, which extended over a period of years, were not discovered, and the failure to discover them resulted in this loss which the defendant company sustained, which has been reduced by payments to $927.30, then it seems to me you would be justified in rendering a verdict in the defendant's favor against the plaintiffs for that amount, less of course the $75 which defendant now concedes plaintiffs are entitled to receive."

We have examined the other assignments relative to the admission of testimony objected to by counsel for defendant and are satisfied no reversible error was committed by the trial judge in his rulings upon the admission or rejection of evidence.

We think the counterclaim was submitted to the jury in a manner as favorable to the defendant as it had any right to expect. As the jury rejected the entire counterclaim, nothing further need be said. The assignments of error are severally overruled.

Judgment affirmed.

In re LONDON AND GENERAL BANK *

Court of Appeal, 1895. 2 Ch. 673.

Lord Justice LINDLEY: This is an appeal by Mr. Theobald, one of the auditors of the London and General Bank, which is being wound up,

* This case is discussed at p. 17 *supra*.

against an order made by Mr. Justice Vaughan Williams, under Section 10 of the Companies Act, 1890. By this order Mr. Theobald and the directors of the bank are declared jointly and severally liable to pay to the Official Receiver of the company two sums of £5,946 12s. 0d. and £8,486 11s. 0d., being respectively the amounts of dividends declared and paid by the bank for the years 1890 and 1891, with interest on those sums. The grounds on which this order was made on Mr. Theobald are that these dividends were paid out of capital, and that such payment was made pursuant to resolutions of the shareholders based upon recommendations of the directors of the bank and upon balance sheets prepared and certified by Mr. Theobald, and which did not truly represent the financial position of the company.

Mr. Theobald's appeal was supported by arguments to the effect: (1) that Mr. Theobald was not an officer of the company within the meaning of Section 10 of the Winding-up Act, 1890; (2) that the balance sheets and certificates given by Mr. Theobald were in accordance with the books of the bank, and that Mr. Theobald's duty as auditor was confined to framing the balance sheets, which showed the position of the bank as disclosed by its books; (3) that the dividends in question were not really paid out of capital and that, however imprudent and reckless it may have been to pay them, Mr. Theobald, as auditor, is not legally responsible for such payment; (4) that even if Mr. Theobald, as auditor, failed adequately to discharge his duty, and even if the dividends were paid out of capital, his failure to discharge his duty was the remote and not the proximate cause of the non-payment (sic) of the dividends, and that he, consequently, is not legally liable to make good the amount so paid; (5) that at any rate the order is wrong in declaring him liable jointly and severally with the directors to repay the dividends in question.

The first of these contentions was argued and decided last April, and the Court then held that an auditor of a banking company governed by the Companies Act, 1879, and by such articles as regulated the present company, was an officer of the company within the meaning of Section 10 of the Winding-up Act, 1890, and was liable to have proceedings taken against him under that section. This point, having been thus decided, was, of course, not again raised, and nothing further need be said about it.

It remains, however, to consider what the duties of an auditor are as respects companies governed by the Companies Act, 1879, and by such articles as regulate this particular company. It will be convenient to do this before examining the facts relied upon by the liquidator as making Mr. Theobald liable to make good the dividends which he has been ordered to pay. Section 7 of the Companies Act of 1879, clauses 1, 5 and 6, are material. '7.—(1) Once at least in every year the accounts of every banking company registered after the passing of this Act as a limited company shall be examined by an auditor or auditors, who shall be elected annually by the company in general meeting.' Then clause 5 is: 'Every auditor shall have a list delivered to him of all books kept by the company, and shall at all reasonable times have access to the books and accounts of the company; and any auditor may, in relation to such books and accounts, examine the directors or any other officer of the company.' Then there is a proviso, which one need not read, about banks beyond the limits of Europe. Then 6 is: 'The auditor or auditors shall make a report to the members on the accounts examined by him or them, and on every balance sheet laid before the company in general meeting during his or their tenure of office; and in every such report shall state whether, in his or their opinion, the balance sheet referred to in the report is a full and fair balance sheet properly drawn up, so as to exhibit a true and correct view of the state of the company's affairs, as shown by the books of the company, and such report shall be read before the company in general meeting.' Then '7. The remuneration of the auditor or auditors shall be fixed by the general meeting appointing such auditor or auditors, and shall be paid by the company.' It is necessary also to read articles 106, 107 and 114. Article 106, which is under the head 'Accounts,' runs thus: 'At every ordinary meeting the directors shall lay before the meeting a balance sheet showing the financial state of the company for the previous financial year, duly audited, and every such balance sheet shall be accompanied by a report of the directors as to the state and condition of the company, and as to the amount which they recommend to be paid out of the profits by way of dividend or bonus to the shareholders, after allowing for any interim dividend which the directors may have declared, and any sum which they may have set aside under article 116 hereof.' Then article 107, which is under the head 'Audit,' runs thus: 'The accounts of the company shall be from time to time examined and the correctness of the statements shall be from time to time ascertained, by two or more auditors, in accordance with these presents.' Then article 114, which, I think, is the only further one I need read at this moment, runs thus: 'The auditors shall be supplied with copies of the statement of accounts intended to be laid before the meeting, and it shall be their duty to examine the same with the accounts and vouchers relating thereto.' These are the enactments and regulations which bear directly on the duties of the auditors, and although articles 107 and 114 are in terms more explicit than Section 7 of the statute as regards the duty of the auditors to examine and ascertain the correctness of the statements laid before them, and of the accounts laid before the shareholders, yet it is tolerably plain from the language of Section 7 of the Act, clause 5, that the articles add little, if anything, to the duties imposed on the auditors by the statute alone.

In connection with these articles, and in order to save repetition, it should be stated that by the articles of this bank it is the duty of the directors, and not of the auditors, to recommend to the shareholders the amounts to be appropriated for dividends; and it is the duty of the directors to have proper accounts kept so as to show the true state and position of the company. Lastly, it is for the shareholders, but only on the recommendation of the directors, to declare a dividend.

It is impossible to read Section 7 of the Companies Act, 1879, without being struck with the importance of the enactment that the auditors are to be appointed by the shareholders, and are to report to them directly, and not to, or through, the directors. The object of this enactment is obvious. It evidently is to secure to the shareholders independent and reliable information respecting the true financial position of the company at the time of the audit. The articles of this particular company are even more explicit on this point than the statute itself, and remove any possible ambiguity to which the language of the statute, taken alone, may be open if very narrowly criticised.

It is no part of an auditor's duty to give advice either to directors or shareholders as to what they ought to do. An auditor has nothing to do with the prudence or imprudence of making loans with or without security. It is nothing to him whether the business of a company is being conducted prudently or imprudently, profitably or unprofitably; it is nothing to him whether dividends are properly or improperly declared, provided he discharges his own duty to the shareholders. His business is to ascertain and state the true financial position of the company at the time of the audit, and his duty is confined to that. But then comes the question: How is he to ascertain such positions? The answer is: By examining the books of the company. But he does not discharge his duty by doing this without inquiry and without taking any trouble to see that the books of the company themselves show the company's true position. He must take reasonable care to ascertain that they do. Unless he does this, his duty will be worse than a farce. Assuming the books to be so kept as to show the true position of the company, the auditor has to frame a balance sheet showing that position according to the books, and to certify that the balance sheet presented is correct in that sense. But his first duty is to examine the books, not merely for the purpose of ascertaining what they do show, but also for the purpose of satisfying himself that they show the true financial position of the company. This is quite in accordance with the decision of Mr. Justice Stirling in *The Leeds Estate Company* v. *Shepherd* in 36 Chancery Division, page 802. An auditor, however, is not bound to do more than exercise reasonable care and skill in making inquiries and investigations. He is not an insurer; he does not guarantee that the books do correctly show the true position of the company's affairs; he does not guarantee that his balance sheet is accurate according to the books of the company. If he did he would be responsible for an error on his part, even if he were himself deceived, without any want of reasonable care on his part—say, by the fraudulent concealment of a book from him. His obligation is not so onerous as this.

Such I take to be the duty of the auditor; he must be honest—that is, he must not certify what he does not believe to be true, and he must take reasonable care and skill before he believes that what he certifies is true. What is reasonable care in any particular case must depend upon the circumstances of that case. Where there is nothing to excite suspicion, very little inquiry will be reasonable and sufficient; and in practice, I believe, business men select a few cases haphazard, see that they are right, and assume that others like them are correct also. Where suspicion is aroused more care is obviously necessary, but still an auditor is not bound to exercise more than reasonable care and skill even in a case of suspicion; and he is perfectly justified in acting on the opinion of an expert where special knowledge is required.

Mr. Theobald's evidence satisfies me that he took the same view as myself of his duty in investigating the company's books and preparing his balance sheet. He did not content himself with making his balance sheet from the books without troubling himself about the truth of what they showed. He checked the cash, examined vouchers for payments, saw that the bills and securities entered in the books were correct, took reasonable care to ascertain their value, and in one case obtained a solicitor's opinion on the validity of an equitable charge. I see no trace whatever of any failure by him in the performance of this part of his duty. It is satisfactory to find that the legal standard of duty is not too high for business purposes, and is recognised as correct by business men.

The balance sheet and certificate of February, 1892, that is, for the year

1891, was accompanied by a report to the directors of the bank. Taking the balance sheet, the certificate, and report together, Mr. Theobald stated to the directors the true financial position of the bank, and if this report had been laid before the shareholders, Mr. Theobald would have completely discharged his duty to them. Unfortunately, however, this report was not laid before the shareholders, and it becomes necessary to consider the legal consequences to Mr. Theobald of this circumstance.

A person whose duty it is to convey information to others does not discharge that duty by simply giving them so much information as is calculated to induce them, or some of them, to ask for more. Information and means of information are by no means equivalent terms. Still, there may be circumstances under which information given in the shape of a printed document circulated amongst a large body of shareholders would by its consequent publicity be very injurious to their interests, and in such a case I am not prepared to say that an auditor would fail to discharge his duty if, instead of publishing his report in such a way as to ensure publicity, he made a confidential report to the shareholders, and invited their attention to it, and told them where they could see it. The auditor is to make a report to the shareholders, but the mode of doing so, and the form of the report, are not prescribed. If, therefore, Mr. Theobald had laid before the shareholders the balance sheet and the profit and loss account accompanied by a certificate in the form in which he had prepared it, he would perhaps have done enough, under the peculiar circumstances of the case. I feel, however, the great danger of acting on such a principle, and in order not to be misunderstood, I will add that an auditor who gives shareholders means of information instead of information in respect of a company's financial position does so at his peril, and runs the very serious risk of being held, judicially, to have failed to discharge his duty.

In this case I have no hesitation in saying that Mr. Theobald did fail to discharge his duty to the shareholders in certifying and laying before them the balance sheet of February, 1892, without any reference to the report which he laid before the directors, and with no other warning than is conveyed by the words 'The value of the assets as shown on the balance sheet is dependent upon realisation.' The most important asset on that balance sheet is put down as 'Loans to customers and other securities, £346,975,' and on those a full and detailed report was made to the directors, showing the very unsatisfactory state of these loans and securities, and it is impossible to read the oral evidence, the report of Mr. Balfour and Mr. Brock, dated the 22nd December, 1891, and the report of the auditor to the directors of the 3rd February, 1892, without coming to the conclusion that the entry of that large sum as a good asset without explanation was unjustifiable. It is a mere truism to say that the value of loans and securities depends upon their realisation. We are told that a statement to that effect is so unusual that the mere presence of those words is enough to excite suspicion. But, as already stated, the duty of an auditor is to convey information, not to arouse inquiry, and although an auditor might infer from an unusual statement that something was seriously wrong, it by no means follows that ordinary people would have their suspicions aroused by a similar statement if, as in this case, its language expresses no more than any ordinary person would infer without it.

But Mr. Theobald relies on the fact that he was induced to omit from his certificate all reference to the report which he made to the directors because Mr. Balfour, the chairman, promised to mention such report in his speech to the shareholders, and he did so. But although Mr. Balfour twice alluded to the report, he did so in such a way as to avoid attracting attention to it. The second time he mentioned it was after a dividend had been declared, and when a motion to reappoint the auditors was before the meeting. The truth is that not a word was said to convey to the shareholders the substance of the information contained in the report, or to induce them to ask any question about it. The balance sheet and the profit and loss account were true and correct in this sense, that they were in accordance with the books. But they were, nevertheless, entirely misleading, and misrepresented the real position of the company. Under these circumstances, I am compelled to hold that Mr. Theobald failed to discharge his duty to the shareholders with respect to the balance sheet and certificate of February, 1892. Possibly he did not realise the extent of his duty to the shareholders as distinguished from the directors, and he, unfortunately, consented to leave the chairman to explain the true state of the company to the shareholders instead of doing so himself. The fact, however, remains, and cannot be got over, that the balance sheet and certificate of February, 1892, did not show the true position of the company at the end of 1891, and that this was owing to the omission by the auditor to lay before the shareholders material information which he had obtained in the course of his employment as auditor of the company, and to which he called the attention of the directors.

But then it is contended that, even if this be so, there was, after all, no payment of a dividend out of capital; and further that, even if there was, still that such payment was not the natural or immediate result of Mr. Theobald's certificate, and of the accounts which he prepared.

Whether the payment was made out of capital or not is a question of fact. It was professedly made out of profits made by the bank by charging its customers with interest and commission on loans and discounts. The books showed such profit, but the question is, where did the money come from with which the dividends were paid? The money came from cash at the bankers or in hand, but this cash could not be properly treated as profit, and the directors and auditors knew this perfectly well. This part of the case has been most carefully investigated by the learned judge whose decision we are reviewing, and after attending most attentively to the observations of counsel on the reasonings and conclusions contained in the judgment appealed from, I see no reason whatever for dissenting from them. On the contrary, I entirely agree with him in saying that the profits for the year 1891 never really existed except on paper—that, to use his words, 'Whatever may be the right line to draw as to when profit not received may be carried to profit for the purpose of the annual revenue account, it is plain that there was no justification for so doing in the present case'. The real truth is that the assets of the bank were put down in the balance sheet at far too high a figure, and this entry, though not misleading if explained (as it was to the directors), was seriously misleading in the absence of explanation. Mr. Theobald says that he regarded the assets of the bank as only locked up, but his report and the schedule to it go far beyond this. The value of the principal asset depended on the probability of the Balfour group of companies and some of the other large borrowers repaying their loans. They were financing each other, their indebtedness to the bank increased largely during the year, the securities held by the bank for these loans were, to say the least, of very doubtful character, and yet the total amount due to the bank in respect of these loans is inserted in the balance sheet as a good asset without any deduction, and without a word of explanation to the shareholders. We now know that these assets have realised a comparatively small sum, and we were very properly warned against the danger of doing injustice by being wise after the event. But disregarding the result of realisation and attending only to what was known to the auditors in February, 1892, the entry in the balance sheet of the sum of £346,975 as a good asset was wholly unjustifiable unless explained.

We are now in a position to understand the true meaning of a passage contained in the auditors' report to the directors of the 3rd February, 1892, and which runs thus: 'We cannot conclude without expressing our opinion unhesitatingly that no dividend should be paid this year'. I find it impossible to treat this as a statement by the auditors that there are profits divisible among the shareholders, but that the auditors cannot recommend a dividend. I can only regard the passage as meaning that there are no funds out of which the dividend can properly be paid, and, therefore, no dividend ought to be paid this year. A dividend of 7 per cent. was, nevertheless, recommended by the directors, and was resolved upon by the shareholders at a meeting furnished with the balance sheet and profit and loss account certified by the auditors, and at which meeting the auditors were present, but silent. Not a word was said to inform the shareholders of the true state of affairs. It is idle to say that these accounts are so remotely connected with the payment of the dividend as to render the auditors legally irresponsible for such payment. The balance sheet and account certified by the auditors as showing a profit available for dividend were, in my judgment, not the remote, but the real operating cause of the motion for the payment of the dividend which the directors improperly recommended. The auditors' account and certificate gave weight to such recommendation and rendered it acceptable to the meeting. It was wholly unnecessary for the Official Receiver to call a shareholder to say that he was induced by the auditors' certificate to concur in the resolution to pay a dividend. As to this part of the case *res ipsa loquitur*.

The point was made that the form of the order was wrong. But there was nothing in this. Mr. Theobald could obviously be sued alone in an action at law for breach of his statutory duty as auditor, and the measure of damages would be the sum which he has been ordered to pay. Whether a similar action at law could be maintained against him and the directors jointly is more open to question. I am by no means satisfied that it could not, seeing that the wrongful payment of the dividend was caused by his improper certificate and accounts, and by the use made of them by the directors. But, be this as it may, there was a clear breach of trust by the directors, facilitated, and, indeed, only rendered possible by the auditor, who failed in discharging his own duty to the shareholders; and I have no doubt that in equity both he and they could be held jointly and severally liable for the misapplication of the company's moneys, which constituted a breach of trust. In respect, therefore, to the sum of £8,486 11s. wrongfully paid as dividend in 1892 in respect of the alleged profits made in 1891, the appeal in my opinion fails.

I pass now to the accounts and balance sheet prepared by the auditors in February, 1891, and showing the state of affairs in 1890. A profit for that year was shown and a dividend of £5,946 12s. was declared and paid, and Mr. Theobald has been held liable for this sum also. I agree with Mr. Justice Vaughan Williams in holding that the dividend for 1890 was in fact improperly declared and paid. But the evidence that Mr. Theobald was guilty of any breach of duty in certifying the accounts in February, 1891, is far less cogent than that which presses so heavily against him with reference to the accounts of February, 1892. The truth is that the conviction that the bank's affairs were every year getting worse and worse grew upon him year by year. This state of things was shown by the decrease of its reserve capital and the increase of its loans to customers. But the loans to customers were, speaking roughly, £100,000 less at the end of the year 1890 than at the end of 1891, and seeing that the accounts prepared by the auditors did accurately represent the position of the company as shown by the books, and that it is not proved that Mr. Theobald really knew, or ought then to have known, that the position of the bank was not correctly shown by the books, I think Mr. Justice Vaughan Williams has gone too far in holding Mr. Theobald liable for this sum. The reasons which induced the learned judge to decide that Mr. Theobald was not liable for the dividends paid in 1889 and 1890 appear to me to apply also to the dividends paid in 1891 in respect of the profits of 1890. No doubt the change made by the auditors in 1886 in the form of the certificate that they gave is really significant, and, unexplained, leads to the inference that the auditors did not believe that the books of the company and the balance sheet prepared from them correctly showed the position of the bank. But Mr. Theobald's evidence does, in my opinion, show that in February, 1891, matters were not known or believed to be so bad as to lead him to the conclusion that there were then no profits out of which a dividend could properly be paid. It is true that the position of the bank was very unsatisfactory in 1890, and the auditors knew it to be so. This, however, appeared from the balance sheet and accounts which they laid before the shareholders. It is known now that the assets were put down at too high a figure; but it is not proved that the auditors knew it or ought to have known it. The Balfour group of companies, though dependent upon each other, were by no means in so tottering a state as they were a year later. Mr. Wilkinson's debt was still treated by the directors as bearing interest and as a good, or at all events not a bad, debt. Mr. Benham's debt was unsatisfactory, but the auditors can hardly be blamed for treating it as good, having regard to the solicitor's statement as to the security held for it. This part of the case is very near the line, but having carefully considered it, I do not think that the evidence is sufficiently strong to establish a case of misfeasance on the part of Mr. Theobald in February, 1891. I am not satisfied that he was then guilty of more than an excusable error of judgment; although now that all the facts are known the error is seen to have been very serious in its consequences. As to the sum of £5,946 12s. 0d., therefore, the appeal must be allowed. As regards costs, Mr. Theobald's appeal has resulted in reducing the sum for which he has been held liable; but, in other respects, and as regards his main contention, it has failed. Under these circumstances he ought not to receive or pay any costs of the appeal, and the only order as to costs will be that the Official Receiver be paid his costs out of the assets of the company.

Lord Justice Lopes has read and considered this judgment and concurs in it.

Lord Justice Rigby: I have had the advantage of reading and considering the judgment just delivered by Lord Justice Lindley, and I might have confined myself to saying I concur in it, but as I have gone carefully into the evidence as against the appellant, I think that I shall do well to show how I have come to the conclusion on which my judgment is founded. I shall not attempt to repeat all that is contained in Lord Justice Lindley's judgment. Where no reference is made to a particular topic it must be taken that I have nothing to add, though I do not wish to detract from anything said. The appeal is against that part of the order of the 20th December, 1894, of Mr. Justice Vaughan Williams, which finds Mr. Theobald liable as one of the auditors of the London and General Bank Ltd. to make good to the assets of the company, jointly with other persons, and severally the amount with interest from the date of the order of two sums, £6,768 6s. 9d. and £9,328 17s. 4d., being the dividends with interest thereon down to the date of the order recommended by the directors and declared by meetings of the company in the years 1891 and 1892 for the years 1890 and 1891. I have not taken the same figures as Lord Justice Lindley did, because there has been added to the dividends the amount of interest down to the date of the order. I think it will be the exact figure.

The order was made on a summons taken out by the liquidator of the company in the matter of the Companies Acts and in the matter of the bank, asking, so far as is material for the present appeal, for a declaration of the joint and several liability of the directors and auditors of the company on the ground that the dividends before mentioned were not paid out of profits but out of capital, and so far as the auditors were concerned on the ground that they certified and reported that the balance sheets which were laid before the company at the said meetings purported to show profits in excess of the sum paid as dividends. I understand the application to have been in substance an application against the auditors as officers of the company under the 10th Section of the Act of 1890 to compel them to contribute to the assets of the company by way of compensation for their misfeasance, such sums as the Court may think just.

The main issues, therefore, seem to be whether the auditors have been guilty of any misfeasance in relation to the company; whether the misfeasance has occasioned loss to the company for which compensation ought to be directed to be made. This will involve the question whether the dividends were, in fact, paid not out of profits, but out of capital, and whether such payment was the fault of the auditor. Then there will be the question of the amount of compensation which ought to be directed. To determine the first question, I think it will be necessary to consider in some detail the position and duties of the auditors, what they ought to have done, and what they have done. Then I refer to subsection 6 of Section 7 of the Companies Act of 1879, and to those articles of association which have been referred to by Lord Justice Lindley. I do not think it necessary here to read them out. The articles of association cannot absolve the auditors from any obligation imposed upon them by the statute, and it may be that they do not in this case impose any greater obligations as to the balance sheet, though they make it clear that similar obligations extend to all accounts placed before the company, including profit and loss account as well as the balance sheet. Under the statute, the members of the company are entitled to have the safeguard of an expression of opinion of the auditors to the effect, first, that the balance sheet is a full and fair balance sheet; and, secondly, that it, the balance sheet, is properly drawn up so as to exhibit a true and correct view of the state of the company's affairs. The words 'as shown by the books of the company' seem to me to be introduced to relieve the auditors from any responsibility as to affairs of the company kept out of the books and concealed from them, but not to confine it to a mere statement of the correspondence of the balance sheet with the entries in the books. Now, a full and fair balance sheet must be such a balance sheet as to convey a truthful statement as to the company's position. It must not conceal any known cause of weakness in the financial position, or suggest anything which cannot be supported as fairly correct in a business point of view. The provision as to the balance sheet being properly drawn up so as to exhibit a correct view of the state of the company's affairs is taken from, though it does not go quite so far as, article 94, Table A, of the schedule to the Companies Act of 1862. Treated as an addition to the requisition of a full and fair balance sheet, it may not be easy to define the full extent of the obligation which it imposes, nor is it necessary to do so in this case, for it certainly requires, as will hereafter appear, a more detailed statement of facts, or a more detailed explanation of the affairs of the bank, than is contained in any of the balance sheets of this company.

It will be important to see what information the auditors actually acquired as to the business of the company, and the way in which they reported upon the successive balance sheets. Mr. Theobald and Mr. Timms were auditors of the bank from its incorporation in 1882, and they made the audit for successive years down to and including the audit for 1891.

The reports of the auditors to the members always took the form of a certificate or memorandum written on the balance sheet for the year. Their reports on the accounts for the years 1882 and 1883 contained a statement to the effect that in their opinion the balance sheet exhibited a true and correct view of the position of the bank. In their report on the accounts of 1885 a somewhat less emphatic statement to the same effect appears, but in the subsequent report no such statement is to be found. In a report to the directors dated the 11th February, 1886, which refers to the accounts for 1885, Mr. Theobald, after noticing that the first-class investments, kept by bankers for quick realisation in case of need, stood at a considerably reduced sum, and that more than the whole capital of the company was invested in four accounts, viz. the accounts of the Liberator, the Lands Allotment Co., the House and Land Co., and the Building Estates Co., and that these investments could not be easily realised in critical times, proceeds to say: 'You are doubtless aware that it is a rule with bankers to have at hand in cash or easily realisable securities an amount equal to at least one-third of the customers' current accounts. Considering the whole amount of uncalled capital, I consider that in this case the proportion is scarcely sufficient.' There can be no doubt that even at this time Mr. Theobald was aware that the state of affairs of the bank was unsatisfactory in the important points of lock-up of capital and consequent deficiency of realisable securities. At this date the cash in hand appeared to be £28,000—I only give the round figures—and the easily realisable securities were worth £12,600, making together £41,000 odd, while the current accounts and deposit accounts of customers together reached £107,000. I have not been able to distinguish the separate amounts of current and deposit accounts at that time. In the balance sheet for 1891, more particularly dealt with hereafter, the cash had fallen to £25,000, and the easily realisable securities to £7,820, making together £32,000 odd; hardly more than one-sixth of the sum due to customers on current accounts alone, which had increased to £189,000 odd, the amount due on current and deposit accounts taken together being £282,000. No other report of the auditors to the directors is put in evidence until that of 1892 as to the accounts of 1891. The report of the auditors to the members on the accounts for 1886 to 1890, both inclusive, are simply to the effect that the cash and bills receivable are correct, that securities had been produced for the investments and loans (no information being given as to the securities so produced) and that the balance sheet is a correct summary of the accounts recorded in the books. In the last-mentioned report is contained for the first time a statement, 'The value of the assets as shown on the balance sheet is dependent on realisation.'

Great stress has been laid on this by counsel for the appellants. They argue that it was sufficient to put members upon inquiry, and that from the course taken at the trial they were debarred from giving the evidence of experts as to the importance and signification of this. I may at once say that it was the duty of the auditors to convey in direct and express terms to the members any information which they thought proper to be communicated, that the words of the statement are perfectly clear in their meaning, but also entirely unimportant, amounting to a mere truism, and that no evidence of experts would have been of the slightest use for the purpose of giving them a greater importance or signification than they possessed in themselves, even if such evidence were admissible. To me it appears that all the reports from 1886 onwards were imperfect, and that the auditors in giving reports in such form failed entirely to fulfil the statutory duties imposed upon them. Counsel for the appellants argued that such a failure would not amount to misfeasance but only to negligence, and that the appellant is not charged by the summons with negligence, but I cannot admit the cogency of this argument. The reports were made in order to fulfil the statutory obligation, and to be read to the meetings in accordance with the statute. Mr. Theobald, with reference to this matter, says at page 74 of the evidence, 'My evidence means the same as the Act'. Then he is asked, 'Do you say you could have given the certificate required by the Act of 1891?' (I think that question must have been meant and understood to mean, 'Could you have given the certificate for 1891 required by the Act?') ' (A), Yes, certainly. (Q) Then why did you not do so? (A) Because I was not aware that it was considered necessary for me to give the certificate either in the words of the Act or not at all.' Mr. Theobald's interpretation of his own certificate cannot be received either in his favour or against him, and we should not unduly press against him apparent admissions made in the course of a very trying cross-examination. But this evidence of his does, I think, go so far as to show that the certificates were in fact given as reports under the Act, and independent of that evidence I think there can be no doubt that they were intended to be and were received and acted upon as reports under the Act.

I consider the giving of the certificates (assuming them to be to the knowledge of the auditors misleading certificates, a question which I shall deal with separately) to be a misfeasance within the meaning of Section 10 of the Act of 1890, and not a mere act of negligence; and that this was a fair meaning of the charge contained in the summons I can have no doubt, having regard to the terms of the certificates given and the explanations of Mr. Theobald himself, that there was a strong and growing feeling of dissatisfaction in the mind of Mr. Theobald at the state of the affairs of the bank as shown by the books, and I find no sufficient communication of the facts causing this dissatisfaction in the reports. The balance sheets when examined do not in my opinion fulfil the statutory requirements of being full and fair balance sheets, and they are not properly drawn up so as to exhibit a true and correct view of the state of the company's affairs as shown by the books of the company. To establish this, I think it is necessary to give a short summary of the evidence, as to the years 1889, 1890 and 1891, the only years as to which we have sufficient evidence to be able to arrive at definite conclusions. From the tables set out at page 7 of the Official Receiver's report it appears that during the years 1889, 1890 and 1891, the greater part of the business of the bank consisted in making loans to and discounting bills for a group of companies, nine in number, conveniently referred to as the Balfour group, or the Balfour companies. Loans were also made or discounting facilities afforded to other companies allied to the Balfour companies, to certain directors of the bank, and customers, including Wilkinson and Benham, who are named in the table, by reason of special considerations affecting their accounts. These accounts of allied companies and the persons last mentioned are for convenience hereinafter referred to as 'the special accounts.'

The balances due from the Balfour companies at the end of the years 1889, 1890 and 1891 were, for 1889 £119,000, for 1890 £218,000, and for 1891 £308,000. Corresponding balances in the 'special accounts' were, for 1889 £77,000, for 1890 £112,000, for 1891 £121,000, the aggregate balances from the Balfour companies and on the special accounts being for 1889 £196,000, for 1890 £321,000, for 1891 £429,000. The corresponding balances due from all other customers and persons were, for 1889 £135,000, for 1890 £103,000, for 1891 £100,000. Roughly speaking, the proportion of what may be called the outside business that with the Balfour companies and on the special accounts was, at the end of 1889 two-thirds, at the end of 1890 one-third, and at the end of 1891 one-fourth. The paid-up capital increased in 1890 by about £67,000, and in 1891 by about £43,000, or altogether £120,000, but the whole of this, and considerably more than £100,000 in addition, had been absorbed into the accounts of the Balfour companies and the special accounts.

It has already been pointed out that the amount of cash and easily realisable securities at the end of 1891 was hardly more than one-sixth of the amount due to customers on current accounts, or about one-half of what Mr. Theobald had in 1886 pointed out to be required according to the usual practice of bankers.

These figures show an alarming absorption during the three years of the available assets of the company in advances to the Balfour companies and on the special accounts, and a perilous diminution of easily realisable assets. As is usual with banking companies, profits alleged to have been earned by the bank consisted, with unsubstantial exceptions, of interest on loans, discounting of bills, and commissions.

The gross profits entered in the books as having been earned from the Balfour companies, between the incorporation of the bank and the end of 1891, amounted to upwards of £84,000. The amount distributed in dividends during the same period was upwards of £58,000 and the amount carried to reserve fund £13,000. I include there £3,000 carried to reserve fund in accordance with the report on the accounts of 1891, making together £71,000.

The reserve fund, however, was not required by the articles of associa tion to be kept separate, and was not kept separate from the general funds of the bank. It was employed in the bank's business, quite rightly, no doubt.

Subject to an argument as to appropriation of payments dealt with hereafter, the profits supposed to have been earned from the Balfour companies were not actually paid, but they were only debited in the accounts current of the different companies, and, speaking generally, the moneys owing by the different companies went on increasing from year to year. It is evident that, unless these profits could be fairly treated as not only earned but payable within a reasonable time, there would at the end of 1891 be no profits out of which a dividend could be paid, but, on the contrary, a large deficiency.

The learned judge, after a careful consideration and investigation of the evidence before him, has found, as a fact, that the credits of these companies at the end of each year were generally credits created temporarily for the purpose of audit, and that such credits, in the majority of cases, were created either by the discounting of bills of companies like Hobbs & Co., which bills constituted a mere paper asset, or by loans direct or indirect from the bank itself, the bulk of which were ill-secured.

I see no reason to differ from this conclusion, but it is a conclusion arrived at to an important extent from comparing the books of the bank with the books of other companies of the Balfour group to which the auditors had no access, and it is only to the extent to which it is founded on entries in the books of the bank itself that it can be used for the purpose of charging the appellant with knowledge of the facts, though it is very important on the question whether the dividends were really paid out of capital or not. The books themselves show that in many instances the accounts were put in credit in the manner described by the learned judge, but in other cases, and especially with reference to the indirect loans, that is to say, loans made by the bank to one of the companies out of which that company made an advance to another of the group for the purpose of putting the accounts of the latter in credit at the end of the year, the auditors would have no sufficient means of tracing the transactions.

Having made these general observations I will go on to examine more completely the important case of the accounts for the year 1891. For that purpose, as being more fair to the auditors, I will assume without at all deciding that, down to the end of 1890, no knowledge that the former balance sheets were misleading has been brought home to the auditors, and will endeavour to ascertain what additional information the auditors acquired during the audit for 1891. In the year 1891 the indebtedness of the Balfour companies to the bank as appearing by the bank books was increased by the sum of between £89,000 and £90,000 without any additional securities of importance being given, though, no doubt, to a considerable but unascertained extent money was expended on buildings already charged to the bank, which would make the property charged, though not necessarily the charges in favour of the bank, more valuable.

The securities consisted in the main of charges on buildings being constructed under building agreements. on which large sums had already been charged in priority to the bank. The buildings were unfinished, and required further expenditure of very large sums before they could advantageously be disposed of, and in my judgment there was abundant evidence to show that these securities of the bank were very insufficient, and not realisable at all without the expenditure of further money, which the bank was unable to advance. The sums due on the special accounts had increased from £102,000 to £121,000, that is to say, between £18,000 and £19,000. With regard to these special accounts, I do not think it necessary to go in detail through the list, but I find that the auditors comment very unfavourably on the security for the following debts: That of William Blewitt for £7,849; that of Blewitt and Balfour for £2,148; and that of Balfour for £12,000. I think, however, that they may have considered the personal security in these cases sufficient, and I do not found anything on those cases. Wilkinson, at the end of 1890, was indebted to the bank in the sum of £24,000 practically unsecured. Mr. Theobald complained about interest being debited on the ground that the directors had then more definite information as to the security. This was going through the audit for 1890. The fact is that the security consisted of debentures of a tramway company whose tramway was never built. Interest accordingly ceased to be debited to this account in March, 1891. When Mr. Theobald was pressed to explain why the full sum was returned as an asset, he replied that it would have to be provided for out of the reserve fund. He further explained that he thought the account wanted watching, but that it was likely to turn out all right. In examination before the judge with reference to this debt, he said that he had conferred with the manager, who knew all about the circumstances. 'First of all,' says he, 'I suggested the whole should be written off, but afterwards, Mr. Brock, I think it was, sent for Mr. Blewitt. We had a very serious conference about it, and they convinced me that the time had not come to do that (write off the whole), and they might yet get the whole of the amount back, but I thought it was not wise to charge interest.'

This, I think, falls very far indeed short of showing that the auditor believed, or could have believed, that the debt was a good debt, though it might have justified the carrying of it to a suspense account, instead of writing it off as bad. The importance of the case depends upon the fact that if the debt had not been entered in the balance sheet as a good debt, there would have been no profit at all to show for the year 1891. At the end of 1891, Mr. Wilkinson's debt, which had risen from discounting bills, all of which would appear by the dates to have been dishonoured, was reduced to £16,000 on account of discount by a loan of £10,000, but the indebtedness remained unaffected. With regard to Benham's debt which increased in the year 1891 from £31,635 to £47,745, it was proved that in 1891 Mr. Theobald refused to pass the security for another year, and, to satisfy him, a letter purporting to come from Benham's solicitor, Mr. Waring, containing an undertaking to pay off £15,000 within a week, was produced. He had also been told, during the audit for 1890, that there was a security under a supposed will which had not been proved, and that they expected to get the will proved very soon. During the audit for 1891 he ascertained that the debt had increased from £31,000 to £47,000, that the £15,000 promised to be repaid had not been repaid, and that the alleged will had not been proved—indeed, it turned out afterwards that such a will never existed. The explanation of Mr. Theobald, that he trusted to the solicitor seeing that the security was all right, is not, under circumstances, altogether satisfactory, but I think it is safer to allow Mr. Theobald the benefit of the defence, though his own report sufficiently shows that he was not himself thoroughly satisfied. I wish to make it plain, so far as I can, that I am only relying on matters which Mr. Theobald ought to have known and must be presumed to have known. The debt of £7,300 from the Medway Portland Cement Co. had, like Wilkinson's, ceased to be charged with interest, and could not properly have been treated as a fund for the payment of dividend. With reference to that of the Public Works Co. Ltd., amounting to £8,105, the auditors, in their schedule to their report to the directors, say this: 'The realisation of this is very doubtful.' There could, therefore, be no justification for treating this as a fund for payment of dividend. Whilst Mr. Theobald was engaged upon the audit of the accounts for 1891, or previously, a report of Messrs. Balfour & Brock, dated 22nd of December, 1891, was produced to him as to the way of putting into credit current accounts of Hobbs & Co. Ltd., George Newman & Co. Ltd., the London, Edinburgh & Glasgow Insurance Co., and C. H. Wilkinson, by loans from the bank. With reference to Mr. Wilkinson's account, the proposal 'that the overdraft should be made in part by a loan and in part by fresh acceptances of both secured as may be arranged, we think the further loan should be £10,000 on loan and £15,000 on bills'. The loan was made, and, apparently, £16,000 was left on security of acceptances, but it does not appear that any security was then arranged for or given, or that Mr. Theobald investigated this matter. Attention was, therefore, called in this particular case to the mode in which the accounts were put in credit as found by the learned judge. Several facts which appear to me to be most material with reference to the debt of 1891 are to be gathered from the text of the report. I have dealt, to a certain extent, with the schedule in the remarks I have previously made, but as to the text of the report of the auditors of February, 1892, almost every sentence is full of serious meaning. In it they state 'that they are unable to give a more satisfactory certificate than the one set forth,' which is a mere statement that the balance sheet is a correct summary of the accounts as recorded in the books, followed by a statement that the value of the assets as shown on the balance sheet is dependent upon realisation, which I have already commented upon, an important sentence: 'On this subject we have reported specifically to the board.' This may mean they have reported as to the value of the assets, or as to their realisation, or (as I think is the true construction) as to both. The auditors were induced to withdraw this sentence, which, though it would have given no information of the slightest value to the members, yet would have been calculated to put them upon inquiry. They go on: 'We are not qualified, nor is it the province of the auditors, to estimate with exactitude the value of the securities.' The words 'with exactitude' seem to me to be emphatic, and to point out that they had, as appears by the report, made a general estimate of the securities, which was very unfavourable. They say, 'Nevertheless, we feel it our duty to send you herewith a schedule of the securities amounting to £487,000, which we desire should have the special and very serious consideration of the directors.'

In the £487,000 are included every one of the sums owing by the Balfour companies and on the special accounts, and nearly £60,000 more out of the £100,000 owing by other customers of the bank. Auditors who feel it their duty to call the special and very serious consideration of their directors to £487,000 out of a total of£530,000 of the debts due to the bank must indeed have arrived at the opinion that the state of affairs of the company was critical and dangerous, but, as will appear, Mr. Theobald does not deny this, though he attempts, unsuccessfully, I think, to explain it away by saying that all his anxiety arose from the fact of the assets being locked up. Further on in the report the auditors say, 'The gravity of the situation is enhanced by the fact, as we believe it to be, that the board is in many cases powerless to decline further help because they are powerless to realise.' This appears to me to be a very just but a very serious statement. The Balfour companies were indeed so much bound up with one another by a system of inter-financing, and some of them had committed themselves so deeply in the building schemes of Hobbs & Co., Newman & Co. and others, that they would only be kept going in the future, as they had been in the past, by continued advances from the funds of the bank. The last quoted extract from the report seems to me to show that the auditors fully appreciated this view of the state of affairs of the company. They continue as follows: 'We beg also respectfully to point out that the quarters from which the bank obtains by far the larger proportion of its business'—meaning, I conclude, the Balfour companies, and some of the special accounts—'are such that the constitution of the board must make it difficult, if not impossible, to obtain a sufficiently independent judgment upon many vital questions which have to be decided in its management.' No doubt this refers to the fact that some members of the board of the bank, the financing company, were members also of the board of different Balfour companies requiring advances, and the difficulty arising from this is obvious and serious. Then follows a sentence which forms an appropriate ending to such a report: 'We cannot conclude without expressing the opinion unhesitatingly that no dividend should be paid this year.' The auditors were, unfortunately, persuaded by Mr. Balfour, assisted by Mr. Brock, to strike out this clause, I believe, before the report reached the hands of the other directors of the bank. Mr. Theobald explains this by saying that he came to the conclusion that it was beyond the province of the auditors to express an opinion as to the policy of declaring a dividend, and if that were all, I should be disposed to agree with him. It is no part of the auditors' duty to consider what is good or what is bad policy. They have only to examine into facts and see that the members have their opinion as to the balance sheet showing the state of affairs of the company. But the context seems to oblige me to read the excised sentence as meaning not that it was impolitic, but that it would be improper, having regard to the state of affairs of the company, to declare a dividend. Having regard to the explanations given by Mr. Theobald in his evidence, I think the postscript to this report very significant. It runs thus: 'We do not wish it to be understood that we consider all the accounts in the schedule are unsecured, but as a whole the capital therein represented is locked up.' That is the defence, that all their alarm arose from the capital being locked up. This is not, I think, the language that would have been used if the auditors had thought that the only mischief was in the locking-up, and an examination of the schedlue to my mind confirms this conclusion. To a great extent the memoranda in the schedule explain themselves, and I have already dealt with many of the items. The accounts of each one of the Balfour companies is referred to in such a way as to show the unsatisfactory state of the securities Mr. Theobald now says that he had no doubt as to the solvency of any of the Balfour companies, and in a certain sense I am ready to believe this; that is to say, he thought that if they continued to be financed in the future as they had been in the past, and so were enabled to complete the buildings which had been commenced, they might ultimately be able to repay the advances to them with interest and commission. But this is not the meaning of solvency in a legal or business sense, and it is quite plain that Mr. Theobald knew perfectly well that some at least of these companies were, and were likely to remain for an indefinite period, unable to meet their liabilities as they became due. In no other way can the memoranda as to the want of security, or the defective nature of the securities, of the several Balfour companies be explained. Similar observations apply to the memoranda as to the special accounts. Notwithstanding this report, every item of the £487,000 was entered as a good debt in the balance sheet for 1891. No valuation was made of any one of the debts, or of the securities for them. If any such valuation had, in fact, been made, I think it plain that there could have been no profit shown for the year. Mr. Theobald gave evidence several times over to the effect that whilst he was engaged in the audit for 1891 he felt that it was a very important crisis in the bank's affairs, and that if they could only get over the next month or so they would save it. His explanation of his withdrawal of the words in the proposed report to the members is that on this point he had reported specifically to the board. In explanation he gave, among other carefully prepared and considered reasons, the following: That 'Mr. Balfour was so thoroughly aroused to the necessity for taking the affairs of the bank resolutely in hand as to lead me to believe that he would do so, and being a man of great financial resource, he would be able to save the bank'; and that Mr. Balfour also spoke of an amalgamation. 'Mr. Balfour said that, while doing this, he would confer with me continuously, and that no interim dividend should be paid without consultation with me.' The first intimation received of payment of the interim dividend was an announcement in the Press of an interim dividend for 1892, for which it is not suggested Mr. Theobald was in any way liable. This would have given twelve months to work, during which time it would have been quite possible for Mr. Balfour to obtain very large repayments from the borrowing companies with which he was connected, and thus for the bank to be saved. That is a very important point to make.

In another place he says, 'My main point is this, that the bank could be saved if many of these accounts were collected. Mr. Balfour had absolute power over most of these companies, and he was so thoroughly alarmed that I quite believed that if we could only tide over that period he would use his influence over other companies to bring the money into the bank. I quite imagined he would do that, even if it meant that some of the other companies would have to go to the wall. What becomes of his statement that he thought the companies were solvent? He says it is a critical time; if you can tide over the next month or two—as to which he never expresses an opinion—if you can do that, then the resources of Mr. Balfour are so great, his influence with the other companies so great, that it is quite possible he may collect a number of the accounts, even if the other companies have got to go to the wall. I think it is impossible to avoid the conclusion that Mr. Theobald, when about to make his report on the accounts of 1891, was thoroughly alarmed at the critical position of the bank, as he thought it more than likely the bank would not tide over another month or two, but that if it did, it could only be saved by extraordinary exertions on Mr. Balfour's part, and that in the process some of the other Balfour companies might have to go to the wall. He represents Mr. Balfour as fully sharing his alarm. If we turn to the balance sheet to see whether the state of the company's affairs, as apprehended by Mr. Theobald, was in any way indicated therein, we shall, I think, be obliged to answer the question in the negative.

The liabilities appear to be sufficiently set forth. It is the statement of the assets which most calls for criticism. The cash at the bank was correctly stated and so are the bills receivable, though the amount of £180,000 there appears only to have been arrived at by transferring £58,000, on 31st December, 1891, from bills receivable to a loan account for unpaid expenses. Disregarding the small item for stamps, the only other items on the credit side are as follows: 'Investments including reserve fund'—the reserve fund at that time was £10,000—'2¾ per cent. Consols and Prescott and Arizona Railway bonds, £7,820.' That could not be the investments which included the reserve fund of £10,000. 'Loans to customers and other securities, £346,000.' In the two items, 'bills receivable' and 'loans to customers and other securities,' are, as above pointed out, included the whole of the sums, amounting to £487,000, the subject of the report of the auditors to the directors, at their full value. This item, 'loans to customers and other securities,' is, of course, altogether inaccurate and may be very misleading. What the £346,000 really consists of is 'loans to customers partly secured,' which is a very different matter. It would be open to any ordinary reader of the balance sheet to suppose that there were securities to an indefinite amount apart from loans to customers, and available to meet moneys due on the current accounts of customers. I am at a loss to understand for what purpose this item could have been so entered. It was not through inadvertence, for it was a correction of a still more misleading entry occurring in former balance sheets. It was suggested that such an item frequently appears in balance sheets. It may be so for anything I know, but it is none the less improper in the particular balance sheet which we have to consider. In short, the balance sheet, as it stands, would have given no hint to any ordinary reader of the critical position arising either from the locking-up of capital or from the doubtful nature of many of the debts entered at their full value. In reporting this balance sheet without explanation the auditors were, in my judgment, guilty of a misfeasance within the meaning of the 10th Section of the Act of 1890, as charged in the summons, and were in this case, at any rate thoroughly alive to the unsatisfactory state of the affairs of the bank as shown by the books. The next question is whether the misfeasance was the cause of loss to the company. On examination of the evidence there set forth, I should be led to the conclusion that the auditors did not know that a dividend could not properly be paid out of profits.

See how the figures stand from another point of view. The profit and loss account shows a gross profit of £24,000. After making provision for bad and doubtful debts, and after deduction of £6,600 for expenses of management and other charges, there is carried over to the balance sheet a net profit of £18,000 odd, out of which there had already been applied £6,000 and more in payment of an interim dividend, leaving a balance of between £11,000 and £12,000 and nothing more. £3,000 of that was to be carried to reserve; so you have only about between £8,000 and £9,000, according to the books, for dividends. But of the gross profits for the year 1891 shown by the books £16,788 were book entries debited to the Balfour companies, £2,462 a book entry debited to Benham's account, and £275 a book entry debited to Wilkinson's account. That, of course, was in the early part of the year, Wilkinson's account being treated as a debit. Assuming all the Balfour companies, and Benham and Wilkinson, to have been able to pay the whole sums due from them, except the amount debited in 1891 for interest and commission, not only the profits available for dividend would be swept away, but of the reserve fund itself little or nothing would be left. Such an assumption however, in my judgment, would have been extravagantly favourable to the auditors, and it only required that one of the debts owing by Mr. Wilkinson (I leave out Benham because I do not want to found on Benham any charge against Mr. Theobald), or almost any one of the Balfour companies should turn out to be bad, it would exhaust everything belonging to the bank which was not capital. It turned out that each of the Balfour companies as well as Wilkinson and Benham, as well as other debtors of the bank, were insolvent. In my judgment it is established that the bank had no funds out of which the dividends could in any point of view be properly paid. I think the auditors might well be held to have known, but I do not rely upon that conclusion in my judgment; what I do rely upon is that the auditors must have known and did know that the balance sheet was not properly drawn up so as to show the state of affairs, and that was a misfeasance. If they were guilty of misfeasance in relation to the company, they must be responsible for the consequences of such misfeasance, whether they had arrived at the conclusion that the dividend if paid at all would be payable out of capital or not. That dividends were, in fact, paid out of capital cannot, I think, be doubted. It was argued that before the stoppage of the bank the profits entered in the 1891 balance sheet were, in fact, paid by appropriation of moneys paid into current accounts. This would not apply to a case like Wilkinson's, where there was no current account, but in my judgment the rule in Clayton's case has no sort of application under the circumstances. If it had, a bank might always pay profits by mere book entries, though the customers against whom interest and commission were charged might all be hopelessly insolvent. Was, then, the loss occasioned by the misfeasance of the auditors? It had been argued that the payment of the dividend was not the proximate result of the auditors' report, as the recommendation of the directors and the vote of the meeting had to intervene. This appears to me to misrepresent the true state of things. The report of the auditors was a continuing representation, made indeed before, but in law and in good sense to be treated as repeated after, the recommendation of the directors. It was perfectly well known to Mr. Theobald (at any rate at the meeting where he was present and heard the reading of the report recommending a dividend, and the speech of Mr. Balfour) that this report was intended to be relied upon as justifying the recommendation and as an invitation to vote the dividend. How far the judgment should go against the appellant has given me considerable difficulty. A great deal of the reasoning which has led me to hold that their reporting on the accounts of 1891 is a misfeasance in relation to the company applies only to the case of that report. The learned judge has held Mr. Theobald liable not only for the 1891, but also for the 1890, dividend. I am far from saying that he is clearly wrong, but I cannot satisfy myself that he is clearly right.

In the case of the 1890 dividend it cannot, on the evidence, be made out to my full satisfaction that the auditors knew the balance sheet to be substantially misleading, and I think it safer to confine the order to the dividend in respect of 1891.

Lord Justice LINDLEY: The order will stand as to one dividend with interest but not as to the other.

In re KINGSTON COTTON MILL CO.*

Court of Appeal, 1896. 2 Ch. 279.

Lord Justice LINDLEY said: This is an appeal from an order made by Mr. Justice Vaughan Williams under Section 10 the Companies (Winding-up) Act, 1890, on Mr. Pickering and Mr. Peasegood, the auditors of the company, ordering them to pay the liquidator certain sums of money, being the amounts of dividends improperly declared and paid out of the assets of the company on the faith of certain balance sheets prepared and signed by the auditors. The appeal is made upon two grounds: (1) that the auditors have not failed to discharge their duty to the company and are under no liability to make good the money misapplied; (2) that even if they have, the proper remedy is by action and not by the summary process to which the liquidator has had recourse. It will be convenient to dispose of the second point first. It has already been decided that the auditors of this company are 'officers' within the meaning of Section 10 of the Companies (Winding-up) Act, 1890 (see [1896] 1 Ch. 6; *The Times* Law Reports, Vol. XII, p. 60). The object of that section is the same as that of Section 165 of the Companies Act, 1862, which it has replaced. That object was to facilitate the recovery by the liquidator of assets of a company improperly dealt with by its promoters, directors, or other officers. The section applies to breaches of trust and misfeasance by such persons. I agree that the section does not apply to all cases in which actions by the company will lie for the recovery of damages against the persons named; it is easy to imagine cases of breach of contract, trespasses, negligences, or other wrongs to which the section is inapplicable, and some such have been the subject of judicial decision; but I am not aware of any authority to the effect that the section does not apply to the case of an officer who has committed a breach of his duty to the company, the direct consequence of which has been a misapplication of its assets, for which he could be made responsible by an action at law or in equity. Such a breach of duty, if established, is a 'misfeasance' within the meaning of the section, or, to adopt the language used in *Cavendish-Bentinck v. Fenn* (12 A. C. 652), such a breach of duty is a misfeasance in the nature of a breach of trust. This view of the section was adopted by this Court in *In re The London & General Bank* ([1895] 2 Ch. 166, 673; *The Times* Law Reports, Vol. XI, pp. 374-573), and is, in my opinion, correct. On this preliminary point, therefore, which, however, does not touch the merits of the case, the appellants are not entitled to succeed. I come now to the real question in this controversy, and that is, whether the appellants have been guilty of any breach of duty to the company. To decide this question it is necessary to consider: (1) What their duty was; (2) How

---

* This case is discussed at p. 18 *supra*.

they performed it, and in what respects (if any) they failed to perform it. The duty of an auditor generally was very carefully considered by this Court in *In re The London and General Bank* ([1895] 2 Ch. 673), and I cannot usefully add anything to what will be found on pages 682-684. It was there pointed out that an auditor's duty is to examine the books, ascertain that they are right, and to prepare a balance sheet showing the true financial position of the company at the time to which the balance sheet refers. But it was also pointed out that an auditor is not an insurer, and that in the discharge of his duty he is only bound to exercise a reasonable amount of care and skill. It was further pointed out that what in any particular case is a reasonable amount of care and skill depends on the circumstances of that case; that if there is nothing which ought to excite suspicion, less care may properly be considered reasonable than could be so considered if suspicion was or ought to have been aroused. These are the general principles which have to be applied to cases of this description. I protest, however, against the notion that an auditor is bound to be suspicious, as distinguished from being reasonably careful. To substitute the one expression for the other may easily lead to serious error. I pass now to consider the complaint made against the auditors in this particular case. The complaint is that they failed to detect certain frauds. There is no charge of dishonesty on the part of the auditors. They did not certify or pass anything which they did not honestly believe to be true. It is said, however, that they were culpably careless. The circumstances are as follows: For several years frauds were committed by the manager, who, in order to bolster up the company and make it appear flourishing when it was the reverse, deliberately exaggerated both the quantities and values of the cotton and yarn in the company's mills. He did this at the end of the years 1890, 1891, 1892 and 1893. There was no book or account (except the stock journal, to which I will refer presently) showing the quantity or value of the cotton or yarn in the mill at any one time. It would not be easy to keep such a book. Nor is it wanted for ordinary purposes. There is considerable waste (20 or 25 per cent. on the average) in the manufacture of yarn from cotton, and the market prices of both cotton and yarn are subject to great fluctuations. The balance sheets of each year contained on the asset side entries of the values of the stock-in-trade at the end of the year, and those entries were stated to be 'as per manager's certificate.' There were also in the balance sheets entries on the opposite side of the values of the stock-in-trade at the beginning of the year. The quantities did not appear in either case. The auditors took the entry of the stock-in-trade at the beginning of the year from the last preceding balance sheet, and they took the values of the stock-in-trade at the end of the year from the stock journal. The book contained a series of accounts under various heads purporting to show the quantities and values of the company's stock-in-trade at the end of each year, and a summary of all the accounts showing the total value of such stock-in-trade. The summary was signed by the manager, and the value as shown by it was adopted by the auditors and was inserted as an asset in the balance sheet, but 'as per manager's certificate.' The summary always corresponded with the accounts summarised, and the auditors ascertained that this was the case. But they did not examine further into the accuracy of the accounts summarised. The auditors did not profess to guarantee the correctness of this item. They assumed no responsibility for it. They took the item from the manager, and the entry in the balance sheet showed that they did so. I confess I cannot see that their omission to check his returns was a breach of their duty to the company. It is no part of an auditor's duty to take stock. No one contends that it is. He must rely on other people for details of the stock-in-trade in hand. In the case of a cotton mill he must rely on some skilled person for the materials necessary to enable him to enter the stock-in-trade at its proper value in the balance sheet. In this case the auditors relied on the manager. He was a man of high character and of unquestioned competence. He was trusted by everyone who knew him. The learned judge has held that the directors are not to be blamed for trusting him. The auditors had no suspicion that he was not to be trusted to give accurate information as to the stock-in-trade in hand, and they trusted him accordingly in that matter. But it is said they ought not to have done so, and for this reason. The stock journal showed the quantities —that is, the weight in pounds—of the cotton and yarn at the end of each year. Other books showed the quantities of cotton bought during the year and the quantities of yarn sold during the year. If these books had been compared by the auditors they would have found that the quantity of cotton and yarn in hand at the end of the year ought to be much less than the quantity shown in the stock journal, and so much less that the value of the cotton and yarn entered in the stock journal could not be right, or, at all events, was so abnormally large as to excite suspicion and demand further inquiry. This is the view taken by the learned judge. But, although it is no doubt true that such a process might have been gone through, and that, if gone through, the fraud would have been discovered, can it be truly said that the auditors were wanting in reasonable care in not thinking it necessary to test the managing director's returns? I cannot bring myself to think they were, nor do I think any jury of business men would take a different view. It is not sufficient to say that the frauds must have been detected if the entries in the books had been put together in a way which never occurred to anyone before suspicion was aroused. The question is whether, no suspicion of anything wrong being entertained, there was a want of reasonable care on the part of the auditors in relying on the returns made by a competent and trusted expert relating to matters on which information from such a person was essential. I cannot think there was. The manager had no apparent conflict between his interest and his duty. His position was not similar to that of a cashier who has to account for the cash which he receives, and whose own account of his receipts and payments could not reasonably be taken by an auditor without further inquiry. The auditor's duty is not so onerous as the learned judge has held it to be. The order appealed from must be discharged with costs.

Lopes, L. J., in the course of his judgment, made the following observations upon the duties of auditors: It is the duty of an auditor to bring to bear on the work he has to perform that skill, care, and caution which a reasonably competent, careful and cautious auditor would use. What is reasonable skill, care and caution must depend on the particular circumstances of each case. An auditor is not bound to be a detective, or as was said, to approach his work with suspicion or with a foregone conclusion that there is something wrong. He is a watch-dog, but not a bloodhound. He is justified in believing tried servants of the company in whom confidence is placed by the company. He is entitled to assume that they are honest, and to rely upon their representations, provided he takes reasonable care. If there is anything calculated to excite suspicion he should probe it to the bottom, but, in the absence of anything of that kind, he is only bound to be reasonably cautious and careful. His lordship then referred to the circumstances which led to the auditors being deceived, and came to the conclusion that they were not wanting in skill, care or caution, in accepting the figures of the manager, and he concluded as follows: The duties of auditors must not be rendered too onerous. Their work is responsible and laborious, and the remuneration moderate. I should be sorry to see the liability of auditors extended any further than in *In re The London and General Bank.* Indeed, I only assented to that decision on account of the inconsistency of the statement made to the directors with the balance sheet certified by the auditors and presented to the shareholders. This satisfied my mind that the auditors deliberately concealed that from the shareholders which they had communicated to the directors. It would be difficult to say this was not a breach of duty. Auditors must not be made liable for not tracking out ingenious and carefully-laid schemes of fraud, when there is nothing to arouse their suspicion and when those frauds are perpetrated by tried servants of the company and are undetected for years by the directors. So to hold would make the position of an auditor intolerable.

* * * *

THE IRISH WOOLLEN CO. v. TYSON *

Irish Court of Appeal, 1900. 26 The Accountant L. R. 13.

[The question before the court was whether Mr. Kevans, the accountant, was, or was not, responsible for the non-detection of the frauds.]

* * * *

Lord Justice Holmes, in delivering his judgment, referred to the career of the company which, he said, was formed in June, 1887, for the purpose of promoting the woollen industry in Ireland, the original capital being £6,000. For some time at the commencement the business was almost entirely confined to the purchase of woollen goods from Irish manufacturers. In the year 1889 the directors resolved to develop their undertaking by seeking to establish their home trade, and for this purpose they increased their capital. The prospectus announcing this resolution alluded to the success that had attended the operations of the company up to that time, and held out more brilliant prospects for the future. The whole of the additional capital, however, was required to pay off debts previously incurred, and could hardly be used for the purpose of opening up new business. Between the years 1888 to 1895 nine balance sheets were presented to the shareholders, each showing considerable net profit; and during all this period dividends were paid which never once fell as low as 5 per cent., amounting to £4,649. There is not the slightest evidence of the soundness of the financial position of the company until its operations were suspended, when Mr. Carnegie—the auditor's representative, who was examining the accounts—noticed a double entry. The mistake was a trifling one, and he was satisfied with the explanation given by Mr. Crawford, who had been for some time the accountant of the

* This case is discussed at p. 18 *supra.*

company. Crawford and Johnson abandoned their positions, and the balance sheet for the last period (1895) showed a deficiency of £11,107. The company, by order of the Court, was directed to be wound up compulsorily, and Mr. Garde—who was himself formerly in the employment of the defendant auditor—found that, although the company was just solvent as regards its creditors, its capital had entirely disappeared, and I presume it was his report that led to the bringing of the present action. It appears that Crawford, acting either by himself or with Johnston, the warehouseman, was a defaulter to a very large extent. Mr. Kevans says, in his letters of the 22nd and 24th January, 1896, 'that although the whole of the items that made up Crawford's definciency were apparently received within the three months ending 31st December, 1895, it is highly improbable that he could have abstracted all that money in so short a period of time, but that it was impossible to say how far back exactly the defalcations extended.' The defendant was held guilty in connection with Crawford's fraud, and I therefore pass away from this portion of the case, which relates to only a small part of the losses sustained by the company. To account for the rest it is necessary to go more fully into the way the business was carried on. The directors, who were paid no fees for the first two or three years, were originally selected by lot; and Mr. Peter White was appointed managing director; Mr. Tyson was appointed secretary at £250 per annum; and the rest of the staff—examiner and packer—at £150 and £75 per annum respectively. Mr. Tyson did not long remain secretary, and was succeeded by Mr. McDonough, and subsequently by Crawford. Mr. White, in one of his letters, referred in a somewhat gloomy manner to the large annual amount of money paid to the officers in the shape of salaries, and recommended such a change being made as would reduce the annual expenses to £600. White's recommendation was accepted, and from that date Crawford was appointed secretary. He only received 35s. per week, and his income from the company never seemed to come up to £150 a year. I presume that Johnston did not receive more. Mr. Kevans was the first auditor of the company, and he provided the books which, in his judgment, were necessary for keeping the accounts. They consisted of: (1) cash book; (2) customers' ledger; (3) creditors' ledger; (4) day book; (5) invoice guard book; (6) petty cash book. It cannot be denied that these were sufficient to show the true financial position of the business of the company, if they had been honestly kept. Mr. MacDermot commented upon the absence of one book, but I attach no importance to this. The multiplication of books, if written up by different parties, may be a check upon fraud, but in this case all the bookkeeping was done by a single officer who, if dishonest, would take care to make the books appear perfectly straight. There was another book, referred to in the evidence, kept for the private use of the directors, but whatever its significance may be it could not affect Mr. Kevans. In February, 1891, there occurred a circumstance materially bearing upon the case. After that time the auditor's fee was increased to £40, the consideration being a 'monthly audit.' It was not understood by this that a balance sheet or profit and loss account was to be prepared for each month, or that a monthly statement was to be submitted to the directors. It was a monthly investigation for the purpose of checking fraud or error. It was, as Mr. Kevans himself says, 'a system of monthly checking with a view to the half-yearly audit.' Mr. Kevans seems to have done little of the actual work himself, and the evidence varies as to the nature of the supervision which he gave to it; the investigation of the books he deputed to his assistants—namely Mr. Roche, Mr. Garde and Mr. Carnegie, and it must be on the faith of their representations that he certified the balance sheets. I presume this course is not unusual, and that an accountant with a large business is not supposed to do everything himself. The auditor is bound to give reasonable care and skill but this can also be exercised by his deputy. I do not think there is anything to be gained by considering in the abstract the duties of an auditor of a joint stock company. He is entitled to see the company's books and the materials for their books, and also to ask for explanations. But he is not called on to seek for knowledge outside the company, or to communicate with customers or creditors. He is not an insurer against fraud or error; and if fraud is alleged it must be shown with precision the acts of negligence for which he is said to be responsible. Nine balance sheets were prepared, and the figures on some represent the aggregate amount of many items, but I propose to deal only with matters that have been referred to during the hearing. There are three sets of figures with which I will deal: (1) stock-in-trade; (2) sundry debtors; (3) sundry creditors on the liability side of the balance sheet. Taking these in order, I find that Mr. Garde, in his evidence, drew a distinction between the home stock and the stock in America, which was never mentioned in this Court. I do not fully understand this, as Mr. Kevans can only be held responsible from the 4th January, 1892, and at that date the American trade had been abandoned. The Master of the Rolls expressed a doubt, with which I agree, as to whether it was the duty of the directors to take stock with their own hands. It was taken by Mr. O'Callaghan, and I agree with the Master of the Rolls that he (Mr. O'Callaghan) did quite as much as he could be expected to do. There was certainly no duty cast on the auditor to take stock. What he did was to have the calculations checked in his office, and this was done with proper care. Mr. Kevans said he was particularly careful as to the deduction for discount, and, as far as I could gather, the universal rate of 10 per cent. seems reasonable. Moreover, an auditor has nothing to do with the terms upon which the company or a trader buys or sells. As to No. 2, the charge in this is that the allowance made for the trade discount of 2½ per cent. was omitted. This is a purely technical question. Mr. Kevans says that the proper method of dealing with these debts was to return them as they stood in the books, and to bring the discount, when it was allowed, to the profit and loss account. Mr. Pixley said it would not be scientifically correct to deduct these discounts. This seems to be in accordance with common sense, and it is to be noted that although Mr. Garde, as liquidator, corrected the balance sheets by marking off these discounts, he never thought of doing so when conducting the audit. As to the provision for the 'bad debts,' if there is any one thing upon which an auditor is dependent upon the officers it is the writing-off or the making of a prospective allowance for, bad debts. He has no personal knowledge of the customers, and Mr. Kevans seems to have taken particular attention in reference to this. (See questions 2,125 to 2,127 in the evidence.) He said 'he had some special knowledge on the subject, that he saw all ascertained bad debts duly written off, and that there was a fund amounting to £500 as a provision therefor.' For the foregoing reasons there is no ground for alleging negligence against Mr. Kevans on the 'assets side' of the balance sheet. As far as this portion is concerned, I think the balance sheets were properly and carefully prepared, and there was nothing dishonest or negligent on the part of anyone; but if there was, it was not on the part of Mr. Kevans or of his representative. Now dealing with 'sundry creditors'; here evidently there is a fraud, and a curious thing is that no one seemed to have derived any benefit from the fraud. Dealing with the invoices, the learned judge detailed the practice in connection with the statements of accounts being laid before the meeting, and said the ledger was used for the purchases made and for the payments on account thereof. If, then, all this were rightly done it would be easy for the auditor to ascertain the amounts due to the creditors, but unfortunately the books were not properly kept. The creditors' accounts in the ledger did not show all the goods purchased up to the time of the audit, nor could the auditor discover the omissions on account of many of the invoices being either 'suppressed' or not put into the book until a later date—a process described as 'carrying over.' There is some doubt as to whether the deficiency arose from the suppression or the carrying over, but my impression is that the whole of it comes within the last mentioned class, for at the end of 1894 we find they amounted to £4,095. Mr. Peter White is now dead, and he should not be condemned unheard, but it is difficult to believe that this system was not within his own knowledge. As chief promoter he was no doubt anxious to see that the company was successful; Crawford, who was the secretary, appears to have continued the process. It seems strange that a system of fraud so long continued, and for so extensive a period, was never detected by the auditor. Once or twice he noticed something, and the explanation that was given was 'that the goods were not taken into stock.' The question is, was it negligent not to have seen this? There is no doubt that both the suppression and carrying over of invoices would have been detected if the auditor had called for the creditors' statements of accounts upon which payment was ordered, and compared them with the ledger. I should have thought this was part of the auditor's duty for many reasons; but all the accountants examined, except Mr. Southworth, stated that this course is never taken unless there is something to arouse suspicion. Mr. Pixley, the eminent London accountant, says it could not well be done except in the case of a very small concern. In the face of such evidence I should not leave myself at liberty to hold that Mr. Kevan's assistants were guilty of negligence in not looking at these statements of account if they were engaged in an ordinary audit. Little time is allowed for doing so; but in this case there was this system of monthly checking. From the time that Crawford was accountant in 1890 the accounts of the company were completely in his hands. Now White, for the two years following, may have given general directions, but he was often away in America for months at a time, and it is clear that the monthly audit was instituted for the purpose of seeing that he (Crawford) would do his work regularly and honestly. I am unable to conceive how, if there was nothing wrong about this monthly checking, it did not lead at an early period to the detection of the frauds in this ledger. Mr. Kevans ought to have found out, by the accounts, the payments that were made—and no better means could be adopted than that of a comparison with the statements of accounts. It ought to have been done in some way, and, if it had, detection would have been certain. I do not base my decision on this alone; apart altogether from the statements of account and the monthly check, I do not understand how the carrying over of the invocies could have escaped detection by the accountant, who should have used due care and skill and who was not a mere machine. The invoices carried over were ultimately posted to the ledger. If they were posted to their true dates it would be at once apparent that they were not entered in at the proper time. If they were posted under false dates, why was this not detected when the ledger accounts were checked with the invoices? And when no invoices came into the books, it is admitted that this ought to have excited suspicion. For these reasons I am of opinion that if due care and skill had been exercised, the carrying over and the suppression of invoices would have been discovered, and the auditor is liable for any damage the company has sustained from the understatement of liabilities in the balance sheet due to this cause since 4th January, 1892. I consider that not only are Mr. Kevans and his assistants not free from blame for this, but also for the mechanical way the audit was carried out. I desire to say that, although I have carefully read the evidence, I have not attempted to examine the books of the company out of Court. I, at one time, thought of doing so, but, on consideration, feared that they might lead me into error. That some damage has been sustained by the company is clear; and it will be observed that I have said nothing about the measure of the damages. Theoretically, damages resulting from negligence has been assessed in money, but it would be premature to consider it now.

Lord Justice FITZGIBBON: I entirely concur with the judgment that Lord Justice Holmes has delivered, and there are a few matters on which I desire to offer some independent observations:

First.—What is the measure of the defendant auditor's duty in a case such as this?

Second.—What is the evidence of the particular case of the breach of that duty?

Third.—A few words upon the question of damages.

As regards the measure of the duty of a gentleman employed, as Mr. Kevans was in this case, the result is the same, as it occurs to me, in all cases in which professional skill is employed, except one, the peculiar instance of a barrister. The measure of duty is the bringing of reasonable care and skill to the performance of the business directed to be done, having regard, first to the contract of employment, then to the character of the business itself, to the remuneration of the defendant, and to all the other circumstances of the case. In strict rule, however, the measure of the duty is to be ascertained by applying to all the circumstances of the case the best consideration, so as to ascertain what ought to have been done under the circumstances. Now, in all the three English cases, and also in this case, the auditor was bound by the articles of association of the company. In one English case it was put forward for the auditor that he had never seen the articles of association, and it was admitted that he had never read them, but, nevertheless, it was held that if he did not see them, he was at least bound to do all that was required just as if he had seen them. In this case Rules 150 and 157 of the articles of association prescribe the duties of the auditor, and it is not suggested that Mr. Kevans did not see them. 'Once at least in every year the accounts of the company shall be examined, and the correctness of the statement and balance sheet ascertained by one or more auditor or auditors.' Now, it appears that half-yearly statements were submitted to the directors, and I gather that Mr. Kevans discharged his duties half-yearly, but I shall deal with the case entirely on the assumption that he did it only once a year, because his half-yearly examination probably would not be as complete as the one completed at the end of the year. The 157th rule of the article provides: 'That the auditor shall be supplied with copies of the statements of accounts *seven* days before the intended meeting, and it shall be his duty to examine the same with the accounts and vouchers relating thereto, and to report to the company in general meeting thereon.' These are the two rules that define his duty. Rule 158 is, however, important, as showing the materials that were to be placed at his disposal. 'The auditor shall have a list delivered to him by the directors of all the books kept by the company, and shall have reasonable access to the books and accounts of the company, and may in relation thereto examine the directors, or other officers of the company.' Now, there are two specific things that Mr. Kevans was charged with. In the first place, it was practically left to him to say what books the company ought to keep, and therefore he, in the position of a skilled accountant, was really made an adviser as to what the set of books were that he was to examine, and I take it for granted that the books recommended were sufficient. Another matter was, that in the course of the business they had to some extent ascertained by actual experience what was necessary for their protection. They (the directors) made an arrangement with the auditor that there should be a monthly checking ,and therefore he was bound, dealing with the set of books that he himself provided, to check these books once a month and to audit them once a year. Now, I am not going to minimise the distinction between checking and auditing. I do not agree at all with a great deal of what has been presented to us that Mr. Kevans was to have done in the monthly checking, but the monthly checking was a 'checking at the time,' a preparation for the future, and a security that the books were carried forward from month to month in the state in which they should be audited. His remuneration was not very large, but it must not be taken to have been inadequate. He also must be taken to have had a knowledge of the business. It was not a business to which any of the directors could have been expected to devote anything like their whole time; and it was a business where, to Mr. Kevans' own knowledge, the clerical staff was cut down to a very low point. Therefore, he must have known that there was more reliance placed upon him, upon his checking, and upon the audit, than might be expected in the case of an ordinary company. That being the measure of his duty—it is the same rule that applies to all, with the exception I have mentioned—what is the nature of the breach of that duty? It is curious that in one English case the breach of duty for which the auditor was said to be held liable was exactly as here—a breach of duty in not detecting the case of misfeasance on the part of others, which was not for the purpose of putting money into their own pockets, but for the purpose of giving a fictitious appearance of prosperity to a company that really was not prosperous. I shall have to say more about that when I come to the question of damages. I think the fairest way to deal with Mr. Kevans in this case is to treat him as being charged with having failed to find just cause of suspicion on the face of these books which, if found, would have imposed on him the duty of pursuing his suspicion until he found whether it was or was not well founded; and in that I am only following the example of Lord Justice Keane, who in his judgment, took as an example one particular instance of one particular year, and applied all the rest of the case to that. I am fortunate in the present case to have an instance which was discussed as a fair example of the mode in which the fraud in question was carried out; as an example of the grounds of suspicion—that there were grounds of suspicion—appearing on the face of the books themselves; and also the means that these books would have supplied (had the suspicion been entertained), in order to detect the frauds. Now, I must entirely disclaim from myself the intention of going to do anything more than what any ordinary intelligent juror would be bound to do if he was trying Mr. Kevans on his indictment for having failed to discover what appears on the face of the books themselves. This is not a question of technical knowledge, nor a question in which it could be capable of misleading anyone. The English cases have established that the auditor is entitled, in the absence of the elements of suspicion, to assume that the books are honestly kept, and that, therefore, unless on the face of a presumably honest book something appears to excite his suspicion, he is not guilty of negligence, whatever other people might be in their departments, if he does not discover that something was wrong. Now, the one example is the case of Hill & Sons, for the period where the balance was struck as of the 31st December, 1892, and the 31st December, 1893. In that year there was an increase, as now appears, in the suppressed invoices and in the carried over invoices, and this account is one of those in which that increase took place, and it has been taken and discussed as an instance and as an example of others in the book (creditors' ledger), presumably dealt with in the same way. At page 108 of the ledger the account of Hill & Sons—if I use a technical word wrongly I hope I may be forgiven—is ruled on the 31st December, 1892. The figures immediately below the ruling indicate to my mind that, when it was ruled, all the items for that year were then written up. From the 12th August to the 20th December, 1892, there were, altogether, items that amount only to £57 3s. 9d., and all of these items are on the one date, 20th December. There were no transactions with Hill & Sons between the 12th August and the 31st December, except whatever is covered by the entries of the 20th December. Therefore, if there was anything written in it could only be the £57 3s. 9d.; but I think it is admitted that these were not written afterwards, because after that, and the very last item above the ruling, is the correction of an error of £500, which is taken from the contra side of the account; and there is a ruling on the top of £736 4s. 9d., and there the account ends for the year 1892. On the face of the book there is no subsequent entry in Hill & Sons' account at all going back into 1892. It is a perfectly legible account for 1892, closed on the 31st December, balanced by the correction of an error, and, as I call it, closed in every sense. I will assume that all the transactions of 1892 were included in the accounts of 1892, and that there was nothing carried forward. Now, there is also a ruling on the 31st December, 1893—there is on the face of the book, as it stands, an undoubted ruling as of the 31st December, 1893. But what is the case? It is conceded that in striking a trial balance for the purpose of statements of account for the year 1893, three items that only appear on the right side of page 150 were in the book at the time. In the book now, before we come to the ruling, there were inserted below these and after them half a column of items totting to no less than £698 19s. 11d., and the whole of that is included in the amount of these 'kept-back invoices' for the year 1893. Well, I will admit that it is not the business of an auditor, when he comes to strike his trial balance, on the 31st December for the purpose of a meeting, to have every account closed and balanced, but he must strike a trial balance, and he did so; but at a figure, 15th December. I do not agree with the monthly check that was taken. Some of these items now introduced must have been there, and therefore within a month of the 31st December, 1893, if the monthly check had been carried out, the representative of Mr. Kevans would have found that after the figure which he had taken for ascertaining the financial position of this company, a string of figures had been put in, all in December, and all within a day or two of the 15th, the day at which the financial position of the company had been ascertained. I think that was something; but it is nothing to what follows, because between that time and whatever time this book was ruled there then follows a further string of items—nearly £600 in amount—that go up to the 3rd November and go down as far as the 14th December. I cannot conceive any more clear or glaring grounds of suspicion than to discover in the account of a single customer items amounting to such a sum having got into the books after the trial balance is struck under dates going back two months prior to the period of the ascertaining of the trial balance. There appears to be a further thing—a monthly check was to be adopted, and that would have put an auditor on inquiry. It appears to me that the moment I come to the conclusion that that was on the face of it a suspicious mode of dealing with Hill & Sons' figures, I am bound to show how it would be corrected. I can add nothing to the judgment of Lord Justice Holmes—viz. that it would then have been necessary to call for the creditors' statements of account, and at that moment they would have disclosed on the face of them not merely those post-dated items, but the suppressed invoices also; and at the instant that this discovery was made there is an absolute conviction of something wrong forced upon the mind of the auditor. It, therefore, occurs to me that, upon those two branches, all that is required, both to show the negligence, to arouse suspicion and to supply the means of putting a stop to the frauds is to be found on the face of the book, and for all I have said I have no foundation except what is upon the face of that book (creditors' ledger). I now take the three English cases, in order to make a few observations on each. In 36 Ch.D., in the *Leeds Estate Building Investment Co.,* Mr. Justice Stirling held that the manager and auditor were liable. It is right to say that the procedure in the other cases was different from this Leeds case; and it is important to bear in mind that the other two were under the 10th Section of the Winding-up Act. In this case the auditor was held liable, and Mr. Justice Stirling held him liable, saying that it was his duty to see that no part of the capital was applied to any other than the proper purpose, and, in particular, that no part of the capital was returned to the creditors—that is, in dividends—except in the cases in which a reduction of capital was permitted by various Acts of Parliament. The next case, and the most important one, is the *London and General Bank* ([1895] 2 Ch.D. 681). That was a procedure under this 10th Section Mr. Justice Lindley says, 'An auditor has nothing to do with the prudence or imprudence of the way in which the business has been carried on; nothing to say as to whether it was properly, improprely, profitably or unprofitably carried on, provided he discharges his own duties to the shareholders. His business is to ascertain and state the true financial position of the company at the time of the audit, and his duty is confined to that.' But then comes the question, 'How is he to ascertain that?' The answer is by examining the books of the company. But he does not discharge his duty by doing this without inquiry and without taking the common trouble to see that the books show the company's true position. He must take reasonable care to see that this is done (page 682), otherwise the audit reduces itself to an 'idle farce.' I have endeavoured to keep myself within that, and think that the principle is the very lowest upon which we can define the duties of an auditor. In the *Kingston Cotton Mills* case (1 Ch.D. 96, 279), Mr. Justice Vaughan Williams held, 'that it was the duty of the auditor to have made a calculation outside the books which, if made, would have shown that the amount of the stock was overstated on the books.' In this case of the stocktaking and the over-valuing, &c., Mr. Kevans is exonerated. Now, time after time, this passage about the 'watch-dog and the bloodhound' has been made use of, and I would wish to say a word regarding it too. His lordship then read from Lord Justice Lindley's judgment the passages dealing with the duties of auditors, in one of which it was laid down that 'an auditor was a watch-dog, but not a bloodhound.' This, Lord Justice Fitzgibbon remarked, was very unfair to the bloodhound, who was just as little likely to have his sense of suspicion aroused as the watch-dog. Applying this instance of the dogs to the present case, was not the watch-dog bound to bark? And if, when sniffing round, you hit upon a trail of something wrong, surely you must follow it up, and there is just as much obligation on the auditor, who is bound to keep his eyes open, and his nose, too. As in the case of the hound, the auditor will follow up this trail to the end, and the first things he will 'root up' are those statements of account, and then the fraud is discovered. On the question of damages—the damage here—and I guard myself against expressing any individual opinion upon anything more than is necessary—is sufficiently supplied for the purpose of showing the existence of pecuniary losses. In the first place, there has been a paying away of a large amount of money in dividends to the shareholders that had not been earned, and therefore at the time that that was stopped the company ought to have been in possession of a money capital, which they had parted with by paying it away to their shareholders. It would be premature to discuss the pecuniary damage until the financial position of the company is finally ascertained. Then, again, had this system of the suppression—the carrying forward—of invoices been detected sooner, it would have been open to the directors to have done something to stop it. They had several ways, either to increase their percentages or diminish their dealings—in the latter case thereby producing a less loss; or they could have stopped the business and wound it up. On the question of the amount of the damages, that depends on the amount of the losses the plaintiff has suffered, taking all the circumstances of the case into consideration. We have not all these circumstances before us, and it is, I say, premature to discuss damages at all beyond the point I have discussed them. I have come with much reluctance to the conclusion that a professional man has failed in his duty, and I am glad to be able to think that the worst that could be said of the case is this: That, in what is so small a company, Mr. Kevans and his representative, who went there to do this audit (for which Mr. Kevans received a very small fee), were deceived not by any glaring or probable fraud such as they would be on the watch against, but by a thing that was done more for the purpose of giving an appearance of fictitious prosperity to a company which did not exist than that of putting money into the pockets of shareholders. That, however, cannot alter the legal liability if it is based, as I am satisfied it is, upon the failure to have suspicion aroused.

THE LORD CHANCELLOR also concurred, and the appeal was accordingly dismissed.

CRAIG v. ANYON *

Appellate Division of the Supreme Court of New York, First Department, 1925. 212 App. Div. 55, 208 N. Y. Supp. 259, aff'd, 242 N. Y. 569, 152 N. E. 431 (1926).

MARTIN, J. The plaintiffs during the years 1913 to 1917, inclusive, were engaged in business in New York city as brokers in stocks and commodities such as cotton, wheat and coffee. Their transactions on behalf of customers were conducted on the New York Stock Exchange, the Cotton Exchanges in New York and New Orleans, the Chicago Board of Trade and similar exchanges in which they had membership. The business was apparently prosperous and the partners had enjoyed a large income therefrom. On May 26, 1917, through the confession of Robert Moore, an employee of their commodities department, following an office investigation, they learned that their prosperity had been an illusion, and that their books had been falsified by Moore throughout a period of nearly five years, during which they had been defrauded of over $1,250,000.

During the entire five years' period, the defendants, composing an accounting firm well known both in the United States and England, were under retainer from the plaintiffs. Each three months throughout this period the books were audited by them and a report submitted, by which reports the plaintiffs say they were assured the books were properly kept, no reference being made to any irregularity.

The action is founded upon the charge that these audits were negligently made; that, had any audit been made with reasonable care, the falsification of the books would have been discovered, Moore would have been discharged and no further loss would have occurred.

The complaint alleges a contract whereby the defendants undertook periodically to audit the plaintiffs' books and accounts and to report any errors or omissions therein, and negligence by the defendants in the performance of the contract and damage to the plaintiffs amounting to the sum of $1,280,233.61. This is made up of sums paid to customers to whom, it is alleged, nothing would have been paid except for the defendants' negligent failure to report that similar unauthorized payments had previously been made, and of other sums paid to brokers, and not charged to any customer, upon transactions which, as it is alleged, would not have been permitted were it not for the defendants' negligence in failing to report irregularities consisting of similar transactions previously made.

The answer admits the employment of the defendants to audit the plaintiffs' books "subject to certain instructions and limitations imposed" by the plaintiffs and their predecessor firms; denies the allegation of negligent performance of the contract; and sets up as a defense negligence on the part of the plaintiffs and both negligence and "larceny, embezzlement and criminal acts and practices" on the part of employees of the plaintiffs.

The action was tried in May, 1922. At the end of plaintiffs' case a

* This case is discussed at p. 19 ff. *supra*.

motion to dismiss was denied except as to six defendants who had become members of the firm after 1917.

The defense rested without offering evidence and the motion to dismiss was renewed. The court reserved decision in accordance with the practice set forth in section 1187 of the Code of Civil Procedure (Civ. Prac. Act, § § 459, 585), and submitted two specific questions to the jury, as follows:

"Were the defendants negligent in the performance of their agreement with Craig & Co.?"

"If so, what damages to the plaintiffs resulted directly and proximately from such negligence?"

The court charged that if the defendants were found liable the verdict must be either for $2,000, the amount paid as compensation for the defendants' services; or for $1,177,805.26, the amount of plaintiffs' actual loss as proved. To the first question the jury answered, "Yes;" to the second question, "$1,177,805.26."

Upon the rendition of the verdict the defendants' motion to set aside the answer to the second question was granted; the defendants' motion to set aside the answer to the first question was denied; and a general verdict was directed in favor of the plaintiffs for $2,000, appropriate exceptions being noted by the plaintiffs. The order recites that the court proceeded "on the ground that as a matter of law the only loss which resulted directly and proximately from the negligence of the defendants was the sum of $2,000."

The three main questions litigated were (1) the degree of care actually used by the defendants; (2) the understanding or agreement of the parties with respect to the scope of the audits to be made; (3) the degree of care used by the plaintiffs. The three questions are closely interlocked and are to be answered by the inferences to be drawn from practically undisputed evidence.

It is apparent from an examination of the record that the jury found the defendants were negligent and the court agreed with the jury on that question, but disagreed with it as to the damages resulting from such negligence.

Three questions are before us on this appeal: (1) Were the defendants negligent; (2) did the plaintiffs' negligence contribute to the loss, and (3) assuming defendants were negligent, what damages resulted therefrom? The first question has been resolved in favor the plaintiffs both by the jury and the court. With reference to that question, therefore, it is necessary only to inquire whether the evidence warranted a finding of negligence.

The plaintiffs contend that defendants are chargeable wth negligence by reason of the carelessly conducted audit of the plaintiffs' books. It is asserted that one or more books were in the custody of the plaintiffs when each audit was made, an examination of which would have disclosed the account of one Zabriskie as reflecting an indebtedness to the plaintiffs of many thousands of dollars.

The defendants offered no evidence and no defense, except the cross-examination which developed the fact that an inspection of all the books in the office would have disclosed irregularities; whereas the auditors, in making investigations and reports, relied on books, papers and carbon copies of statements to customers furnished by one Moore, who apparently had charge of a division of the business.

There can be very little doubt as to carelessness by the auditors. Whether it caused the loss is a more difficult question. Although a proper audit would have disclosed facts leading to the discovery of Moore's wrongdoing, there are a number of other elements entering into this case which show that the plaintiffs are not without blame and might have avoided the loss.

They now seek to make Moore a mere clerk. He was much more. He was in charge of plaintiffs' commodities department. He was permitted to absolutely control that department; and the real cause of the loss is to be found in the fact that he was given a free hand, without any supervision, to deal with the accounts of Zabriskie and others at will. He decided what entries were to be made by the bookkeepers and how they were to be made, so far as transactions in his division of the business were concerned. He was permitted to give directions for the firm to outside brokers as to whether transactions should be closed or carried as "open."

This appears to have been of great assistance in enabling him to keep the actual condition of the Zabriskie account concealed. To this customer large sums of money were paid time to time, the payment of which was unwarranted, for the accounts with him would have shown the absence of a sufficient balance to meet margins. Money was paid to him at a time when he must have been heavily indebted to plaintiffs.

Should the plaintiffs have relied on Moore who was dealing with the Zabriskie account for Zabriskie and at the same time taking care of the account for the plaintiffs? Certainly they were called upon to exercise some supervision in the matter. Having left a branch of their business to an employee, it does not seem reasonable that although there was no supervision they should now be permitted to charge the loss to the auditors who, apparently on account of the dishonesty of such employee, failed to uncover defalcations.

In his charge to the jury the court said: "These defendants rendered such reports every three months. These reports undoubtedly contained mistakes and inaccuracies. They were based on what Moore wanted them to believe was the position of the firm and not on the true position of the firm."

The auditors relied on Moore. They were deceived by him. So were the plaintiffs. The auditors could have performed their work independently of what they were told by Moore. But Moore was the employee who dealt with them and who gave them the books and papers upon which they were to work. They did not suspect any wrongdoing and believed they were justified in taking the information given them by the firm's representative, who exercised without interference, power to deal with them in reference to their work in the commodities department. Defendants relied on Moore's honesty, but no more than did plaintiffs.

In *Matter of Kingston Cotton Mill Company (No. 2)* (L. R. [1896] 2 Ch. Div. 279) Lord Justice Lindley said: "In this case the auditors relied on the manager. He was a man of high character and of unquestioned competence. He was trusted by everyone who knew him. The learned judge has held that the directors are not to be blamed for trusting him. The auditors had no suspicion that he was not to be trusted to give accurate information as to the stock-in-trade in hand, and they trusted him accordingly in that matter. But it is said they ought not to have done so, and for this reason. The stock journal shewed the quantities—that is, the weight in pounds—of the cotton and yarn at the end of each year.

Other books shewed the quantities of cotton bought during the year and the quantities of yarn sold during the year. If these books had been compared by the auditors they would have found that the quantity of cotton and yarn in hand at the end of the year ought to be much less than the quantity shewn in the stock journal, and so much less that the value of the cotton and yarn entered in the stock journal could not be right, or at all events was so abnormally large as to excite suspicion and demand further inquiry. This is the view taken by the learned judge. But ,although it is no doubt true that such a process might have been gone through, and that, if gone through, the fraud would have been discovered, can it be truly said that the auditors were wanting in reasonable care in not thinking it necessary to test the managing director's return? I cannot bring myself to think they were, nor do I think that any jury of business men would take a different view. It is not sufficient to say that the frauds must have been detected if the entries in the books had been put together in a way which never occurred to any one before suspicion was aroused. The question is whether, no suspicion of anything wrong being entertained, there was a want of reasonable care on the part of the auditors in relying on the returns made by a competent and trusted expert relating to matters on which information from such a person was essential. I cannot think there was. The manager had no apparent conflict between his interest and his duty. His position was not similar to that of a cashier who has to account for the cash which he receives, and whose own account of his receipts and payments could not reasonably be taken by an auditor without further inquiry. The auditor's duty is not so onerous as the learned judge has held it to be."

Lord Justice LOPES said (at p. 290): "The duties of auditors must not be rendered too onerous. Their work is responsible and laborious, and the remuneration moderate. I should be sorry to see the liability of auditors extended any further than in *In re London and General Bank* (L. R. [1895] 2 Ch. 673). Indeed, I only assented to that decision on account of the inconsistency of the statement made to the directors with the balance-sheet certified by the auditors and presented to the shareholders. This satisfied my mind that the auditors deliberately concealed that from the shareholders which they had communicated to the directors. It would be difficult to say this was not a breach of duty. Auditors must not be made liable for not tracking out ingenious and carefully laid schemes of fraud when there is nothing to arouse their suspicion, and when those frauds are perpetrated by tried servants of the company and are undetected for years by the directors. So to hold would make the position of an auditor intolerable."

Lord Justice KAY said (at p. 293): "It is said that it is easy to be wise after the event. In former years when the stock journal was correctly entered the alterations in value in a year were frequently very considerable. The increase in the years now in question did not excite any suspicion in the directors. Why should it in the auditors? They had no reason to distrust the manager. Moreover, he had, or was supposed to have, taken the stock which was actually on the premises at the date to which the balance-sheets referred. The auditors could not do this. The only book from which they could obtain information as to the quantities received in the year other than the stock journal was a book called the 'invoice guard book,' in which were pasted the invoices received with goods supplied. But this was not necessarily accurate. Invoices received might have been omitted. Goods might in some cases have been received without invoices. Were the auditors bound to enter upon an investigation which could not bring out an accurate result in order to test the truth of a statement by the manager which no one had any reason to discredit?"

The court instructed the jury that these auditors did not guarantee the correctness of their accounts. "They do not say to the public, 'Let us examine your books and vouchers and we will with absolute certainty discover every dishonesty, every mistake that exists in those books, and we will protect you against that.' " That is not what they undertook to do. They agreed to use such skill in the performance of their agreement as reasonably prudent, skillful accountants would use under the circumstances.

One of the plaintiffs, Mr. Craig, said that when defendants originally began their duties for a predecessor firm they agreed to supervise, superintend and send out certain statements to customers. Mr. Craig knew that was never done. Plaintiffs refused to allow statements to be sent to customers. It is further asserted that the defendants agreed to take the open contracts and to calculate the actual liability of the customers thereon at the time of each audit. It was known that defendants never made such calculations.

The plaintiff Craig says that they told him, "We have to make that calculation both for straddles and open accounts before we can tell you what is the actual standing of this firm." Craig's statements with reference to the contract were made to a man who has since died, leaving no way of directly meeting his testimony in this respect. Craig was aware that there had been for several years a failure to strictly live up to arrangements and agreements as to what was to be accomplished.

Zabriskie started his account in 1909, writing the brokers a letter that he was sending them $200 for margin, and that Moore, the plaintiffs' employee, should have the right to give directions to buy and sell for his account. In other words, it became what is known as a discretionary account. He directed that as soon as the $200 margin was exhausted, the account should be closed. Moore thereafter gave orders to buy and sell for Zabriskie's account. The relationship between Moore and Zabriskie does not appear, but it does appear that the loss could not have occurred if Zabriskie's account had been closed out when his margin had become exhausted.

When Moore gave an order to a broker in Chicago to sell wheat, he would sometimes charge that order to the account of Zabriskie but at other times he would not. He always entered the transactions or had them entered in the blotter. He told the clerks what entries they were to make in the charge ledger. At times he gave an order to enter such contracts against Zabriskie in this ledger and at other times he did not. If these books were all examined at the end of the three months, any accountant, skilled or unskilled, would have discovered something was wrong, or that some entry remained to be made. Items not entered in the proper place were entered in the back of the book on pages beyond the charge account in the customers' open contract ledger. They were made against Zabriskie but with instructions that they were not to be entered as actual charges against him. This was feasible because Moore was allowed to deal to the extent of very great sums in Zabriskie's account for Zabriskie and at the same time had charge of the branch office to the extent of deciding what bookkeeping entries should be made. Though Moore was directing these very extensive dealings from both sides, nothing was ever done to check up and see whether the transactions were in order. Moore arranged for payments to Zabriskie from time to time. These payments should never have been made; for with the true condition of his account known it would have been apparent that margins on hand did not warrant them. Had the "opens" been properly checked it could have been seen whether Zabriskie had balances due him and whether they warranted the payments made to him. Craig made large payments to him without attempting to ascertain how his accounts stood. Moore had the sole control in a department of plaintiffs' activities and therein plaintiffs allowed him to represent their interests as well as the interests of some of those dealing with them. He was permitted to represent conflicting interests. This was true when the accountants were there and when they were not. During the whole of the three months' period between audits, being a major part of the time, the plaintiffs paid out large sums of money without any investigation or examination of the books, though an examination would have disclosed the irregularities for which they now attempt to hold the defendants.

The actual liability of Mr. Zabriskie on open transactions and the amount to be paid out should have been ascertainable from the customers' ledger. The evidence shows that between February 28, 1917, and May 26, 1917, there was an actual change of position of something like $500,000. Were plaintiffs justified in relying, as reasonably prudent business men, on Moore's honesty, though he was allowed to exercise discretionary powers on behalf of customers? Moore was trusted with supervision over the department where the loss occurred and, at the same time, was permitted to deal at will for Zabriskie. He was left in the same position as to at least one other account. He was also margin clerk. As such it was for him to decide what margins should be maintained.

His various and diverse duties and powers put him in a position to keep records and papers or cause them to be kept so as to deceive the accountants who relied on him. If it be assumed that they should not have done so, it is nevertheless true that the plaintiffs also relied upon them to an extent beyond all reason in view of all the circumstances. They were guilty of the same kind of negligence of which they now complain. It may be true that a proper accounting would have put the plaintiffs on guard with reference to Moore's wrongdoing, but it is also true that, if the plaintiffs had attended to their business and, in view of the large transactions involved, had looked up Zabriskie's account when payments were being made to him, the dishonesty of Moore would have been discovered.

The plaintiffs admit that they never inquired into the "opens" of Zabriskie when he asked for money, nor when he placed orders to be executed. Had they done so, nothing would have been paid to him other than as his margins warranted, and losing trades would have resulted in his account being closed. Instead they left these matters to an employee, who, though not a partner or principal, had full authority in his department.

It also appears that the accountants notified the plaintiffs in writing that a certain ledger should not be taken out of the control of one Hodge and that, if it took up too much of his time, an assistant should be engaged under his control. The accountants wrote the plaintiffs, "as this ledger is now operated, it is practically a check on the subsidiary departments and we see no advantage in establishing a separate ledger." Notwithstanding this advice, one of the partners put that ledger under Moore's direction, leaving him with control of every book in the office necessary to work his schemes and, at the same time, conceal his misdeeds.

Craig had knowledge that Moore was to have discretion as to Zabriskie's account. This is shown by a letter: "I enclosed herewith check for $200 which please place to the credit of my account. I am not fully acquainted with the method of trading in cotton and wish to leave the operation of my account entirely in Mr. Moore's hands—with instructions to close out if the margin becomes exhausted."

It seems to us, therefore, that the loss was due ot the failure of Moore to close out the account when the margin became insufficient. No matter what the accountants had reported, if Zabriskie's account had been closed there would have been no loss. True, it was not closed out because of the wrongdoing of Moore; but slight supervision would have disclosed Moore's wrongdoing.

Counsel for plaintiffs in his opening stated: "Moore got a man by the name of Zabriskie—we do not know Zabriskie except as a name on the books and as a witness in litigation that grew out of those transactions—that is our total acquaintance with Zabriskie—since Zabriskie wrote a letter to the plaintiff firm as then constituted—and you will understand me, of course, when I say the plaintiff firm I mean Craig's firm, in which he enclosed a check for $200 which he said he wanted to trade in commodities, $200 will constitute a margin, that Moore was to do the trading for him, and that if the margin of $200 was exhausted, that was the end of the transaction."

Zabriskie was in fact better known to the plaintiffs than they would admit. Craig knew Zabriskie for about ten years, having spoken to him a number of times. In 1910 he took Zabriskie to a dinner of the Stock Exchange members, to which he invited all of his best customers. Craig raised Moore's salary because Zabriskie, a valuable customer, desired it and said he could obtain for Moore better compensation elsewhere.

Moreover, the Zabriskie account was the most active the plaintiffs carried. He did from seventy-five per cent to eighty-five per cent of their Chicago commodities business. Notwithstanding the tremendous loss which such an active account might bring to the plaintiffs, they never investigated the financial standing of Zabriskie; they never received a mercantile report on him; they never asked him for references in the face of the fact that his initial margin was about $200. During this period the plaintiffs paid Zabriskie $123,689.04 without once making an examination of the books to see whether anything was due him.

We are of the opinion that the loss was not entirely the result of the negligence of the defendants, but also resulted from the careless and negligent manner in which the plaintiffs conducted their business.

The verdict embraces two items: Money paid to Zabriskie and subsequent losses to his account which he failed to meet. These losses were paid to other brokers by Moore. They would not have been incurred if Zabriskie's account had been investigated. The purchases to which they relate would not have been made for there was no margin in Zabriskie's account to make them.

Before a payment was made to Zabriskie or an order given by or for him was executed, the "opens" and the sufficiency of his margin should have been investigated. This should have been done from day to day, at times from hour to hour, even though plaintiffs had audits from the accountants.

In *Deyo v. Hudson* (225 N. Y. 602, 615) the court said: "If they had no right to rely exclusively upon the assurance of Mitchell when they might have prevented the loss themselves they cannot recover."

There is no doubt in this case that plaintiffs could have prevented the loss by the exercise of reasonable care, and that they should not have relied exclusively on the accountants.

We think the damages cannot be said to flow naturally and directly from defendants' negligence or breach of contract. Plaintiffs should not be allowed to recover for losses which they could have avoided by the exercise of reasonable care.

In *City of East Grand Forks* v. *Steele* (121 Minn. 296) the court said (at pp. 298-300): "This is not an action in tort, but an action to recover damages for breach of contract. As said by Justice MITCHELL in *Whittaker* v. *Collins,* 34 Minn. 299, 25 N. W. 632, 57 Am. Rep. 55 (an action brought to recover for the negligence of a physician): 'Where the action is not maintainable without pleading and proving the contract, where the gist of the action is the breach of the contract, either by malfeasance or nonfeasance, it is in substance, whatever may be the form of the pleading, an action on the contract. * * * The foundation of the action is the contract, and the gravamen of it its breach.'

"The rule governing liability for breach of contract is given in the syllabus to *Sargent* v. *Mason,* 101 Minn. 319, 112 N. W. 255, as follows: 'In an action for damages for breach of contract, the defaulting party is liable only for the direct consequences of the breach, such as usually occur from the infraction of like contracts, and within the contemplation of the parties when the contract was entered into as likely to result from its non-performance.' * * *

"The damages claimed on account of the losses resulting from the defalcations of the clerk and the insolvency of his surety are too remote to be recovered, without showing the existence of special circumstances, known to defendants, from which they ought to have known that such losses were likely to result from a failure to disclose the true condition of affairs. Such losses are neither the natural nor the proximate consequences of the failure of defendants to make a proper audit. Neither are any facts shown from which it may be inferred that a loss from either of these causes was or ought to have been contemplated, when the contract was made, as likely to result from a breach of duty on the part of defendants."

In *Saugerties Bank* v. *Delaware & Hudson Co.* (236 N. Y. 425, 430) the court said: "As I say this criminal act made it possible to use them; without it they could not have been used and the defendant's omission would have resulted in no harm.

"Under these circumstances I fail to see how it can be said that its omission was the proximate cause of plaintiff's injury. In the first place it has been found as matter of fact that it was not such proximate cause and ordinarily it is to be determined as a question of fact whether there has been such a connection between cause and effect as to make the former proximate. (*Milwaukee & St. Paul Ry. Co.* v. *Kellogg,* 94 U. S. 469, 475.) But if we disregard this particular finding of fact we then have it on other findings that between defendant's omission and plaintiff's injury there has intervened the criminal act of a third party without which the injury could not have occurred. There has been produced a great amount of legal literature and numberless opinions on this subject of proximate cause which it is impossible and undesirable to attempt to review. But I think that there is one fundamental rule which has been clearly established in the discussion of the subject which is decisive of this case, and that is the one that the act of a party sought to be charged is not to be regarded as a proximate cause unless it is in clear sequence with the result and unless it could have been reasonably anticipated that the consequences complained of would result from the alleged wrongful act; that if the consequences were only made possible by the intervening act of a third party which could not have reasonably been anticipated then the sequential relation between act and results would not be regarded as so established as to come within the rule of proximate cause."

In Sutherland on Damages (Vol. 1 [4th ed.], p. 158, § 41) it is said: "If there intervenes between the defendant's act or omission a wilful, malicious and criminal act committed by a third person, which act defendant had no reason to apprehend, the connection between the original wrong and the result is broken."

The plaintiffs, in effect, contend that defendants are chargeable with negligence because of failure to detect Moore's wrongdoing, wholly overlooking the fact that although they were closely affiliated with Moore, who was constantly under their supervision, they were negligent in failing properly to supervise his acts or to learn the true condition of their own business and to detect his wrongdoing.

We have reached the conclusion that the judgment is right and should be affirmed.

MERRELL and FINCH, JJ., concur; CLARKE, P. J., dissents.

CLARKE, P. J. (dissenting):

I dissent from the affirmance of so much of the judgment as sets aside the verdict of the jury assessing the damages at $1,177,805.26. The contract of audit was not one merely to discover if inadvertent clerical errors had been made in the bookkeeping, but was one of protection of the plaintiff's firm from their own failure to find any error in their books of account. This contract the defendants failed to perform. Admitting the neglect of the plaintiffs to discover the embezzlement and falsification of the accounts through an examination of the books on their own part, the defendants' work in pursuance of the contract, owing to the manner in which it was performed, failed to save plaintiffs from the consequences of such failure and neglect, which was the very subject of the contract.

Judgment and order affirmed, without costs to either party as against the other.

BOARD OF COUNTY COMMISSIONERS v. BAKER *

Supreme Court of Kansas. 152 Kan. 164, 102 P.2d 1006.

HOCH, Justice. This was an action to recover damages for breach of contract. The trial court made certain findings favorable to the plaintiff but awarded only nominal damages, holding that no actual damage had been shown. Plaintiff appeals, contending that additional findings of fact should have been made and that the judgment for nominal damages only was inconsistent with findings of fact and conclusions of law theretofore made.

---

* See footnote 32 *supra*.

The appellant, the Board of County Commissioners of Allen County, Kansas, entered into a contract on August 8, 1936, with appellees, Baker & Miller, licensed municipal accountants, for an audit of the accounts and records of the various county offices. The audit was to be made in compliance with the statutory requirement of an annual county audit. G. S. 1935, 75-1122. The appellees agreed to make the audit in accordance with the "Minimum Standard Audit Program" approved by the State Municipal Accounting Board as required by the statute. The cost of the audit was not to exceed $850.

The appellees proceeded to make the audit. The audit of the county treasurer's office covered the period from October 8, 1935, to October 12, 1936, and that of the other county offices from January 1, 1936, to January 11, 1937. The appellees were paid the full amount of $850 in three payments, the last one of which was made on March 1, 1937. Certain inaccuracies and irregularities were discovered in the report of the auditors, further audit being made of three county offices. Following these disclosures, this action was brought.

After preliminary recitals, it was alleged in the petition that the defendants failed to discover or report shortages later found to have then existed in the "emergency fund" maintained in the office of the county engineer; that as a result of carelessness, negligence and wantonness in making the audit, the defendants had erroneously reported that the county treasurer had collected about $15,000 in taxes in excess of what should have been collected, and that the county clerk had about $500 in cash on hand, whereas nearly all of the amount reported as cash consisted of checks. Other allegations not material to the present discussion need not be narrated, except to add that the plaintiffs alleged that by reason of the careless, negligent and wanton manner in which the audit had been made and of the incorrect audit report, the audit was "worthless to and of no value" to the county, and that plaintiffs had been damaged in the amount paid for the audit for which amount judgment was asked.

Defendant Miller was not served with summons being out of the jurisdiction of the state. The answer of defendant Baker admitted the execution of the written contract and the making of the audit. It alleged that the "emergency fund" in the office of the county engineer was created without authority of law and that the defendants were under no obligation to examine or audit it, but that in their report they did call attention to the fact that such fund was in existence, and alleged that the reimbursement vouchers of this fund were sworn to by the county engineer and approved by the county attorney; that the audit was made in good faith and "that the purpose of said contract and audit report was to enable plaintiff to comply with the provisions of the General Statutes of Kansas of 1935, which require the governing body of each county in the State of Kansas to have the accounts of such county examined and audited by a licensed municipal accountant or accountants, or certified public accountant or acountants; that said audit report was filed with the county clerk of Allen county, Kansas, and in the State Accountant's office, Capitol Building, Topeka, Kansas, as alleged in said third amended petition, and thereby said contract and said audit report completely and fully fulfilled the purpose for which they were intended, as provided by the 1935 General Statutes of the State of Kansas pertaining thereto; that plaintiff has received and retained all the benefits of said contract and audit report and plaintiff therefore has no cause of action for damages against the defendant for breach of said audit contract."

The case was heard by the court, after which sixteen findings of fact and certain conclusions of law were made. It will be sufficient for this review to refer to the findings of fact only to the extent necessary in connection with the "conclusions of law." The conclusions of law were as follows:

"I. That in making the audit in question the defendants were guilty of negligence in the preparation of their report,—

"(a) In not reconciling, within a reasonable degree of accuracy in the first instance, the total taxes collected and uncollected, charged to the treasurer, with the abstract of taxes furnished by the county clerk;

"(b) In not setting out the items of cash on hand in the county clerk's office, as required by the Minimum Standard Audit program;

"(c) In wholly failing to check the A. W. Young emergency fund and include same in their audit.

"II. That Allen county, Kansas, had the benefit of the audit of the offices concerning which no question has been raised; that said audit is not entirely worthless, but was of some value to said county.

"III. That plaintiff has failed to prove any substantial damage that it has suffered by reason of the negligence of the defendants; but that because of the negligence of defendants the plaintiff is entitled to recover nominal damages of one dollar.

"IV. That plaintiff is entitled to recover its costs herein."

This opinion will be simplified if we state at the outset the principal conclusions to which we have arrived after examination of the record, and particularly after analysis of the findings of the trial court. Those conclusions are that the trial court failed in its final determination, to evaluate one of the primary purposes for which the audit was made; that it proceeded upon the erroneous theory that unless the plaintiff established a money loss, apart from the payments made to the defendants, it had shown no substantial damage. The purpose of a county audit is not merely to "comply with the statute" as the defendants rather indicate in their answer. Its primary purpose—the purpose of the statute itself—is to determine whether the accounts and records of the county are being accurately and honestly kept. When the county commissioners, who are charged with responsibility in the matter, employ accountants to make the audit, they contract for skill, accuracy and fidelity on the part of those who represent themselves as experts in this line of work. If service which measures up to that high standard is not furnished, the breach of the contract is fundamental—it goes to the very heart of the contract. If gross inaccuracies are discovered in the report; if disclosure is made that the accountants have failed to report material facts of serious import, bearing upon questions of efficiency and honesty, the report becomes of little if any value. If those employing the accountants cannot rely upon an assumption that the audit and the report have been made with reasonable accuracy and with complete fidelity they have failed to receive the principal thing they were to get under the contract. When confidence in the report is gone, very little is left. In the light of these elementary and fundamental propositions, let us examine the record.

We first note the court's findings (a) (b) (c) under its "conclusions of law." Finding (a) was that the defendants were "guilty of negligence in not reconciling, within a reasonable degree of accuracy in the first instance, the total taxes collected and uncollected, charged to the treasurer, with the abstract of taxes furnished by the county clerk." This conclusion was based upon the court's findings of fact numbered 10 and 12, which we need only summarize. The court there found that the defendants erroneously reported that the county treasurer's books showed the tax roll to be in excess of the tax abstract in the sum of $14,995.30; that subsequently Mr. Bartlett, a bookkeeper in the county clerks office, examined the county treasurer's records and discovered that the correct amount of the difference between the tax roll and the tax abstract was only $44.62; that the attention of the defendants was called to the finding by Mr. Bartlett, after which they wrote to the county clerk and submitted pages to be substituted in their report, showing the difference to be $44.62 as found by Mr. Bartlett, and on this matter the court found that "the evidence does not disclose that the defendants ever checked their records to determine their accuracy."

The court's finding (b) was that the defendants were "guilty of negligence in not setting out the items of cash on hand in the county clerk's office, as required by the Minimum Standard Audit Program." This is based upon the court's finding of fact No. 14, the substance of which is that the auditors reported the "cash count, January 11, 1937 (noon)," to be $494.38, whereas the defendant's work sheets which were placed into the record as an exhibit by the plaintiff, showed the following:

"Cash on hand, January 11, 1937, (noon)		
Coin	$ 7.75	
Bills	12.00	
Checks	416.88	
Cash items (express)	2.00	
I. O. U. (Elarton)	55.75	
		$494.38"

(The item of $416.88, on the same page of their work sheets, is made up as follows)

"A. W. Young Emergency Fund No. 517, 1-11-37	$ .25	
Elarton, Ralph, 1-2-37	391.63	
Palace Ready to Wear, 9-4-36	25.00	
		$416.88"

In this connection we note the testimony of W. L. Warnica. Mr. Warnica was employed by the defendants to help make the audit. He identified an exhibit by the plaintiff as sheets made in his handwriting, signed and turned over by him to his employer Miller. One of these sheets reads as follows: "Allen county, county clerk. County clerk claims the 47 cigarette licenses issued and covered by his personal check on January 2, 1937, have now been collected on except for ten for which he secured a bank loan. The balance of the check represents funds diverted to his own use. The balance of $109.63 is supposed to be covered by another check."

It is also pertinent to note the following testimony of Barton Avery: "I am now and was in September 1937, a Senior Accountant in the State Accountant's Office. I made an investigation of the accounts of Ralph Elarton, County Clerk, from the period January 3, 1936, to January 8, 1937, which showed a difference of $381.95, which had not been reported. I also made a check on the discrepancy as to the cash on hand in the county clerk's office between the Cornell Audit and the Baker-Miller Audit. We asked Mr. Miller about the difference and he said that he omitted the $258.00; that Mr. Elarton stated that it was for an item to be remitted direct to the Department of Inspection and Registration. Mr. Austin Logan was in Iola with me also, and we made a check to see if the personal check of $394.00 of Ralph Elarton, which was in the cash drawer, was ever cashed and cleared the bank, and we learned that Mr. Elarton did not even maintain a bank account at that time."

While the trial court made no specific findings relative to the testimony of witnesses Warnica and Avery, their testimony was not disputed.

It thus appears that the item reported as "cash, $494.38" in the county clerk's office was not cash. Most of it consisted of checks, and the principal check was the personal check of the county clerk, Elarton, whose resignation subsequently followed after disclosures of irregularities. It is hardly necessary to say that of course the county commissioners were entitled to know that checks were being carried as cash. A pertinent provision of the Minimum Standard Audit Program which appellees contracted to observe reads as follows: "Count all cash and cash items on hand. List checks and note date of making. Note checks signed by officers, deputies or employees. Insist upon all checks being deposited in the bank not later than the next business day and see that there is no off-setting withdrawal. Request depository to make direct report of any items not cleared for any reason." (Audit Procedure 1-12a.)

But no recourse to the audit program is required. Had it contained no such specific provision it would none the less have been the plain duty of appellees to report the facts. The county commissioners were certainly entitled to know that a county officer was substituting his own check for cash in the cash drawer. What confidence in the report could remain after disclosure of such a serious failure to do their work carefully and faithfully?

We next note the trial court's "conclusion of law" (c), which was that "the defendants were guilty of negligence in wholly failing to check the A. W. Young emergency fund and include same in their audit." This is based upon the evidence covered by the court's findings of fact numbered 15 and 16. The substance of those findings is that no audit was made of the "emergency fund" in the county engineer's office, the defendants doing little more than report the existence of the fund; but that the work sheets, submitted as an exhibit by the plaintiff, showed, "no funds on hand January 11, 1937. An emergency account has been set up under the name of A. W. Young emergency fund. The amount, $389.49"; that as a result of an audit subsequently made of this emergency fund by an accountant from the State Accountant's office, and covering the same period, unexplained expenditures were disclosed in the amount of $196.77. In other words, it is the plain implication of the court's findings that if the appellees had not been guilty of negligence in failing to audit this fund, they would have discovered a shortage of about $200.

The appellees made no objection at the time, and make none now, to any of the findings heretofore narrated.

We now come to the court's "conclusion of law" No. 2, to which the appellant objected at the time and now objects, which reads as follows: "Allen county, Kansas, had the benefit of the audit of the offices concerning which no question has been raised; that said audit is not entirely worthless, but was of some value to said county."

The theory of the trial court seems to have been that since the audit as to the other county offices had not been attacked, the disclosure and proof of inaccuracies and irregularities in the report as to only three county offices do not seriously injure the value of the report. The unsoundness of such a theory is sufficiently indicated, we think, by the general comments made at the start of this opinion. When reliance can no longer be placed in an auditor's report, the coin of the audit's value has become counterfeit. Moreover, it is pertinent to note that the contract was for a county audit, and this was in harmony with the emphasis placed upon the proposition in the audit program, that county audits are based upon the county as a unit. The "Introductory Comment" therein reads as follows: "The audit contemplated herein comprehends the financial position and financial management of the county. The financial position and management of a county is based on the county as a unit. It may seem trite to indicate as a basic principle that an audit program must consider the county as a composite unit made up of various offices."

The only way the county commissioners could have discovered inaccuracies and irregularities, if any existed, in the other county offices, would have been to have other auditors make another audit. Faults of the audit made by defendants were not discovered until September 1937. Another year, subsequent to the period covered by appellee's audit, had almost expired. In view of the fact that the statute requires that a county audit be made annually, the time for another regular audit would soon arrive. In the meantime, the county commissioners had secured the services of an accountant from the State Accountant's office. Under such circumstances, it would be unreasonable to say that the appellant was under obligation, immediately upon the disclosures in September 1937, to have another audit made of all county offices for 1936, and having failed to do so it cannot recover.

The only remaining question is whether the amount paid for the audit is a proper measure of damages. What other measure could be used? On what scales may some hypothetical residue of reliance be weighed when confidence in an auditor's report has been largely destroyed? We do not say that minor inaccuracies in an audit and slight errors in an auditor's report may not be overlooked, nor that under some circumstances substantial value from an audit may not remain in spite of its errors. But in view of the negligence, the inaccuracies, the inexcusable failure to report facts of serious character, found by the trial court in the instant case, on a record which amply supports such findings, we must conclude that the appellees failed, in a fundamental and essential particular, to furnish the expert and faithful service which they contracted to furnish. Whether this was due to personal fault of the appellees themselves or to that of employees working for them is not material. As in other like situations, public accountants are liable for the failure of their subordinates to make a proper audit. *Ultramares Corporation* v. *George A. Touche,* 255 N. Y. 170, 174 N. E. 441, 74 A. L. R. 1139.

The general rule is that the measure of damages for defective performance of a contract is the difference in the value between what is tendered as performance and what is due as performance under the contract; and that if what is tendered is unsuitable for the purpose contemplated, the measure of damages may be the amount required to remedy the defect. 17 C. J. 853; Sutherland Damages, Vol. 1., p. 48. In the instant case what was called for as performance was an audit and report in which reliance could be placed. What was furnished was an audit and report in which reliance could not be placed. In the case of *City of East Grand Forks* v. *Steele,* 121 Minn. 296, 141 N. W. 181, 182, 45 L. R. A., N. S., 205, Ann. Cas. 1914C, 720, which involved a faulty audit and report by public accountants, it was said:

"5. Defendants represented themselves as expert accountants, which implied that they were skilled in that class of work. In acecpting employment as expert accountants, they undertook, and the plaintiff had the right to expect, that in the performance of their duties they would exercise the average ability and skill of those engaged in that branch of skilled labor. They were employed to ascertain, among other things, whether any irregularities had occurred in the financial transactions of the city clerk, and, if so, the nature and extent of such irregularities. If, from want of proper skill, or from negligence, they did not disclose the true situation, they failed to perform the duty which they had assumed, and failed to earn the compensation which plaintiff had agreed to pay them for the proper performance of such duty.

"6. The work of an expert accountant is of such technical character and requires such peculiar skill that the ordinary person cannot be expected to know whether he performs his duties properly or otherwise, but must rely upon his report as to the thoroughness and accuracy of his work. The full contract price having been paid in the belief, induced by defendants' report, that such report disclosed fully and accurately the condition of the city's accounts, the city is entitled to recover back the amounts so paid, upon proving that, through the incompetence or the negligence of defendants, the report was in substance misleading and false."

In substantial particulars, both in what the appellees reported and in what they failed to report, the instant audit and report were "misleading and false," and the plaintiff is entitled to recover the amount paid under the contract.

The judgment for nominal damages only is set aside, and the case remanded with direction to render judgment for the plaintiff in the sum of $850 together with interest from the dates the installment payments were made.

NATIONAL SURETY CORP. v. LYBRAND *

Appellate Division of the Supreme Court of New York, 1939. 256 App. Div. 226, 9 N.Y.S.2d 554

UNTERMYER, J. The plaintiff surety company maintains this action against three firms of certified public accountants for their failure to discover and report substantial cash shortages after auditing and examining the books and accounts of Halle & Stieglitz, members of the New York Stock Exchange. One Wallach, cashier in the main office of Halle & Stieglitz, confessed on May 2, 1934, to defalcations over a period of years aggregating $329,300. The plaintiff, surety on a fidelity bond, paid the loss to Halle & Stieglitz and now sues as its assignee.

During the period involved Halle & Stieglitz maintained about twenty-seven bank accounts, nine of which were in New York city. It had over 2,500 customers' accounts, a large volume of daily transactions and substantial bank loans. Many of the firm's records were kept in the "cage" of which Wallach, the cashier, had complete charge. Wallach determined when and in what amounts to transfer funds from one bank to another.

His system of embezzlements from about 1925 to May, 1934, consisted of a series of abstractions from petty cash. The ever-accumulating shortage of cash in banks was concealed by delaying and substituting bank deposits from day to day, and, when outside audits were made, by "kiting" checks from one bank to another on the audit date. The effect was that the sums covered thereby appeared in two banks at the same time. This "lapping" or "kiting" practice resulted in a credit at the payee bank on the same day that the check was deposited, making up a shortage previously existing there, while the amount would not be debited at the drawee bank until at least a day thereafter. Wallach knew when audits were to be made and, by the use of this system, effectually concealed his steadily-increasing thefts for several years.

Defendant George R. Bowden & Company (referred to as Bowden) examined the books of Halle & Stieglitz as of January 31, 1928, at which time the cash shortage amounted to $28,350. Wallach's subsequent thefts amounted to $300,950.

Defendants Lybrand, Ross Bros. & Montgomery (referred to as Lybrand) made examinations as of September 30, 1929, September 30, 1930, October 31, 1931, and September 30, 1932. The shortages existing at and arising after those various audit dates were as follows:

Date	Shortage	Subsequent thefts
Sept. 30, 1929	$123,328.50	$205,971.50
Sept. 30, 1930	197,000.00	132,300.00
Oct. 31, 1931	245,000.00	84,300.00
Sept. 30, 1932	273,000.00	56,300.00

Defendant McHeffey & McDonough made an examination as of November 30, 1933. The shortage then amounted to $315,000. Wallach's thefts between that date and the date of his confession in the first week of May, 1934, amounted to $14,300. In all, his peculations aggregated $329,300.

* This case is discussed at p. 22 ff. *supra.*

Lybrand had made an earlier examination in 1926, as had Bowden in 1927, but causes of action thereon were withdrawn as within the Statute of Limitations.

The defendants are charged with failure properly to perform their contracts to audit, with breach of warranty in their reports, with negligence in their work, and with fraudulently misrepresenting material facts in their reports as to the financial condition of Halle & Stieglitz. It is claimed that if the defendants had discovered and reported Wallach's misappropriations, Halle & Stieglitz would not have continued him in their employ or sustained the subsequent losses. It is also claimed that they might then have recovered previous losses from Wallach.

The defendants Lybrand deny the material allegations of the complaint and assert that Halle & Stieglitz knew or should have known of Wallach's dishonesty but failed to advise the defendants of it; that the proximate cause of the loss was the contributory negligence of Halle & Stieglitz; that the damage was not attributable to any reasonable reliance on the acts or omissions of these defendants; and that the defalcations and damages were not within the contemplation of the parties to the contracts. Bowden's answer contains the same defenses, while that of McHeffey & McDonough interposes only denials.

The trial course concluded that the plaintiff failed to make out a case for submission to the jury. The first question is whether there were circumstances which should have put the defendants on their guard so that they, as professional accountants, might have ascertained the true situation in the course of their investigations.

It was Wallach's practice usually to take the "kiting" checks from the check books of the firm, but out of numerical order, so that the stubs pertaining to the checks would appear beyond the last stub regularly dated for the month. Then, when the check stubs for the previous months were totaled in the check books the "kited" checks would not be included in the footings for that month.

The circumstances surrounding "late" deposits are significant in that the deposit was often constituted differently than reflected in the books of the firm. For example, the deposit book would disclose the deposit of several individual items, and although the total sum would be deposited in the bank it would consist of a different number of checks in different amounts and usually drawn by different makers. This practice developed because it was a part of Wallach's system to place a customer's check in the petty cash box, instead of immediately depositing it, then extract from the petty cash the amount of that check in cash, and deposit the check in the bank one or more days later. The accumulating shortage in that bank would then be covered by the deposit of a check or checks drawn on another of the firm's banks for the amount necessary to conceal the shortage. At times Wallach would make up the aggregate of the shortage by depositing his own check along with the checks of others.

The difference between the items on deposit slips and the entries in the deposit books was never observed. The bookkeeping department of Halle & Stieglitz is blamed by the defendants for allowing this to remain unnoticed and unchallenged. Yet these accountants themselves apparently never undertook to examine the deposit slips, which were retained by the several banks, nor to obtain duplicates thereof.

Another office custom of Halle & Stieglitz is criticized by the defendants. Memoranda were prepared in pencil by the bookkeeping department intended to show daily bank balances or the cash totals which the firm was supposed to have in banks. These memoranda would be given to Wallach, who would change the amounts so as to reflect approximately the actual amount of cash in banks. However, these slips were not permanent records. They were information memoranda used solely for the consideration of bank loans. As they were immediately destroyed they could not have been the basis for a check-up of cash shortages. The defendants otherwise charge Halle & Stieglitz with carelessness in the conduct of their bookkeeping department, but there is no evidence that this firm differed in its office practice from that of other Wall Street brokers or that the defendants ever made any suggestions relating thereto.

During the years of Wallach's pilferings one or the other of the defendant firms of certified public accountants was employed by Halle & Stieglitz to make audits which included the verification of cash. For the audit of January 31, 1928, Bowen received fees of $2,800. He specifically reported to Halle & Stieglitz that they had on that date a balance in Guaranty Trust Company of $73,109.20 and in Hanover National Bank of $185,708.17, when in fact the balances were $72,829.20 and $157,638.17, respectively. The shortages in those two bank accounts, aggregating $28,350, were concealed by delayed deposits recorded January 31, 1928, but actually made February first with substituted items.

Djorup, plaintiff's expert, testified that comparison of the bank statements and the deposit books showed a number of delayed deposits between January 14, 1928, and February 4, 1928. The late deposits, before and after the audit date, range as high as $33,684.70, with delays varying from one to three business days. With respect to late deposits, this witness testified that he would have checked the larger items among them by obtaining the deposit slips. It is apparent that inquiries at the time of audit might have revealed the shortages.

Bowden, who rested his case without proof, contends that he did not undertake to verify the bank accounts. His report indicates no such limitation. On the contrary, his balance sheet clearly separates cash in banks and on hand and cash borrowed from customers' accounts. It contains the various bank balances, and cash in banks is listed among assets as amounting to $522,719.69. Even if the words "verify" and "verification" are not used, the fact of verification follows from the specific statement of the balances and total cash.

The Lybrand firm, in contrast to Bowden, concedes that their engagements for the 1929, 1930, 1931 and 1932 audits included the verification of cash. The arrangements for the 1929 and 1930 examinations were in writing, it being stated that the examination was to be "along the lines followed by us in prior audits of your accounts" and would embrace "the *verification of cash,* securities, customers' accounts, etc., without verification of income and expense accounts or the preparation of the questionnaire of the New York Stock Exchange." The arrangements for the 1931 and 1932 examinations were oral and followed the scope of the two previous years. For the four years involved, 1929 to 1932, inclusive, Lybrand received fees of $11,000, $5,000, $2,850 and $2,400 respectively.

The cash shortage on September 30, 1929, amounting to $123,328.50, was concealed by four checks in the amounts of $13,000, $10,000, $100,000 and $328.50. The first three of these checks were taken from the stubs of October first. All were deposited October 1, 1929, to take the place of a deposit of same amount, though of different items, recorded in the books on September thirtieth.

The shortage on September 30, 1930, of $197,000 was concealed by two checks for $102,000 and $95,000, which were drawn from stubs of October first, but deposited in the Guaranty Trust Company on September thirtieth.

On October 31, 1931, the shortage amounted to $245,000. The method of concealment was a deposit of $245,023.11 recorded October thirtieth and actually made October thirty-first with substituted items, including two checks for $120,000 and $125,000, respectively, which were drawn from stubs of November 2, 1931.

On September 30, 1932, with intervening defalcations of $28,000, the shortage had increased to $273,000. It was concealed by two checks of Halle & Stieglitz for $138,000 and $135,000 drawn on National City Bank and Commercial National Bank, respectively, representing the exact amount of the shortage. They had been taken out of numerical order from check stubs which were later dated October 3, 1932, and were deposited in Guaranty Trust Company on September 30, 1932.

Throughout these years there were continual lapped and delayed deposits, and instances of substitution of deposited items. These, plaintiff insists, are well-known danger signals to skilled auditors, but were disregarded or not recognized by the defendants, who never requested duplicate deposit slips, never pointed out late deposits or bank transfers, nor made any suggestion to Halle & Stieglitz as to their methods relative to cash, yet charge Halle & Stieglitz with negligence in the failure to make investigations which are within the ordinary realm of professional accountants. The defendants say Halle & Stieglitz were negligent in failing to observe the differences between the details of the deposits actually made and those recorded in the books during the periods when Halle & Stieglitz made their reconciliations of bank accounts. The employees of Halle & Stieglitz who made such reconciliations were not auditors skilled in their profession, and their methods were purely mechanical checking to arrive at an arithmetical balance. The defendants' employment, however, was the verification of the sums then actually on deposit in the banks.

Aside from accepting the engagement and reviewing the report, the Lybrand partners did not participate in the audits. Their employees were supervised by a senior accountant who made assignments and gave instructions. The only Lybrand employee who "verified" the cash in banks was the witness Brushaber, who was called by the plaintiff. Brushaber had not listed "Transfers between banks" on previous audits, but he made such a list during the period covered by his reconciliation in 1932 and was examined in connection therewith. However, even after compiling such a list, Lybrand's employee either disregarded the very items which had become Wallach's expedient in concealing his defalcations or did not understand their significance. The plaintiff asserts that the procedure followed was mere mechanical routine, with no attempt to guard against the use of checks drawn from the check book out of numerical order and beyond the last check of the current month; that no notice was taken of delayed deposits nor effort made to guard against "lapped" deposits or "kited" checks; that Brushaber did nothing on the audit dates to ascertain the last checks drawn by Halle & Stieglitz for the previous month.

For the audit of November 30, 1933, McHeffey & McDonough received fees of $2,000. The shortage had then reached the sum of $315,000 and was concealed by two checks for $150,000 and $165,000 drawn on National City Bank and Commercial National Bank, respectively, the total covering the exact amount of cash defalcations to that date. These two checks were taken from the stubs of December first, but were deposited in the Guaranty Trust Company on November twenty-ninth, the deposits being recorded as made on December first.

On May 3, 1934, after Wallach had confessed his thefts, McHeffey & McDonough were employed to verify the defalcations and later submitted a detailed report showing the accumulation of the loss over a period of years. The account with Guaranty Trust Company was then short a total of $329,300.

In a letter writen by defendant McHeffey & McDonough on November 8, 1933, they stated that "the details of our audit will include: * * * 6. Verification of Bank Balances." They contend that their report is distinguished from the report of the other defendants in that there was no delayed deposit on the audit date. The plaintiff concedes that there was no delayed deposit between November 29 and December 1, 1933, but there was a deposit of the two "kited" checks of $150,000 and $165,000, above referred to, for which no entry appeared in the deposit book. The only items corresponding in amount were entered on December first. Furthermore, there are instances of substantial delayed deposits in the latter part of November, 1933, and later, investigation of any of which would have disclosed that the shortage was then being concealed by "lapping."

McHeffey & McDonough also contend that they are exonerated because, notwithstanding the shortage, Halle & Stieglitz retained them to verify the amount of defalcations and to prepare a claim against the surety. The subsequent employment, however, did not condone any prior negligence of these defendants. The purpose was solely to verify the shortage and fix the dates of its occurrence. Except for the expert, Klein, who was called by Lybrand, the defendants "rested without calling any witnesses, although there would naturally be available the men who made the audit, those who prepared or supervised the preparation of the working papers or the certified balance sheet and experts to refute the testimony offered by the experts called by plaintiff." (*State Street Trust Co.* v. *Ernst,* 278 N. Y. 104, 111.)

It is contended that the defendants' engagements called for only partial examinations, of limited scope and nature, and that the fees were fixed accordingly. Conceding that the audits and examinations were limited in scope, the loss here did not involve bank loans, customers' accounts, partners' accounts, expense accounts or other liabilities. It resulted from a shortage of cash in banks due to pilferings of petty cash. The question, then, is whether the defendants' duty was performed by a mere book reconciliation of cash or whether it did not require the ascertainment of the actual cash in bank.

It is undisputed that cash in bank can be verified absolutely. The contracts for the services of the defendants were plain and their engagements required the exercise of reasonable skill and diligence in making an actual determination of the cash position of Halle & Stieglitz and not a mere arithmetical bookkeeping computation. When they accepted the employment, though it may be at a low rate of compensation, they assumed the risk of non-performance of contracts contemplating actual verification of cash in banks.

To "verify" as defined in Corpus Juris, volume 67, page 230, is to "ascertain to be correct; * * * to confirm or establish the truth of." In Dicksee's Manual on Auditing (Am. ed. 1909), edited by Robert H. Montgomery, one of the defendants herein, it is said (p. 40): "A list of cheques outstanding should be retained, and it should be ascertained afterwards, either by a second writing up of the pass book or by inquiry of the bank, whether the amounts agree. If the time of the proposed audit is known, fraud may easily be committed and the cash inflated by drawing a cheque at the last moment which will be 'outstanding.'"

In Montgomery's own treatise on "Auditing—Theory and Practice" (1912), he says (p. 94): "When the cash balance consists of several bank accounts or funds, care must be taken to see that the entire balance is verified simultaneously. Instances are known where auditors have been deceived through one balance, after being inspected, having been transferred and used on a later day in connection with another balance."

Safeguards against fraud are discussed in Bell and Powelson on Auditing (1932), at page 71:

"The reason for thus testing individual deposits, and especially the composition thereof, is to detect any evidence of temporary misappropriations of cash which have been restored, or of the somewhat similar form of fraud known as 'kiting,' which involves a series of unauthorized 'borrowings,' one being used to repay the other. * * *

"When there is more than one bank account, a test should always be made of deposits during the last days of the audit period. The particular purpose of this is to detect a deposit in one bank of an unrecorded check on another bank to conceal a shortage in the first bank, which check cannot reach the second bank in time to be charged by it in the audit period and will not appear as outstanding."

And (at p. 73) it is said: "For the same reason that all checks supposed to have been issued should be accounted for, it is necessary, so far as practicable, to determine that none have been issued which were not supposed to have been. Knowing that all current numbers of checks would be accounted for by the auditor, the person desiring to issue a fraudulent check would be likely to use one that was not current. For that reason, the auditor should see that no checks have been abstracted from the back of the check book, if they are in book form."

The extent of an accountant's duty is well defined in *Matter of London & General Bank* (L. R. [1895] 2 Ch. 673, 682). Not only must he examine the books but, if that be his contract, he must satisfy himself with reasonable diligence that the books "show the true financial position of the company."

The evidence in this case discloses similar conditions at the time of all the audits in question. It was for the jury to say whether the practice of "lapping" and "kiting" of checks should have put the defendants upon inquiry which would have led to discovery of the defalcations, and whether, if defendants had exercised ordinary care and used proper methods of accounting as established by the expert testimony, they would have observed checks drawn out of numerical order. If they had checked "outstandings" they would have noted that the check or checks used by Wallach at the audit dates were returned with the canceled vouchers accompanying the next bank statement. Again, if there had been any substantial compliance with the requirements for verifying cash in banks the cash shortages would have been detected, as the jury might have found. Their representations that there had been a verification of cash was a pretense of knowledge when they did not know the condition of the bank accounts and had no reasonable basis to assume that they did. This, the jury could have found, amounted at least to a constructive fraud. (*Ultramares Corp.* v. *Touche,* 255 N. Y. 170, 190, 191; *State Street Trust Co.* v. *Ernst, supra,* p. 112.)

The defendants assert that they are not liable, no matter how negligent they may have been, because Halle & Stieglitz were guilty of contributory negligence. If it be true that Halle & Stieglitz so conducted their business as to make possible Wallach's defalcations, it did not necessarily excuse the defendants from the consequences of their negligence in failing to discover and report the facts. The action here, it must be remembered, is not to recover for the thefts committed by Wallach as it would be if it were against Wallach or against the surety. The action is for errors of the accountants in failing to discover Wallach's defalcations, thereby making further defalcations possible and rendering more difficult recovery for defalcations of the past. The measure of damages in two such classes of actions is not the same.

We are, therefore, not prepared to admit that accountants are immune from the consequences of their negligence because those who employ them have conducted their own business negligently. The situation in this respect is not unlike that of a workman injured by a dangerous condition which he has been employed to rectify. (*Kowalsky* v. *Conreco Company,* 264 N. Y. 125.) Accountants, as we know, are commonly employed for the very purpose of detecting defalcations which the employer's negligence has made possible. Accordingly, we see no reason to hold that the accountant is not liable to his employer in such cases. Negligence of the employer is a defense only when it has contributed to the accountant's failure to perform his contract and to report the truth. Thus, by way of illustration, if it were found that the members of the firm of Halle & Stieglitz had been negligent in connection with the transfer of funds which occurred at about the time of each audit and that such negligence contributed to the defendants' false reports, it would be a defense to the action, for it could then be said that the defendants' failure to perform their contracts was attributable, in part, at least, to the negligent conduct of the firm. That was the principle applied in *Craig* v. *Anyon* (212 App. Div. 55; affd., 242 N. Y. 569) where the embezzler had been negligently represented to the accountants as a person to be trusted. In the present case the loss consisted of thefts by a cashier not so represented "whose own account of his receipts and payments could not reasonably be taken by an auditor without further inquiry." (*Matter of Kingston Cotton Mill Co.* [*No. 2*], L. R. [1896] 2 Ch. Div. 279.)

We are, therefore, of opinion that the plaintiff established a *prima facie* case. The question of the defendants' liability on the various theories set forth in the complaint should have been submitted to the jury. It was also for the jury to say whether the defendants were liable for defalcations subsequent to their audits, depending upon whether such losses could reasonably have been anticipated at the time they were engaged in the performance of the work. (*Critten* v. *Chemical National*

Bank, 171 N.Y. 219; *Smith* v. *London Assurance Corp.,* 109 App. Div. 882.)

It may be prudent, though perhaps unnecessary, to say that we have stated the facts as they might have been found if the case had been submitted to the jury. We do this because, the complaint having been dismissed, the plaintiff is entitled to the most favorable inferences fairly to be drawn from the evidence. We do not intend to suggest that the facts, as we have stated them, would have been accepted by the jury or that upon a new trial other facts may not appear. We merely hold that on the present record the issues of fact, including negligence and contributory negligence, were for the jury.

[Judgment reversed and a new trial ordered.]

DANTZLER LUMBER & EXPORT CO. v. COLUMBIA CASUALTY CO.*

Supreme Court of Florida, 1934. 115 Fla. 541, 156 So. 116.

BUFORD, Justice. We adopt the statement of the case as presented by counsel for respective parties.

The appellee, Columbia Casualty Company, filed bill of complaint against the appellants, Dantzler Lumber & Export Company, a Florida Corporation, L. N. Dantzler, Jr., and Alvin C. Ernst, Lester W. Blyth, Harry C. Royal, and Forrest H. Figsby, copartners doing business under the firm name of Ernst & Ernst.

Summarized, the bill of complaint alleged:

(a) That the Columbia Casualty Company is a corporation organized under the laws of the state of New York, and authorized to do business in the state of Florida, as a surety company for compensation.

(b) That Dantzler Lumber & Export Company is a corporation organized under the laws of Florida, engaged in the lumber export business at Tampa, Hillsborough county, Fla.

(c) That L. N. Dantzler, Jr., is vice president and treasurer of Dantzler Lumber & Export Company, and resides at Tampa, Hillsborough county, Fla.

(d) That Ernst & Ernst is a copartnership composed of the persons named in the bill, all of the members of the copartnership being nonresidents of the state of Florida; said copartnership being engaged in business as public accountants and maintaining an office in the state of Florida.

(e) That Ernst & Ernst contracted with Dantzler Lumber & Export Company to make annual audits of books and accounts of said company, and did make audits of said books and accounts for the period from September 20, 1926, to August 7, 1931, and reported said audits of the books and accounts to said Dantzler Lumber & Export Company, said audits being made at or near the end of each calendar year, and that said audits were made by auditors or accountants in the employ of said Ernst & Ernst, and that said auditors were unrestricted in making and reporting said annual audits, and were required to make complete and detailed

* See footnote 36 *supra.*

audits and reports, and were under agreement with said Dantzler Lumber & Export Company to make examination of all cash transactions for the period covered by each audit, including inspection of vouchers and other supporting data.

(f) That one W. Frank Alderman was employed as bookkeeper by Dantzler Lumber & Export Company during the period above mentioned, and that said Alderman, by means of issuing certain checks against the bank accounts of said Dantzler Lumber & Export Company fraudulently obtained possession of and embezzled moneys of said Dantzler Lumber & Export Company to the aggregate amount of $39,425.61; that of said sum $1,670.09 was embezzled during the year 1927, $4,716.62 in the year 1928, $15,670.70 in the year 1929, $8,693.20 in the year 1930, and $8,675 in the year 1931.

(g) That said Ernst & Ernst was negligent and careless in making its audits of the books and accounts of said Dantzler Lumber & Export Company, and that by the exercise of due care, caution, and vigilance, as they were in duty bound to do, they would have discovered the embezzlement, that it was the duty of said auditors, pursuant to their contract of employment, to examine every cash transaction and to investigate supporting data, and that, had said auditors, in making said audits, examined the cash transactions wherein the cash above mentioned as withdrawn by said Alderman by the checks above mentioned, with due care and accuracy required of auditors, and pursuant to their contract of employment, the embezzlement committed by Alderman would have been discovered at the time of the audit in 1927, which would have terminated the said embezzlements and resulted in a loss of only $1,670.09, which was the amount of the embezzlement committed by said Alderman prior to the 1927 audit, but that, through the failure of said Ernst & Ernst to use due care and vigilance, and to properly perform their contract to examine all cash transactions and supporting data and report the same in their annual audits, the said embezzlements committed by the said Alderman were not discovered and were permitted to continue until August, 1931, during which time the amount of the embezzlements so committed by the said Alderman aggregated the sum of $39,425.61.

(h) It is further alleged in the bill that in each report of the audit of the books and accounts of Dantzler Lumber & Export Company by Ernst & Ernst, commencing the year 1927 and continuing through succeeding years including 1930, it was certified by the auditors that "all record cash receipts for the year under review were traced directly into the bank deposits and disbursements through the bank account were verified by an examination of said checks, invoices or other supporting data on file." It is alleged that, had the auditors compared the checks with the invoices and other supporting data, it would have been found that Alderman was wrongfully and fraudulently withdrawing the money from his employer, Dantzler Lumber & Export Company, from the bank account on checks made payable to "Yourselves," and that said checks were cashed by the paying teller of the bank; that a careful, reasonable, and intelligent audit of said accounts and the tracing of said checks would have disclosed that there was no supporting data for them and that they were not connected with any business transactions of Dantzler Lumber & Export Company; that Dantzler Lumber & Export Company relied upon the accuracy of said auditors' reports and believed them to have been made in good faith as stated therein; that, had the auditors, Ernst & Ernst, made the examination it reported to Dantzler Lumber & Export Company it had made, the defalcation of Alderman would have been discovered, Alderman would have been discharged and further loss obviated. And it is alleged that by and through the fraud of Ernst & Ernst the Dantzler Lumber & Export Company sustained losses in the approximate sum of $37,755.52 in excess of that occurring prior to the time of the first audit in 1927 when the defalcation should have been discovered and disclosed.

(i) That the Columbia Casualty Company had executed a surety bond in the sum of $10,000, payable to said Dantzler Lumber & Export Company, protecting said Dantzler Lumber & Export Company against loss through embezzlements by certain of its employees, including the said Alderman, and that, in accordance with the terms of its bond, for the making of which it received an annual premium of $75 from Dantzler Lumber & Export Company, it responded to its said liability and paid the full penalty of said bond, to wit, the sum of $10,000, to said Dantzler Lumber & Export Company, whereas, if the said embezzlements had been discovered by said auditors at the end of the year 1927, as the bill charges should have been done if said auditors had exercised due diligence and had not been careless in the performance of their contract, the liability of said Columbia Casualty Company on its bond would have been limited to said sum of $1,670.09, being the total of the embezzlements committed by the said Alderman up to that time.

(j) That, at the time of making payment of the amount of its bond to Dantzler Lumber & Export Company, it notified said Dantzler Lumber & Export Company and said Ernst & Ernst that it made claim against said Ernst & Ernst for reimbursement to it of the loss so sustained by it, and that it would claim to be subrogated to the rights of Dantzler Lumber & Export Company to the extent of the payment so made by it against said Ernst & Ernst, and warned said Dantzler Lumber & Export Company and said Ernst & Ernst against making any settlement between themselves without taking into consideration and providing for reimbursement to said Columbia Casualty Company for its said loss.

(k) The bill further alleges that, disregarding the notices so given, said Dantzler Lumber & Export Company and Ernst & Ernst settled and adjusted the claim which Dantzler Lumber & Export Company made against Ernst & Ernst for a sum of money unknown to Columbia Casualty Company, but that said settlement was made by way of compromise for less than the total claim, and that Dantzler Lumber & Export Company and Ernst & Ernst have refused to disclose to Columbia Casualty Company the nature and terms of said settlement and the amount of money paid in settlement of said claim.

The bill prays that Dantzler Lumber & Export Company and N. L. Dantzler, Jr., be required to make answer to certain interrogatories propounded by the bill, and disclose whether or not settlement of the claim of Dantzler Lumber & Export Company against Ernst & Ernst was made, and, if so, the amount of the settlement. Certain other interrogatories are propounded by the bill which are not of material importance on this appeal.

The bill prayed that Columbia Casualty Company be decreed to be subrogated to the rights and claims of Dantzler Lumber & Export Company against Ernst & Ernst as to all liability of Ernst & Ernst to Dantzler Lumber & Export Company on account of the loss sustained by reason of the alleged neglect of Ernst & Ernst as set forth in the bill to the extent of the loss sustained by Columbia Casualty Company and that the persons constituting the copartnership of Ernst & Ernst be decreed to pay to Columbia Casualty Company such sums as might be found to be due upon an accounting.

The defendants in the court below filed motion to dismiss. The motion was overruled, and appeal was entered.

Appellants have filed their assignments in error, being four in number. The assignments of error present for our determination two questions: First, Did the bill of complaint set forth a statement of facts showing liability of the appellant copartnership Ernst & Ernst to the appellant Dantzler Lumber & Export Company? If that question is answered in the affirmative, the second question is: "Did the bill show a right in the appellee Columbia Casualty Company to subrogate pro tanto to the rights of Dantzler Lumber & Export Company against Ernst & Ernst?" If this question is also answered in the affirmative, then order appealed from should be affirmed.

The allegations of the bill are sufficient to show that the firm of Ernst & Ernst carried on a business in the state of Florida of accounting and auditing; that as such accountants and auditors they undertook to make annual audits of the books and accounts of Dantzler Lumber & Export Company, and in pursuance of such undertaking they made an audit of the books and accounts of that corporation from 1927 until 1930, inclusive. It alleges that a careful and proper audit of the books and accounts would have shown that Alderman embezzled $1,670.09 in 1927, $4,716.62 in 1928, $15,670.70 in 1929, $8,693.20 in 1930, and $8,675 in 1931.

The allegations are sufficient to show that Ernst & Ernst negligently and fraudulently misrepresented the financial condition of the business and the status of the accounts of Dantzler Lumber & Export Company in each and every of the reports of audits made. Public accountants and auditors hold themselves out to be skilled and competent to perform the duties and services which they undertake to perform as accountants and auditors, and they are bound in law to perform such services in an accurate and skillful manner. When auditors and accountants are employed for the purpose of auditing books and accounts they occupy a relation of trust and confidence to their employer based up on the superior knowledge of the business of accounting and auditing possessed by the auditors and accountants.

The bill of complaint presents a case of gross negligence if not of legal fraud on the part of the accountants in the performance of their services. It alleges a loss by reason of such negligence and therefore the right of action ex delicto, notwithstanding the injury complained of might also be ground for action ex contractu. The action here is not for mere nonperformance, but it is based upon an alleged breach of duty to skillfully perform and truly report the condition of accounts, in reporting a condition which did not in truth and in fact exist and the true status of which could and would have been discovered and disclosed by a careful, skillful, and proper audit of the books of account.

In 26 R. C. L. 758, it is said:

"Whenever a negligent breach of a contract is also a violation of a common law duty, an action ex delicto will lie. Accompanying every contract is a common law duty to perform the thing agreed to be done with care, skill, reasonable expediency, and faithfulness, and a negligent failure to observe any of these conditions is a tort, as well as a breach of the contract. If the transaction complained of had its origin in a contract which placed the parties in such a relation that in attempting to perform the promised service the tort was committed, then the breach of the contract is not the gravamen of the suit. The contract in such case is mere inducement, creating the state of things which furnishes the occasion of the tort. And in all such cases the remedy is an action on the case. Based on the principle above indicated, the firmly established rule is that for injuries resulting from the unskilful or otherwise negligent performance of a thing agreed to be done, an action ex delicto will lie, notwithstanding the act complained of would also be ground for an action ex contractu."

In 45 C. J. 1093, it is said:

"In an action ex delicto for negligence in the performance of a contract, the fact of negligence must be alleged as in other cases of negligence, and an allegation only of a breach of a contractual duty is not sufficient, although it describes such breach as negligence. As an element of such allegation facts should be averred to show the contractual relation between the parties and the consequent duty owing by defendant to plaintiff; and, when necessary for this purpose the contract out of which such duty and the consequent negligence arose should be stated, although it is not necessary to allege the terms of the contract in detail."

In *Smith et al.* v. *London Assurance Corporation,* 109 App. Div. 882, 96 N. Y. S. 820, the court held:

"Where public accountants were employed on the express agreement that they should frequently check the defendant's cash account in one branch of its business and verify the items thereon, and they negligently and willfully failed to do so, and on account of such failure its cashier was enabled to embezzle large amounts of money, they were liable for the sums embezzled."

In *Banfield et ux.* v. *Addington et ux.,* 104 Fla. 661, 140 So. 893, 895, we quoted with approval from *Mobile Life Ins. Co.* v. *Randall,* 74 Ala. 170, saying:

"Wherever there is carelessness, recklessness, want of reasonable skill, or the violation or disregard of a duty which the law implies from the conditions or attendant circumstances, and individual injury results therefrom, an action on the case lies in favor of the party injured; and if the transaction had its origin in a contract, which places the parties in such relation as that, in performing or attempting to perform the service promised, the tort or wrong is committed, then the breach of the contract is not the gravamen of the suit. There may be no technical breach of the letter of the contract. The contract, in such case, is mere inducement, and should be so stated in pleading. It induces, causes, creates the conditions or state of things, which furnishes the occasion of the tort. The wrongful act, outside of the letter of the contract, is the gravamen of the complaint; and in all such cases, the remedy is an action on the case."

In that same opinion, we also said:

"The reason for this is the firmly established rule that for injuries resulting from the unskilled or otherwise negligent performance of a thing agreed to be done, an action ex delicto will lie, notwithstanding the injury complained of would also be ground for an action ex contractu. In such cases the distinction made is that the action ex delicto can be maintained where the action is founded on something more than mere nonfeasance in the performance of an alleged contract."

Numerous cases are there cited to support this enunciation which is known as the American Rule, as distinguished from the English Rule which prevails in some jurisdictions.

We therefore answer the first question in the affirmative.

As to the nature and doctrine of subrogation, in 25 R. C. L. 1313, it is said:

"The doctrine of subrogation is generally considered to have been derived, and the term itself borrowed, from the civil law, though some authorities regard the Roman Law as its source. However this may be, it has long been an established branch of equity jurisprudence. It does not owe its origin to statute or custom, but it is a creature of courts of equity, having for its basis the doing of complete and perfect justice between the parties without regard to form. It is a doctrine, therefore, which will be applied or not according to the dictates of equity and good conscience, and considerations of public policy, and will be allowed in all cases where the equities of the case demand it. It rests upon the maxim that no one shall be enriched by another's loss, and may be invoked wherever justice demands its application, in opposition to the technical rules of law which liberate, securities with the extinguishment of the original debt. The right to it depends upon the facts and circumstances of each particular case, and to which must be applied the principles of justice. In the administration of relief by subrogation, it will be found that the jurisdiction of equity rests largely on the prevention of frauds and on relief against mistakes; and the expression of the rule has so nearly covered the field that it may now be said that, wherever a court of equity will relieve against a transaction, it will do so by the remedy of subrogation, if that be the most efficient and complete that can be afforded."

Our court is committed to a liberal application of the rule of equitable subrogation. See *Federal Land Bank* v. *Dekle,* 108 Fla. 555, 148 So. 756, and cases there cited.

In 25 R. C. L. 1316, it is said:

"Subrogation is a consequence which equity jurisprudence attaches to certain conditions. The parties may not have contracted for it either expressly or by legal implication; but if, in the performance of that contract which they did make, certain conditions have resulted which make it necessary for equity to interpose its authority in this respect, it will do so, provided that in so doing it will violate no law and not alter the contract. It is accordingly the universal rule that the right of legal subrogation need not rest upon any formal contract or written agreement, nor does it follow from any fixed law; but it exists on principles of mere equity and benevolence, and is founded on the relationship of the parties."

In the same volume (page 1372), it is said:

"One who has indemnified another in pursuance of his obligations so to do succeeds to, and is entitled to, a cession of all the means of redress held by the party indemnified against the party who has occasioned the loss. Thus the rule is well settled in fire insurance as well as in marine insurance, that the insurer, upon paying to the assured the amount of a loss on the property insured, is subrogated in a corresponding amount to the assured's right of action against any other person responsible for the loss; this right of the insurer against such other person not resting upon any relation of contract or of privity between them, but arising out of the nature of the contract of insurance as a contract of indemnity, derived from the assured alone, and enforceable in his right only."

To like effect is 33 C. J. 43.

In *Chickasaw County Farmers' Mutual Fire Insurance Co.* v. *Weller*, 98 Iowa, 731, 68 N. W. 443, it was held:

"Payment by a fire insurance company of a claim for property destroyed by the negligence of a railroad company, is not voluntary, and may be recovered back, where the insured had previously made a settlement with the railroad company, receiving payment in full, which fact he concealed from the insurance company, although the latter knew that he was making a claim against the railroad company.

"One who has ben paid by a railroad company, the full value of property destroyed by its negligence, cannot recover insurance on such property, as the insurance company would be entitled to be subrogated to the rights of the insured to recover from the railroad company."

In Joyce on Insurance (2d Ed.) vol. 5, p. 5888, § 3544, the writer says:

"If third parties who may be liable to the insured for the loss effect a settlement with the latter and obtain a release from all liability, and this is done with knowledge of the fact that the insurers have already paid to the insured the amount of their liability to him, such settlement and release will in no way affect the insurer's right of subrogation as against such third parties, since the settlement and release will be in fraud of the insurer's rights, and consequently void."

In 14 R. C. L. 1404, it is said:

"On payment of a loss the insurer acquires the right to be subrogated pro tanto to any right of action which the insured may have against any third person whose wrongful act or neglect caused the loss. This right includes the subrogation of the insurer to any cause of action which the insured has against a carrier whose failure of duty caused the loss, as the carrier is primarily and the insurer only secondly liable, and the insurer also is subrogated to the property owner's statutory right of recovery against a railroad company for setting out fire by the operation of its road. Likewise an insurer of internal revenue stamps may recover, in the name of the owner, from the government for their loss. The insurer is subrogated only to such rights as the insured possessed, and the right of the insurer against the wrongdoer may be defeated by the act of the insured, prior to the loss, or even after the loss, in releasing the wrongdoer from any liability or giving him the benefit of any insurance, or by a recovery of the amount of the loss by the insured, unless, in the case of a release after loss, the wrongdoer settles with the insured with full knowledge of the insurer's right of subrogation."

To like effect in Cooley's Briefs on Insurance (2d Ed.) vol. 7, p. 6713.

It therefore appears that the allegations of the bill of complaint are sufficient to constitute the basis for a suit to enforce subrogation.

We have examined and considered the argument and authorities cited in brief for plaintiff in error, but we hold that the authorities herein cited enunciate the law as it is in this jurisdiction, and therefore, we answer the second question also in the affirmative.

The contention is made that the appellants have the right to trial by jury as to the rights of parties. The contention is not tenable for the reason that subrogation is a matter of equitable cognizance, and, aside from this, the bill of complaint seeks discovery of the terms, amount, and condition of the settlement had between the appellants. It was therefore necessary for the appellee to seek its relief in a court of equity. The court of equity, having acquired jurisdiction to determine rights cognizable in equity between the parties, it will reach out and draw unto its consideration and determination the entire subject-matter bringing before it all the parties interested therein and will retain such jurisdiction until all matters involved in litigation between the parties or growing out of and connected with the subject-matter of the suit are fully disposed of. See *Hitchcolk* v. *Mortgage Securities Corporation,* 95 Fla. 147, 116 So. 244, and cases there cited.

In *Norris et ux.* v. *Eikenberry,* 103 Fla. 104, 137 So. 128, 130, we said: "While a court of equity, having once obtained jurisdiction of a cause, will retain it for all purposes and administer complete relief, yet, in order to authorize relief which can be obtained in a suit at law, there must be some substantial ground of equitable jurisdiction both alleged and proven; otherwise, a court of equity will not retain jurisdiction and grant a purely legal remedy."

As we have heretofore indicated, "Subrogation is a consequence which equity jurisprudence attaches to certain conditions. The parties may not have contracted for it either expressly or by legal implication, but if in the performance of that contract which they did make, certain conditions have resulted which make it necessary for equity to interpose its authority in this respect it will do so." It may be said to be the universal rule "that the right to legal subrogation need not rest upon any formal contract or written agreement, nor does it follow from any fixed law, but it exists on principles of mere equity and benevolence and is founded on relationship of the parties." It therefore appears that it was not necessary that there should have been any privity between Columbia Casualty Company and Ernst & Ernst to create the liability of Ernst & Ernst under the principle of equitable subrogation to Columbia Casualty Company. It appears to be also well settled that "the insurer upon paying to the insured the amount of loss, is subrogated in a corresponding amount to the assured's right of action against any other person responsible for the loss." This right of insured against such other person does not rest upon any relation of contract or privity between the insurer and such other person, but it arises out of the nature of the contract of insurance as a contract of indemnity, and, being derived from the contract with the insured alone, it is enforceable in his right only. See 25 R. C. L. p. 1372, and cases there cited. See, also, 33 C. J. 43; also *Chickasaw County Farmers' Mutual Fire Ins. Co.* v. *Weller, supra;* 14 R. C. L. 1404.

Columbia Casualty Company's right to recover rests upon principles of subrogation, and only by the enforcement of its right to subrogation may it recover. The matter of enforcing subrogation is of equitable cognizance.

It therefore appears that, inasmuch as the bill of complaint contains sufficient allegations to show that the complainant in the court below was entitled to an accounting because of funds having been received by

Dantzler Lumber & Export Company from Ernst & Ernst and that the bill of complaint also contains sufficient allegations to show that the insurer has the right to be subrogated pro tanto to any right of action which the insured may have had against Ernst & Ernst, whose alleged wrongful act or negligence caused the loss, the bill is not without equity.

For the reasons stated, the order appealed from should be affirmed. It is so ordered.

Affirmed.

Ellis and Terrell, JJ., concur.

Davis, C. J., and Whitfield, J., concur in part and dissent in part.

Brown, J., dissents.

Davis, Chief Justice (concurring in part; dissenting in part).

There was a general motion to dismiss for want of equity in the bill, which was overruled. Since that motion is the equivalent of a general demurrer and there is equity in the bill, in my opinion, at least to the extent of the discovery sought against Dantzler Lumber & Export Company, I concur in the result which is an affirmance of the order from which this appeal is taken.

But there is no justification in law, as I see it, for holding that, in a case of this kind, the alleged tort-feasor's right to a jury trial of a tort action can be defeated by the fact that the right sought to be enforced by plaintiff is a subrogated right and not the original right. Our own cases so hold. See *Atlantic Coast Line R. Co.* v. *Campbell,* 104 Fla. 274, 139 So. 886. Compare *Royal Indemnity Co.* v. *Knott,* 101 Fla. 1495, 1502, 136 So. 474.

If a tort was committed by the negligent audit of the Dantzler Lumber & Export Company's books by Ernst & Ernst as alleged, it gave rise to a legal right to a tort action by Dantzler Lumber & Export Company against Ernst & Ernst. On that tort action Ernst & Ernst are constitutionally entitled to a jury trial. Their right to a trial by jury ought not to be, on principle, defeated by the fact that Columbia Casualty Company has acquired a right to subrogation under its contract of suretyship entered into with Dantzler Lumber & Export Company, to which contract Ernst & Ernst is not a party. As I see it, Columbia Casualty Company, as the new plaintiff by reason of subrogation, must step into the shoes of Dantzler Lumber & Export Company and must submit its claim to a jury trial just as Dantzler Lumber & Export Company would have had to do had no subrogation taken place.

Can it be said that, where A has a claim against B for damages by reason of tort committed by A against B, B loses his right to a jury trial because C, by reason of the doctrine of subrogation as applied between A and C, has acquired A's claim against B?

My view is that, under the principles stated in *Atlantic Coast Line R. Co.* v. *Campbell,* 104 Fla. 274, 139 So. 886, Columbia Casualty Company is, as a matter of law, a subrogated plaintiff and is entitled to maintain a suit at law against Ernst & Ernst as tort-feasors, to the same extent that Dantzler Lumber & Export Company could have done had no subrogation taken place, but that subrogation in favor of Columbia Casualty Company against Dantzler Lumber & Export Company cannot operate so as to destroy the right to a jury trial which was at all times possessed by Ernst & Ernst as against the subrogated claim.

I concur as to the finding of some equity in the bill, to wit, the right to subrogation and to a discovery by the surety as to material facts relating to its suretyship. I dissent from all other portions of the opinion prepared by Mr. Justice BUFORD.

The rule that a court of equity once having assumed jurisdiction of a cause on any equitable ground will reach out and draw into its consideration and determination the entire subject-matter, bringing before it all the parties interested therein, means no more than that, where there is a distinct equitable controversy and a substantial ground of equitable jurisdiction, a court of equity will render complainant full relief even to the extent of passing upon strictly legal questions and granting strictly legal remedies. It does not mean a bill in equity can bring into a court of equity, as incident to the right to discovery, separate cause of action cognizable in a court of law. *Russell* v. *Clark,* 7 Cranch, 69, 3 L. Ed. 271; *Buzard* v. *Houston,* 119 U. S. 347, 7 S. Ct. 249, 30 L. Ed. 451.

In this case there is no equitable controversy between Columbia Casualty Company and Ernst & Ernst, no privity of contract between them, and no right of discovery from them. The equitable controversy is wholly between Columbia Casualty Company, on the one hand, and Dantzler Lumber & Export Company, on the other. To join in Ernst & Ernst for the purpose of settling an alleged action at law against them to which Columbia Casualty Company has by operation of law become subrogated is not sustained by any authority other than the general rule above cited in the preceding paragraph, and, as will be seen, the general rule does not mean that third parties not in privity to an equitable right can be brought in as an incident to it, and thereby deprived of the right to a trial by jury. *Hitchcolk* v. *Mortgage Securities Corp.,* 95 Fla. 147, 116 So. 244, cited in the majority opinion, in so far as it held to the contrary, has been by this court expressly overruled in a recent decision of this court. See *Norris* v. *Eikenberry,* 103 Fla. 104, 137 So. 128, text page 134, column 1.

I therefore concur in part and dissent in part to the extent indicated.

WHITFIELD, J., concurs.

BROWN, Justice (dissenting).

Although the bill may show a right of action on the part of the Dantzler Company against Ernst & Ernst, either ex contractu for breach of contract or ex delicto for breach of duty arising out of the contract between those parties, I cannot see how the doctrine of subrogation can be resorted to in support of a right of action, either legal or equitable, on behalf of the Columbia Casualty Company against Ernst & Ernst. The contract between Ernst & Ernst and the Dantzler Company was not made for the benefit of the casualty company. Of course, upon payment to the Dantzler Company of the loss occasioned by the embezzlement of its funds by one of its employees, for whose fidelity to his trust the casualty company had executed a surety bond to the Dantzler Company to the extent of the amount named in the policy, the casualty company became subrogated to the extent of such payment to any right of action which the Dantzler Company may have had against the defaulting employee whose faithfulness the casualty company had in effect guaranteed, but this right of subrogation did not extend to any cause of action the Dantzler Company may have had against the firm of accountants whom they had employed for some years to make an annual audit of the company's books. The Dantzler Company was under no obligation to the Columbia Casualty Company to employ Ernst & Ernst or any one else to audit their books. They apparently made this contract for annual auditing for their own benefit. The Columbia Casualty Company was in no way a party to the contract between the Dantzler Company and Ernst & Ernst, nor does it appear that, in writing the surety contract with the Dantzler Company, the casualty company were relying upon or had any knowledge of the fact that the Dantzler Company were employing Ernst & Ernst to make an annual audit of their books. See *Ultramares Corporation* v. *Touche,* 225 N. Y. 170, 174 N. E. 441, 74 A. L. R. 1139. Nor is there any question of conventional subrogation involved in this case.

Cases involving the right of insurance companies to subrogation to the rights of the insured party against tort-feasors causing loss to the insured subject-matter are not in point here, as in those cases the liability of the insurance company is based on the destruction or damage to the subject-matter of the contract, and there is a direct relationship between the subject-matter of the contract and the tort of the third party. But here there is no direct relationship between the contract of suretyship entered into between the casualty company and the Dantzler Company and the contract for auditing services entered into between Dantzler Company and Ernst & Ernst. So far as the casualty company is concerned, its liability and its loss would have been the same if the Dantzler Company had never made a contract with Ernst & Ernst and had never had its books audited. There being no privity of contract nor any duty owed by the auditors to the casualty company, the latter certainly had no right of direct action against such auditors.

Nor is there any showing of a right to equitable or legal subrogation; nor does the writer know of any rule of law under which the casualty company could have compelled the Dantzler Company to prosecute an action for damages against Ernst & Ernst, and so, if the Dantzler Company saw fit to compromise or waive any claim they may have had against the auditors, the casualty company had no right to complain.

See, in this general connection, 25 R. C. L. 1831; *Marianna National Farm Loan Association* v. *Braswell,* 95 Fla. 510, 116, So. 639.

Furthermore, as pointed out by Mr. Chief Justice DAVIS in his opinion herein, the procedure here attempted to be put in motion, even if there was a right of subrogation, would deprive Ernst & Ernst of their right to a trial by jury.

I think, therefore, the order overruling the motion to dismiss the bill should be reversed.

FLAGG v. SENG *

California District Court of Appeal, Fourth District, 1936. 16 Cal. App. 2d 545, 60 P.2d 1004.

BARNARD, Presiding Justice. The California Land Buyers Syndicate was organized in June, 1926, for the purpose of buying real property in San Diego county with the intention of later selling the same at a profit. With the permission of the state corporation department one R. L. Stewart was appointed as the corporation's agent for the sale of stock at a commission of 20 per cent. A large amount of stock was sold, and the

* This case is discussed at p. 25 *supra.*

corporation acquired some thirty-one separate properties. Stewart opened an office for the sale of stock, and the syndicate sublet from him a portion of that space, in which it conducted its business under an arrangement by which it allowed Stewart a certain sum each month to cover certain expenses. The syndicate had its own bookkeepers and other employees, some of whom also worked for Stewart. The directors of the corporation held regular meetings and kept careful minutes. Any purchase of property was made only on the unanimous approval of the directors and after the property had been examined and appraised by each director. All papers in connection with each transaction were kept together, and the directors were familiar with these and with the manner in which the books of account were kept.

The defendants, who were accountants, were employed to open up a set of books and thereafter from time to time to audit the books and report to the directors. Four such audits were made, the first on September 8, 1927, and the last on January 21, 1930. In addition, the defendants took a trial balance at the end of each three months and reported to the directors. These audits and reports all indicated the amount of the surplus at the respective dates as shown by books of the corporation. A number of sales and exchanges of lands were made, all of which were entered on the books in accordance with values fixed by the board of directors. When a parcel was traded in on another property at a figure higher than its cost, the difference was carried on the books as surplus, with the knowledge and approval of the directors. Dividends at 2 per cent. were paid quarterly on the preferred stock from April 19, 1927, to and including June 30, 1929. On November 12, 1929, the syndicate closed its office and ceased operations. An auditor sent by the state corporation department made an examination early in 1930 and found no irregularities in the books and records of the corporation.

As stated by the appellant, he "seeks to recover on behalf of his bankrupt the funds withdrawn from its treasury through the frauds of Stewart; respondents having participated in these frauds are equally liable with Stewart in answering for the loss sustained."

The complaint alleges that the respondents were employed by the syndicate to audit the corporation's books and accounts and submit to the directors annual reports as to the corporation's financial condition and such other reports as might be requested; that the respondents did audit the books of accounts of the corporation and made reports of its financial condition as disclosed by those books and accounts from December, 1926, until November, 1929; that the respondents well knew that Stewart was the manager of said corporation, that he had control of the entire business of said corporation, that all books and records were in his exclusive charge, that all financial transactions were handled by him, and that all audits and reports were required for the purpose of informing the board of directors of the actual condition of the corporation as disclosed by its books and accounts; that the respondents well knew that Stewart was engaged in a stock-selling campaign and that the continued payment of regular quarterly dividends of 2 per cent. was essential to the continuance of this campaign; that the respondents submitted to the directors various audits and reports purporting to show that the corporation then had a surplus available for the payment of dividends; that these audits and reports were false and did not set forth the true condition of the corporation as disclosed by its books and accounts; that the respondents knew that these audits and reports were false and did not set forth the true condition of the corporation; that the board of directors, believing said audits and reports to contain a true and correct statement of the condition of the corporation as disclosed by its books and records, declared and paid various specified dividends; that at no time since its incorporation did the syndicate have any surplus for the payment of dividends; that the respondents knew that the books of the corporation disclosed this fact; that the respondents knew that these reports and audits were submitted to the directors for the purpose of inducing them to declare and pay dividends so that Stewart might continue his stock sales; that the board of directors relied and acted upon the information furnished by the defendants as to the condition of said corporation; and that all payments of dividends were illegal and constituted an impairment of the capital of the corporation.

The defendants answered, denying all of the plaintiff's charges, and setting up several special defenses. After a trial the court found in all respects in favor of the defendants, and this appeal is from the judgment which followed.

The appellant states that his right to recover a judgment herein "depends upon whether or not he has, by a preponderance of the evidence, established that approximately $68,000.00 of his bankrupt's assets have been unlawfully distributed among the Syndicate's preferred stockholders to its prejudice and the prejudice of its creditors, by the frauds and deceptions practiced upon the corporation by its fiscal agent and manager, R. L. Stewart, and those associated with him and that respondents, with guilty knowledge, aided and participated in such frauds and deceptions by suppressing all information in relation thereto while employed by the Syndicate as its auditors and by certifying in their audit reports and statements submitted to Syndicate to the truth and reality of transaction set up by false and fictitious entries in Syndicate's books and records made to conceal and cover the illegal and wrongful acts and conducts of Stewart and his associates." The case was tried on the issue as to whether the defendants knowingly submitted false reports which deceived the directors and which caused them to declare dividends which could not be legally declared.

The court found, among other things, that it was not true that the sole source from which the corporation produced funds for the operation of its business was from the sale of shares of its capital stock; that Stewart had the exclusive right to sell stock for which he was paid a commission of 20 per cent.; that with that exception it was not true that he had control of any of the business affairs of the corporation or that any of the records of the corporation were kept or maintained by him; that the stenographers and bookkeepers when engaged on the business and books of the corporation were the employees of its directors and said books, records, and accounts were at all times kept and maintained by and under the control of the directors; that the directors hired Stewart to see that these accounts and records correctly reflected the transactions had or entered into by the company; that said books, records, and accounts correctly reflected these transactions; that the directors were familiar with these books and knew how the same were being kept and maintained; that the respondents from time to time were employed by the directors to make, and did make, to them audit reports, trial balances, and statements reflecting the financial condition of the corporation as shown by its books and records; that the various audits and reports made by the respondents were neither false nor fraudulently prepared, and that each of the same correctly set forth the true condition of said Corporation at the time the same was made; that it was not true that the corporation did not have a surplus at any time but that the corporation did have a surplus as shown by its books of account on the dates and in the amounts set forth in the various audits and reports; that the directors were familiar with the books and with the condition of the corporation and in ordering the various dividends to be paid did not rely upon the reports and audits submitted by the respondents; that it was not true that the respondents or any of them knew that any of the reports or audits was made or submitted for the purpose of inducing the directors to declare or to pay dividends so that Stewart might proceed with his stock sale, or for the purpose of inducing any one to do anything whatsoever for any purpose; that it was not true that any of the dividends paid were illegally declared, or that by reason of any such payments the corporation has had its capital investment impaired, or that by reason thereof it became, or now is, insolvent; that none of the letters, audits, reports, or statements prepared by the respondents or submitted to the directors was false or fraudulent, and that none thereof was made, prepared or submitted for any purpose except in good faith to furnish the directors, in compliance with the terms of their employment, with true and correct reports of the financial condition of the corporation for the period covered therein as shown by the books, accounts, and records of the corporation; and that all of said audits and reports were faithfully and diligently made.

The transcript and the briefs are voluminous, and it is a little difficult to follow the appellant's contentions. Disregarding immaterial matters, the gist of appellant's case is that Stewart, rather than the directors, was in actual control and direction of the business of the corporation; that Stewart sold stock in an illegal manner, claimed a fictitious profit on unsold real estate, and deceived the directors by manipulating the books; that the respondents assisted Stewart in this deception by suppressing information and by falsely reporting the condition of the corporation; that this was intentionally and knowingly done; that the directors, relying on these reports and being deceived thereby, declared dividends which were not warranted by the condition of the corporation; that the corporation was damaged; and that the respondents are liable therefor. The court found that Stewart was not in charge of the business of the corporation or of its books; that its transactions and business were conducted by the directors; that the directors were familiar with the books and the manner in which they were kept and with the facts in connection with each of the transactions; that the audits and reports were correctly made; and that the directors were not deceived by any of these reports and audits. These findings are fully sustained by the evidence, and the appellant has failed to establish the facts which he admitted throughout the trial were essential to his recovery. Most of these findings and other material findings are not directly attacked, and the contention seems to be that the court should have drawn different conclusions. It is argued, however, that some of the findings are not supported by the evidence because, while the audits and reports correctly reflected the condition of the corporation as shown by its books, the respondents could have discovered through further investigation that the books did not show the actual situation, that stock was being sold in an illegal manner, and that profits supposedly accruing from the sales of real property were in fact nonexistent.

Several of these contentions relate to the theory of bookkeeping and accounting, and involve the question as to whether certain items were properly carried on the books as assets. All of the expert witnesses called by the respondents testified against the appellant's contentions in this regard, and this testimony was confirmed, at least in part, by the appellant's own experts. Conceding that any conflict here appears, the court's findings are sustained by a part, and apparently by a preponderance, of the evidence.

Appellant's main contention seems to be that stock in the corporation was exchanged for real estate in violation of the permit issued by the state corporation department, and that, when a parcel of real estate was exchanged for other property at a price in excess of its original cost, the difference was entered on the books as a profit before the second piece was sold. The matter last referred to represents an established policy on the part of the directors, the books were thus kept on their order, and they were in no way deceived by anything done by the respondents in this connection. With respect to the other matter it appears that stock was, in effect, exchanged for real property. This was done by putting through escrows whereby the corporation's check was given in payment for the land and the other party's check was given in payment for the stock. While there is some evidence that certain papers in the files of the corporation indicated the true situation, although the same was not indicated by the books of the corporation, there is other evidence to the effect that this could not be learned from an examination of the books and records of the corporation, that it was unknown to the respondents except in one instance, and that in that case the respondents took the matter up with the attorney for the corporation who assured them that the matter was perfectly legal. It further appears that whatever illegality existed and whatever harm arose therefrom was caused directly by the action of the board of directors, and that all such exchanges were made with their full knowledge and consent and in accordance with their fixed policy, and no inference could be drawn that anything done by the respondents had any casual relation to any part of this situation.

Not only are the findings sustained by the evidence, but we are unable to see how the matters particularly relied upon by the appellant can justify or compel any other conclusions than those drawn by the court. Conceding that certain sales of stock were illegally made, this was not only well known to the directors, but was intentionally done by them. They were not only not deceived by the audits and reports, but they had intentionally handled the transactions in such a manner as to make them appear on the books as a cash transaction. While the court found upon sufficient evidence that the respondents had no knowledge of those parts of those transactions which had been thus covered up, and conceding, for the sake of argument, that the respondents might have found out the true situation by a more extensive investigation, it in no way appears that any discovery they might have made would have affected the result. The method pursued by the directors was followed on the advice of their attorneys, and, although the same has since been declared illegal, no such blame can be attached to the respondents, under the circumstances here appearing, as would justify a reversal of the judgment.

Some contention is made that the trial court committed prejudicial error in limiting the appellant's cross-examination of a certain witness. The cross-examination of this witness takes up more than a thousand pages of the transcript, and it abundantly appears therefrom that the court did not abuse its discretion in this regard.

The judgment is affirmed.

FIDELITY & DEPOSIT CO. OF MARYLAND v. ATHERTON *

Supreme Court of New Mexico. 47 N. M. 443, 144 P.2d 157.

Brice, Justice. The questions are: (1) Whether the appellant (plaintiff below), who as surety upon the official bond of the treasurer of Bernalillo County, paid the shortage of a defaulting deputy county treasurer, is subrogated to the county's rights and remedies (if any) against the appellees Horton & Bixler (hereafter referred to as appellees), whose negligence as public accountants (it is charged) was the proximate cause of the loss: and (2) should appellees be required to pay appellant, whose loss has been partially paid and the balance well secured, by the county treasurer who is the principal debtor?

The appellees demurred to appellant's complaint, asserting that it did not state a cause of action. The demurrer was overruled and thereafter appellee answered. This action of the court is assigned as error, but we are of the opinion that the trial court did not err in overruling the demurrer. Our reasons therefor will sufficiently appear from a determination of the merits of the case.

The facts as found by the trial court, material to a decision, are as follows:

The appellees, a co-partnership, are certified public accountants. They entered into a written contract with Bernalillo County, wherein they agreed for considerations named, to conduct a continuous audit of the books and records of account of Bernalillo County and to act as consulting accountants for the period from July 1, 1936, to and including June 30, 1937; to furnish to the appellee Board of County Commissioners (hereafter called the Board), upon demand, a certified statement of cash receipts and disbursements of the county treasurer from July 1, 1936 to and including June 30, 1937; to prepare typewritten reports of a final audit for the period ending June 30, 1937; to meet with the Board at least once a month and furnish it the balances to the credit of the various funds over which the Board had control and against which it could draw warrants; to place accountants on the assignment who were skilled and experienced in municipal accounting; to make audits in conformity with existing laws, and render reports as required by the Board, and—"Party of the Second Part agrees to furnish evidence to the Board of County Commissioners and to file evidence with the County Clerk, indicating that the County will be protected for the faithful performance of the terms of this agreement, and also protected against defalcations or other misdeeds of employees of Party of the Second Part, such evidence being a blanket accountant's Liability Policy of $60,000.00—34682-K American

---

* This case is discussed at p. 27 *supra*.

Surety Company of New York, protecting all clients of Party of the Second Part. This above Policy expires June 1, 1937."

This contract was extended by agreement of the parties to June 30, 1938. During the existence of this contract David J. Armijo was the county treasurer of Bernalillo County and the appellant surety on his official bond, payable to the State of New Mexico and conditioned that he would well and faithfully perform his duties as county treasurer; that he would render true accounts of his office and pay over all monies that might come into his hands by virtue of his office to the persons authorized to receive the same by law, and carefully keep and preserve all books and papers and other property pertaining to his office and deliver them to his successor.

Virgil G. Webster was deputy county treasurer, and he as principal, and the appellant as his surety, executed a bond for $10,000 payable to the State of New Mexico, conditioned substantially as that of the treasurer's bond. This bond was not required by law, and was executed for the protection of the county treasurer as against his deputy.

From the period of July 1, 1937, to January 22, 1938, deputy county treasurer Webster embezzled from the treasurer's office funds aggregating $21,611.57. The appellant paid to county treasurer Armijo $10,000 as surety on his deputy's bond, which sum of money was delivered back to it, and appellant thereupon paid to the county of Bernalillo the total amount of the defalcation.

After endorsing to appellant the $10,000 check received from it, treasurer Armijo executed and delivered to appellant his promissory note in the principal sum of $11,611.57 (the balance due the County by treasurer Armijo) secured by a mortgage on certain real estate, the value of which is ample security for the payment of the note, and much in excess of the principal sum thereof. Thereafter treasurer Armijo paid to appellant on that note sums aggregating $3,393.43. No effort has been made by appellant to enforce collection of this indebtedness, although long past due.

The duties of the treasurer of Bernalillo County required him to and he did collect monies for payment of taxes upon real and personal property in said county as well as to collect and receive other monies due said county.

In the collection of tax monies by the county treasurer of Bernalillo County, at all times material, the method and procedure used was as follow: Upon receipt of the tax rolls from the county assessor, the county treasurer prepared a form of tax receipt in triplicate, in white, blue and pink, for each taxpayer shown on the tax rolls. These receipts were numbered consecutively and bound in books each containing one hundred receipts, not dated or signed by the treasurer at the time of their preparation. The blue and pink sheets were carbon impressions of the white sheet made at the same time as the white sheet was typed. The white and blue receipts were perforated, permitting them to be torn out of the tax receipt book. When taxes were paid the receipts were signed in triplicate by the treasurer or his employee and the date of payment was inserted. The white receipt was then delivered to the taxpayer, the blue receipt was removed from the receipt book and retained by the treasurer. The pink receipt was not perforated for tearing out of the bound book, and it remained in the receipt book after the taxes were paid. It was a permanent record of the cash received.

Appellees each month sent their employee to the County Treasurer's office to audit the books and records of account of the treasurer, and to prepare data for quarterly and annual audit reports, required to be made under the auditing contract. They compared the blue receipts and the adding machine tapes which then remained in the treasurer's office with the entries in the tax cash record and the tax cash journal; totaled the amounts in the tax cash record and the tax cash journal and checked the distributions to the various funds in the tax cash journal.

The pink receipts were permanently bound records of the treasurer's office containing a record of the actual cash received by the treasurer from taxes.

The tax cash record book and the tax cash journal kept during 1937 did not contain any details showing the name of the taxpayer who paid taxes, the number of the receipt issued to the taxpayer, or the amount of money for which each receipt was issued, but only the total sum received daily as shown by the entries purporting to have been made by the bookkeeper from the blue receipts which ostensibly remained available in the treasurer's office. The books did not contain entries showing any money received upon blue receipts which had been lost or destroyed.

Appellees did not test check any of the pink receipts by comparing them with the available blue receipts or the tax cash record or the tax cash journal, or the tax roll at any time prior to January 1, 1938, to determine whether or not all cash received by the country treasurer for which tax receipts were issued and for which pink receipts remained had been accounted for in the tax cash record and the tax cash journal, and did not at any time during 1937 check the pink receipts in the bound volume against the blue receipts available in the treasurer's office or against the tax rolls, or against the tax cash record or against the tax cash journal.

Between January 1, 1937, and January 22, 1938, during which time the audit contract was in force, deputy treasurer Webster embezzled from monies collected for taxes $21,176.20, and $435.28 from other monies received in the treasurer's office. To cover this defalcation Webster destroyed the blue receipts equal in amount to the funds embezzled, and made new adding machine tapes to correspond with the amount received less the amount embezzled. As the amounts evidenced by the blue receipts destroyed were not entered in the cash record or the tax cash journal, the amounts of the retained receipts corresponded with those evidenced by these records and the adding machine tape.

Appellees did not check the pink receipts nor begin the special investigation agreed upon, in September, 1937, at any time during 1937, but commenced work thereunder on January 1, 1938, to ascertain if there was any shortage in the treasurer's office.

The trial court concluded that appellees were not negligent in the performance of their contract with the County of Bernalillo; and they "did not cause, or contribute to the cause of, any loss sustained by the plaintiff."

The appellees assert that the complaint does not state a cause of action; that as the State of New Mexico is the obligee named in the bond, it is an indispensable party to the action; that as there was no privity of contract between appellees and appellant it could not be subrogated to the rights and remedies (if any) of the county of Bernalillo; that mere actionable negligence resulting from the breach of a contract creates no right to subrogation in favor of one who is neither a party nor a privy to the contract. These questions for the purpose of this suit only will be resolved in favor of the appellant. The writer is of the opinion that these assumptions are legally correct, but this is not necessarily the view of any other members of the court, and the questions are not decided.

Subrogation is not necessarily founded upon contract. *Crippen* v. *Chappel,* 35 Kan. 495, 11 P. 453 Am. Rep. 187; *Fourth Nat. Bank* v. *Board of Com'rs of Craig County,* 186 Okl. 102, 95 P.2d 878. It is an equitable remedy of civil law origin whereby through a supposed succession to the legal rights of another, a loss is put ultimately on that one who in equity and good conscience should pay. *American Surety Co. of New York* v. *Robinson,* 5 Cir., 53 F.2d 22, 23; *Northern Trust Co.* v. *Consolidated Elevator Co.,* 142 Minn. 132, 171 N.W. 265, 4 A.L.R. 510. It is a remedy for the benefit of one secondarily liable, who has paid the debt of another and to whom in equity and good conscience should be assigned the rights and remedies of the original creditor, *Andrew* v. *Bevington Sav. Bank,* 206 Iowa 869, 221 N.W. 668.

Treasurer Armijo was primarily liable to the county for his deputy's defalcation. He paid $10,000 which was paid to him by appellant as surety on his unfaithful deputy's official bond. True, the appellant's check to Armijo was endorsed by him, returned to appellant and delivered to the county; but it was Armijo's money and he, not appellant, paid the county the $10,000. The balance of $11,611.57 was paid to the county by appellant, of which amount Armijo has repaid $3,393.43, and appellant has accepted Armijo's note secured by a mortgage on property the value of which is much in excess of the debt, which, though long past due, appellant has made no effort to collect.

If, in equity and good conscience, the appellees, under any circumstances, should pay this debt (a question we do not decide), they should not be required to do so under the facts stated. The appellant has refused to enforce collection of the amount due it from the treasurer Armijo, who is primarily liable therefor, and the collection of which could be enforced if not paid upon demand.

We do not hold that a surety who has paid his principal's obligation is not ordinarily entitled to be subrogated to all rights and remedies of the insured, including those based upon ordinary negligence; we do not decide the question; but see *United States F. & G. Co.* v. *Citizens' Nat. Bank,* D.C., N.M., 13 F.2d 213; *Dantzler Lumber & Export Co.* v. *Columbia Casualty Co.,* 115 Fla. 541, 156 So. 116, 95 A. L. R. 258; *Maryland Casualty Co. v. Cook,* D. C., Mich., 35 F.Supp. 160; *Fourth Nat. Bank* v. *Board of Com'rs,* 186 Okl. 102, 95 P.2d 878; *Martin* v. *Federal Surety Co.,* 8 Cir., 58 F.2d 79. We do hold that where, as in this case, the surety has been paid approximately two-thirds of its outlay by the principal debtor, and has accepted for the balance its principal's note, so well secured that there can be no question of ultimate payment, which it refuses to enforce, it would be inequitable to require a third person to pay it.

No general rule can be laid down which will afford a test in every case in which subrogation is sought. The underlying principle is that the right flows from principles of justice and equity. Every case depends upon its particular facts, and we can see no reason in equity or justice to require a third person to pay this particular debt with such a background of facts. *Richardson* v. *American Surety Co.,* 97 Okl. 264, 223 P. 389; *American Surety Co.* v. *Citizens' Nat. Bank of Roswell,* D.C., N.M., 294 F. 609.

The appellees owed to the board of county commissioners a legal duty to make their reports without fraud, and a contractual duty to make them, under the terms of their contract, with the care and caution required of experts. They likewise owed a duty to third persons, if any, to whom they knew, or reasonably should have known, their employer intended to exhibit their reports, and upon which they might act to their injury, to make such reports without fraud. But there is no finding that appellees made a fraudulent report, or of a reliance upon appellees' report by either the appellant or Armijo, nor, of course, that they, or either of them, was injured by such reliance, so as to bring the case within the doctrine of *Ultramares Corp.* v. *Touche,* 255 N.Y. 170, 174 N.E. 441, 74 A.L.R. 1139.

We are entirely satisfied that appellant could have collected from Armijo the balance due it, without the necessity of a suit, and certainly with much less trouble and expense than it has incurred in this proceeding against appellees. Its negligence in failing or refusing to collect from Armijo does not appeal to this court as a reason for requiring third persons to pay the debt.

It should be stated in behalf of the appellees that the trial court found that they performed their contract; that they were not negligent, and that no act or default of theirs caused or contributed to the loss of the county's funds.

The decree of the district court should be affirmed, and it is so ordered.

DEFALCATION IN RELATION TO AUDIT, INTERNAL CONTROL AND FIDELITY BONDS *

By John L. Carey, Executive Director of the American Institute of Accountants

Losses running into millions of dollars are suffered each year by American business through defalcation by employees, of which only a small percentage are covered by fidelity bonds. Every businessman naturally trusts his own employees or he would not continue to employ them. He often enjoys an unwarranted sense of security, which is shattered when a theft occurs. Then he locks the stable door after the horse has been stolen by taking precautionary measures that should have been taken long before.

Studies have shown that most defaulters are not habitual criminals, or even fundamentally dishonest. They often begin by "borrowing" company money to meet financial emergencies. Then if they find it easy to continue without discovery, they cannot resist the temptation.

Employers are sometimes to blame for permitting strong temptation to dishonesty to confront their employees.

There are three major preventives of losses through defalcation. They are internal control, audits, and fidelity bonds. A book could be written about each of them. The purpose of this discussion is only to emphasize the fact that the most economical and effective defense against defalcations requires an integration of the three major preventives.

Internal Control: The best defense against defalcation is an adequate

---

* Published in 83 Journal of Accountancy 353 (1947) and 15 The Controller 127 (1947).

system of internal control, which basically is simply a division of duties among employees in such a manner that no one person alone should be able to defraud the company without early detection. Independent auditors review their clients' systems of internal control in the course of their audits, and they often make recommendations to a client as to how his system could be strengthened. These recommendations are often placed in the file for future reference and then forgotten. The busy executive has many other things to do. But it would be good business in every instance to carry out the recommendations of the accountants for strengthening the system. It is the cheapest and most effective way of minimizing losses.

Audits: Audits by independent public accountants are sometimes assumed to be a satisfactory defense against defalcations. This is not a wholly valid assumption. Today the primary purpose of most audits of business of any size is to provide an expert, independent opinion on the financial position and results of operations of the company concerned. The usual audit is based on testing and sampling procedures which may incidentally, but will not necessarily, disclose defalcations. Unless there has been collusion between several of the principal executives, an independent audit should disclose theft of amounts having a material effect on the reported financial position or earnings. The accounting profession has stated publicly again and again that the customary type of audit (financial examination) cannot be expected to catch minor irregularities, and that the auditor cannot take responsibility for detecting them, although the deterrent effect of audits may minimize frauds.

It is possible to make detailed audits that would give reasonable assurance of the detection of even minor irregularities (though it would not necessarily prevent them, unless such audits were made at frequent intervals throughout the year), but such detailed audits would be so expensive that the game would not be worth the candle. The cost of such detailed auditing in companies of any size might be greater than probable losses through defalcation.

Fidelity Bonds: Even a good system of internal control, however, does not always prevent collusive fraud. If two or more employees conspire to defraud the employer they may be successful for some time without discovery. Again, many companies are too small to be able to afford an internal accounting staff of a size which would permit the installation of a satisfactory system of internal control. Accountants generally recommend, as a matter of broad policy, that fidelity bonds be taken out on all employees who have positions of any importance from the viewpoint of fraud prevention. At the present time most accountants believe that fidelity bond coverage in many companies is inadequate in relation to risks involved, and recommend extension of such coverage. Adequate coverage not only assures recovery of losses from discovered defalcations, but it has a preventive effect, in that the underwriters usually investigate the past records of bonded employees, and employees may sometimes be deterred from theft by the thought that they might be prosecuted by the surety company, no matter how merciful their boss might be.

One complication has occurred in recent years that the accounting profession has been attempting, with some success, to resolve. Some surety companies, under their rights of subrogation, have asserted claims against independent public accountants on the ground that all or a part of the loss insured by the company under a fidelity bond would not have occurred if the independent public accountant had not failed to make early discovery of the defalcation.

Auditor's Responsibility

If an independent public accountant should be guilty of an affirmatively dishonest act or wilful failure to follow accepted audit procedures, he should be held responsible. This, however, is quite a different thing from holding him financially responsible for not discovering defalcations which generally accepted auditing procedures are not expected to disclose.

Unless an independent auditor has reasonable confidence that he will not be held responsible by the surety company concerned for failure to detect defalcations (except in case of gross negligence or dishonesty) he may feel it necessary to protect himself by extending the scope of detailed auditing. This would substantially increase the audit fee. The client might decide that he was paying twice for the same protection. He might dispense with the audit, or drop fidelity coverage, or transfer the bond to a surety company which will provide the auditor with the reasonable assurance that will permit him to confine his work to the scope necessary for certification of the financial statements.

Surety companies generally have recognized the position of the accounting profession. In December, 1945, twenty-three of the companies issuing fidelity bonds signed a form of letter to the American Institute of Accountants under which they have agreed that they will not assert claims against accountants in any cases not involving affirmatively dishonest or criminal acts or gross negligence on the part of accountants, and that claims shall in no case be asserted except after a hearing of the matter by an impartial committee of three persons who are not accountants. If this committee concludes that such a case does not involve affirmatively dishonest or criminal acts or gross negligence, then the companies have agreed that they will not assert claims against the accountants. If the committee reaches a contrary conclusion, then the surety company quite properly may assert its claim. In the past year, eleven additional surety companies have signed similar letters, bringing the total number to thirty-four.

It is hoped that other surety companies will participate in this general agreement which, it is belived, will help greatly to avoid unnecessary increase in the cost of audits, to encourage adequate fidelity bond coverage, and to bring about better integration of audit, internal control, and fidelity bonds as a defense against defalcation.

SECTION 3

LIABILITY TO THIRD PARTIES AT COMMON LAW

LANDELL v. LYBRAND *

Supreme Court of Pennsylvania, 1919. 264 Pa. 406, 107 Atl. 783.

PER CURIAM. Appellees, defendants below, are certified public accountants, and, as such, audited the books and accounts of the Employers' Indemnity Company for the year 1911. The appellant, plaintiff below, averred in his statement of claim that he had been induced to buy 11 shares of the capital stock of that company, at the price of $200 per share, on the strength of the report made by the appellees as to its assets and liabilities at the close of the year 1911; the report having been shown to him by some one who suggested that he purchase the stock. A further averment was that the report was false and untrue, that the stock purchased by him on the strength of it is valueless, and for the loss he sustained he averred the defendants were liable. To enforce this liability an action in trespass was brought against them. In their affidavit of defense they averred that the statement of claim disclose no cause of action, and asked that this be disposed of by the court below as a matter of law, under the provisions of section 20 of the Practice Act of May 14, 1915 (P. L. 483). It was so disposed of by the court below in entering judgment for the defendants.

There were no contractual relations between the plaintiff and defendants, and, if there is any liability from them to him, it must arise out of some breach of duty, for there is no averment that they made the report with intent to deceive him. The averment in the statement of claim is that the defendants were careless and negligent in making their report; but the plaintiff was a stranger to them and to it, and, as no duty rested upon them to him, they cannot be guilty of any negligence of which he can complain. *Schiffer* v. *Sauer Co.* et al., 238 Pa. 550, 86 Atl. 479. This was the correct view of the court below, and the judgment is accordingly affirmed.

ULTRAMARES CORP. v. TOUCHE **

Appellate Division of the Supreme Court of New York, First Department, 1930. 229 App. Div. 581, 243 N. Y. Supp. 179, rev'd, 255 N. Y. 170, 174 N. E. 441 (1931).

MCAVOY, J. The defendants, public accountants, have been held liable to the plaintiff, to whom they owed no contractual duty through any con-

* This case is discussed at p. 29 *supra*.

** This case is discussed at p. 30 ff. *supra*.

tract of employment which the plaintiff intrusted to them. Whether a duty arises here, in the absence of direct contractual relation, out of the situation shown by the evidence, is the problem for solution.

The general principle involved, and upon which plaintiff relies for imposition of liability, is that if one undertakes to discharge any duty by which the conduct of others may be governed, he is bound to perform it in such a manner that those who are thus led to action in the faith that such duty will be properly performed shall not suffer loss through improper performance of the duty or neglect in its execution. Thus in *Glanzer* v. *Shepard* (233 N. Y. 236) we have the buyers of merchandise given recovery against public weighers who were to make return of the weight and to furnish buyers with a copy. The public weighers certified the weight and the buyers paid the sellers on that basis. Discovery that the weight had been incorrectly certified as a result of defendants' negligence was found to give the plaintiffs the right to the resulting damage.

It was decided there that the use of the certificates was not an indirect or collateral consequence of the action of the weighers; and "it was a consequence which, to the weighers' knowledge, was the end and aim of the transaction." The sellers ordered, but the buyers were to use the certificates. Public weighers hold themselves out to the public as "skilled and careful in their calling." (*Glanzer* v. *Shepard, supra,* 238.)

The duty there was held not be found in terms of contract, nor of privity; although arising from contract, its origin is not exclusive from that realm. If the contract and the relation are found, the duty follows by rule of law. Diligence—it was pointed out—was owing not only to the person who ordered the employment, but also to those who relied thereon.

Plaintiff here is in the business of factoring. The defendants were engaged by Fred Stern & Co., Inc., to audit its books and accounts and certify a balance sheet as of the end of the year 1923. They prepared a balance sheet and attached it to a certificate signed by them, which they dated February 26, 1924. This balance sheet stated that Fred Stern & Co., Inc., had a net worth amounting to $1,070, 715.26, when the fact (as thereafter found) was that at the very time of this certification the firm was insolvent, with impairment of thousands of dollars in its assets and credit and much enhancement of its reported liabilities.

The finding of the jury would justify a conclusion that defendants were guilty of a gross degree of negligence in their audit, and it is even urged that the evidence also warranted the finding that the balance sheet was made up in fraud of the rights and obligations which accountants, engaged in public calling, would owe to those to whom they had reason to believe such balance sheets would be exhibited for purposes of obtaining loans, extending credit, or to induce the sale of merchandise.

The evidence showed that these accountants knew for four years that their client (Fred Stern & Co., Inc.) was a borrower from banks in large sums; that these banks required certified balance sheets as a basis for making loans; and that Fred Stern & Co., Inc., would require these certified balance sheets for continuing existing loans and securing new loans. So that this might be done, some thirty-two original counterparts of the certified balance sheet were requested by the client, Fred Stern & Co., Inc., and furnished by the accountants (defendants).

The jury's verdict thus imports that defendants knew that the certified balance sheets would be used by Fred Stern & Co., Inc., for the purpose of procuring loans, and that the very purpose of employment in the transaction between Fred Stern & Co., Inc., and Touche, Niven & Co., the accountants, was to allow Fred Stern & Co., Inc., to bring it about through these balance sheets, the result that loans on the faith thereof would be made by persons who would be governed by its declarations. Financial statements in the course of trade have come to be used customarily for the purpose of securing credit, and accountants indicate in their public advertisements that makers of loans should require the safeguard of an independent audit prepared by public accountants, so a corelative obligation is placed upon them. It is their duty—if they do not wish their audit to be so used—to qualify the statement of their balance sheet and the certificate which accompanies it in such a way as to prevent its use. One cannot issue an unqualified statement which will be so used, and then disclaim responsibility for his work.

Banks and merchants, to the knowledge of these defendants, require certified balance sheets from independent accountants, and upon these audits they make their loans. Thus, the duty arises to these banks and merchants of an exercise of reasonable care in the making and uttering of certified balance sheets.

The facts here are brought within the rule in the case of *International Products Co.* v. *Erie R. R. Co.* (244 N. Y. 331) that "there must be knowledge, or its equivalent, that the information is desired for a serious purpose; that he to whom it is given intends to rely and act upon it; that if false or erroneous he will, because of it, be injured in person or property. * * * The relationship of the parties, arising out of contract or otherwise, must be such that in morals and good conscience the one has the right to rely upon the other for information, and the other giving the information owes a duty to give it with care."

The certificate which these accountants attached to the balance sheet reads:

"TOUCHE, NIVEN & CO.,
"Public Accountants,
"Eighty Maiden Lane,
"New York

February 26, 1924.

"CERTIFICATE OF AUDITORS.

"We have examined the accounts of Fred Stern & Co., Inc., for the year ended December 31, 1923, and hereby certify that the annexed balance sheet is in accordance therewith and with the information and explanations given us. We further certify that, subject to provision for Federal taxes on income, the said statement in our opinion, presents a true and correct view of the financial condition of Fred Stern & Co., Inc., as at December 31, 1923.

"TOUCHE, NIVEN & CO.,
"Public Accountants."

From the certificate and the findings made by the jury which are entitled to be held conclusive in behalf of the plaintiff there is established: That the defendants knew that the result of the audit would be used by Fred Stern & Co., Inc., to represent its financial condition to persons from whom Fred Stern & Co., Inc., might seek to borrow money, and that the balance sheet would be relied upon by such persons as indicating the true financial condition of Fred Stern & Co., Inc.; that defendants, in exercising their public calling as auditors, did not exercise that care and skill required of them, but acted in a negligent and careless manner, as a consequence of which the balance sheet made by them was incorrect, and that such negligence was the proximate cause of the loss sustained by plaintiff, *i. e.,* that there was a causal relation between the neglect and the loss sustained which could reasonably have been anticipated, and that the presentation of the balance sheets, as certified by defendants, was the inducing cause for making these loans to Fred Stern & Co., Inc., which plaintiff made, and that the loss was not caused by reason of any change in the financial condition of Fred Stern & Co., Inc., from the time of the presentation of the audit to the plaintiff, or because of any reliance of plaintiff on other intervening causes; and that plaintiff's conduct was free from contributory negligence, and we, therefore, conclude that a liability was properly found, arising out of a duty owed by the defendants to plaintiff not to misrepresent, willfully or negligently, the financial condition of Fred Stern & Co., Inc., and that the judgment for the plaintiff was correct and should not have been set aside.

That the particular person who was to be influenced by defendants' act was unknown to the defendants is not material to a right to recovery, for it is not necessary that there should be an intent to defraud any particular person. In this case there was no mere casual representation made as a matter of courtesy; there was a certificate intended to sway conduct. There was "the careless performance of a service * * * which happens to have found in the words of a certificate its culmination and its summary." (*Glanzer* v. *Shepard, supra,* 241.) Here is an act performed carelessly, intended to influence the actions of third parties, and one that reasonably might be expected, when carelessly performed, to cause substantial loss.

A duty exists towards those whom the accountants know will act on the faith of their certificates. The loss occurring here was the very result which reasonably was to be anticipated if the balance sheet was carelessly prepared.

While negligence was established and was the proximate cause of the loss, and, as we have seen, the duty arose out of this situation which, while not contractual, was, nevertheless, a ground of liability, yet we do not think that there was sufficient proof upon which to found a liability in fraud. We think that there was no error at the close of the entire case, in the court's decision to dismiss the second cause of action based upon that ground. Misjudgment, however gross, or want of caution, however marked, is not fraud. The mere breach of duty, or the omission to use due care is not fraud. Intentional fraud, as distinguished from a mere breach of duty or the omission to use due care, is an essential factor in an action for deceit. (*Kountze* v. *Kennedy,* 147 N. Y. 124.)

We think that there was a proper conclusion with respect to damages. The amount of cash loans made to Fred Stern & Co., Inc., with interest thereon, credited with all moneys repaid or collected by plaintiff, whether through voluntary action or suit, without deduction of costs of collection, was the approximate damage, and while other proof of damage was excluded by the trial court, no appeal has been taken by plaintiff which raises a construction of that rule.

The judgment and order appealed from should, therefore, be modified by reversing so much thereof as sets aside the verdict and dismisses the amended complaint as to the first cause of action, and by directing that the verdict be reinstated and judgment entered thereon, with costs to the plaintiff, and as so modified affirmed without costs.

DOWLING, P. J., and O'MALLEY, J., concur; FINCH and MARTIN, JJ., dissent.

FINCH, J. (dissenting). Assuming that the defendants may be held liable for the negligence of their employees where they undertake a duty to a definite plaintiff (*Glanzer* v. *Shepard,* 233 N. Y. 236), or to a definite class (*Doyle* v. *Chatham & Phenix Nat. Bank,* 253 N. Y. 369), yet, for the following reasons the defendants are not liable to this plaintiff: *First,* because they undertook to make only a "balance sheet audit" at the request of their client; *second,* because in their certificate the defendants purported only to furnish their opinion based upon an examination in connection with " the information and explanations given us." But even more important, the defendants furnished such a report and certificate without reference to any particular person or class of persons.

The plaintiff seeks to liken the facts in the case at bar to a case where the defendants were to make an audit which to their knowledge was for a definite plaintiff, to induce such plaintiff to make loans thereon. (*Glanzer* v. *Shepard, supra.*) This record does not sustain such a contention. The courts have not gone to the length of holding that defendants in a case like the case at bar can be held liable in negligence to the whole world, or, as has been aptly said, liable for "negligence in the air."

In other words, not only the purpose for which the statement is to be used, but the person or class of persons who is to rely thereon, must be definite to the knowledge of the defendants. The plaintiff relies upon the stipulation in the record that the defendants "knew generally that these reports would be used as financial statements to banks or to creditors or to stockholders or to purchasers or sellers." In accordance with the authorities, this general knowledge is not sufficient.

As Judge ANDREWS said in *International Products Co.* v. *Erie R. R. Co.* (244 N. Y. 331), speaking of the information given, "that he to whom it is given intends to rely and act upon it; that if false or erroneous he will because of it be injured in person or property." In *Courteen Seed Co.* v. *Hong Kong & S. B. Corp.* (245 N. Y. 377) Judge POUND writes: "It [the defendant] did not deal with appellant, had no relations with it and was under no duty of care to it." (See, also, *Savings Bank* v. *Ward,* 100 U. S. 195.)

The professional man, be he accountant or otherwise, certifies for his client and not for all the world. If the client makes it clear to such a man that the statement is to be used in a particular transaction in which a third party is involved, such circumstance should create a duty from the professional man to such third party. If the accountant is to be held to an unlimited liability to all persons who may act on the faith of the certificate, the accountant would be obliged to protect himself by a verification so rigid that its cost might well be prohibitive and a limited but useful field of service thus closed to him. The smallness of the compensation paid to the defendants for the services requested is in striking contrast to the enormity of the liability now sought to be imposed upon them. If in the case at bar the plaintiff had inquired of the accountants whether they might rely upon the certificate in making a loan, then the accountants would have had the opportunity to gauge their responsibility and risk, and determine with knowledge how thorough their verification of the account should be before assuming the responsibility of making the certificate run to the plaintiff.

It also appears in the case at bar that the loss of the plaintiff resulted because of its own contributory negligence in failing to check the collateral. (*Craig* v. *Anyon,* 212 App. Div. 55: aff'd., 242 N. Y. 569.)

In so far as the claim of actual fraud is concerned, there is no proof in this record sufficient to support such a finding by a jury. The court, therefore, properly dismissed this cause of action. (Civ. Prac. Act, § 457-a.) This is so, even assuming that personal connivance and fraud on the part of the employees of defendants could be held within the scope of the authority given to these employees by the defendants, which at least is doubtful. (*Henry* v. *Allen,* 151 N. Y. 1; *Credit Alliance Corp.* v. *Sheridan Theatre Co.,* 241 id. 216; *Martin* v. *Gotham Nat. Bank,* 248 id. 313.)

It follows that the judgment and order should be affirmed.

MARTIN, J., concurs.

Judgment and order modified by reversing so much thereof as sets aside the verdict and dismisses the amended complaint as to the first cause of action, and by directing that the verdict be reinstated and judgment entered thereon, with costs to the plaintiff, and as so modified affirmed, without costs.

ULTRAMARES CORP. v. TOUCHE *

Court of Appeals of New York, 1931. 255 N. Y. 170, 174 N. E. 441.

[Cross-appeals from a judgment of the Appellate Division of the Supreme Court in the first judicial department, entered June 18, 1930, which modified and affirmed as modified a judgment in favor of defendants, entered upon an order of the court at a Trial Term setting aside a verdict in favor of plaintiff and dismissing the complaint. The defendants appeal from so much of the judgment as reversed the judgment dismissing the complaint as to the first cause of action and directed reinstatement of the verdict; and the plaintiff appeals from so much of said judgment as affirmed the judgment of the Trial Term dismissing the complaint as to the second cause of action.]

CARDOZO, Ch. J. The action is in tort for damages suffered through the misrepresentations of accountants, the first cause of action being for misrepresentations that were merely negligent and the second for misrepresentations charged to have been fraudulent.

In January, 1924, the defendants, a firm of public accountants, were employed by Fred Stern & Co., Inc., to prepare and certify a balance sheet exhibiting the condition of its business as of December 31, 1923. They had been employed at the end of each of the three years preceding to render a like service. Fred Stern & Co., Inc., which was in substance Stern himself, was engaged in the importation and sale of rubber. To finance its operations, it required extensive credit and borrowed large sums of money from banks and other lenders. All this was known

* This decision reverses the Appellate Division decision reprinted at p. 175 *supra.* It is discussed at p. 30 ff. *supra.*

to the defendants. The defendants knew also that in the usual course of business the balance sheet when certified would be exhibited by the Stern company to banks, creditors, stockholders, purchasers or sellers, according to the needs of the occasion, as the basis of financial dealings. Accordingly, when the balance sheet was made up, the defendants supplied the Stern company with thirty-two copies certified with serial numbers as counterpart originals. Nothing was said as to the persons to whom these counterparts would be shown or the extent or number of the transactions in which they would be used. In particular there was no mention of the plaintiff, a corporation doing business chiefly as a factor, which till then had never made advances to the Stern company, though it had sold merchandise in small amounts. The range of the transactions in which a certificate of audit might be expected to play a part was as indefinite and wide as the possibilities of the business that was mirrored in the summary.

By February 26, 1924, the audit was finished and the balance sheet made up. It stated assets in the sum of $2,550,671.88 and liabilities other than capital and surplus in the sum of $1,479,956.62, thus showing a net worth of $1,070,715.26. Attached to the balance sheet was a certificate as follows:

"Touche, Niven & Co.
"Public Accountants
"Eighty Maiden Lane
"New York

"February 26, 1924.

"Certificate of Auditors

"We have examined the accounts of Fred Stern & Co., Inc., for the year ending December 31, 1923, and hereby certify that the annexed balance sheet is in accordance therewith and with the information and explanations given us. We further certify that, subject to provision for federal taxes on income, the said statement, in our opinion, presents a true and correct view of the financial condition of Fred Stern & Co., Inc., as at December 31, 1923.

"TOUCHE, NIVEN & CO.
"Public Accountants."

Capital and surplus were intact if the balance sheet was accurate. In reality both had been wiped out, and the corporation was insolvent. The books had been falsified by those in charge of the business so as to set forth accounts receivable and other assets which turned out to be fictitious. The plaintiff maintains that the certificate of audit was erroneous in both its branches. The first branch, the asserted correspondence between the accounts and the balance sheet, is one purporting to be made as of the knowledge of the auditors. The second branch, which certifies to a belief that the condition reflected in the balance sheet presents a true and correct picture of the resources of the business, is stated as a matter of opinion. In the view of the plaintiff, both branches of the certificate are either fraudulent or negligent. As to one class of assets, the item of accounts receivable, if not also as to others, there was no real correspondence, we are told, between balance sheet and books, or so the triers of the facts might find If correspondence, however, be assumed, a closer examination of supporting invoices and records, or a fuller inquiry directed to the persons appearing on the books as creditors or debtors, would have exhibited the truth.

The plaintiff, a corporation engaged in business as a factor, was approached by Stern in March, 1924, with a request for loans of money to finance the sales of rubber. Up to that time the dealings between the two houses were on a cash basis and trifling in amount. As a condition of any loans the plaintiff insisted that it receive a balance sheet certified by public accountants, and in response to that demand it was given one of the certificates signed by the defendants and then in Stern's possession. On the faith of that certificate the plaintiff made a loan which was followed by many others. The course of business was for Stern to deliver to the plaintiff documents described as trust receipts which in effect were executory assignments of the moneys payable by purchasers for goods thereafter to be sold. When the purchase price was due, the plaintiff received the payment, reimbursing itself therefrom for its advances and commissions. Some of these transactions were effected without loss. Nearly a year later, in December, 1924, the house of cards collapsed. In that month, plaintiff made three loans to the Stern company, one of $100,000, a second of $25,000, and a third of $40,000. For some of these loans no security was received. For some of the earlier loans the security was inadequate. On January 2, 1925, the Stern company was declared a bankrupt.

This action, brought against the accountants in November, 1926, to recover the loss suffered by the plaintiff in reliance upon the audit, was in its inception one for negligence. On the trial there was added a second cause of action asserting fraud also. The trial judge dismissed the second cause of action without submitting it to the jury. As to the first cause of action, he reserved his decision on the defendants' motion to dismiss and took the jury's verdict. They were told that the defendants might be held liable if with knowledge that the results of the audit would be communicated to creditors they did the work negligently, and that negligence was the omission to use reasonable and ordinary care. The verdict was in favor of the plaintiff for $187,576.32. On the coming in of the verdict, the judge granted the reserved motion. The Appellate Division affirmed the dismissal of the cause of action for fraud, but reversed the dismissal of the cause of action for negligence, and reinstated the verdict. The case is here on cross-appeals.

The two causes of action will be considered in succession, first the one for negligence and second that for fraud.

(1) We think the evidence supports a finding that the audit was negligently made, though in so saying we put aside for the moment the question whether negligence, even if it existed, was a wrong to the plaintiff. To explain fully or adequately how the defendants were at fault would carry this opinion beyond reasonable bounds. A sketch, however, there must be, at least in respect of some features of the audit, for the nature of the fault, when understood, is helpful in defining the ambit of the duty.

We begin with the item of accounts receivable. At the start of the defendants' audit, there had been no posting of the general ledger since April, 1923. Siess, a junior accountant, was assigned by the defendants to the performance of that work. On Sunday, February 3, 1924, he had finished the task of posting, and was ready the next day to begin with his associates the preparation of the balance sheet and the audit of its items. The total of the accounts receivable for December, 1923, as thus posted by Siess from the entries in the journal, was $644,758.17. At some time on February 3, Romberg, an employee of the Stern company, who had general charge of its accounts, placed below that total another item to represent additional accounts receivable growing out of the transactions of the month. This new item, $706,843.07, Romberg entered in his own handwriting. The sales that it represented were, each and all, fictitious. Opposite the entry were placed other figures (12-29), indicating or supposed to indicate a reference to the journal. Siess when he resumed his work saw the entries thus added, and included the new item in making up his footings, with the result of an apparent increase of over $700,000 in the assets of the business. He says that in doing this he supposed the entries to be correct, and that his task at the moment being merely to post the books, he thought the work of audit or verification might come later, and put it off accordingly. The time sheets, which are in evidence, show very clearly that this was the order of time in which the parts of the work were done. Verification, however, there never was either by Siess or by his superiors, or so the triers of the facts might say. If any had been attempted, or any that was adequate, an examiner would have found that the entry in the ledger was not supported by any entry in the journal. If from the journal he had gone to the book from which the journal was made up, described as "the debit memo book," support would still have failed. Going farther, he would have found invoices, seventeen in number, which amounted in the aggregate to the interpolated item, but scrutiny of these invoices would have disclosed suspicious features in that they had no shipping number nor a customer's order number and varied in terms of credit and in other respects from those usual in the business. A mere glance reveals the difference.

The December entry of accounts receivable was not the only item that a careful and skillful auditor would have desired to investigate. There was ground for suspicion as to an item of $113,199.60, included in the accounts payable as due from the Baltic Corporation. As to this the defendants received an explanation, not very convincing, from Stern and Romberg. A cautious auditor might have been dissatisfied and have uncovered what was wrong. There was ground for suspicion also because of the inflation of the inventory. The inventory as it was given to the auditors, was totaled at $347,219.08. The defendants discovered errors in the sum of $303,863.20, and adjusted the balance sheet accordingly. Both the extent of the discrepancy and its causes might have been found to cast discredit upon the business and the books. There was ground for suspicion again in the record of assigned accounts. Inquiry of the creditors gave notice to the defendants that the same accounts had been pledged to two, three and four banks at the same time. The pledges did not diminish the value of the assets, but made in such circumstances they might well evoke a doubt as to the solvency of a business where such conduct was permitted. There was an explanation by Romberg which the defendants accepted as sufficient. Caution and diligence might have pressed investigation farther.

If the defendants owed a duty to the plaintiff to act with the same care that would have been due under a contract of employment, a jury was at liberty to find a verdict of negligence upon a showing of a scrutiny so imperfect and perfunctory. No doubt the extent to which inquiry must be pressed beyond appearances is a question of judgment, as to which opinions will often differ. No doubt the wisdom that is born after the event will engender suspicion and distrust when old acquaintance and good repute may have silenced doubt at the beginning. All this is to be weighed by a jury in applying its standard of behavior, the state of mind and conduct of the reasonable man. Even so, the adverse verdict, when rendered, imports an alignment of the weights in their proper places in the balance and a reckoning thereafter. The reckoning was not wrong upon the evidence before us, if duty be assumed.

We are brought to the question of duty, its origin and measure.

The defendants owed to their employer a duty imposed by law to make their certificate without fraud, and a duty growing out of contract to make it with the care and caution proper to their calling. Fraud includes the pretense of knowledge when knowledge there is none. To creditors and investors to whom the employer exhibited the certificate, the defendants owed a like duty to make it without fraud, since there was notice in the circumstances of its making that the employer did not intend to keep it to himself (*Eaton, Cole & Burnham Co.* v. *Avery,* 83 N. Y. 31; *Tindle* v. *Birkett,* 171 N. Y. 520). A different question develops when we ask whether they owed a duty to these to make it without negligence. If liability for negligence exists, a thoughtless slip or blunder, the failure to detect a theft or forgery beneath the cover of deceptive entries, may expose accountants to a liability in an indeterminate amount for an indeterminate time to an indeterminate class. The hazards of a business conducted on these terms are so extreme as to enkindle doubt whether a flaw may not exist in the implication of a duty that exposes to these consequences. We put aside for the moment any statement in the certificate which involves the representation of a fact as true to the knowledge of the auditors. If such a statement was made, whether believed to be true or not, the defendants are liable for deceit in the event that it was false. The plaintiff does not need the invention of novel doctrine to help it out in such conditions. The case was submitted to the jury and the verdict was returned upon the theory that even in the absence of a misstatement of a fact there is a liability also for erroneous opinion. The expression of an opinion is to be subject to a warranty implied by law. What, then, is the warranty, as yet unformulated, to be? Is it merely that the opinion is honestly conceived and that the preliminary inquiry has been honestly pursued, that a halt has not been made without a genuine belief that the search has been reasonably adequate to bring disclosure of the truth? Or does it go farther and involve the assumption of a liability for any blunder or inattention that could fairly be spoken of as negligence if the controversy were one between accountant and employer for breach of a contract to render services for pay?

The assault upon the citadel of privity is proceeding in these days apace. How far the inroads shall extend is now a favorite subject of juridical discussion (Williston, Liability for Honest Misrepresentation, 24 Harv. L. Rev. 415, 433; Bohlen, Studies in the Law of Torts, pp. 150, 151; Bohlen, Misrepresentation as Deceit, Negligence or Warranty, 42 Harv. L. Rev. 733; Smith, Liability for Negligent Language, 14 Harv. L. Rev. 184; Green, Judge and Jury, chapter Deceit, p. 280; 16 Va. Law Rev. 749). In the field of the law of contract there has been a gradual widening of the doctrine of *Lawrence* v. *Fox* (20 N. Y. 268), until today the beneficiary of a promise, clearly designated as such, is seldom left without a remedy (*Seaver* v. *Ransom,* 224 N. Y. 233, 238). Even in that field, however, the remedy is narrower where the beneficiaries of the promise are indeterminate or general. Something more must then appear than an intention that the promise shall redound to the benefit of the public or to that of a class of indefinite extension. The promise must be such as to "bespeak the assumption of a duty to make reparation directly to the individual members of the public if the benefit is lost" (*Moch Co.* v. *Rensselaer Water Co.,* 247 N. Y. 160, 164; American Law Institute, Restatement of the Law of Contracts, § 145). In the field of the law of torts a manufacturer who is negligent in the manufacture of a chattel in circumstances pointing to an unreasonable risk of serious bodily harm to those using it thereafter may be liable for negligence though privity is lacking between manufacturer and user (*MacPherson* v. *Buick Motor Co.,* 217 N. Y. 382; American Law Institute, Restatement of the Law of Torts, § 262). A force or instrument of harm having been launched with potentialities of danger manifest to the eye of prudence, the one who launches it is under a duty to keep it within bounds (*Moch Co.* v. *Rensselaer Water Co., supra,* at p. 168). Even so, the question is still open whether the potentialities of danger that will charge with liability are confined to harm to the person, or include injury to property (*Pine Grove Poultry Farm* v. *Newton B.-P. Mfg. Co.,* 248 N. Y. 293, 296; *Robins Dry Dock & Repair Co.* v. *Flint,* 275 U. S. 303; American Law Institute, Restatement of the Law of Torts, *supra*). In either view, however, what is released or set in motion is a physical force. We are now asked to say that a like liability attaches to the circulation of a thought or a release of the explosive power resident in words.

Three cases in this court are said by the plaintiff to have committed us to the doctrine that words, written or oral, if negligently published with the expectation that the reader or listener will transmit them to another, will lay a basis for liability though privity be lacking. These are *Glanzer* v. *Shepard* (233 N. Y. 236); *International Products Co.* v. *Erie R. R. Co.* (244 N. Y. 331), and *Doyle* v. *Chatham & Phenix Nat. Bank* (253 N. Y. 369).

In *Glanzer* v. *Shepard* the seller of beans requested the defendants, public weighers, to make return of the weight and furnish the buyer with a copy. This the defendants did. Their return, which was made out in duplicate, one copy to the seller and the other to the buyer, recites that it was made by order of the former for the use of the latter. The buyer paid the seller on the faith of the certificate which turned out to be erroneous. We held that the weighers were liable at the suit of the buyer for the moneys overpaid. Here was something more than the rendition of a service in the expectation that the one who ordered the certificate would use it thereafter in the operations of his business as occasion might require. Here was a case where the transmission of the certificate to another was not merely one possibility among many, but the "end and aim of the transaction," as certain and immediate and deliberately willed as if a husband were to order a gown to be delivered to his wife, or a telegraph company, contracting with the sender of a message, were to telegraph it wrongly to the damage of the person expected to receive it (*Wolfskehl* v. *Western Union Tel. Co.,* 46 Hun, 542; *DeRuth* v. *New York, etc., Tel. Co.,* 1 Daly, 547; *Milliken* v. *Western Union Tel. Co.,* 110 N. Y. 403, 410). The intimacy of the resulting nexus is attested by the fact that after stating the case in terms of legal duty, we went on to point that viewing it as a phase or extension of *Lawrence* v. *Fox* (*supra*), or *Seaver* v. *Ransom* (*supra*), we could reach the same result by stating it in terms of contract (cf. *Economy Building & Loan Assn.* v. *West Jersey Title Co.,* 64 N. J. L. 27; *Young* v. *Lohr,* 118 Iowa, 624; *Murphy* v. *Fidelity, Abstract & Title Co.,* 114 Wash. 77). The bond was so close as to approach that of privity, if not completely one with it. Not so in the case at hand. No one would be likely to urge that there was a contractual relation, or even one approaching it, at the root of any duty that was owing from the defendants now before us to the indeterminate class of persons who, presently or in the future, might deal with the Stern company in reliance on the audit. In a word, the service rendered by the defendant in *Glanzer* v. *Shepard* was primarily for the information of a third person, in effect, if not in name, a party to the contract, and only incidentally for that of the formal promisee. In the case at hand, the service was primarily for the benefit of the Stern company, a convenient instrumentality for use in the development of the business, and only incidentally or collaterally for the use of those to whom Stern and his associates might exhibit it thereafter. Foresight of these possibilities may charge with liability for fraud. The conclusion does not follow that it will charge with liability for negligence.

In the next of the three cases (*International Products Co.* v. *Erie R. R. Co., supra)* the plaintiff, an importer, had an agreement with the defendant, a railroad company, that the latter would act as bailee of goods arriving from abroad. The importer, to protect the goods by suitable insurance, made inquiry of the bailee as to the location of the storage. The warehouse was incorrectly named, and the policy did not attach. Here was a determinate relation, that of bailor and bailee, either present or prospective, with peculiar opportunity for knowledge on the part of the bailee as to the subject-matter of the statement and with a continuing duty to correct it if erroneous. Even the narrowest holdings as to liability for unintentional misstatement concede that a representation in such circumstances may be equivalent to a warranty. There is a class of cases "where a person within whose special province it lay to know a particular fact, has given an erroneous answer to an inquiry made with regard to it by a person desirous of ascertaining the fact for the purpose of determining his course accordingly, and has been held bound to make good the assurance he has given" (HERSCHELL, L. C., in *Derry* v. *Peek,* [L. R.] 14 A. C. 337, 360). So in *Burrowes* v. *Lock* (10 Ves. 470), a trustee was asked by one who expected to make a loan upon the security of a trust fund whether notice of any prior incumbrance upon the fund had been given to him. An action for damages was upheld though the false answer was made honestly in the belief that it was true (cf. *Brownlie* v. *Campbell,* [L. R.] 5 A. C. 925, 935; *Doyle* v. *Chatham & Phenix Nat. Bank, supra,* at p. 379).

In one respect the decision in *International Products Co.* v. *Erie R. R. Co.* is in advance of anything decided in *Glanzer* v. *Shepard.* The latter case suggests that the liability there enforced was not one for the mere utterance of words without due consideration, but for a negligent service, the act of weighing, which happened to find in the words of the certificate its culmination and its summary. This was said in the endeavor to emphasize the character of the certificate as a business transaction, an act in the law, and not a mere casual response to a request for information. The ruling in the case of the *Erie Railroad* shows that the rendition of a service is at most a mere circumstance and not an indispensable condition. The Erie was not held for negligence in the rendition of a service. It was held for words and nothing more. So in the case at hand. If liability for the consequences of a negligent certificate may be enforced by any member of an indeterminate class of creditors, present and prospective, known and unknown, the existence or non-existence of a preliminary act of service will not affect the cause of action. The service may have been rendered as carefully as you please, and its quality will count for nothing if there was negligence thereafter in distributing the summary.

Doyle v. *Chatham & Phenix Nat. Bank* (*supra*), the third of the cases cited, is even more plainly indecisive. A trust company was a trustee under a deed of trust to secure an issue of bonds. It was held liable to a subscriber for the bonds when it certified them falsely. A representation by a trustee intended to sway action had been addressed to a person who by the act of subscription was to become a party to the deed and a *cestui que trust*.

The antidote to these decisions and to the over-use of the doctrine of liability for negligent misstatement may be found in *Jaillet* v. *Cashman* (235 N. Y. 511) and *Courteen Seed Co.* v. *Hong Kong & Shanghai Banking P. Corp.* (245 N. Y. 377). In the first of these cases the defendant supplying ticker service to brokers was held not liable in damages to one of the broker's customers for the consequences of reliance upon a report negligently published on the ticker. If liability had been upheld, the step would have been a short one to the declaration of a like liability on the part of proprietors of newspapers. In the second the principle was clearly stated by POUND, J., that "negligent words are not actionable unless they are uttered directly, with knowledge or notice that they will be acted on, to one to whom the speaker is bound by some relation of duty, arising out of public calling, contract or otherwise, to act with care if he acts at all."

From the foregoing analysis the conclusion is, we think, inevitable that nothing in our previous decisions commits us to a holding of liability for negligence in the circumstances of the case at hand, and that such liability, if recognized, will be an extension of the principle of those decisions to different conditions, even if more or less analogous. The question then is whether such an extension shall be made.

The extension, if made, will so expand the field of liability for negligent speech as to make it nearly, if not quite, coterminous with that of liability for fraud. Again and again, in decisions of this court, the bounds of this latter liability have been set up, with futility the fate of every endeavor to dislodge them. Scienter has been declared to be an indispensable element except where the representation has been put forward as true of one's own knowledge (*Hadcock* v. *Osmer*, 153 N. Y. 604), or in circumstances where the expression of opinion was a dishonorable pretense (3 Williston, Contracts, § 1494; *Smith* v. *Land & House Prop. Corp.*, [L. R.] 28 Ch. Div. 7, 15; *Sleeper* v. *Smith*, 77 N. H. 337; *Andrews* v. *Jackson*, 168 Mass. 266; *People ex rel. Gellis* v. *Sheriff*, 251 N. Y. 33, 37; *Hickey* v. *Morrell*, 102 N. Y. 454, 463; *Merry Realty Co.* v. *Martin*, 103 Misc. Rep. 9, 14; 186 App. Div. 538). Even an opinion especially an opinion by an expert, may be found to be fraudulent if the grounds supporting it are so flimsy as to lead to the conclusion that there was no genuine belief back of it. Further than that this court has never gone. Directors of corporations have been acquitted of liability for deceit though they have been lax in investigation and negligent in speech (*Reno* v. *Bull,* 226 N. Y. 546, and cases there cited; *Kountze* v. *Kennedy,* 147 N. Y. 124). This has not meant, to be sure, that negligence may not be evidence from which a trier of the facts may draw an inference of fraud (*Derry* v. *Peek,* [L. R.] 14 A. C. 337, 369, 375, 376), but merely that if that inference is rejected, or, in the light of all the circumstances, is found to be unreasonable, negligence alone is not a substitute for fraud. Many also are the cases that have distinguished between the willful or reckless representation essential to the maintenance at law of an action for deceit, and the misrepresentation, negligent or innocent, that will lay a sufficient basis for rescission in equity (*Bloomquist* v. *Farson,* 222 N. Y. 375; *Seneca Wire & Mfg. Co.* v. *Leach & Co.,* 247 N. Y. 1). If this action is well conceived, all these principles and distinctions, so nicely wrought and formulated, have been a waste of time and effort. They have even been a snare, entrapping litigants and lawyers into an abandonment of the true remedy lying ready to the call. The suitors thrown out of court because they proved negligence, and nothing else, in an action for deceit, might have ridden to triumphant victory if they had proved the self-same facts, but had given the wrong another label, and all this in a State where forms of action have been abolished. So to hold is near to saying that we have been paltering with justice. A word of caution or suggestion would have set the erring suitor right. Many pages of opinion were written by judges the most eminent, yet the word was never spoken. We may not speak it now. A change so revolutionary, if expedient, must be wrought by legislation (*Landell* v. *Lybrand,* 264 Penn. St. 406).

We have said that the duty to refrain from negligent representation would become coincident or nearly so with the duty to refrain from fraud if this action could be maintained. A representation even though knowingly false does not constitute ground for an action of deceit unless made with the intent to be communicated to the persons or class of persons who act upon it to their prejudice (*Eaton, Cole & Burnham Co.* v. *Avery, supra*). Affirmance of this judgment would require us to hold that all or nearly all the persons so situated would suffer an impairment of an interest legally protected if the representation had been negligent. We speak of all "or nearly all," for cases can be imagined where a casual response, made in circumstances insufficient to indicate that care should be expected, would permit recovery for fraud if willfully deceitful. Cases of fraud between persons so circumstanced are, however, too infrequent and exceptional to make the radii greatly different if the fields of liability for negligence and deceit be figured as concentric circles. The like may be said of the possibility that the negligence of the injured party, contributing to the result, may avail to overcome the one remedy, though unavailing to defeat the other.

Neither of these possibilities is noted by the plaintiff in its answer to the suggestion that the two fields would be coincident. Its answer has been merely this, *first,* that the duty to speak with care does not arise unless the words are the culmination of a service, and *second,* that it does not arise unless the service is rendered in the pursuit of an independent calling, characterized as public. As to the first of these suggestions, we have already had occasion to observe that given a relation making diligence a duty, speech as well as conduct must conform to that exacting standard (*International Products Co.* v. *Erie R. R. Co., supra*). As to the second of the two suggestions, public accountants are public only in the sense that their services are offered to any one who chooses to employ them. This is far from saying that those who do not employ them are in the same position as those who do.

Liability for negligence if adjudged in this case will extend to many callings other than an auditor's. Lawyers who certify their opinion as to the validity of municipal or corporate bonds with knowledge that the opinion will be brought to the notice of the public, will become liable to the investors, if they have overlooked a statute or a decision, to the same extent as if the controversy were one between client and adviser. Title companies insuring titles to a tract of land, with knowledge that at an approaching auction the fact that they have insured will be stated to the bidders, will become liable to purchasers who may wish the benefit of a policy without payment of a premium. These illustrations may seem to be extreme, but they go little, if any, farther than we are invited to go now. Negligence, moreover, will have one standard when viewed in relation to the employer, and another and at times a stricter standard when viewed in relation to the public. Explanations that might seem plausible, omissions that might be reasonable, if the duty is confined to the employer, conducting a business that presumably at least is not a fraud upon his creditors, might wear another aspect if an independent duty to be suspicious even of one's principal is owing to investors. "Every one making a promise having the quality of a contract will be under a duty to the promisee by virtue of the promise, but under another duty, apart from contract, to an indefinite number of potential beneficiaries when performance has begun. The assumption of one relation will mean the involuntary assumption of a series of new relations, inescapably hooked together" (*Moch Co.* v. *Rensselaer Water Co., supra,* at p. 168). "The law does not spread its protection so far" (*Robins Dry Dock & Repair Co.* v. *Flint, supra,* at p. 309).

Our holding does not emancipate accountants from the consequences of fraud. It does not relieve them if their audit has been so negligent as to justify a finding that they had no genuine belief in its adequacy, for this again is fraud. It does no more than say that if less than this is proved, if there has been neither reckless misstatement nor insincere profession of an opinion, but only honest blunder, the ensuing liability for negligence is one that is bounded by the contract, and is to be enforced between the parties by whom the contract has been made. We doubt whether the average business man receiving a certificate without paying for it and receiving it merely as one among a multitude of possible investors, would look for anything more.

(2) The second cause of action is yet to be considered.

The defendants certified as a fact, true to their own knowledge, that the balance sheet was in accordance with the books of account. If their statement was false, they are not to be exonerated because they believed it to be true (*Hadcock* v. *Osmer, supra; Lehigh Zinc & Iron Co.* v. *Bamford,* 150 U. S. 665, 673; *Chatham Furnace Co.* v. *Moffatt,* 147 Mass. 403; *Arnold* v. *Richardson,* 74 App. Div. 581). We think the triers of the facts might hold it to be false.

Correspondence between the balance sheet and the books imports something more, or so the triers of the facts might say, than correspondence between the balance sheet and the general ledger, unsupported or even contradicted by every other record. The correspondence to be of any moment may not unreasonably be held to signify a correspondence between the statement and the books of original entry, the books taken as a whole. If that is what the certificate means, a jury could find that the correspondence did not exist and that the defendants signed the certificates without knowing it to exist and even without reasonable grounds for belief in its existence. The item of $706,000, representing fictitious accounts receivable, was entered in the ledger after defendant's employee Siess had posted the December sales. He knew of the interpolation, and knew that there was need to verify the entry by reference to books other than the ledger before the books could be found to be in agreement with the balance sheet. The evidence would sustain a finding that this was never done. By concession the interpolated item had no support in the journal, or in any journal voucher, or in the debit memo book, which was a summary of the invoices, or in any thing except the invoices themselves. The defendants do not say that they ever looked at the invoices, seventeen in number, representing these accounts. They profess to be unable to recall whether they did so or not. They admit, however, that if they had looked, they would have found omissions and irregularities so many and unusual as to have called for further investigation. When we couple the refusal to say that they did look with the admission that if they had looked, they would or could have seen, the situation is revealed as one in which a jury might reasonably find that in truth they did not look, but certified the correspondence without testing its existence.

In this connection we are to bear in mind the principle already stated in the course of this opinion that negligence or blindness, even when not equivalent to fraud, is none the less evidence to sustain an inference of fraud. At least this is so if the negligence is gross. Not a little confusion has at times resulted from an undiscriminating quotation of statements in *Kountze* v. *Kennedy* (*supra*), statements proper enough in their setting, but capable of misleading when extracted and considered by themselves. "Misjudgment, however gross," it was there observed, "or want of caution, however marked, is not fraud." This was said in a case where the trier of the facts had held the defendants guiltless. The judgment in this court amounted merely to a holding that a finding of fraud did not follow as an inference of law. There was no holding that the evidence would have required a reversal of the judgment if the finding as to guilt had been the other way. Even *Derry* v. *Peek,* as we have seen, asserts the probative effect of negligence as an evidentiary fact. We had no thought in *Kountze* v. *Kennedy* of upholding a doctrine more favorable to wrongdoers, though there was a reservation suggesting the approval of a rule more rigorous. The opinion of this court cites *Derry* v. *Peek,* and states the holding there made that an action would not lie if the defendant believed the representation made by him to be true, although without reasonable cause for such belief. "It is not necessary," we said, "to go to this extent to uphold the present judgment, for the referee, as has been stated, found that the belief of Kennedy * * * was based upon reasonable grounds." The setting of the occasion justified the inference that the representations did not involve a profession of knowledge as distinguished from belief (147 N. Y. at p. 133). No such charity of construction exonerates accountants, who by the very nature of their calling profess to speak with knowledge when certifying to an agreement between the audit and the entries.

The defendants attempt to excuse the omission of an inspection of the invoices proved to be fictitious by invoking a practice known as that of testing and sampling. A random choice of accounts is made from the total number on the books, and these, if found to be regular when inspected and investigated, are taken as a fair indication of the quality of the mass. The defendants say that about 200 invoices were examined in accordance with this practice, but they do not assert that any of the seventeen invoices supporting the fictitious sales were among the number so selected. Verification by test and sample was very likely a sufficient audit as to accounts regularly entered upon the books in the usual course of business. It was plainly insufficient, however, as to accounts not entered upon the books where inspection of the invoices was necessary, not as a check upon accounts fair upon their face, but in order to ascertain whether there were any accounts at all. If the only invoices inspected were invoices unrelated to the interpolated entry, the result was to certify a correspondence between the books and the balance sheet without any effort by the auditors, as to $706,000 of accounts, to ascertain whether the certified agreement was in accordance with the truth. How far books of account fair upon their face are to be probed by accountants in an effort to ascertain whether the transactions back of them are in accordance with the entries, involves to some extent the exercise of judgment and discretion. Not so, however, the inquiry whether the entries certified as there, are there in very truth, there in the form and in the places where men of business training would expect them to be. The defendants were put on their guard by the circumstances touching the December accounts receivable to scrutinize with special care. A jury might find that with suspicions thus awakened, they closed their eyes to the obvious, and blindly gave assent.

We conclude, to sum up the situation, that in certifying to the correspondence between balance sheet and accounts the defendants made a statement as true to their own knowledge, when they had, as a jury might find, no knowledge on the subject. If that is so, they may also be found to have acted without information leading to a sincere or genuine belief when they certified to an opinion that the balance sheet faithfully reflected the condition of the business.

Whatever wrong was committed by the defendants was not their personal act or omission, but that of their subordinates. This does not relieve them, however, of liability to answer in damages for the consequences of the wrong, if wrong there shall be found to be. It is not a question of constructive notice, as where facts are brought home to the knowledge of subordinates whose interests are adverse to those of the employer *(Henry* v. *Allen,* 151 N. Y. 1; see, however, American Law Institute, Restatement of the Law of Agency, § 506, subd. 2-a). These subordinates, so far as the record shows, had no interests adverse to the defendants', nor any thought in what they did to be unfaithful to their trust. The question is merely this, whether the defendants, having delegated the performance of this work to agents of their own selection, are responsible for the manner in which the business of the agency was done. As to that the answer is not doubtful *(Fifth Ave. Bank* v. *42d St., etc., R. R. Co.,* 137 N. Y. 231; *Gleason* v. *Seaboard Air Line Ry. Co.,* 278 U. S. 349, 356; American Law Institute, Restatement of the Law of Agency, § 481).

Upon the defendants' appeal as to the first cause of action, the judgment of the Appellate Division should be reversed, and that of the Trial Term affirmed, with costs in the Appellate Division and in this court.

Upon the plaintiff's appeal as to the second cause of action, the judgment of the Appellate Division and that of the Trial Term should be reversed, and a new trial granted, with costs to abide the event.

POUND, CRANE, LEHMAN, KELLOGG, O'BRIEN and HUBBS, JJ., concur. Judgment accordingly.

BEARDSLEY v. ERNST *

Court of Appeals of Ohio, Cuyahoga County, 1934. 47 Ohio App. 241, 191 N. E. 808.

Syllabus by the Court.

In an action for damages for fraudulent misrepresentations of accountants, brought by one purchasing stocks and bonds, relying on such accounts' certified balance sheet, fraud is not established, where it is shown by the accountants' certificate that the statements "were based upon statments from abroad with respect to the foreign constituent companies." Such statement gives rise to the indisputable inference that the accountants had not examined the records of the foreign constituent companies.

MCGILL, Judge. This is a proceeding in error to reverse a judgment of the court of common pleas wherein Martha R. Beardsley was plaintiff and Alwin C. Ernst and others were defendants.

The petition in substance alleged that the defendants were copartners doing business as Ernst & Ernst, who were certified public accountants. It further alleged that the plaintiff in 1931 purchased at different times two bonds and twenty-one shares of preferred stock in the International Match Corporation. The petition set forth that the plaintiff acted upon her own initiative and relied upon the certification made by the expert accountants to the consolidated balance sheet and consolidated income and surplus account of the International Match Corporation for the year 1929 and for the year 1930.

It was further alleged by the plaintiff that the certificates made by the defendants were fraudulent, in that the defendants purported to have knowledge of the facts when in truth the defendants had no such knowledge; that the fraud was not discovered until after the suicide and death of Ivar Krueger, which occurred in Paris on March 12, 1932; and, further, that the bonds and stocks were at said time worthless and the International Match Corporation was bankrupt, although not so officially declared at the time of the purchases. By reason of these facts plaintiff claimed damages resulting from the alleged fraud in the sum of $2,339.99.

The defendants filed a joint answer, which, in substance, admitted the partnership; admitted the execution of the certificates; and also pleaded a general denial. A jury having been waived, the court below heard the evidence and rendered judgment for the defendants.

An examination of the record discloses that each certificate executed by the defendants was as follows:

"We hereby certify that we have examined the books of account and record of International Match Corporation and its American Subsidiary company at December 31, 1929, and have received statements from abroad with respect to the foreign constitutent companies as of the same date.

* See footnote 47 *supra*.

Based upon our examination and information submitted to us it is our opinion that the annexed Consolidated Balance Sheet sets forth the financial condition of the combined companies at the date stated, and that the related Consolidated Income and Surplus Account is correct.

"Ernst & Ernst."

On behalf of the plaintiff, proof was introduced that the International Match Corporation was adjudicated bankrupt by the United States District Court of the Southern District of New York on April 9, 1932. There were introduced by stipulation copies of an audit made by Price, Waterhouse & Co., who were employed to audit the affairs of the International Match Corporation, and these audits had been filed with the referee in bankruptcy.

The audit made by Price, Waterhouse & Co. revealed annual net earnings of the International Match Corporation for the years involved to be approximately $8,000,000, whereas the defendants had certified the net income for 1929 and 1930 respectively to have been in excess of $20,000,000.

The plaintiff relies largely upon the case of *Ultramares Corporation* v. *Touche,* 255 N. Y. 170, 174 N. E. 441, 442, 74 A. L. R. 1139. In that case a certificate was made by Touche, Niven & Co., who were public accountants, to the effect that they had examined the accounts of Fred Stern & Co., Incorporated, and the certificate stated "that the annexed balance sheet is in accordance therewith and * * * the said statement, in our opinion, presents a true and correct view of the financial condition of Fred Stern & Co., Inc., as at December 31, 1923."

The lower court, in the *Touche* Case, held the accountants liable for negligence and not liable for fraud. Both sides appealed, and Judge Cardozo reversed both holdings and found that the accountants were not liable for negligence, but were liable for fraud. In that case, syllabus 8 reads as follows:

"8. In action for damages for fraudulent misrepresentations of accountants, brought by person making advances relying on certified balance sheet, dismissal without submission to jury held error.

"The evidence indicated that, in certifying to the correspondence between balance sheet and accounts, the defendant accountants made a statement as true to their own knowledge when they had no knowledge on the subject."

If certified public accountants examine the books and records of a corporation and certify that the balance sheet reflects the true condition of the books and records examined, and there is a substantial variation between the balance sheet and such books and records, an action would no doubt lie against the accountants, where the certification was made knowingly, or where there was a pretense of knowledge when in fact they had no knowledge.

In the instant case, however, the certificate made by Ernst & Ernst clearly states that it is based both upon an examination of records and upon statements received from abroad with respect to the foreign constituent companies. The language used in these certificates gives rise to the indisputable inference that the accountants had not examined the books and records of the foreign constituent companies.

The record does not establish fraud or any false or fraudulent statements in relation to the examination actually made of the books and records in this country. We do not think that the defendants can be charged with fraud under these certificates by the very language used therein, when they in fact disclose that some of the information and statements came from abroad. It is obvious that the accountants in this case could not know whether or not the information from abroad was accurate or inaccurate, and, inasmuch as they disclose that these certificates were based partly upon information so received, there was no pretense of knowledge as to the information received which would make defendants liable.

Accordingly, the judgment of the common pleas court is affirmed.

Judgment affirmed.

GLANZER v. SHEPARD *

Court of Appeals of New York, 1922. 233 N. Y. 236, 135 N. E. 275.

APPEAL, by permission, from a judgment entered January 21, 1921, upon an order of the Appellate Division of the Supreme Court in the first judicial department, which reversed a determination of the Appellate Term, reversing a judgment of the City Court of the city of New York in favor of plaintiffs entered upon a verdict directed by the court and affirmed said City Court judgment.

CARDOZO, J. Plaintiffs bought of Bech, Van Siclen & Co., a corporation, 905 bags of beans. The beans were to be paid for in accordance with weight sheets certified by public weighers. Bech, Van Siclen & Co., the seller, requested the defendants, who are engaged in business as public weighers, to make return of the weight and furnish the buyers with a copy. A letter to the weighers, dated July 20, 1918, informed them that the bags were on the dock, that the beans had been sold to Glanzer Bros., the plaintiffs, who would accept delivery Tuesday, July 23, and that the defendants were to communicate with the plaintiffs, and ascertain whether it would "be in order" to be on the pier Tuesday morning to weigh the beans before delivery. The defendants did as bidden. They certified the weight of the 905 bags to be 228,380 pounds, and were paid for the service by the seller. Their return recites that it has been made "by order of" Bech, Van Siclen & Co., "for G. Bros." One copy of the return they sent to the seller, and a duplicate to the buyers. Later, 17 bags, containing 4,136 pounds, were withdrawn from the shipment. The others were accepted and paid for on the faith of the certificates. The plaintiffs, upon attempting a resale, found that the actual weight was less by 11,854 pounds than the weight as certified in the return. Upon learning this, they brought suit against the defendants in the City Court of New York for $1,261.26, the amount overpaid. The trial judge, upon motions made by each side for the direction of a verdict, ordered judgment for the plaintiffs. The Appellate Term reversed upon the ground that the plaintiffs had no contract with the defendants, and must seek their remedy against the seller. The Appellate Division reversed the Appellate Term, and reinstated the verdict. The defendants are the appellants here.

We think the law imposes a duty toward buyer as well as seller in the situation here disclosed. The plaintiffs' use of the certificates was not an

* This case is discussed at p. 31 f. *supra*.

indirect or collateral consequence of the action of the weighers. It was a consequence, which, to the weighers' knowledge, was the end and aim of the transaction. Bech, Van Siclen & Co. ordered, but Glanzer Brothers were to use. The defendants held themselves out to the public as skilled and careful in their calling. They knew that the beans had been sold, and that on the faith of their certificate payment would be made. They sent a copy to the plaintiffs for the very purpose of inducing action. All this they admit. In such circumstances, assumption of the task of weighing was the assumption of a duty to weigh carefully for the benefit of all whose conduct was to be governed. We do not need to state the duty in terms of contract or of privity. Growing out of a contract, it has none the less an origin not exclusively contractual. Given the contract and the relation, the duty is imposed by law (cf. *MacPherson* v. *Buick Motor Co.,* 217 N. Y. 382, 390).

There is nothing new here in principle. If there is novelty, it is in the instance only. One who follows a common calling may come under a duty to another whom he serves, though a third may give the order or make the payment (1 Street, Foundations of Legal Liability, pp. 187, 188; Bohlen, Affirmative Obligations in the Law of Torts, 44 Am. Law Reg. [N. S.] 209, 218, 293, 294; 3 Holdsworth, History of English Law, p. 332). "It is the duty of every artificer to exercise his art rightly and truly as he ought" (Fitzherbert Abr., Trespass sue le Case, 94d, quoted by Bohlen, *supra,* p. 293). The surgeon who unskillfully sets the wounded arm of a child is liable for his negligence, though the father pays the bill (*Gladwell* v. *Steggall,* 5 Bing. N. C. 733; *Pippin* v. *Sheppard,* 11 Price, 400-411). The bailee who is careless in the keeping of the goods which he receives as those of A, does not escape liability though the deposit may have been made by B. It is ancient learning that one who assumes to act, even though gratuitously, may thereby become subject to the duty of acting carefully, if he acts at all (*Coggs* v. *Bernard,* 2 Ld. Raymond, 909; *Shiells* v. *Blackburne,* 1 H. Bl. 158; Willes, J., in *Skelton* v. *L. & N. W. Ry. Co.,* L. R. 2 C. P. 631, 636; Kent, Ch. J., in *Thorne* v. *Deas,* 4 Johns. 84, 96). The most common examples of such a duty are cases where action is directed toward the person of another or his property (Street, *supra*). A like principle applies, however, where action is directed toward the governance of conduct. The controlling circumstance is not the character of the consequence, but its proximity or remoteness in the thought and purpose of the actor. There are decisions that a lawyer who supplies a certificate of title to a client is not answerable to a third person whom he did not mean to serve (*Savings Bank* v. *Ward,* 100 U. S. 195; cf. *Glawatz* v. *People's Guaranty Search Co.,* 49 App. Div. 465; *Day* v. *Reynolds,* 23 Hun, 131). "Neither fraud nor collusion is alleged or proved; and it is conceded that the certificates were made by the defendant at the request of the applicant for the loan, without any knowledge on the part of the defendant what use was to be made of the same or to whom they were to be presented" (*Savings Bank* v. *Ward, supra,* p. 199). No such immunity, it has been held, protects the searcher of a title who, preparing an abstract at the order of a client, delivers it to another to induce action on the faith of it (*Economy Bldg. & Loan Ass'n.* v. *West Jersey Title Co.,* 64 N. J. L. 27; *Denton* v. *Nashville Title Co.,* 112 Tenn. 320; *Anderson* v. *Spriestersbach,* 69 Wash. 393; *Murphy* v. *Fidelity Abstract & Title Co.,* 114 Wash. 77; *Brown* v. *Sims,* 22 Ind. App. 317; *Western Loan Co.* v. *Silver Bow Abstract Co.,* 31 Mont. 448; *Lawall* v. *Groman,* 180 Penn. St. 532;

cf. *Scholes* v. *Brook,* 63 L. T. [N. S.] 837, 838; aff'd., 64 id. 674). Constantly the bounds of duty are enlarged by knowledge of a prospective use (*MacPherson* v. *Buick Motor Co., supra,* p. 393; Brett, M. R., in *Coventry, Sheppard & Co.* v. *Great Eastern Ry Co.,* L. R. 11 Q. B. D. 776, 780; cf. *Bank of Batavia* v. *N. Y., L. E. & W. R. R. Co.,* 106 N. Y. 195, 199). We must view the act in its setting, which will include the implications and the promptings of usage and fair dealing. The casual response, made in mere friendliness or courtesy (*Fish* v. *Kelly,* 17 C. B. [N. S.] 194, 205, 207; Bohlen, *supra,* p. 374; Street, *supra,* p. 408) may not stand on the same plane, when we come to consider who is to assume the risk of negligence or error, as the deliberate certificate, indisputably an "act in the law" (Pollock, Contracts [8th ed.] p. 3), intended to sway conduct. Here the defendants are held, not merely for careless words (*Le Lievre* v. *Gould,* 1893, 1 Q. B. D. 491; Pollock, Torts [10th ed.], pp. 301, 302; Jeremiah Smith, Liability for Negligent Language, 14 Harvard Law Review, 184, 195), but for the careless performance of a service—the act of weighing—which happens to have found in the words of a certificate its culmination and its summary (cf. *Corey* v. *Eastman,* 166 Mass. 279, 287). The line of separation between these diverse liabilities is difficult to draw. It does not lose for that reason its correspondence with realities. Life has relations not capable always of division into inflexible compartments. The moulds expand and shrink.

We state the defendants' obligation, therefore, in terms, not of contract merely, but of duty. Other forms of statement are possible. They involve, at most, a change of emphasis. We may see here, if we please, a phase or an extension of the rule in *Lawrence* v. *Fox.* (20 N. Y. 268) as amplified recently in *Seaver* v. *Ransom* (224 N. Y. 233). If we fix our gaze upon that aspect, we shall stress the element of contract, and treat the defendants' promise as embracing the rendition of a service, which though ordered and paid for by one, was either wholly or in part for the benefit of another (*DeCicco* v. *Schweizer,* 221 N. Y. 431; *Rector, etc., St. Mark's Church* v. *Teed,* 120 N. Y. 583). We may find analogies again in the decisions which treat the sender of a telegram as the agent of the recipient (*Wolfskehl* v. *W. U. Tel. Co.,* 46 Hun, 542; *Milliken* v. *W. U. Tel. Co.,* 110 N. Y. 403). These other methods of approach arrive at the same goal, though the paths may seem at times to be artificial or circuitous. We have preferred to reach the goal more simply. The defendants, acting, not casually nor as mere servants, but in the pursuit of an independent calling, weighed and certified at the order of one with the very end and aim of shaping the conduct of another. Diligence was owing, not only to him who ordered, but to him also who relied.

Other points are made by counsel. We have not failed to consider them, but they do not alter our conclusion. Both sides having moved for direction of a verdict without other request, the ruling of the trial judge stands with the same force as the verdict of a jury (*Adams* v. *Roscoe Lumber Co.,* 159 N. Y. 176). If the purpose of the parties, the relation that arose between them and the significance of the transaction may be the subject of conflicting inferences, those most favorable to the plaintiffs must be deemed to have been accepted.

The judgment should be affirmed with costs.

Hiscock, Ch. J., Pound, McLaughlin, Crane and Andrews, JJ., concur; Hogan, J., dissents.

Judgment affirmed.

DOYLE v. CHATHAM & PHENIX NATIONAL BANK *

Court of Appeals of New York, 1930. 253 N. Y. 369, 171 N. E. 574.

APPEAL from a judgment of the Appellate Division of the Supreme Court in the second judicial department, entered July 17, 1929, affirming a judgment in favor of defendant entered upon a decision of the court at a Trial Term, a jury having been waived.

KELLOGG, J. The plaintiff is the owner of "Collateral Trust Gold Bonds" executed by the Motor Guaranty Corporation, a Delaware corporation. Certain bonds were issued directly to the plaintiff for value paid; others were issued for value to persons from whom the plaintiff purchased. The bonds are expressed to have been issued in pursuance of the provisions of a certain indenture of trust entered into between the Motor Guaranty Corporation and the defendant, the Chatham and Phenix National Bank of the City of New York, as trustee. Each of the bonds bears a certificate, signed by the defendant as trustee, which reads as follows: "This bond is one of the series of bonds described in the Collateral Trust Indenture mentioned therein." The securities pledged by the Motor Guaranty Corporation to protect its bond issue, which were deposited with the defendant as trustee, have proven worthless and the bonds are uncollectible. The plaintiff, as assignee of all causes of action accruing to the persons from whom he purchased, and in his own right, brings this action to recover from the defendant trustee the losses sustained, on the ground that its certificates were issued negligently and without authority, and that the plaintiff and his assignors were thereby induced to acquire worthless bonds and pay value therefor.

The collateral trust indenture was executed on the 1st day of February, 1922. It recites that the Motor Guaranty Corporation proposes from time to time to issue its collateral trust gold bonds, to draw interest at eight per cent, payable semi-annually; that each bond is to be written in accordance with a form of bond set up in the indenture. This form, with which the bonds of the plaintiff comply, contains the statement that the bond is "secured by the trade acceptances or notes of dealers, guaranteed by the Motor Guaranty Corporation; cash or notes of purchasers in part payment for motor vehicles, or other first lien mortgages, such purchasers' notes being endorsed by dealers and guaranteed by the Motor Guaranty Corporation." It also contains the following: "This bond is secured by said collateral of a face value of at least one hundred and ten percentum (110%) of the principal amount of the bond." It also states: "This bond shall not be valid for any purpose until the Trustee's certificate endorsed hereon shall have been duly executed." The form of the prescribed certificate, to be signed by the defendant as trustee, is identical with each of the certificates attached to the plaintiff's bonds, the reading of which has already been given.

The indenture provides that bonds shall from time to time be executed by the Motor Guaranty Corporation and delivered to the defendant as trustee for authentication by it; that the delivery shall be accompanied by a request, signed by an appropriate officer of the corporation, stating the amount, date and denomination of bonds to be issued, and demanding

* See footnote 50 *supra*.

authentication of the bonds requested to be issued. It further provides that the trustee shall thereupon, without further action by the corporation, authenticate the bonds and deliver them back to the corporation, "provided, however, there shall be delivered to and pledged with the Trustee" certain named collateral. The collateral to be pledged is as follows: "(a) Cash or current funds, and/or (b) Trade acceptances or notes of dealers guaranteed by the Motor Guaranty Corporation, or notes of purchasers in part payment for motor vehicles, or other first lien mortgages, such purchasers' notes being endorsed by dealers and guaranteed by the Motor Guaranty Corporation." It also provides: "The aggregate principal amount of cash and/or of securities delivered and pledged under subsection (b) shall always be at least equal to 110% of the amount of the Bonds to be issued hereunder in respect thereto." It further provides: "Upon receipt of cash and/or notes, and/or first lien mortgages, all as provided and described in this article, the Trustee shall be fully protected and is authorized without further inquiry, to authenticate and deliver the Bonds specified in such request and shall in no way be responsible to see to the application of the proceeds of any such Bond."

The identure further provides that the trustee may require from time to time that the corporation furnish a certificate or certificates of the president or a vice-president, attested by the secretary or assistant secretary, under the corporate seal, setting forth all or any information "concerning names and addresses of makers, acceptors, and other pertinent data regarding such collateral and/or first lien mortgages, such lists, descriptions and tabulations of collateral delivered or to be delivered to the Trustee." It contains this: "Such certificate or certificates shall be conclusive evidence to the Trustee of all statements therein contained and full warrant and protection to it for any and all action taken on the faith thereof under the terms of this indenture."

During the year 1922 the Motor Guaranty Corporation delivered to the defendant, for its certification as trustee, bonds of an aggregate par value in excess of $110,000. The defendant executed the requested certificates and returned the bonds to the corporation, which issued them to various persons upon payment of value therefor. Among these bonds were the bonds now owned by the plaintiff. In January, 1923, the corporation defaulted in the payment of interest and the defendant resigned as trustee. The fact then appeared that the corporation had, during the course of the year 1922, deposited with the trustee, as collateral for the bonds certified by it, the notes of various persons or corporations expressing an aggregate par value in excess of $130,000, all of which, with the exception of one note for $300, were in fact utterly valueless. With the same exception, none of the notes given were for the purchase of an automobile; none were made by an automobile dealer, or, for that matter, by a dealer in goods, wares and merchandise of any description. The makers comprised a lawyer, a bond salesman, a ticket agent, a mining corporation, and a construction company. The maker of two notes, aggregating $75,000, had no occupation, business or other visible means of support, although judgments in excess of $900,000 were outstanding against him. None of the securities held by the trustee defendant, at the time the bonds now owned by the plaintiff were issued, with the exception noted, were the notes or acceptances of dealers or automobile purchasers. Subsequently to January, 1923, all the assets of the Motor Guaranty Corporation were sold for the sum of $143.30.

We agree that the defendant cannot be held as the guarantor of the sufficiency or legality of the securities pledged with it, or for negligence in not ascertaining that the securities were worthless. (*Tschetinian* v. *City Trust Co.,* 186 N. Y. 432; *Green* v. *Title Guarantee & Trust Co.,* 223 App. Div. 12; aff'd., 248 N. Y. 627; *Byers* v. *Union Trust Co.,* 175 Penn. St. 318; Jones on Corporate Bonds & Mortgages, § 287a.) "The purpose of the certification was not to insure the sufficiency of the security. It was to prevent an overissue." (*Ainsa* v. *Mercantile Trust Co.,* 174 Cal. 504, 512.) If the defendant, without investigation, chose to lend its name to the swindling operations of a bogus finance corporation, by acting as its trustee and certifying its bonds, provided it certified with authority and without actual knowledge of the fraud intended, it was well within its legal rights. The question before us for decision is this: May the defendant be held in damages if, without authority, it certified the bonds now owned by the plaintiff, thereby inducing the plaintiff and his assignors to advance moneys upon the faith of securities which were worthless?

It is clear that the defendant signed the certificates without authority. As we have seen, it was authorized to certify "provided, however, there shall be delivered to and pledged with the Trustee" certain securities. The securities enumerated were the acceptances or notes of dealers or automobile buyers. No such securities were ever delivered to the defendant. If the defendant had requested and obtained a statement from the appropriate officers of the corporation, certifying to the "pertinent data regarding such collateral" possessed by them, its authority, without further investigation, to execute the certificates could not have been questioned. However, it requested and received no such statement. Its authority, therefore, remained conditional upon the fact that the notes of dealers had been precedently deposited with it. No such securities having been deposited, it had no authority to execute the certificates.

In *Conover* v. *Guarantee Trust Co.,* (88 N. J. Eq. 450; aff'd., 89 N. J. Eq. 584) the facts considered were these: A trust agreement provided that the mortgagor would assign to a trustee bonds and mortgages acquired by it, which had been appraised and guaranteed by a corporation associated in interest with the mortgagor; that, as the securities were deposited, the trustee would certify bonds of the mortgagor to an equal amount and deliver them to it for issuance to purchasers. The trustee accepted bonds secured by mortgages upon the lands of the mortgagor, rather than bonds and mortgages owned by the mortgagor and assigned to the trustee, and thereupon certified an equal amount of bonds which were sold subsequently by the mortgagor. It was held that the trustee was without authority to execute the certificates and was, therefore, liable to compensate the takers of the bonds for their money losses occasioned by the acquisition thereof. In *Rhinelander* v. *Farmers Loan & Trust Co.* (172 N. Y. 519) this court expressed the opinion that where a corporate mortgage provides for a certification of bonds, only upon the making by the directors of the mortgagor of a written instrument setting forth the purposes of the issue, the certification, without such a statement made, would afford to a taker of the bonds thus certified a cause of action against the certifying trustee for damages resulting from the investment. Such a recovery was there withheld, but only for the reason that the cause of action had been barred by the Statute of Limitations. In *Mullen* v. *Banking Co.* (108 Me. 498) the facts considered were these: All the bonds authorized by a trust indenture had been certified by the trustee and issued by the mortgagor. Nevertheless, on the request of a director of the mortgagor, the trustee certified two additional bonds, which were issued for value to the plaintiff. It was held that the plaintiff might recover from the trustee the difference between the value of an authorized bond and the value of the bond actually received, which was nil. The court said: "Under these circumstances the responsibility rests upon the trustee to authenticate no bond that should not be authenticated."

In *Conover* v. *Guarantee Trust Co.* (*supra*) the opinion was expressed that the right of the takers of the bonds to recover damages from the trustee, on account of its unauthorized certification, rested upon a breach of the duty owed by the trustee to the takers as *cestui que trustent.* A similar view was expressed in *Rhinelander* v. *Farmers Loan & Trust Co.* (*supra*), where the court said of the acceptance by the trustee of its trust position: "In executing that acceptance the defendant created the relation of trustee and *cestui que trust* between it and the future bondholders." Notwithstanding these expressions, it is obvious that a trustee, in wrongly certifying bonds to prospective takers, in order that they may become *cestui que trust,* cannot at that moment and before the relationship is established, have violated a trust duty owed to them. Manifestly this is true: "There is no trust or other relation between a trustee and a stranger about to deal with a *cestui que trust.*" (LINDLEY, L. J., in *Low* v. *Bouverie,* L. R. [1891] 3 Ch. 82.) In *Mullen* v. *Banking Co.* (*supra*) the court held that an unauthorized certificate executed by a trustee was a false representation that the bond was properly issued, rendering the trustee liable upon a cause of action in deceit. The fact that the representation was innocently made was not material, said the court, since the trustee, by its certificate, made an assertion of fact which, according to information which was or should have been within its own knowledge, was not true. In the case before us, however, it is clear that the plaintiff may not recover damages for a false representation, as in an action for deceit. In the first place, no such cause of action is alleged. In the second place, there is no proof that the trustee, in issuing its certicates, intended to defraud the plaintiff or his assignors. "Intentional fraud, as distinguished from a mere breach of duty or the omission to use due care, is an essential factor in an action for deceit." (*Kountze* v. *Kennedy,* 147 N. Y. 124; *Reno* v. *Bull,* 226 N. Y. 546.)

That there may be liability for damages resulting from the negligent utterance of words is now the settled doctrine in this jurisdiction. (*Glanzer* v. *Shepard,* 233 N. Y. 236; *International Products Co.* v. *Erie R. R. Co.,* 244 N. Y. 331.) In the first of the cited cases a buyer of merchandise, in reliance upon an erroneous certificate of a public weigher employed by the seller, made an overpayment for the goods purchased, and was permitted to recover from the weigher the equivalent of the moneys overpaid. In the second, a consignee of merchandise, desiring to insure the same, inquired of a carrier, which was to warehouse them, where the goods would be stored. The carrier, although the goods had not yet been received, replied that they were stored upon a certain dock, and the consignee insured them at that place. They were subsequently received by the carrier and stored at another dock where they were destroyed by fire. In consequence the consignee lost its insurance. It was permitted a recovery from the carrier for the amount of its loss. No relationship had been established, between the plaintiff and the defendant, in either of these cases, when the careless statement was made. In the one, the plaintiff had no contract relationship with the weigher; in the other the relationship of bailor and bailee had not been initiated, for the goods had not been received. Nevertheless the negligent statements gave rise to causes of action.

In *Glanzer* v. *Shepard* (*supra*) Judge CARDOZO said: "The defendants, acting, not casually nor as mere servants, but in the pursuit of an independent calling, weighed and certified at the order of one with the very end and aim of shaping the conduct of another. Diligence was owing, not only to him who ordered, but to him also who relied." In *International Products Co.* v. *Erie R. R. Co.* (*supra*) Judge ANDREWS named certain elements which must be present, in order that a cause of action for negligent speaking might lie. The utterer of the statement must have knowledge that the statement is required for a serious purpose; that those for whom it is made intend to rely and act thereupon; that if it be false they may be damaged. Finally, the relationship of the parties, arising out of contract or otherwise, must be such that in morals and good conscience the one has the right to rely upon the other for information, and the other, giving the information, owes a duty to give it with care. "An inquiry made of a stranger is one thing; of a person with whom the inquirer has entered or is about to enter into a contract concerning the goods which are or are to be its subject is another. Even here the inquiry must be made as the basis of independent action. We do not touch the doctrine of *caveat emptor*." The case of *Derry* v. *Peek* (L. R. 14 A. C. 337) was cited by Judge ANDREWS as establishing the principle, for application in the courts of England, that no action lies for a statement, negligently but not fraudulently made. However, even in that case, Lord HERSCHELL, in laying down the general rule, made this noteworthy exception: "There is another class of actions which I must refer to also for the purpose of putting it aside. I mean those cases where a person within whose special province it lay to know a particular fact, has given an erroneous answer to an inquiry made with regard to it by a person desirous of ascertaining the fact for the purpose of determining his course accordingly, and has been held bound to make good the assurance he has given."

The defendant here, like the defendant in *Glanzer* v. *Shepard* (*supra*), occupied an independent position, and issued its certificates at the behest of a third person. We may say with Judge CARDOZO that the certificates were made "with the very end and aim of shaping the conduct of another." Like the utterer of the statement in the assumed case in Lord HERSCHELL's exception, it was the "special province" of the defendant "to know a particular fact;" it imparted information, by its certificates, to persons "desirous of ascertaining the fact for the purpose of determining" their course accordingly. Within the requirements laid down by Judge ANDREWS, the defendant knew that the certificates were desired for a serious purpose by persons who intended to rely and act thereupon. They were issued for the very purpose of establishing a relationship of trustee and *cestui que trust* between the defendant and the persons who might rely thereon. It must be remembered that this is not the case of a buyer and seller to whose transactions the principle of *caveat emptor* might apply. It is a case where the creator of a trust, accepted by the defendant, in a solemn instrument signed by both, named the defendant as trustee, for the special purpose, among others, that it might certify bonds to prospective investors, to the very end that the takers of the bonds might receive definite assurance that the bonds were issued pursuant to the terms of the indenture. It seems clear, therefore, that, within the authorities cited, the defendant, in so far as its certificates constituted misrepresentations of fact, innocently though negligently made, became liable to the takers of the bonds, who invested their moneys upon the faith of the certificates.

The certificates were not to be issued, as we have seen, unless acceptances and notes of dealers and automobile buyers, in excess of bonds to be issued, had been deposited with the defendant as security therefor. Necessarily, therefore, the certificates constituted representations that the deposits had been made. Clearly, if the defendant, as trustee, had issued the certificates when no securities whatever had been deposited with it, liability for the damage done would have arisen. Equally must this follow where, as in this case, the securities deposited were not the securities specified in the trust indenture from which alone the defendant derived its power to certify. In not ascertaining that the securities deposited were not securities of the character named in the indenture, the defendant was guilty of negligence. In certifying the bonds, as issued pursuant to the terms of the indenture, it was guilty of negligently making a misrepresentation of fact. The plaintiff and certain assignors were induced by the certificates to invest in the worthless bonds. If the certificates had not been executed the bonds could not have been issued and no loss would have accrued. Therefore, the false certificates were the proximate cause of the losses sustained. (*Conover* v. *Guarantee Trust Co., supra; Mullen* v. *Banking Co., supra; Rhinelander* v. *Farmers Loan & Trust Co., supra.*)

The provisions of the trust indenture in certain instances exempting the defendant from liability for its acts or omissions as trustee, do not, in this instance, apply. (*Conover* v. *Guarantee Trust Co., supra; Mullen* v. *Banking Co., supra; Rhinelander* v. *Farmers Loan & Trust Co., supra.*) In *Conover* v. *Guarantee Trust Co.* (*supra*) the vice chancellor said: "It accordingly seems impossible to construe an immunity clause as intended to exempt a trustee from liability for transcending his powers as clearly defined by the trust agreement; his engagement is to exercise the powers, and only the powers conferred upon him, and the appropriate office and purpose of an immunity clause forming a part of a trust agreement which specifically and clearly defines the trustee's powers appears to be to limit his responsibility in matters of judgment and discretion committed to him in the execution of those defined powers."

The record indicates that the plaintiff and many of his assignors took their bonds in reliance upon the certificates and in ignorance of the character of the securities deposited. The plaintiff is entitled to recover damages on account of the investments thus induced, on the basis of the consideration paid therefor plus interest, less the value of the bonds acquired, if any. (*Reno* v. *Bull, supra.*) The record leaves it in doubt whether certain other assignors were not fully aware of the character of the securities deposited and of the shady nature of the financial transactions in which the Motor Guaranty Corporation was engaged and, therefore, whether or not they in good faith relied upon the certificates in making their investments. For the determination of these questions a new trial is necessary.

The judgment of the Appellate Division and that of the Trial Term should be reversed and a new trial granted, with costs to abide the event.

Cardozo, Ch. J., Pound, Crane, Lehman, O'Brien and Hubbs, JJ., concur.

Judgments reversed, etc.

STATE STREET TRUST CO. v. ERNST *

Court of Appeals of New York, 1938. 278 N. Y. 104, 15 N. E. 2d 416.

Appeal, by permission, from a judgment of the Appellate Division of the Supreme Court in the first judicial department, entered June 4, 1937, which unanimously affirmed a judgment in favor of defendants entered upon an order of the court at a Trial Term granting motions by the defendants to set aside a verdict in favor of plaintiff and for the direction of a verdict in favor of defendants.

Finch, J. Was the evidence introduced by plaintiff so inadequate that, resolving all contested issues and drawing all possible inferences in plaintiff's favor, a jury could not find that defendants were guilty of gross negligence raising an inference of fraud, and that plaintiff relied upon the certified balance sheet prepared by defendants, thereby suffering damage?

The Pelz-Greenstein Company was organized in 1922 to engage in the business of financing wholesalers or mills. Its sole business was lending money, taking back, as collateral, inventory of the borrower and assignments of accounts receivable. Each borrower was referred to as a "department." Advances were made by Pelz-Greenstein to its borrowers to enable them to purchase or manufacture merchandise. Pelz-Greenstein was repaid in large part by the assignment of accounts receivable resulting from the sales of such merchandise. The collectibility of these advances thus depended in the first instance on the salability of the merchandise manufactured or purchased by the funds so advanced. If the merchandise failed to sell, not only was the repayment of the advances jeopardized, but likewise the income of Pelz-Greenstein, for its major item of income, to wit, commissions, was a percentage of the assigned accounts.

On January 19, 1929, the president of Pelz-Greenstein applied to plaintiff for a line of credit and a loan of $300,000. He presented an estimated balance sheet of the business as of December 31, 1928, and stated that defendants, a firm of accountants, were making an audit of the condition of the company as of that date and that a balance sheet certified by defendants would be submitted to plaintiff when it had been prepared. Plaintiff refused to grant the application of Pelz-Greenstein for a time loan until it had received the certified balance sheet of defendants and had found that it substantially corroborated the estimated balance sheet. Pending the receipt of the certified balance sheet of defendants plaintiff made a demand loan to Pelz-Greenstein of $300,000.

This certified balance sheet prepared by defendants was dated April 2, 1929, and issued in ten counterparts. The defendants admit that they knew it was to be used to obtain credit. On April 9 a copy was given by Pelz-Greenstein to plaintiff. Plaintiff found that the certified balance sheet substantially corroborated the estimated balance sheet. The demand note was then surrendered and a three months' time note taken in its place. This note was renewed for three months' periods, the last renewal

* This case is discussed at p. 34 ff. *supra*.

being made January 9, 1930. Morgan, the lending officer of plaintiff, testifies that he relied upon this certified balance sheet in passing upon the application for the loan and in making the renewals. On April 26, 1930, Pelz-Greenstein was petitioned into bankruptcy. Plaintiff has received back only a portion of its loan and brings this action for the difference.

With the certified balance sheet defendants issued the following certificate:

"We hereby certify that we examined the books of account and record pertaining to the assets and liabilities of Pelz-Greenstein Co., Inc., New York City, as of the close of business December 31, 1928, and, based on the records examined, information submitted to us, and subject to the foregoing notes [not here material], it is our opinion that the above condensed statement shows the financial condition of the company at the date stated and that the related income and surplus account is correct."

On May 9, 1929, a month after supplying ten copies of the balance sheet to be used, to the knowledge of the defendants, to obtain credit, defendants sent a letter to the Pelz-Greenstein Company containing comments on and explanations of the balance sheet. Apparently only one copy of this letter was sent, and it did not come to the attention of plaintiff nor, so far as the evidence shows, to any one else until after the bankruptcy of Pelz-Greenstein. This accompanying letter contained statements of facts discovered by defendants in the course of their audit, and, therefore, known to them when they prepared the original certified balance sheet, but which were not mentioned therein. One of the defendants testified before trial that the certified balance sheet was subject to the comments contained in the letter and the letter was sent for the purpose of trying to prevent any one from using this balance sheet without knowing the scope of the examination which was made.

At the close of plaintiff's case defendants moved to dismiss the complaint. The trial judge reserved decision. Defendants thereupon rested without calling any witnesses, although there would naturally be available the men who made the audit, those who prepared or supervised the preparation of the working papers or the certified balance sheet and experts to refute the testimony offered by the experts called by plaintiff. Defendants renewed their motion to dismiss and also moved for a directed verdict. The court reserved decision and submitted the case to the jury. After the jury rendered a verdict for plaintiff the trial judge denied the reserved motion to dismiss, but granted a motion to set aside the verdict, and directed a verdict for defendants. The Appellate Division has unanimously affirmed, and the appeal is here by permission of this court.

In the brief of respondents, Pelz and Greenstein are denominated as deliberately dishonest. It is there conceded that they made old and probably uncollectible accounts appear good by causing payments to be made to Pelz-Greenstein, Inc., by another corporation owned by themselves, which payments, credited to such old accounts, made it appear as if the debtors had been paying their debts. They induced one Saqui, who freely admitted his own dishonesty and testified on behalf of plaintiff, to furnish false inventories and to assign to Pelz-Greenstein large numbers of false and fictitious accounts. In one account of $800,000 there were $300,000 of wholly fictitious sales. At the time Pelz-Greenstein was hopelessly insolvent.

To what extent may accountants be held liable for their failure to reveal this condition? We have held that in the absence of a contractual relationship or its equivalent, accountants cannot be held liable for ordinary negligence in preparing a certified balance sheet even though they are aware that the balance sheet will be used to obtain credit. (*Ultramares Corp.* v. *Touche,* 255 N. Y. 170.) Accountants, however, may be liable to third parties, even where there is lacking deliberate or active fraud. A representation certified as true to the knowledge of the accountants when knowledge there is none, a reckless misstatement, or an opinion based on grounds so flimsy as to lead to the conclusion that there was no genuine belief in its truth, are all sufficient upon which to base liability. A refusal to see the obvious, a failure to investigate the doubtful, if sufficiently gross, may furnish evidence leading to an inference of fraud so as to impose liability for losses suffered by those who rely on the balance sheet. In other words, heedlessness and reckless disregard of consequence may take the place of deliberate intention.

In *Ultramares Corp.* v. *Touche* (255 N. Y. 170) we said with no uncertainty that negligence, if gross, or blindness, even though not equivalent to fraud, was sufficient to sustain an inference of fraud. Our exact words were: "In this connection we are to bear in mind the principle already stated in the course of this opinion that negligence or blindness, even when not equivalent to fraud, is none the less evidence to sustain an inference of fraud. At least this is so if the negligence is gross" (p. 190).

To emphasize our holding that active and deliberate fraud was not necessary to create liability, and that gross negligence, and even blindness to the obvious may be evidence to sustain an inference of fraud, we were careful to point out that the language in *Kountze* v. *Kennedy* (147 N. Y. 124), saying that misjudgment, however gross, or want of caution, however marked, is not fraud, must be confined to the facts of that case, where the trier of the facts had found the defendants guiltless, and the ruling "amounted merely to a holding that a finding of fraud did not follow as an inference of law." (*Ultramares Corp.* v. *Touche, supra,* p. 191.)

The defendants, however, contend that they may escape all liability by insisting that the balance sheet merely purported to reflect the condition of the books and that it did this correctly. The balance sheet, however, did not correctly reflect the condition of the company even as shown by the books, as will later appear. Nor is the duty of an accountant in preparing a balance sheet confined to a mere setting up of the items from the books. Such duties have been defined

"His [the author's] business is to ascertain and state the true financial position of the company at the time of the audit, and his duty is confined to that. But then comes the question, 'How is he to ascertain that position?' The answer is, 'By examining the books of the company.' But he does not discharge his duty by doing this without inquiry and without taking any trouble to see that the books themselves shew the company's true position. He must take reasonable care to ascertain that they do so. Unless he does this his audit would be worse than an idle farce. Assuming the books to be so kept as to shew the true position of a company, the auditor has to frame a balance-sheet shewing that position according to the books and to certify that the balance sheet presented is correct in that sense. But his first duty is to examine the books, not merely for the purpose of ascertaining what they do shew, but also for the purpose of satisfying himself that they shew the true financial position of the company." (*Matter of London & General Bank,* [1895] 2 Ch. 673, 682.)

The record is, indeed, replete with evidence, both oral and documentary, to make a prima facie case against the defendants. In the first place, we have these accountants guilty of an act which is the equivalent of active misrepresentation. On April 2, 1929, they sent to Pelz-Greenstein the certified balance sheet, with ten additional copies, knowing that it was to be used to obtain credit. "Nothing was said as to the persons to whom these counterparts would be shown or the extent or number of the transactions in which they would be used * * * The range of the transactions in which a certificate of audit might be expected to play a part was as indefinite and wide as the possibilities of the business that was mirrored in the summary." (*Ultramares Corp.* v. *Touche,* 255 N. Y. 170, 174.) Not until thirty days later did the accountants send to Pelz-Greenstein a letter of explanation of this balance sheet, and then apparently only one copy. So important was this covering letter in the minds of defendants that, although the balance sheet attached to the covering letter was in other respects substantially identical with the original balance sheet, it contained the following notation, which did not appear at all on the original balance sheet released thirty days earlier: "This balance sheet is subject to the comments contained in the letter attached to and made a part of this report." One of the copartners, testifying before trial, said: "We want to try to prevent anyone using this balance sheet, without knowing the scope of the examination which we made, which is set forth in paragraph 2 of the full report. * * * We have had cases where our entire covering letter had been deleted from these reports and just the balance sheet used." Yet, in effect, these defendants themselves did just this. They held back this covering letter for thirty days and issued the balance sheet alone to the world of possible lenders. The loan by the plaintiff was made long before this important covering letter was even sent.

The above act of the accountants, in placing in circulation a certified balance sheet which they practically conceded should not be used without knowing the scope of the examination set forth in the covering letter, and then allowing a period of thirty days to elapse before sending the covering letter, and then only one copy, whereas there had been ten copies of the certified balance sheet issued, was itself gross negligence and an important piece of evidence raising an inference of fraud.

The certified balance sheet, outside of capital, showed a small surplus of $83,000. According to the evidence and the reasonable inferences deductible therefrom, a jury might have found that instead of a surplus of $83,000 the balance sheet should have shown a deficit and impairment of capital of over half a million. A jury could also have found that in addition over $768,000 of its commission accounts were in a condition indicating the likelihood of substantial losses.

Turning now to the specific items. The second largest item in the balance sheet was the item:

"Commission Accounts Receivable — secured by merchandise	
Advances	$2,043,337.81
Less allowance	19,767.15
	$2,023,570.66"

The above item represented the advances made by Pelz-Greenstein to its borrowers to finance their operations in the purchase or manufacture of merchandise. These accounts, amounting to over one-fourth of Pelz-Greenstein's total assets, were shown on the certified balance sheet as good after deducting the $19,000 allowance. Yet, to the knowledge of defendants, according to their own statement, in the delayed covering letter, a very large proportion of these commission accounts receivable "were comparatively inactive during the year and appeared slow of collection." Out of the total of $2,043,000 an aggregate of $768,000, or over 38 per cent of the total amount, had unpaid advances at the end of the year 1928, amounting to 125 per cent of the total sales during the year. This meant that these borrowers owed Pelz-Greenstein more money at the end of the year than their total sales during the year by 25 per cent, thus indicating stagnation of inventories. Not only did these stagnant accounts represent over 38 per cent in amount, but they included 27 out of 55 borrowers. The defendants had knowledge of this condition as shown by the delayed covering letter, and this knowledge was brought home to them by their report for the prior year, when they referred in the following manner to similar accounts, although the percentage of advances to sales then was only 65 per cent, as compared with 125 per cent in 1928: "The following accounts had excessive advances as measured by their sales volume which indicated probably excessive or slow moving inventories." It was conceded that this was the third consecutive audit by the defendants of the books of Pelz-Greenstein.

One of the experts for the plaintiff testified without contradiction that the percentage of unpaid advances, amounting to 125 per cent of sales, indicated that the accounts were in an over-extended condition and were badly out of proportion to the amount of merchandise sold during the year, indicating that the inventories were either excessive, slow moving or unsalable. In his opinion this condition indicated the likelihood of excessive losses. Furthermore, this expert testified unequivocally that the financial condition of Pelz-Greenstein could not be truthfully expressed without mention of this condition in the balance sheet. Professor Cole, the other expert called by plaintiff, testified that proper accounting practice required that defendants either establish a very large allowance for uncollectible accounts or indicate, in connection with the balance sheet, the existence of approximately $768,000 with a ratio of advances to sales of 125 per cent. The best corroboration of the testimony of both these experts is what defendants themselves said of this condition in the delayed covering letter. In spite of this a reserve of a mere $19,767.15 was set up against this account. This was to cover not only those accounts of $768,000, showing the stagnation of inventories described above, but all other commission accounts in a total of over $2,000,000.

This small reserve of $19,000 was practically absorbed in the one account of W. K. Wardener, which had gone into bankruptcy in 1924 and from which account Pelz-Greenstein had received nothing since May, 1924. Even if the accountants had not been informed that the Wardener account was in bankruptcy yet a warning that this account required a substantial reserve was given to them by the fact that an account upon which nothing had been received since May, 1924, was being padded year after year by monthly interest charges. From a failure to note on the balance sheet the stagnant condition of over three-quarters of a million of these accounts and the setting up of a totally inadequate reserve, a jury might reasonably draw the inference that these defendants had no genuine belief in these figures in the balance sheet to which they certified.

We next come to a very substantial item entitled

"Commission Account Advances—
Inactive and in Liquidation ....$215,124.72."

This item appeared on the certified balance sheet without any reserve. The books of Pelz-Greenstein showed on their face that many of the accounts included in this item had had no transactions for many years, neither sales nor relaizations upon security. Furthermore, within this time the books showed systematic inflation of these accounts by steadily increasing interest charges. In fact, these charges were added to one account, even though the account appeared on the face of the books to have been in bankruptcy. The covering letter set forth the real condition of these accounts in detail, thus showing full knowledge on the part of the defendants. Defendants seek to sustain the integrity of this item on the ground that they placed it "below the line" and characterized it as "inactive and in liquidation." The only evidence in the record concerning the effect of these acts is the uncontradicted evidence of the accounting experts that placing an item below the line means only that it is not current but that otherwise it will be realizable in full. Furthermore, these expert witnesses testified that the failure to set up a reserve against an item, whether it is placed above or below the line, according to the rules of accountancy which any one must apply in reading a balance sheet, means that the accountants represent that they have no knowledge which would indicate to them that these accounts are worth less than "full value" and "that the people certifying to this balance sheet indicate this is the value." The experts went on to testify without contradiction that from the facts as shown on the face of the books a reserve of at least $150,000 should have been set up against these accounts unless investigation showed them to be of full value.

The defendants urge that these defendants were excused from investigation because of a letter from Leon S. Pelz, treasurer of Pelz-Greenstein, in which he stated that Pelz-Greenstein had in its possession "sufficient salable merchandise to completely liquidate" these accounts. In other words, defendants were content to certify a balance sheet knowing it would be used to secure bank credit which contained an item of over $125,000* of apparently dead accounts on the uninvestigated and unsupported statement of the party seeking the credit that these accounts were amply secured, although it appeared on the face of the books that there had been no realization upon this security for years. Where the books indicate the likelihood of a substantial loss, a failure to indicate this on the balance sheet can be justified only by an actual check-up. It does not suffice to rely instead upon the statement of an officer of the firm the books of which are being examined. If an accountant may disregard a situation which indicates substantial losses because he is informed by the person whose books are being examined that there is adequate security, the balance sheet issued by the accountant, by its failure to point this out, contains a misrepresentation. The very purpose of the bank in seeking the balance sheet prepared by the accountant is to check any possible fraud on the part of the person seeking the loan. Yet these

* Sic. should clearly be $215,000. (Ed.)

accountants contend that they may accept as true a statement by the party whose books are being examined, make no check-up or investigation on their own part, and issue a statement omitting entirely any mention of the reason why investigation of the security was omitted.

We have explicit expert testimony, uncontradicted, that under these circumstances it was improper accounting practice for defendants to accept a letter from Pelz-Greenstein, and that they should have investigated these accounts very fully to ascertain whether the companies were still in business and to ascertain definitely and independently what security, if any, Pelz-Greenstein held for the payment of these accounts.

We next come to an item which is not as large as those which have gone before, but as to which there was obvious gross negligence. In the "Accounts Receivable" item of $3,200,000, protected only by a reserve of $15,000, was a group of accounts totaling over $72,000 denominated by defendants on their work sheet as "Ocean Bankrupt Accounts." Defendants stated that the failure to set up a reserve against this $72,000 of bankrupt accounts was justified because they were covered by policies of credit insurance. A mere cursory examination of the policies shows that over $32,000 of these accounts were not covered by the policies at all. Thus the reserve was shown to be inadequate by this one account alone. In addition, defendants' own work sheets showed that $14,000 of these bankrupt accounts had been with the insurance company from three years to fifteen months without action. There was expert testimony which a jury was at liberty to believe that a reserve of at least $46,000 should have been established against this account.

We find, also, a $10,000 demand note listed as part of the assets without reserve although it had been overdue and in the hands of an attorney, who had been unable to collect, for two years.

In connection with the foregoing items we have been concerned with evidence from which a jury might find that defendants had actual knowledge that the condition of the items in the balance sheet was not as represented. In the account of E. Heller & Bros., on the other hand, plaintiff contends that the evidence was sufficient to justify a jury in finding that there were circumstances appearing on the books which were so unusual and suspicious that proper accounting practice required defendants to make an investigation. The Heller account involved over $800,000 of the assets of Pelz-Greenstein. During the first eleven months of 1928 sales by the Heller Company never exceeded $191,000 a month, and averaged about $129,000. In December, just preceding the report of the accountants, sales were listed in the books as having jumped to $491,000. The amount included $300,000 of wholly fictitious sales. Plaintiff contends that this sudden increase of approximately $300,000 for the month should have put defendants on notice that something was wrong. Investigation was at least called for and would have disclosed the fictitious accounts.

We come now to evidence from which a jury could find that these defendants were at least heedless and reckless in purporting to reflect the condition of the books. We have an allowance of $101,000 for "doubtfuls" and "discounts," $86,000 of this $101,000 being for discounts and $15,000 for doubtfuls in the item of Accounts Receivable for $3,200,000. There was evidence that these figures for doubtfuls and discounts were arrived at, not by computation on the basis of business done during the year 1928, but by accepting the figures used for the year 1927. The working papers used by defendants for 1927 showed that in that year the amount of discounts had been based originally upon usual accounting practice, and was much larger than the final figure adopted by the accountants. Also, the original allowance for doubtfuls was greater than the final figure. On the basis of these higher figures, however, the profit for the year 1927 was less than the amount of dividends declared for that year. The reserves for discounts and for doubtfuls were then reduced so as to establish a profit in excess of the dividends for the year. The haphazard method used in arriving at these figures and the failure to follow usual accounting practice supports the contention urged by plaintiff, without answer or explanation upon this record, that defendants, in preparing this balance sheet, were negligent to such an extent as to amount to a reckless disregard for the accuracy necessary for a balance sheet to give the proper reflection of the condition of the business.

The record contains many other important items of evidence to enumerate which would unduly extend this opinion, now beyond reasonable limits.

The foregoing presents abundant evidence from which a jury could find that defendants knew facts which vitally affected the financial worth of Pelz-Greenstein, and which defendants totally suppressed on the certified balance sheet but disclosed to Pelz-Greenstein alone in the one copy of the covering letter sent thirty days later. The jury further could have found that the computation of reserves on the certified balance sheet was a misrepresentation which did not reflect the facts as known to defendants, and which they in good faith should have revealed. Where the record shows acts on the part of the accountants, as outlined above, we cannot say, as a matter of law, that plaintiff has failed to make out a case for the jury.

This brings us to the question of reliance. Defendants contend that the difference between the estimated balance sheet furnished by Pelz-Greenstein and the certified balance sheet prepared by them was such that as a matter of law plaintiff must have disregarded their certified balance sheet in making the loan and decided to make the loan solely on the basis of the estimated balance sheet of Pelz-Greenstein. In so contending defendants disregard the uncontradicted evidence that the certified balance sheet substantially corroborated the estimated balance sheet, the differences being only those which an audit would ordinarily produce. A mere comparison of the two balance sheets discloses that there was ample evidence from which a jury could find that the certified balance sheet was a substantial corroboration of the estimated balance sheet. When the items of cash receivable, commission accounts receivable and subscriptions on the two balance sheets are totaled they show a total for the estimated balance sheet of $7,760,000 and for the certified balance sheet of $7,650,000, the latter figure being net after deducting reserves of about $121,000. As the estimated balance sheet showed no reserves, the actual discrepancy in assets between the estimated and certified balance sheet was only about $11,000. Furthermore, the only substantial difference between the balance sheets was that defendants listed a number of items as non-current assets which the estimated balance sheet had listed as current assets. It cannot be said, therefore, that there was no evidence that the certified balance sheet substantially corroborated the estimated balance sheet. It is undoubtedly true that, in making the loan, there was reliance upon the then reputations of Pelz and Greenstein. But this does not preclude reliance also upon defendants' certified balance sheet. Evidence of such reliance is to be found in the uncontradicted testimony of the witnesses testifying for the plaintiff. Also it is to be found in the fact that the plaintiff would not make any but a demand loan until receipt of the certified balance sheet, and that it was only after it had received and examined the certified balance sheet that it made the time loan. The fraudulent misrepresentations on the part of defendants need not be the sole inducing cause of the damage. It is sufficient if such representations be an inducing cause. (*Ochs* v. *Woods,* 221 N. Y. 335; *Laska* v. *Harris,* 215 N. Y. 554.)

In addition the defendants rely on the fact that plaintiff renewed the note on several occasions so as to extend it for more than a year, and that when the precarious condition of Pelz-Greenstein Company was discovered plaintiff agreed to participate in a pooling of assets agreement with several other banks. Defendants knew that Pelz-Greenstein Company was seeking a line of credit from plaintiff and that the original note, if granted, would be extended subsequently. There is abundant evidence to show that these extensions were made in reliance upon the certified balance sheet, and, although other factors may have been considered, they do not constitute a sole and independent cause which brought about the loss rather than the misstatements in the balance sheet. (See *Hotaling* v. *Leach & Co.,* 247 N. Y. 84, 93.) The pooling agreement was to plaintiff's advantage and helped to minimize the loss.

Finally, defendants argue that plaintiff was not damaged by reason of the balance sheet because at the time it was issued plaintiff already had made a demand loan of $300,000, and the company, according to plaintiff's allegations, was insolvent at that time. There can be no doubt that if at the time the balance sheet was issued plaintiff had been informed of the true condition of Pelz-Greenstein Company it would have insisted upon immediate payment of the demand loan, and there is evidence from which it can be found that at that time full payment of the loan could have been obtained.

Upon all the evidence it cannot be said as a matter of law that plaintiff has failed to make out a prima facie case against defendants.

The judgments should be reversed and a new trial granted, with costs in all courts to abide the event.

LEHMAN, J. (dissenting). The defendants, a firm of accountants, were employed by the Pelz-Greenstein Company to examine the books of the company and to prepare a certified balance sheet of its financial position. To their employers they owed a duty to perform their work with care and with the skill which they represented they had, as professional accountants. They owed no such duty to persons who might deal with Pelz-Greenstein Company, upon the basis of the certified balance sheet prepared by the defendants. To such persons they owed only the duty to refrain from making any fraudulent misrepresentation. (*Ultramares Corp.* v. *Touche,* 225 N. Y. 170.) The courts below have held, without dissent, that the evidence is insufficient to permit an inference of fraud as defined in that case.

The only representations made by the defendants are contained in the balance sheet which they prepared after examining the books of account of the Pelz-Greenstein Company and the certificate appended thereto. The certificate states: "We hereby certify that we examined the books of account and record pertaining to the assets and liabilities of Pelz-Greenstein Co., Inc., New York City, as of the close of business December 31, 1928, and, based on the records examined, information submitted to us, and subject to the foregoing notes [not material here], it is our opinion that the above condensed statement shows the financial condition of the company at the date stated and that the related income and surplus account is correct."

To prepare a balance sheet, accountants must, of course, examine the books and accounts submitted to them, and from such examination and any other information which may be furnished to them, they must prepare a balance sheet which, *in their opinion,* reflects the true financial position of the business. The certificate of the defendants constitutes an express representation of *fact* that they have "examined the books of account and record pertaining to the assets and liabilities of Pelz-Greenstein Co., Inc." The balance sheet itself represents and was understood to represent only the "opinion" of the defendants based "on the records examined" and on information presented to the defendants.

It is undisputed that the defendants did examine the books and accounts of Pelz-Greenstein Company and that the balance sheet is based upon entries in those books and accounts. It is also undisputed that the balance sheet did not show the true financial position of the business. According to the balance sheet, the corporation had assets of about $8,000,000 and debts of less than $5,000,000; its capital of over $3,000,000 was unimpaired and it had, a surplus of about $83,000. In fact the corporation was insolvent; its liabilities exceeded the fair value of its assets. The defendants did not, however, warrant, or certify, the accuracy of the balance sheet; they represented only that the balance sheet was in "their opinion" correct. May they be held responsible for loss caused to the bank by reliance on this expression of opinion? That is the problem presented upon this appeal.

The defendants are not liable for error of judgment; they are not liable even for lack of care in arriving at their opinion. They are liable only if the opinion expressed was not only erroneous, but was fraudulently expressed. Actual bad faith and intent to deceive is not always, it is true, an essential element in a cause of action for deceit. Such a cause of action may be established against the defendants without proof that they expressed an opinion which they knew was incorrect; at least, however, there must be evidence of a ruthless disregard of whether the opinion was correct or not—the expression of an opinion where "the grounds supporting it are so flimsy as to lead to the conclusion that there was no genuine belief back of it." (*Ultramares Corp.* v. *Touche, supra,* p. 186.)

In that case we said that "negligence or blindness, even when not equivalent to fraud, is none the less evidence to sustain an inference of fraud. At least this is so if the negligence is gross" (p. 190). That rule was not new; it had been applied in earlier cases cited in the opinion. Again and again, however, in that opinion, as in the cases cited, the court pointed out that even gross negligence is not equivalent to fraud. It may, in proper case, furnish sufficient evidence to justify an inference of fraud, but that is true only when the proof of gross negligence shows that the grounds supporting the opinion are in fact "so flimsy *as to lead to the conclusion* that there was no genuine belief back of it. *Further than that this court has never gone.*" (Italics are mine.) (*Ultramares Corp.* v. *Touche, supra,* p. 186.)

Judge FINCH has, in his opinion, referred to the evidence upon which he bases his conclusion that it establishes fraud. I shall try to avoid repetition of that evidence. The most important of the alleged errors in the balance sheet is the failure to provide sufficient reserves for the collection of "commission accounts receivable." The amount of reserves which should be set aside to take care of loss that may be suffered by reason of inability to collect such accounts is a matter of judgment. The defendants knew of circumstances which it is said pointed clearly to the conclusion that a reserve of $21,000 is insufficient to take care of these accounts of over $2,043,337.81. Perhaps the defendants here showed a lack of caution. Their letter sent thirty days after the certified balance sheet was sent, shows that they knew that the reserve *might* prove insufficient. None the less, the amount of probable loss even with these circumstances known remained uncertain; the estimate of one per cent loss was doubtless over-optmistic, yet the estimate was based on facts which were not "so flimsy as to lead to the conclusion that there was no honest belief back of it" (p. 186).

The next error which, it is argued, shows negligence so gross as to indicate a lack of honest belief based on substantial grounds is that no allowance was made for "commission account advances." Many of these accounts were old. Again there are circumstances which perhaps should have acted as a warning signal to a cautious accountant. The defendants saw the signal—that is shown by the supplementary letter—but decided, nevertheless, to make no allowance. Again it would, doubtless, have been better if the defendants had given to those who might rely upon the balance sheet, the warning signal they had seen. They did, however, give notice on the balance sheet that accounts were "inactive and in liquidation" and they removed them from the current assets of the business and placed them "below the line." The owners of the business, men who at that time had a fine reputation, assured the defendants that they had sufficient security to liquidate these dead accounts. I can find here no justification for any argument that a balance sheet which shows that no allowance or reserve has been made for inactive accounts in liquidation may be held to be a fraudulent representation that no allowance or reserve is necessary.

I agree that the jury might find gross negligence in failure to provide a reserve of $46,000 against a group of bankrupt accounts aggregating $72,000. Even gross negligence in regard to an item of $46,000 in a balance sheet showing assets of almost $8,000,000 can hardly be regarded as substantial evidence of fraudulent misrepresentation. I do not take up in detail the other items where it is said the jury might find gross negligence. Each one involves the exercise of judgment; in none does it appear that there was no ground for honest exercise of judgment.

Certainly there is here no deliberate intention to deceive, no statement of *fact* made without actual knowledge, no statement of an opinion which the defendants did not honestly hold; nor, with the possible exception of the one item of $46,000, is there any evidence of an expression of opinion made by a person careless as to whether it was based on sufficient knowledge. The case is entirely different from that presented by *Ultramares Corp.* v. *Touche* (*supra*). There the defendants certified that the balance sheet corresponded with accounts which the jury might find had not been examined by the defendants, or had been disregarded by them; and the court pointed out "that in certifying to the correspondence between balance sheet and accounts" (p. 192), the defendants made a statement as true to their own knowledge, when they had, as a jury might find, no knowledge on the subject.

Here the defendants examined adequately the books and data which they certified they had examined, and they are not charged with either bad faith or even neglignce in making their examination. The balance sheet corresponds with the books and if the defendants were negligent, their negligence, whether gross or slight, consisted only in failure to give to the information, which they obtained through such examination, the effect which expert witnesses testify should, in their opinion, be given to it. The defendants realized that this information might reasonably affect their judgment. The explanatory letter which they sent later shows that. The jury might find that the defendants' judgment was bad, but the court pointed out in the *Ultramares* case that liability cannot be predicated upon error however great in the exercise of judgment. The error of judgment does not indicate a willful expression of a false opinion, or an expression of opinion based on grounds so flimsy that the jury might conclude that the opinion was not based on genuine belief. To permit recovery in a case where the evidence does not sustain such a conclusion is to wipe out the distinction which this court has always drawn and which it reiterated in the *Ultramares* case.

The judgment should be affirmed.

O'BRIEN, LOUGHRAN and RIPPEY, JJ., concur with FINCH, J.; LEHMAN, J., dissents in opinion in which CRANE, Ch. J., concurs; HUBBS, J., taking no part.

Judgments reversed, etc. (See 278 N. Y. 704.)

O'CONNOR v. LUDLAM *

Court of Appeals of the United States for the Second Circuit, 1937.
92 F.2d 50, cert. denied, 302 U. S. 758.

SWAN, Circuit Judge. This is an action for deceit brought against the members of the firm of Haskins & Sells, certified public accountants. Haskins & Sells audited the books and accounts of G. L. Miller & Co., Inc., a Delaware corporation, as of the close of business August 31, 1925, and delivered to the corporation a balance sheet purporting to show its financial condition as of that date after giving effect to proposed new financing, namely, the sale of 30,000 shares of preferred stock at par—$3,000,000. This balance sheet was used by the corporation in selling its preferred stock to the public, and Haskins & Sells knew that it was to be so used. The plaintiffs are persons who purchased shares of the preferred stock between October 24, 1925, and June 3, 1926, in reliance upon the balance sheet, which they assert was fraudulently false and misleading. In September, 1926, the corporation was adjudicated bankrupt, its assets were insufficient to pay the allowed claims of creditors, and the plaintiffs lost their investments in their entirety. This action was begun in October, 1928. Jurisdiction of the District Court rests upon diversity of citizenship, and each of the plaintiffs sued on his own behalf for $3,000 or more. Their separate causes of action were tried together for convenience. After a trial lasting thirteen weeks, the jury found a verdict for the defendants.

* This case is discussed at p. 40 ff. *supra.*

Judgment thereon was entered May 18, 1934. Seventeen of the plaintiffs have appealed. The appellees are the original defendants, excepting Charles S. Ludlam, against whom the action had abated by death. The enormous record on appeal, consisting of more than 4,000 printed pages and several hundred documentary exhibits, was not filed until January, 1936, and the case did not come on for argument until a year later. The errors assigned relate solely to refusals to charge as requested, no exceptions having been taken by the appellants to the charge as given.

G. L. Miller & Co., Inc., was organized under the laws of Delaware in October, 1930. It took over the assets, good will, and liabilities of G. L. Miller & Co., a Florida corporation, and issued therefor 1,000 shares of no par value stock. This was issued to Mr. G. L. Miller, who remained throughout the owner of all the common stock of the corporation, except for qualifying shares issued to employee-directors. The net book value of the assets, exclusive of good will, so taken over was about $7,500 after deducting liabilities. In 1923 the corporation declared a common stock dividend of 100 per cent. Thus there were 2,000 shares outstanding at the time of the proposed new financing in 1925. The business of the Miller Company consisted in underwriting mortgage bonds on real estate, usually on buildings to be constructed, acting as trustee under the mortgage indentures, and selling the bonds to the public. The common course of business involved three agreements: An underwriting agreement under which Miller & Co. purchased the mortgagor's bonds; a trust indenture, under which Miller & Co. as trustee was to receive from the mortgagor in equal monthly installments sums sufficient to enable it to pay semiannually to the bondholders the yearly interest, the federal income tax thereon (up to 4 per cent.), and the amount required for annual redemption of the bonds, which matured serially; and a disbursing agreement, under which Miller & Co. agreed to advance the amount of the mortgage loan as construction progressed. For the money thus advanced Miller & Co. depended upon the sale of the mortgage bonds.

At the time of the audit in question Miller & Co. had received from mortgagors for interest, income tax, and bond-redemption payments due under the trust indentures funds totalling approximately $1,377,000. These were held by it as trustee for the bondholders, but were commingled with its own cash, and the audit is claimed to be intentionally fraudulent in not adequately disclosing the amount of cash held in trust. Another ground of attack relates to payments made by Miller & Co. to complete the construction of mortgaged buildings. In selling bonds Miller & Co. represented that the mortgagor had agreed to provide the money necessary to complete the building under construction, and had furnished a surety bond guaranteeing completion free of all liens prior to that of the mortgage indenture. In fact, surety bonds were not furnished, and frequently the mortgagor defaulted in completing the structure. To make good such defaults Miller & Co. advanced very large sums out of its own funds. These were represented by notes of affiliates or subsidiaries of Miller & Co. and were shown in the audit as "secured," although, as the District Judge charged, they were not secured. Furthermore, in numerous instances Miller & Co. had itself guaranteed to bondholders completion of the buildings under construction, and the audit made no mention of such contingent liabilities running into many millions of dollars. It is also charged that the defendants made a false certificate as to the net earnings of Miller & Co. for the year 1924 and the first eight months of 1925. The audit is printed in the margin.[1]

The specific items which are challenged will be referred to hereafter in discussing the alleged errors of the court in refusing to charge as requested.

The charge which Judge Patterson delivered to the jury was an exceptionally clear exposition of the applicable law. Since there was no contractual relationship between the plaintiffs and the defendants, liability could be imposed only for fraud; a mistake in the balance sheet, even if it were the result of negligence, could not be the basis of a recovery. *Ultramares Corp.* v. *Touche, Niven & Co.,* 255 N. Y. 170, 174 N. E. 441, 74 A. L. R. 1139. Fraud presupposes not only an untrue statement but also a fraudulent intent. On the question of falsity of the representations the jury was told that the issue was whether the defendants' representations, "in the sense to be taken by an ordinary reasonable man," were, in fact, true or untrue—whether a true or a false impression was created. On the question of intent, the jury was told that fraud may be established by showing that a false representation has been made, either knowingly, or

---

[1] G. L. MILLER & CO.
Incorporated

General Balance Sheet, August 31, 1925
After Giving Effect to Proposed New Financing

ASSETS

Cash, Including Time Certificates of Deposit		$4,663,099.93
Temporary Investments in Outside Securities:		
Free Securities	$335,861.38	
In Escrow	131,038.44	
Total temporary investments in outside securities		466,899.82
Bonds Secured by First Mortgages on Real Estate		7,621,918.92
Notes and Accounts Receivable and Accrued Interest — Secured		2,987,411.69
Deferred Debit Items		162,126.42
Furniture and Fixtures, Less Reserve for Depreciation		52,038.30
Good-Will		1.00
Total		$15,953,496.08

LIABILITIES

Due to Mortgagors — For Bonds Underwritten — Payable as Construction Progresses		$8,757,379.86
Accounts Payable and Sundry Accruals		88,258.24
Customers' Partial Payments		124,099.69
Funds for Bond Interest and Redemption		1,966,938.40
Deferred Credits to Income		234,624.80
Reserves:		
Bond issue expenses	$116,576.82	
Taxes	171,894.43	
General	30,000.00	
Total reserves		318,471.25

without belief in its truth, or in reckless disregard of whether it be true or false; and that the issue was whether the defendants had an honest belief that the statements made by them were true. "If they did have that honest belief, whether reasonably or unreasonably, they are not liable. If they did not have an honest belief in the truth of their statements, then they are liable, so far as this third element [scienter] is concerned." The jury was also told that an intent to deceive may be inferred from a lack of honest representation; and that, so far as alleged concealments or omissions were concerned, the issue was whether the omission to state certain matters was deliberate and intended to conceal. It was further charged that, if the audit made "was so superficial as to be only a pretended audit and not a real audit, then the element of knowledge of falsity of their representations is present, and they may be held liable." Reading the charge as a whole, it seems to be in strict conformity with the established law. *Ultramares Corp.* v. *Touche, Niven & Co.,* 255 N. Y. 170, 174 N. E. 441, 74 A. L. R. 1139; *Knickerbocker Merchandising Co.* v. *United States,* 13 F. (2d) 544 (C. C. A. 2); *Fidelity & Deposit Co.* v. *Drovers' State Bank,* 15 F. (2d) 306 (C. C. A. 8); *Panther Rubber Mfg. Co.* v. *Commissioner of Int. Rev.,* 45 F. (2d) 314 (C. C. A. 1). And apparently the plaintiffs themselves thought it accurate and satisfactory at the time, for in response to the court's invitation to state exceptions to the charge as delivered, counsel replied that he had none. However, both sides had previously handed to the court requested instructions, and at the conclusion of the charge Judge Patterson remarked that many of the requests had been given in substance and that, to the extent not thus covered, the requests were refused an exception granted in each instance. The requests handed up by the appellants numbered 82; and their assignments of error involve 40 alleged refusals to charge as requested, although they had failed to point out any errors in the charge as given. A similar grant of blanket exceptions has been criticized for the burden it passes to an appellate court. *People* v. *Katz,* 209 N. Y. 311, 103 N. E. 305, Ann. Cas. 1915A, 501. In

---

Capital and Surplus:

Preferred capital stock, 8% cumulative participating (authorized and to be issued 30,000 shares of $100.00 each)	$3,000,000.00	
Common capital stock (authorized 5,000 shares of no par value; issued 2,000 shares)	200,000.00	
Surplus	1,263,723.84	
Total Capital and Surplus		4,463,723.84
Total		$15,953,496.08

Note: The Company carries life insurance on the life of Mr. G. L. Miller, President, for $500,000.00.

Our audit of the books and accounts of the G. L. Miller Company, Incorporated, discloses that the net earnings of the Company for the year ended December 31, 1924, were in excess of 2½ times the dividend requirements of the contemplated issue of 30,000 shares of 8% cumulative preferred stock, and that the net earnings for the eight months ended August 31, 1925, were in excess of 3 times the dividend requirements of said stock for the said eight months.

New York, September 30, 1925.

HASKINS & SELLS
Certified Public Accountants.

the federal courts the doctrine is firmly established that exceptions should be specifically taken so that the trial judge may have an opportunity to reconsider the matter and remove the ground of exception. Where the exceptions are not specific, an appellate court is under no duty laboriously to relate each of the requested instructions to the charge as given, in order to determine that no error was committed. *American Sugar Refining Co.* v. *Nassif,* 45 F. (2d) 321, 326 (C. C. A. 1) and authorities there cited. Nevertheless, if a refused instruction constituted plain error and had resulted in a miscarriage of justice, we should hesitate to ignore it because exceptions were taken as they were in the case at bar. Accordingly, we have examined all of the errors assigned, but we shall discuss only those relating to requested instructions which appear to be the most significant.

The Subject of Trust Funds: The first item of assets on the general balance sheet is "Cash, Including Time Certificates of Deposit ..... $4,663,099.93." This figure was obtained by adding to the actual cash the estimated proceeds from sale of the new preferred stock. The actual cash included $1,477,000 of trust funds which Miller & Co. as trustee had received from mortgagors on account of payments due under trust indentures. Miller & Co. was itself the beneficiary of $100,000 of these trust funds, but the remainder, $1,377,000, was held in trust for other bondholders. The inclusion of this sum as a general cash asset of the company without further explanation would plainly give a false impression as to the company's cash position. The main defense against this charge was the defendants' contention that an adequate explanation was supplied by the item on the liability side of the balance sheet, "Funds for Bond Interest and Redemption ..... $1,966,938.40." In round figures this sum represented the aforesaid amount of $1,477,000 actually received from mortgagors plus an amount of $489,000 which was accrued and treated on the company's books as received, although in fact it had not been. The defendants point out that the word "Funds" necessarily meant trust funds, since the "Bond Interest and Redemption" referred to could relate only to bonds on mortgaged property, Miller & Co. having no bond issue of its own. On the question whether there was ambiguity in this item, there was testimony both ways and the judge so charged, after calling the jury's attention to the respective contentions of the parties. He had previously stated that the sum of about $1,400,000.00 was received by Miller & Co. as trustee under the mortgages.

The appellants complain because their requested instructions numbered 25 to 31, inclusive, were not given. They urge that the jury was simply left with the conflicting contentions of counsel on the subject of trust funds. In substance, their complaint seems to be that the court did not point out with particularity how to apply to this subject the general rules he laid down for determining whether representations were false and made with fraudulent intent. Such a complaint is not well taken. The judge was under no obligation to discuss in detail the evidence relating to each item of the alleged misrepresentations, and particularly is this true where no request was made to amplify the charge as given. Request No. 25 was to the effect that cash received as trustee can form no part of the company's assets. It is incredible that the jury did not so understand. The court had charged that about $1,400,000 was held in trust, and the issues between the parties, as shown by the court's statement of their respective claims and the general charge, was whether the balance sheet disclosed this trust obligation to the ordinary reader, and whether the accountants could honestly believe that it did. Several of the requested instructions, for example, No. 28, assumed that the balance sheet concealed the true financial condition by failure to disclose the trust. This was for the jury to decide, and such requests were properly refused. Request No. 26 asserted that it was the duty of Haskins & Sells to show clearly on the balance sheet that these trust funds did not belong to Miller & Co. As a principle of correct accounting we should suppose this to be true, but the issue for the jury was not that, but was whether a false impression of financial worth was intentionally created. Request No. 31 asserted that prospective investors in the preferred stock were entitled to know whether Miller & Co. had been guilty of breach of trust and that "the misuse of trust funds is the normal incident of a hopeless financial condition." The inclusion of the final sentence, above quoted, was enough to justify refusal of the instruction in the form presented. We think the charge as given was adequate on the subject of trust funds and no prejudicial error occurred in the refusal of requested charges on this subject.

The Subject of Secured Notes: The fourth item of assets in the balance sheet is "Notes and Accounts Receivable and Accrued Interest—Secured ...... $2,987,411.69." The main dispute as to this item relates to notes of corporations amounting to $1,434,764.76. They represented advances made by Miller & Co. for the completion of mortgaged buildings. They were signed by affiliated or subsidiary corporations. Although stated in the balance sheet to be "Secured," they were not secured as a matter of law. The plaintiffs contend that the defendants knew they were not secured. They further claim that the notes were of little value, to the defendants' knowledge, and, finally, that the notes signed by subsidiaries should have been shown as such.

With respect to listing the notes as secured, the defense is that Peed honestly, even if erroneously, believed them to be secured. He testified that he based his opinion on a provision in the trust indentures empowering the trustee to make advances "for payment of taxes, insurance premiums, or any other purpose for preserving the property and the lien of this instrument," or on similar provisions. As to this the trial judge charged: "As matter of law it is my opinion, and I charge you, that these advances to complete unfinished buildings are not the kind of advances that are secured under the trust deeds. The point, however, is not so clear that persons reading such parts of the deed might not, in good faith, entertain different opinions; and the good faith of the defendants in representing these advances as secured is one of the questions of fact for you to determine under all the evidence applicable to these notes, and under the rules which I will later explain to you."

Of their several requests dealing with this subject, the appellants urge No. 38 as the most significant. This informed the jury that, if they should find that the statement as to security was false and "that the defendants represented to the plaintiffs that this was true to their own knowledge, as distinguished from belief or opinion, they are guilty of making a false balance sheet, even if they believed it to be true." It is urged that the *Ultramares* Case in 255 N. Y. 170, 174 N. E. 441, 74 A. L. R. 1139, points directly to the correctness of this request, but we cannot so construe it. Accountants profess to speak with knowledge when certifying to an agreement between the audit and the entries in books audited, but there is no suggestion in the cases relied upon that a statement by an auditor that notes are secured by the provisions of a trust deed is an assertion of knowledge rather than an expression of opinion. To suggest that a title examiner was guilty of fraud if he erroneously certified a title because he had honestly misconceived the legal significance of a provision in a deed would doubtless horrify counsel for the appellants no less than other members of the legal profession. There is no reason to hold accountants to a higher standard, when they deal with legal documents. The issue of the defendants' good faith was rightly left to the jury.

Complaint is made of the refusal to charge request No. 67 to the effect that, if the defendants knowingly overvalued doubtful assets [the notes], then they were guilty of false representations. We cannot doubt that the jury were sufficiently informed of so obvious a proposition by the general charge as given. This request was repeated in various alternative forms covering specific details of the evidence. That the trial judge was under no duty in such a case as this to discuss in detail the evidence relating to each alleged misrepresentation we have already stated.

Request No. 65 relates to the failure to show that the notes were those of subsidiary or affiliated companies. The court made reference to this and to the conflicting testimony of experts as to whether good accounting practice required it. We think this was sufficient. Here also the issue was the defendants' intent, and questions of the effect of concealment and of a pretended rather than real audit were covered in the general charge.

Contingent Liabilities: We can see little excuse for omitting from the balance sheet mention of contingent liabilities. These were principally guaranties of completion of buildings under construction and might run into millions of dollars should the mortgagors default, which was not a remote possibility as shown by Miller & Co.'s prior experience. Nevertheless, Palmer, one of the defendants' experts, testified that it was proper to omit the items; and Klein and Madden said that the showing of contingent liabilities is frequently a matter of judgment and that they need not be shown when, as here, with respect to the guaranties of completion, the primary obligation was shown under the heading "Due to Mortgagors —For Bonds Underwritten—Payable as Construction Progresses ..... $8,757,379.86." The plaintiffs' expert contradicted this. The charge called attention to the conflicting testimony and instructed the jury to weigh it. The refused requests were to the effect that omission of the contingent liabilities made the balance sheet false. In view of the conflicting testimony, such a charge was properly refused. Even if it were an abuse of good accounting practice to omit them, such an abuse was not fraud unless accompanied by an intent to conceal. The issue of fraudulent concealment was fairly put to the jury in the general charge.

Finally, the appellants complain of the refusal to charge that, if the balance sheet represented Miller & Co. to be in a sound financial position when in fact the defendants knew it was not, then they were guilty of fraud. Variations of this proposition were contained in requests 13 and 14. Undoubtedly they were correct statements of law, but they were adequately covered by the general charge.

In conclusion, we may say that the trial was entirely fair to the appellants. A clear and accurate charge was delivered under which the jury might well have found a verdict for the plaintiffs. There was much in the evidence which tended to cast doubt upon the good faith of the accountants, but it did not persuade the jury. An appellate court cannot set at naught a jury's verdict merely because they might have reached a different conclusion had they been sitting as the jury. Finding no error in the charge as given and nothing clearly wrong in refusing requested instructions, we affirm the judgment.

CANDLER v. CRANE, CHRISTMAS & CO. *

Court of Appeal, 1951. 2 K.B. 164, 1 *The Times* L.R. 371.

The defendants, a firm of accountants, had been employed to write up the books and prepare the accounts of a limited liability company, and they instructed F. their clerk to do so. When the accounts had been prepared and were ready for certification by the accountants, F., at the request of the managing director of the limited liability company, showed the accounts to the plaintiff who, to the knowledge of F., was considering whether he should invest money in the company. F. had been careless in the preparation of the accounts so that they were defective and deficient and did not correctly represent the financial position of the company. The plaintiff, after seeing the accounts, invested £2,000 in the company. Subsequently the company was wound up and there were no assets. The plaintiff sued the defendants on the ground that he had lost his investment through breach of duty of care of the defendants to him.

Held, that F. was acting within the scope of his authority in showing the plaintiff the accounts.

There being no contractual or fiduciary relationship between the parties, *Held,* also, by COHEN and ASQUITH, L.JJ. (Denning, L.J., dissenting), that the plaintiff had no cause of action in tort against the defendants.

Le Lievre v. Gould (9 *The Times* L. R. 243; [1893] 1 Q. B. 491) which was held to have been neither overruled nor qualified by *Donoghue* v. *Stevenson* (48 *The Times* L. R. 494; [1932] A. C. 562), followed.

Per ASQUITH, L.J.—There was not a word of disapproval by Lord Atkin in *Donoghue* v. *Stevenson* (*supra*) of the decision in *Le Lievre* v. *Gould* (*supra*) though he referred to the case as annexing a valid and essential qualification to the formula of Lord Esher, M. R., in *Heaven* v. *Pender* ((1883) 11 Q. B. D. 503) . The principle laid down by Lord Atkin in *Donoghue* v. *Stevenson* (*supra*) in answer to the question: "who, then, in law, is my neighbour?" had never yet been applied where the damage complained of was not physical, to either person or property.

Per DENNING, L.J., dissenting: Accountants owed a duty to use care in their reports and in the work which resulted in their reports. Their calling required special knowledge and skill. They owed that duty not only to their employers, but to any third person to whom they showed the accounts or to whom they knew that their employer was going to show them so as to induce him to invest money or take some other action on them. The duty only extended to those transactions for which the accountants knew their accounts were required. He would not call in question the decision in *Le Lievre v. Gould* (*supra*) which was distinguishable from the present case. Surveyors, valuers and analysts were under a similar duty to use care in statement.

This was the appeal of the plaintiff, a Mr. Candler, in an action in which he claimed damages for negligence against the defendants, Messrs.

* See footnote 70 *supra*.

Crane, Christmas and Company, a firm of accountants. The defendants were the accountants to a company called Trevaunance Hydraulic Tin Mines, Limited (referred to as the company). In the circumstances stated in the case the accountants prepared the accounts of the company (which were produced to the plaintiff by an employee of the accountants) and in doing so were, as the trial Judge found, careless in the preparation of them and that accordingly the accounts were "defective and deficient." The plaintiff, relying on the accounts, invested £2,000 in the company and lost it because the company turned out to be a failure.

It was submitted for the plaintiff that, although there was no contract or fiduciary relationship between him and the defendant accountants, nevertheless the relationship between them was so close and direct that the accountants owed him a duty of care within the principles stated in *Donoghue v. Stevenson* (48 *The Times* L. R. 494; [1932] A. C. 562). For the accountants it was submitted that the only duty which they owed was a purely contractual duty which they owed to the company, and therefore that they were not liable for negligence to a person to whom they were under no duty.

By his action against the accountants, the plaintiff pleaded that he had lost his £2,000 through the defendants' breach of duty of care in respect of the accounts which Mr. Fraser placed before him, and he claimed that sum in damages. He also alleged fraud at the trial. Alternatively, the plaintiff alleged that the accountants, as auditors of the company, owed a duty to him as a shareholder to give him the accurate information which they should have given him when he was a prospective investor.

Mr. Justice Lloyd-Jacob dismissed the action. He found that there was no fraud and that no damage flowed from the alternative claim of the plaintiff as a shareholder. On the claim for breach of duty he found that the accounts were defective and deficient and presented a position of the company which was "wholly contrary to the actual position" and that Mr. Fraser was extremely careless in the preparation of the accounts. He said that the damage which the plaintiff suffered was plain, but he held that the accountants were under no duty of care to the plaintiff. Their only duty was to produce accounts which they honestly believed to be the draft accounts of the company.

The plaintiff appealed, but no longer alleged fraud. On the appeal the defendants contended: (1) that Mr. Fraser was not acting in the course of his employment, and (2) that, even if he was, they owed no duty to the plaintiff.

Mr. Neil Lawson appeared for the plaintiff; Mr. John Foster, K. C., and Mr. Phineas Quass for the defendants.

The following judgments were read.

Lord Justice Cohen.—I will ask Lord Justice Denning to read his judgment first.

Lord Justice Denning.—In September, 1946, Mr. Candler invested £2,000 in a company called Trevaunance Hydraulic Tin Mines, Limited (which I will call the company) and he has lost it because the company turned out to be a failure. He now brings this action against the company's accountants and auditors, Crane, Christmas and Company (whom I will call the accountants) claiming that he was induced to invest the money because of erroneous accounts which they put before him and on the faith of which he invested his money. The Judge has found that the accounts were "defective and deficient" and presented a position of the company which was "wholly contrary to the actual position"; that the accountants were "in fact extremely careless in the preparation of the accounts"; and that the damage which Mr. Candler suffered was "plain"; but nevertheless the Judge dismissed his claim because in his opinion the accountants owed no duty of care to Mr. Candler.

The case raises a point of law of much importance, because Mr. Lawson, on behalf of Mr. Candler, submitted that, although there was no contract between Mr. Candler and the accountants, nevertheless the relationship between them was so close and direct that the accountants did owe a duty of care to him within the principles stated in *Donoghue* v. *Stevenson* (48 *The Times* L.R. 494; [1932] A.C. 562); whereas Mr. Foster, on behalf of the accountants, submitted that the duty which the accountants owed was purely a contractual duty owed by them to the company, and therefore they were not liable for negligence to a person to whom they were under no contractual duty.

Before discussing this point of law, I must set out the facts in some detail so as to see what exactly the relationship was between Mr. Candler and the accountants. The story centres round the activities of a Mr. Donald Ogilvie in connexion with some surface tin workings in Cornwall. In November, 1944, he formed the company to work the tin, with himself as chairman and managing director for life. In March, 1946, he told the accountants that he wanted them to prepare the accounts of the company and to write up the books. The accountants entrusted the work to one of their clerks named Henry Fraser, but he had not done much towards it when in June, 1946, Mr. Ogilvie told the accountants that he had decided "to go out for substantially more capital" and asked them to insert an advertisement in a newspaper as quickly as possible. They arranged it for him, and it appeared on July 8, 1946, in these words: "£10,000 established Tin Mine (low capitalization) in Cornwall seeks further capital, instal additional milling plant, directorship and active participation open to suitable applicant.—Apply" &c.

Mr. Candler, the plaintiff, answered that advertisement in these words: "I should be interested to take an active part in a Cornish Tin Mine and have about £2,000 to invest. Will you let me have particulars?" The accountants sent that letter unopened to Mr. Ogilvie, who got into touch with Mr. Candler. As a result, in the first half of September, 1946, Mr. Ogilvie showed Mr. Candler the Cornish workings and told Mr. Candler that, if he invested £2,000, he would get a directorship in the company and a service agreement for two years at £10 a week. Mr. Candler said, however, that he wanted to see the balance-sheet of the company first.

As a result of Mr. Candler's request, Mr. Ogilvie started pressing the accountants to get out the accounts. He told their clerk, Mr. Fraser, that he wanted the accounts got out as quickly as possible, and that the accounts were required to show to a potential investor in the company, whose name was Candler. Mr. Fraser was asked in the witness box: "Did you assume at that time that the accounts that Mr. Ogilvie was pressing for had some relation to his negotiations with Mr. Candler?", and he answered: "I thought there would be a connexion, of course. Yes, I suppose so."

Mr. Fraser accordingly, in the middle of September, 1946, worked on the accounts very intensively, going to Mr. Ogilvie's flat two or three times a day for his explanation of various items. He was, as the Judge found, under the mistaken impression that it was, in substance, Mr. Ogilvie's business, and he accepted Mr. Ogilvie's statements without verification.

On Monday, September 16, 1946, Mr. Ogilvie asked Mr. Fraser to meet Mr. Candler the next day so as to give him information relating to the accounts of the company; and accordingly, on Tuesday, September 17, Mr. Fraser went with Mr. Ogilvie to meet Mr. Candler and took with him the draft accounts which he had by that time prepared. At the meeting Mr. Ogilvie introduced Mr. Fraser to Mr. Candler as the representative of Crane, Christmas and Company, the accountants and auditors of the company, who were preparing the accounts, and he introduced Mr. Candler to Mr. Fraser as a man who was contemplating an investment in the company. Mr. Fraser knew, of course, of the advertisement which his firm had inserted for new capital; and he knew, when the meeting began, that the negotiations depended on Mr. Candler's being satisfied with the balance-sheet of the company.

At that meeting on September 17, Mr. Fraser produced the draft accounts. They already had, on them, at that time, a certificate ready for signature by the accountants, stating in the usual formula: "We have audited the balance-sheet as above set forth. We have obtained all the information and explanations we have required and we report that such balance-sheet is in our opinion properly drawn up so as to exhibit a true and correct view of the state of the company's affairs, according to the best of our information and the explanations given to us and as shown by the books of the company." That certificate was not signed at the time; but Mr. Fraser told Mr. Candler that that certificate would be signed with a clear docket subject to one or two small alterations which he wished to consider for another two or three days.

At that meeting of September 17, Mr. Candler took down in his own handwriting a copy of the accounts, because he wanted to put them before his own accountant for advice. There was a conflict of recollection how he came to take them down, but the judge said that it did not matter because Mr. Fraser clearly assented to Mr. Candler's taking a copy. The Judge said: "Having regard to the fact that Mr. Fraser was plainly aware of the purpose for which the draft accounts were required, I entertain no doubt at all that he was aware of and acquiesced in the showing of these accounts to Mr. Candler: indeed, the meeting would have been wholly pointless but for that purpose." Mr. Fraser drew Mr. Candler's attention to the fact that some of the items in the draft balance-sheet might need revision and the parties arranged to meet again on September 20, 1946. The Judge expressly found that, when the meeting of the 17th broke up, Mr. Fraser must have been satisfied, not only that Mr. Candler was considering an investment in the company, but was taking with him and relying on the draft accounts which Mr. Fraser had prepared.

The parties met again on September 20. By that time Mr. Fraser had concluded his examination of the books and drew Mr. Candler's attention to some modifications which are for present purposes immaterial. Mr. Fraser said that the accounts had been passed by the directors and would be signed in the next few days. Meanwhile Mr. Candler had himself obtained advice from his own accountant and put queries to Mr. Fraser about the accounts which Mr. Fraser answered. Nothing now turns on those queries. At the end of the meeting Mr. Candler told Mr. Ogilvie and Mr. Fraser that he was satisfied and would invest £2,000 in the company. He sent off a cheque for £500 that day to Mr. Ogilvie and the balance of £1,500 on September 25, 1946.

The Judge has found that, to Mr. Fraser's knowledge, Mr. Candler was induced to believe that the accounts, as modified on September 20, 1946, would be the certified accounts as they emerged from the accountants, and that is what did in fact happen. On September 27, 1946, the accounts were certified by the accountants in precisely the same form as Mr. Fraser had shown them to Mr. Candler at the meeting of the 20th without any alteration at all.

It has subsequently turned out that the accounts gave an altogether inaccurate picture of the position of the company. Instances were given to us which show that there was no verification whatever by the accountants of the information which Mr. Ogilvie gave them. Thus, among the assets were inserted "Freehold cottages (at cost) £650." In fact the company had no title deeds for the cottages. The cottages stood in Mr. Ogilvie's name and he had mortgaged them to the bank for his own overdraft. Again, "Leasehold buildings (at cost) £650." The company had no leases, but they stood in Mr. Ogilvie's name and were ultimately forfeited for non-payment of rent. Yet again, the assets were said to include £3,280 expended on capital development, whereas the propriety of that figure depended on whether, out of the total expenditure of the company, a proper allocation had been made between capital and revenue expenditure; and the accounts contained no indication that any such allocation had been necessary, or had indeed been made. It appears that much too high a figure was allocated to capital, thus making the assets appear larger than they in fact were. It was admitted that Mr. Fraser had entirely failed to use proper care and skill in the preparation and presentation of the accounts.

The result was disastrous for Mr. Candler. In September, 1946, he entered the service of the company and moved down to Cornwall and worked at the mine. Indeed, he invested in November, 1946, another £200. But a little later his suspicions became aroused because he discovered that his £2,000 had not been applied for the purposes of the company's business. Ultimately he discovered that the company was in a very bad way. It was not even able to pay his salary. He himself issued writs against the company on May 1, and June 30, 1947, for salary and money lent. On August 11, 1947, he presented a petition for winding up and on December 15, 1947, a winding up order was made. There are no assets. The bank took the freehold cottages for Mr. Ogilvie's debt. The lessors forfeited the leasehold property. Mr. Ogilvie became a bankrupt. Mr. Candler lost his £2,000 altogether, and he says it is due to the carelessness of the accountants, because if they had put before him accounts which had been properly prepared, the true position of affairs would have been disclosed and he would never have invested his money in the company. The only defences raised by the accountants at the hearing of the appeal were: (1) that Mr. Fraser was not acting in the course of his employment; (2) that, even if he was, they owed no duty of care to Mr. Candler.

The Judge seems to have treated it as beyond question that Mr. Fraser was acting in the course of his employment, and I agree with him. There is no doubt that Mr. Fraser was acting within his actual authority in writing up the books and preparing the accounts, and indeed his action in so doing was ratified and confirmed by the senior partner who signed the certificate. But it is said that Mr. Fraser had no authority to show the draft accounts to Mr. Candler, or to answer his queries, at any rate not without asking his principals for permission to do so. The senior partner admitted that it was a very common thing for accountants at the request of the chairman or person in control of a company to give details of the company's accounts to a prospective investor so as to induce him to invest money, but he said that it was for the principal of the firm to do it, and not for a clerk. That may well be so. It may not have been within Mr. Fraser's actual authority, but that is not the point. A master is often made responsible for the unauthorized or forbidden acts of his servant when he has for his own purposes put the servant in a position where he can do the acts. Practical good sense demands that, even though the master is not at fault himself, he should be responsible if the servant conducts himself in a way which is injurious to others. He takes the benefits of the servant's rightful acts and should bear the burden of his wrongful ones; and he is, as a rule, the only one who has the means to pay. So, here, I have no doubt that the accountants are responsible for the way in which Mr. Fraser conducted himself in preparing the accounts and showing them to Mr. Candler who, after all, was perfectly innocent in the matter and had not the slightest idea that Mr. Fraser had no authority to do what he did.

I now come to the great question in the case: did the accountants owe a duty of care to Mr. Candler? If the matter were free from authority, I should have said that they clearly did owe a duty of care to him. They were professional accountants who prepared and put before him these accounts, knowing that he was going to be guided by them in making an investment in the company. On the faith of those accounts he did make the investment, whereas if the accounts had been carefully prepared, he would not have made the investment at all. The result is that he has lost his money. In the circumstances, had he not every right to rely on the accounts being prepared with proper care; and is he not entitled to redress from the accountants on whom he relied? I say that he is, and I would apply to this case the words of Lord Justice Knight Bruce in an analogous case 90 years ago: "A country whose administration of justice did not afford redress in a case of the present description would not be in a state of civilization": *Slim* v. *Croucher* ((1860) 1 De G. F. and J. 518, at p. 527).

Turning now to authority, I can point to many general statements of principle which cover the case made by some of the great names in the law: Lord Eldon, L. C., in *Evans* v. *Bicknell* ((1801) 6 Ves. 174, at p. 183), Lord Campbell, L. C., in *Slim* v. *Croucher* (*supra*), Lord Selborne, L. C., in *Brownlie* v. *Campbell* ((1880) 5 App. Cas. 925, at pp. 935 and 936), Lord Herschell in *Derry* v. *Peek* ((1889) 5 *The Times* L. R. 625, at p. 629; 14 App. Cas. 337, at p. 360), Lord Shaw in *Nocton* v. *Ashburton* (30 *The Times* L. R. 602; [1914] A. C. 932, at p. 972), and Lord Atkin in *Donoghue* v. *Stevenson* (48 *The Times* L. R. 494, at p. 499; [1932] A. C. 562, at p. 580). But it is said that effect cannot be given to those statements of principle because *Le Lievre* v. *Gould* (9 *The Times* L. R. 243; [1893] 1 Q. B. 491) is an actual decision of this Court to the contrary.

Before I consider the decision in *Le Lievre* v. *Gould* (*supra*) itself, I wish to say that, in my opinion, current legal thought at the time it was decided was infected by two cardinal errors. The first error was an error which appeared time and time again in nineteenth-century thought—namely, that no one who is not a party to a contract can sue on it or on anything arising out of it. This error has had unfortunate consequences both in the law of contract and in the law of tort. So far as contract is concerned, I have said something about it in *Smith* v. *River Douglas Catchment Board* (65 *The Times* L. R. 628; [1949] 2 K. B. 500). So far as tort is concerned, it led the lawyers of that day to suppose that, if one of the parties to a contract was negligent in carrying it out, no third person who was injured by that negligence could sue for damages on account of it: see *Winterbottom* v. *Wright* ((1842) 10 M. and W. 109), *Alton* v. *Midland Railway Company* ((1865) 19 C. B. (N. S.) 213), and the notes in *Pasley* v. *Freeman* ((1789) 3 Term. Rep. 51; 2 Sm. L. C. (13th ed., 1929, pp. 103 to 110)); except in the case of things dangerous in themselves, like guns: see *Dixon* v. *Bell* ((1816) 5 M. and S. 198). This error lies at the root of the reasoning of Lord Justice Bowen in *Le Lievre* v. *Gould* ([1893] 1 Q. B., at p. 502) when he said that the law of England "does not consider that what a man writes on paper is like a gun or other dangerous instrument," meaning thereby that, unless it was a thing which was dangerous in itself, no action lay. This error was exploded by the great case of *Donoghue* v. *Stevenson* (*supra*), which decided that the presence of a contract did not defeat an action for negligence by a third person, provided that the circumstances disclosed a duty by the contracting party to him.

The second error was an error as to the effect of *Derry* v. *Peek* (*supra*), an error which persisted for 35 years at least after that decision—namely, that no action ever lies for a negligent statement, even though it is intended that the plaintiff should act on it, and he in fact acts on it to his loss. This error led the Court of Appeal in *Low* v. *Bouverie* (7 *The Times* L. R. 582; [1891] 3 Ch. 82) to deny the correctness of *Slim* v. *Croucher* (*supra*); and in *Le Lievre* v. *Gould* (*supra*) to deny the correctness of *Cann* v. *Willson* ((1888) 4 *The Times* L. R. 588; 39 Ch. 39). The cases thus denied were so plainly just that the very denial of them was itself an error. The error was, however, exposed by the important case of *Nocton* v. *Ashburton* (*supra*), which decided that an action did lie for a negligent statement where the circumstances disclosed a duty to be careful; and that all that is to be deduced from (though not decided by) *Derry* v. *Peek* (*supra*) is that *in the particular circumstances of that case* there was no duty to be careful. Lord Haldane, L. C., observed significantly ([1914] A. C., at p. 947) that the authorities subsequent to *Derry* v. *Peek* (*supra*) had shown "a tendency to assume that it was intended to mean more than it did." In my opinion the decisions of the House of Lords in *Donoghue* v. *Stevenson* (*supra*) and *Nocton* v. *Ashburton* (*supra*) are sufficient to entitle this Court to examine afresh the law as to negligent statements, and that is what I propose to do.

Let me first be destructive and destroy the submissions which Mr. Foster put forward. His first submission was that a duty to be careful in making statements arose only out of a contractual duty to the plaintiff, or a fiduciary relationship to him. Apart from such cases no action, he said, had ever been allowed for negligent statements, and he urged that this want of authority was a reason against its being allowed now. This argument about the novelty of the action does not appeal to me in the least. It has been put forward in all the great cases which have been milestones of progress in our law, and it has always, or nearly always, been rejected. If the great cases of *Ashby* v. *White* ((1703) 2 Ld. Raym. 938), *Pasley* v. *Freeman* (*supra*), and *Donoghue* v. *Stevenson* (*supra*) are read it will be found that in each of them the Judges were divided in opinion. On the one side there were the timorous souls who were fearful of allowing a new cause of action. On the other side there were the bold spirits who were ready to allow it, if justice so required. It was fortunate for the common law that the progressive view prevailed. Whenever this argument of novelty is put forward I call to mind the following emphatic answer which Chief Justice Pratt gave nearly 200 years ago in *Chapman* v. *Pickersgill* ((1762) 2 Wils. 145, at p. 146): "I wish never to hear this objection again. This action is for a tort: torts are infinitely various; not limited or confined, for there is nothing in nature but may be an instrument of mischief." Lord Macmillan gave the same answer in *Donoghue* v. *Stevenson* when he said (48 *The Times* L. R. 494, at p. 510; [1932] A. C., at p. 619): "The criterion of judgment must adjust and adapt itself to the changing circumstances of life. The categories of negligence are never closed." It needs only a little imagination to see how much the common law would have suffered if those decisions had gone the other way.

The second submission of Mr. Foster was that a duty to take care only arose where the result of a failure to take care will cause physical damage to persons or property. It was for this reason that he did not dispute two illustrations of negligent statements which I put in the course of the argument, the case of an analyst who negligently certifies to a manufacturer of food that a particular ingredient is harmless, whereas it is in fact poisonous, or the case of an inspector of lifts who negligently reports that a particular lift is safe, whereas it is in fact dangerous. The analyst and the lift inspector would, I should have thought, be liable to any person who was injured by consuming the food, or using the lift, at any rate if there was no likelihood of intermediate inspection: *Donoghue* v. *Stevenson* (*supra*), *Haseldine* v. *Daw and Son, Limited* (58 *The Times* L. R. 1; [1941] 2 K. B. 343). Mr. Foster said that that might well be so because the negligence there caused physical damage, but that the same would not apply to negligence which caused financial loss. He referred to some observations of Mr. Justice Wrottesley which were in his favour on this point (*Old Gate Estates, Limited* v. *Toplis and Harding and Russell* ((1939) 161 L. T. Rep. 227)). But I must say that I cannot accept this as a valid distinction. I can understand that in some cases of financial loss there may not be a sufficiently proximate relationship to give rise to a duty of care; but if once the duty exists I cannot think that liability depends on the nature of the damage.

The third submission of Mr. Foster was that the duty which the accountants owed was purely a contractual duty, and, therefore, that they were not liable for negligence to a person to whom they were under no contractual obligation. This seems to me to be simply a repetition of the nineteenth century fallacy stated in *Alton* v. *Midland Railway* (*supra*) and exploded by *Donoghue* v. *Stevenson* (*supra*).

Let me now be constructive and suggest the circumstances in which I say that a duty to use care in statement does exist apart from a contract in that behalf. First, what persons are under such duty? My answer is those persons such as accountants, surveyors, valuers and analysts, whose profession and occupation it is to examine books, accounts, and other things, and to make reports on which other people—other than their clients—rely in the ordinary course of business. Their duty is not merely a duty to use care in their reports. They have also a duty to use care in their work which results in their reports. Herein lies the difference between these professional men and other persons who have been held to be under no duty to use care in their statements, such as promoters who issue a prospectus: *Derry* v. *Peek* (*supra*) (now altered by statute), and trustees who answer inquiries about the trust funds: *Low* v. *Bouverie* (7 *The Times* L. R. 582; [1891] 3 Ch. 82). Those persons do not bring and are not expected to bring, any professional knowledge or skill into the preparation of their statements: they can only be made responsible by the law affecting persons generally, such as contract, estoppel, innocent misrepresentation or fraud.

But it is very different with persons who engage in a calling which requires special knowledge and skill. From very early times it has been held that they owe a duty of care to those who are closely and directly affected by their work apart altogether from any contract or undertaking in that behalf. Thus, Fitz-Herbert in his new *Natura Brevium* ((1534) 94D) states that "if a smith prick my horse with a nail, I shall have my action on the case against him, without any warranty by the smith to do it well," and he supports it with an excellent reason: "for it is the duty of every artificer to exercise his art rightly and truly as he ought." This reasoning has been treated as applicable not only to shoeing smiths, surgeons and barbers, who work with hammers, knives and scissors, but also to shipbrokers and clerks in the Custom House who work with figures and make entries in books, "because their situation and employment necessarily imply a competent degree of knowledge in making such entries": see *Shiels* v. *Blackburne* ((1789) 1 Hy. Bl. 159, at p. 163, *per* Lord Loughborough), which was not referred to by Mr. Justice Devlin in *Heskell* v. *Continental Express, Limited* ([1950] 1 All E. R. 1033, at p. 1042).

The same reasoning has been applied to medical men who make reports on the sanity of others: see *Everett* v. *Griffiths* (36 *The Times* L. R. 491, at pp. 493 and 501; [1920] 3 K. B. 163, at pp. 182 and 217). It is, I think, also applicable to professional accountants. They are not liable, of course, for casual remarks made in the course of conversation, nor for other statements made outside their work, or not made in their capacity as accountants: compare *Fish* v. *Kelly* ((1864) 17 C. B. (N. S.) 194). But they are, in my opinion, in proper cases, apart from any contract in the matter, under a duty to use reasonable care in the preparation of their accounts and in the making of their reports. Secondly, to whom do these professional people owe this duty? I will take accountants, but the same reasoning applies to the others. They owe the duty, of course, to their employer or client; and also I think to any third person to whom they themselves show the accounts, or to whom they know their employer is going to show the accounts so as to induce him to invest money or take some other action on them. But I do not think the duty can be extended still further so as to include strangers of whom they have heard nothing and to whom their employer without their knowledge may choose to show their accounts. Once the accountants have handed their accounts to their employer they are not, as a rule, responsible for what he does with them without their knowledge or consent.

A good illustration is afforded by the decision in *Le Lievre v. Gould* (*supra*) itself, which I certainly would not wish to call in question. The facts are somewhat differently stated in the various reports, but collecting them together they come to this: A surveyor there surveyed work for a building owner and handed certificates to him so that he could know the amounts which he had to pay the builder. The building owner then chose to show the certificates to his own mortgagees who advanced money on them instead of on the certificates of their own surveyor. The mortgagees then said that the owner's surveyor owed a duty of care to them. That was obviously untenable, because they should have had the work surveyed by their own surveyor. Indeed, they had actually stipulated for it. The relationship was therefore one in which the inspection of an intermediate person might reasonably be interposed, and was consequently too remote to raise a duty of care: see *per* Lord Atkin in *Donoghue* v. *Stevenson* (48 *The Times* L. R., at p. 499; [1932] A. C., at p. 582). But excluding such cases as those, there are some cases—of which the present is one—where the accountants know all the time, even before they present their accounts, that their employer requires the accounts to show to a third person so as to induce him to act on them; and then they themselves, or their employers, present the accounts to him for the purpose. In such cases I am of opinion that the accountants owe a duty of care to the third person.

The test of proximity in these cases is: Did the accountants know that the accounts were required for submission to the plaintiff and use by him? That appears from *Langridge* v. *Levy* ((1837-8) 2 M. and W. 519) as extended by Baron Cleasby in *George* v. *Skivington* ((1869) L. R. 5 Ex. 1, at p. 5); and from the decision of that good Judge, Mr. Justice Chitty, in *Cann* v. *Willson* (*supra*), which is directly in point. In that case a valuer made a valuation of property for the very purpose of enabling his client to raise a mortgage on it; and, in order to further the transaction, the valuer himself actually put the valuation before the mortgagee's solicitor saying that it was a very moderate valuation and not made in favour of the borrower. The mortgagee advanced money on the faith of the valuation, but it turned out that the valuer had been grossly careless, and the mortgagee lost his money. Mr. Justice Chitty held that the valuer was liable in negligence, apart from any contract at all. He said (39 Ch. D., at p. 42) that the valuation was sent by the valuer direct to the mortgagee's solicitor "for the purpose of inducing the plaintiff and his co-trustee to lay out the trust money on mortgage. It seems to me that the defendants knowlingly placed themselves in that position, and in point of law incurred a duty toward him to use reasonable care in the preparation of the document called a valuation. I think it is like the case of the supply of an article—the supply of the hairwash in the case of *George v. Skivington* (*supra*)."

That reasoning seems to me to be good sense and good law. I know that in *Le Lievre* v. *Gould* (*supra*) the Court of Appeal said that *Cann* v. *Willson* (*supra*) was wrongly decided; but it must be remembered that at that time the general opinion of the profession was that *George* v. *Skivington* (*supra*), on which Mr. Justice Chitty relied, was itself wrongly decided, or at any rate that the principle stated in it by Baron Cleasby was wrong: see *per* Mr. Justice Field and Mr. Justice Cave, and Lord Justice Bowen and Lord Justice Cotton, in *Heaven* v. *Pender* ((1882) 9 Q. B. D. 302, at pp. 306-7; (1883) 11 Q. B. D. 503, at pp. 516-7), and *per* Mr. Justice Hamilton in *Blacker* v. *Lake and Elliott* ((1912) 106 L. T. Rep., at p. 533). If *George* v. *Skivington* (*supra*) was wrong, then, of course, *Cann* v. *Willson* (*supra*) was wrong, for it was based on it. But in *Donoghue* v. *Stevenson* (*supra*) the House of Lords fully restored *George* v. *Skivington* (*supra*), and Lord Atkin himself approved the reasoning of Baron Cleasby (see 48 *The Times* L. R., at p. 500; [1932] A. C., at pp. 584-5). It seems to me that by so doing the House of Lords have implicitly restored *Cann* v. *Willson* (*supra*), because they have restored the case on which it was based; and if *Cann* v. *Willson* (*supra*) is good law, it follows that in the present case the accountants owed a duty of care to Mr. Candler, for the circumstances are indistinguishable.

Thirdly, to what transactions does the duty of care care extend? It extends, I think, only to those transactions for which the accountants knew their accounts were required. For instance, in the present case it extends to the original investment of £2,000 which Mr. Candler made in reliance on the accounts, because the accountants knew that the accounts were required for his guidance in making that investment; but it does not extend to the subsequent £200 which he made after he had been two months with the company. This distinction, that the duty only extends to the very transaction in mind at the time, is implicit in the decided cases. Thus, a doctor, who negligently certifies a man to be a lunatic when he is not, is liable to him, although there is no contract in the matter, because the doctor knows that his certificate is required for the very purpose of deciding whether the man should be detained or not; but an insurance company's doctor owes no duty to the insured person, because he makes his examination only for the purposes of the insurance company: see *Everett* v. *Griffiths* (*supra*), where Lord Justice Atkin proceeded on the self-same principles as he fully expounded later in *Donoghue* v. *Stevenson* (*supra*). So, also, a Lloyd's surveyor who, in surveying for classification purposes negligently passes a mast as sound when it is not, is not liable to the owner for damage caused by its breaking, because the surveyor makes his survey only for the purpose of classifying the ship for the yacht register and not otherwise: *Humphrey* v. *Bowers* ((1929) 45 *The Times* L. R. 297). Again, a scientist or expert (including a marine hydrographer) is not liable to his readers for careless statements in his published works. He publishes his work simply for the purpose of giving information, and not with any particular transaction in mind at all. But when a scientist or an expert makes an investigation and report for the very purpose of a particular transaction, then, in my opinion, he is under a duty of care in respect of that transaction.

It will be noticed that I have confined the duty to cases where the accountant prepares his accounts and makes his report for the guidance of the very person in the very transaction in question. That is sufficient for the decision of this case. I can well understand that it would be going too far to make an accountant liable to any person in the land who chooses to rely on the accounts in matters of business, for that would expose him to "liability in an indeterminate amount for an indtetrminate time to an indeterminate class": see *Ultramares Corporation* v. *Touche* ((1931) 255 N. Y. Rep. 170, at p. 179; 174 N. E. Rep. 441, at p. 444), *per* Chief Justice Cardozo. Whether he would be liable if he prepared his accounts for the guidance of a specific class of persons in a specific class of transactions, I do not say. I should have thought he might be, just as the analyst and lift inspector would be liable in the instances I have given earlier. It is perhaps worth mentioning that Parliament has intervened to make the professional man liable for negligent reports given for the purposes of a prospectus: see sections 40 and 43 of the Companies Act, 1948. That is an instance of liability for reports made for the guidance of a specific class of persons—investors, in a specific class of transactions—applying for shares. That enactment does not help one way or the other to show what result the common law would have reached in the absence of such provisions; but it does show what result it ought to reach.

My conclusion is that a duty to use care in statement is recognized by English law, and that its recognition does not create any dangerous precedent when it is remembered that it is limited in respect of the persons by whom and to whom it is owed and the transactions to which it applies.

One final word. I think that the law would fail to serve the best interests of the community if it should hold that accountants and auditors owe a duty to no one but their client. Its influence would be most marked in cases where their client is a company or firm controlled by one man. It would encourage accountants to accept the information which the one man gives them, without verifying it; and to prepare and present the accounts rather as a lawyer prepares and presents a case, putting the best appearance on the accounts they can without expressing their personal opinion of them. This is, to my way of thinking, an entirely wrong approach. There is a great difference between the lawyer and the accountant. The lawyer is never called upon to express his personal belief in the truth of his client's case; whereas the accountant, who certifies the accounts of his client, is always called upon to express his personal opinion whether the accounts exhibit a true and correct view of his client's affairs; and he is required to do this not so much for the satisfaction of his own client but more for the guidance of shareholders, investors, revenue authorities, and others who may have to rely on the accounts in serious matters of business. If we should decide this case in favour of the accountants there will be no reason why accountants should ever verify the word of the one man in a one-man company, because there will be no one to complain about it. The one man who gives them wrong information will not complain if they do not verify it. He wants their backing for the misleading information he gives them, and he can only get it if they accept his word without verification. It is just what he wants so as to gain his own ends. And the persons who are misled cannot complain because the accountants owe no duty to them. If such be the law, I think it is to be regretted, for it means that the accountants' certificate, which should be a safeguard, becomes a snare for those who rely on it. I do not myself think that it is the law. In my opinion accountants owe a duty of care not only to their own clients, but also to all those whom they know will rely on their accounts in the transactions for which those accounts are prepared.

I would therefore be in favour of allowing the appeal and entering judgment for Mr. Candler for damages in the sum of £2,000.

Lord Justice Asquith.—On two points I entirely agree with the judgment which Lord Justice Denning has delivered and I agree that the cause of action based on an alleged breach of duty occurring after the plaintiff became a shareholder cannot be made out if only because the damaged relied on preceded the breach. I also agree, for the reasons which he has given, that Mr. Fraser was clearly acting within the scope of his employment by the defendant firm in showing the draft accounts and giving certain other information to the plaintiff.

But I have the misfortune to differ from Lord Justice Denning on the more important point raised in this case. The point may be put in this way: Assume that Mr. Fraser's negligent misrepresentations had been made by his employers, the partners in the defendant firm. Assume further, as the fact is, that there was no fraud and no contract or fiduciary relationship between them and the plaintiff. Would they, in those events, have been liable to the plaintiff in respect of damage incurred by him through acting on those negligent misrepresentations? The defendants say, "No." They do not question that in the absence of fraud, contract and fiduciary relationship, there are cases in which A. may be under a legal obligation to B. to use reasonable care for some purposes. Their proposition is that under the conditions assumed in this case the defendants were under no duty, sounding in tort, to the plaintiff to take care that their representations of fact should be true. They rely in support of this contention on *Le Lievre* v. *Gould* (9 *The Times* L. R. 243; [1893] 1 Q. B. 491), a decision binding on this Court. I agree with the trial Judge in considering that authority to be conclusive in their favour unless it can be shown to have been overruled or to be distinguishable.

The plaintiff's case is that whatever may have been the position before *Donoghue* v. *Stevenson* (48 *The Times* L. R. 494; [1932] A. C. 562), the rule which the majority of the House of Lords applied in that case necessarily involves the consequence that (even where fraud, contract and fiduciary relationship are absent) A. will be liable to B. for any negligent misrepresentations on which B. acts to his detriment, provided always that there exists between A. and B. the necessary degree of so-called "proximity." It is argued that there was sufficient proximity on the facts of this case.

It may make for clearness first to consider some of the authorities preceding *Donoghue's* case (*supra*) (as for short I will call it); and, secondly, to inquire what difference, if any, that case has made. I do not think it useful to go back farther than *Derry* v. *Peek* ((1889) 5 *The Times* L. R. 625; 14 App. Cas. 337). In that case the plaintiff subscribed for shares in a limited company in reliance on a prospectus issued by the directors who included the defendants. The prospectus contained a negligent misstatement made in good faith. The claim on the writ as amended was for damages for deceit; for that and nothing else. There was no independent alternative claim in respect of negligent or innocent misrepresentation. The Court of Appeal held that fraud would be sufficiently established by proof that the directors had no reasonable grounds for believing the statement they made. The House of Lords, reversing the Court of Appeal, held that this was not enough to constitute fraud. If the defendants believed what they said it matters not how credulous they were or how groundless their belief. Fraud necessarily connotes dishonesty and no degree of mere stupidity can serve in its place. The case is therefore primarily, and according to one view solely, a decision on the meaning of the word "fraud," and is therefore not directly relevant to the main issue in the present case from which fraud, though originally alleged, has been eliminated. Nevertheless it is indirectly relevant and illuminating. For, although it does not decide in terms, it clearly assumes or implies, that a merely negligent misrepresentation made by a director to potential subscribers for shares, on which some of them act to their detriment, affords the latter no remedy. The notion that *Donoghue's* case (*supra*) was intended parenthetically or *sub silentio* to sweep away this substratum of *Derry* v. *Peek* (*supra*) seems to me quite unconvincing.

After the Court of Appeal had given its decision in *Derry* v. *Peek* (*supra*), but before it had been reversed by the House of Lords, a case came up for determination at first instance on facts not materially distinguishable from those of the present case. In *Cann* v. *Willson* ((1888) 4

The Times L. R. 588; 39 Ch. D. 39) Mr. Justice Chitty, relying on the decision (then unreversed) of the Court of Appeal in *Derry* v. *Peek* (*supra*), held that the plaintiff could recover damages in respect of a negligent but (according to what we now know the word "fraud" means) non-fraudulent misrepresentation. This was the view implicitly condemned by the House of Lords when *Derry* v. *Peek* (*supra*) reached them; and *Cann* v. *Willson* (*supra*) was consequently on this assumption expressly overruled by the Court of Appeal in *Le Lievre* v. *Gould* (*supra*). As I have indicated, this last decision is binding on this Court and disposes of the appeal, in my view, unless it can be shown to have been (*a*) overruled or (*b*) distinguishable.

I will consider these points in turn, premising that the principle on which *Gould's* case (*supra*) was decided was, in the words of Lord Esher, M. R., (9 *The Times* L. R., at p. 244; [1893] 1 Q. B., at p. 498) this: "All that he" (the defendant) "had done was to give untrue certificates negligently. Such negligence, in the absence of contract with the plaintiffs, can give no right of action at law or in equity." Both he and Lord Justice Bowen treated *Derry* v. *Peek* (*supra*) as deciding not merely that fraud was not established in that case, but that nothing short of fraud could in the circumstances of that case have given a cause of action, for example, that negligent misrepresentation could not do so.

That being so, the first question is whether the principle laid down in *Gould's* case (*supra*) has been modified or overruled, either expressly or by necessary implication, by the decision in any other case of superior authority. It has been qualified by *Nocton* v. *Ashburton* (30 *The Times* L. R. 602; [1914] A.C. 932) to this extent, that in the passage cited above, after the words "in the absence of contract with the plaintiff," the further words,"or in some circumstances where a fiduciary relationship exists between the defendant and the plaintiff," ought to be written in. Subject to this gloss, has it been overruled? It has certainly not there been overruled expressly. Has it, then, been overruled by necessary implication? Lord Atkin in *Donoghue's* case (*supra*) referred pointedly to *Gould's* case (*supra*) without a hint or a suggestion that it was wrongly decided, or that the memorable formula which he himself was propounding was inconsistent with it. As regards the two minority judgments, one of them, that of Lord Buckmaster, also mentions the case, and without disapproval.

On the other hand, it is arguable (though the argument does not carry conviction to my mind) that whether or not Lord Atkin realized the fact or directed his mind to the question, the formula which he laid down does in fact logically invalidate the principle laid down, and acted on in *Gould's* case (*supra*). This contention must be squarely faced. Lord Atkin pointed out that the law governing the duty owned by A. to B. in the absence of fraud, contract or fiduciary relationship has been built up piecemeal—built up, if one may pursue the metaphor, in disconnected slabs exhibiting no organic unity of structure. Certain classes owed duties of care to certain other classes: road users to other road users; bailees to person entrusting property to them; doctors and surgeons (and originally barbers) to persons entrusting their bodies to them; occupiers of premises to persons whom they invite or permit to come on the premises; and so on. These categories attracting the duty had been added to and subtracted from from time to time. But no attempt had been made in the past to rationalize them, to find a common denominator between road users, bailees, surgeons, occupiers, and so on, which would explain why they should be bound to a duty of care and some other classes who might be expected equally to be so bound should be exempt —no attempt, that is, save that of Lord Esher, M. R., (from which his colleagues dissociated themselves) in *Heaven* v. *Pender* ((1883) 11 Q. B. D. 503). Yet, said Lord Atkin, there must be such a common denominator, or at any rate some general conception of relations present in the cases in which a duty arises, and absent in cases in which it does not.

Very tentatively (and prefacing his observation with a warning that it might go beyond the province of a Judge to make such an attempt) he suggested the formula which has now become classic, but which nevertheless it is desirable here to quote afresh (48 *The Times* L. R., at p. 499; [1932] A.C., at p. 580): "You must take reasonable care to avoid acts or omissions which you can reasonably foresee would be likely to injure your neighbour. Who, then, in law, is my neighbour? The answer seems to be—persons who are so closely and directly affected by my act that I ought reasonably to have them in contemplation as being so affected when I am directing my mind to the acts or omissions which are called in question. This appears to me to be the doctrine of *Heaven* v. *Pender* *(supra)* as laid down by Lord Esher, when it is limited by the notion of proximity introduced by Lord Esher himself and Lord Justice A. L. Smith in *Le Lievre* v. *Gould* (supra)."

This passage, if read literally and without regard to the qualifying effect of its context, or of the *subjecta materies,* might be taken to comprehend not only conduct causing physical injury to person or property through setting a certain kind of chattels in motion or in circulation (the case immediately under review), but also conduct of any kind through any means (including negligent misstatement) causing *damnum* of any kind recognized by the law, whether physical or not, to anyone who could bring himself within Lord Atkin's definition of a "neighbour." I cannot believe that so broad an application was intended by Lord Atkin himself. The case may not decide quite so little as is contained in the somewhat conservative headnote in the Law Reports, which purports to confine it to the act of a manufacturer launching into circulation a negligently manufactured chattel which is calculated to injure and in fact injures the ultimate consumer or user in circumstances in which neither he nor any intermediate party has a reasonable opportunity of examining it. In fact, it has since been applied somewhat outside this limited ambit: for instance, to physical injury caused by negligent failure to repair a lift: *Haseldine* v. *Daw* (58 *The Times* L. R. 1; [1941] 2 K. B. 343), and to physical injury suffered when unloading timber from a barge: *Denny* v. *Supplies and Transport Company, Limited* (66 *The Times* L. R. (Pt. 1) 1168; [1950] 2 K. B. 374), or by the negligent adoption of a system of working. It has, however, I think, never been applied where the damage complained of was not physical. Mr. Justice Wrottesley in *Old Gate Estates* v. *Toplis and Harding and Russell* ((1939) 161 L. T. 227) held its application was limited to cases where the injury was to life or limb. I think that this is too narrow a view, and that physical injury to property may suffice, but it has never been applied to injury other than physical.

Apart, however, from any limitation which should be read into Lord Atkin's language by reference to the facts of the case before him—the *subjecta materies*—it seems to me incredible that, if he thought that his formula was inconsistent with *Gould's* case (*supra*), he would not have said so. This case, now nearly 60 years old, had at that time stood for nearly 40 years. He must have considered it closely. Yet his only reference to it is as annexing a valid and essential qualification to Lord Esher's formula in *Heaven* v. *Pender* (*supra*). Not a word of disapproval of the decision on its merits. The inference seems to me to be that Lord Atkin continued to accept the distinction between liability in tort for careless (but non-fraudulent) misstatements and liability in tort for some other forms of carelessness, and that his formula defining "who is my neighbour" must be read subject to his acceptance of this overriding distinction.

Counsel for the appellant was unable to point to any clean decided case, standing unreversed, either before or after *Donoghue's* case (*supra*), in which (always apart from fraud, contract and fiduciary relationship) A. had ever been held liable to B. in damages for a careless misrepresentation. But he anchored certain hopes on *George* v. *Skivington* ((1869) L. R. 5 Ex. 1), and on certain observations of Lord Herschell in *Derry* v. *Peek* (*supra*). I will say a word now on each of these cases.

George v. *Skivington* (*supra*), a decision "battered but unbowed," was in the end vindicated by the House of Lords in *Donoghue's* case (*supra*). The case was tried on demurrer. The declaration averred, *inter alia*, "that the defendant carried on the business of a chemist, and in the course of such business professed to sell a chemical compound made of ingredients known only to the defendant, and which he represented and professed to be fit and proper to be used for washing the hair, which could and might be so used without personal injury to the person using the same, and to have been carefully and skilfully and properly compounded by him the defendant; and thereupon the plaintiff Joseph George, bought of the defendant, and the defendant sold to him at a certain price, a bottle of the said compound, to be used by the plaintiff Emma for washing her hair as the defendant then knew, and on the terms that the same was then fit and proper to be used and could be safely used, by her for the purpose aforesaid, without personal injury to her, and had been skilfully, carefully, and properly compounded by the defendant," and that the wife suffered consequent injury.

Thus it was averred that the defendant put into circulation, knowing it was intended to be used by the purchaser's wife, a negligently compounded and deleterious hairwash. She used it, sustained physical injury, and an action was brought by her or on her behalf in which she succeeded on the issue raised by the demurrer. So far, the case is on all fours with *Donoghue's* case (*supra*) according to its narrowest interpretation, and it is not surprising that *Donoghue's* case (*supra*) affirmed it. But the declaration also averred that the defendant had said the hairwash was safe.

The present plaintiff, basing himself on this last averment, contended that it—an averment of negligent misstatement—standing alone would have evoked the same decision—namely, that the facts averred amounted, if proved, to a good cause of action. This I venture to doubt. It seems to me that the essence of the decision resided in the averment of negligent compounding and setting in motion by the defendant of a physical thing with knowledge that the plaintiff would or might use the physical thing so compounded and with resulting injury to the plaintiff; and that the parallel between *Donoghue's* case (*supra*) and the hairwash case lay exclusively in these features.

Turning to the decision in *Derry* v. *Peek* (*supra*), it is said that among decided cases *Derry* v. *Peek* (*supra*) also lends indirect support to the plaintiff's case. This contention is based on a *dictum* of Lord Herschell's (5 *The Times* L. R., at p. 629; 14 App. Cas. at p. 360). Lord Herschell, in deciding that the defendants were not liable for a non-fraudulent misrepresentation in their prospectus, said that he excluded from his purview cases "where a person within whose special province it lay to know a particular fact has given an erroneous answer to an inquiry made with regard to it by a person desirous of ascertaining the fact for the purpose of determining his course."

Here, again, is a statement which if construed in its literal breadth might seem to fit the present case. Lord Herschell's *dictum* was, however, later interpreted both by the Court of Appeal in *Low* v. *Bouverie* (7 *The Times* L. R. 582; [1891] 3 Ch. 82) and later by the House of Lords in *Nocton* v. *Ashburton* (30 *The Times* L. R., at p. 604; [1914] A.C. 932, at p. 950). It seems clear from the latter case (in which the former was also considered and affirmed) that Lord Herschell's proposition has been held only to hold good where (to use its terms) the "person within whose special province it lays to know a particular fact" occupies a contractual or fiduciary position *vis-à-vis* the "person desirous of ascertaining that fact." The cases which had decided otherwise are one by one dismissed by Lord Haldane as defensible if at all only on some other ground: warranty, estoppel, or whatnot. He affirmed that liability for negligence in word had in material respects been developed in our law differently from liability for negligence in act. The cases cited in support of Lord Herschell's *dictum* are all based, according to Lord Dunedin in *Nocton* v. *Ashburton* ([1914] A.C., at p. 964), "upon the existence of a fiduciary relationship, and, subsequently, the breach of duty subsequently arising."

In what has gone before it has been assumed that the two Law Lords who agreed with Lord Atkin's opinion or result accepted the broad formula about "my duty to my neighbour" which he laid down, as well as in the narrow proposition limited to the liability of the negligent manufacturer of a chattel which reaches the consumer without an opportunity of intermediate examination and injures him. This assumption seems to me more than questionable. Lord Thankerton, though he said (48 *The Times* L.R., at p. 506; [1932] A.C., at p. 604) that he entirely agreed with Lord Atkin's discussion of the authorities, was clearly considering the authorities in their application to the narrow ambit of a manufacturer's liability, chattels and physical injury. His judgment does not travel outside those limits. Nor do I read Lord Macmillan's judgment as endorsing the wider proposition. There is a passage in which he laid down certain general propositions (48 *The Times* L. R., at p. 510; [1932] A.C., at p. 619). It would have been easy for him to have adopted Lord Atkin's formula in terms if he had thought so broad a proposition justified. But when he said in an oft-quoted phrase, "the categories of negligence are never closed," he is not, in my view, accepting an acid test of liability valid in all circumstances—he does not mention the word "neighbour"; he is merely saying that in accordance with changing social needs and standards new classes of persons legally bound or entitled to the exercise of care may from time to time emerge—in this case by the addition of a careless manufacturer or circulator of a chattel—as parties bound, *vis-à-vis* consumers or users as parties entitled. In other words, what Lord Macmillan envisaged was the addition of another slab to the existing edifice, not a systematic reconstruction of the edifice on a single logical plan.

For these reasons I am of opinion that *Donoghue's* case (*supra*) neither reverses nor qualifies the principle laid down in *Gould's* case (*supra*).

If I am wrong in thinking that Lord Atkin's formula was not accepted by the majority of the House, there remains the question whether, assuming that *Gould's* case (*supra*) was well decided on its own facts, the facts of the present case are not so far different as to justify and require a different conclusion. The suggestion here is that the conclusion in *Gould's* case (*supra*) could be defended consistently with the principle of *Donoghue's* case (*supra*) being applicable to negligent misrepresentation, if in *Gould's* case (*supra*) there was insufficient "proximity" between the parties to attract the *Donoghue* principle; and that a conclusion favourable to the plaintiff in the present case could properly be reached on the ground that in the present case there was sufficient "proximity." The contention under this head is, in other words, first, that *Donoghue's case* (*supra*) overrules Gould's (*supra*) so far as the latter places careless misstatements on a different and privileged level as compared with some other forms of careless behaviour; but, secondly, that the actual result of *Gould's* case (*supra*) was right because the principle in *Donoghue's* case (*supra*) required "proximity" as a condition of liability and there was in *Gould's* case (*supra*) no sufficient "proximity"; and, thirdly, that this accounts, *inter alia,* for Lord Atkin's omission to say that *Gould's* case (*supra*) was wrongly decided.

This argument also seems to me invalid. The only difference, *quoad* "proximity," between the present case and *Gould's* (*supra*) is that in the present case Mr. Fraser knew when he made his representation the identity of the man who was likely to rely on his representations, whereas Gould did not know this: he did not know that the parties who were to make the advances were the mortgagees, the plaintiffs, or at least he did not know the contents of the mortgage deed. But consider what he did know. He knew before any mortgage was effected that his certificates were required because advances were going to be made by someone to the builder on the security of the work performed up to date as vouched by his certificates. That someone could only be the building owner or some other lender relying on the same security.

I take the following passage from the statement of facts ([1893] 1 Q. B. 492) premising that Hunt was the owner of the land on which two houses were to be built; Lovering was the builder; Dennes was the mortgagee who ultimately made advances; and Le Lievre, the plaintiff, was Dennes' assign. "Hunt arranged with the plaintiff Dennes that he should advance the £850 to Lovering upon the security of a mortgage from him. Hunt also agreed with the defendant Gould, who was an architect and surveyor at Ilfracombe, that he should give certificates from time to time that the work had reached the respective stages at which the respective instalments were to be advanced as provided by the schedule of advances, a copy of which was given to the defendant. This agreement with the defendant was made before the execution of the mortgage."

On those facts, to say that there was insufficient proximity in the *Gould* case (*supra*) seems to me wrong. Lord Atkin, in affirming the *Donoghue* type of liability, and annexing to it the condition of proximity, did not say: "There is no proximity unless the defendant can identify the ultimate victim of his carelessness in advance." The manufacturers of the peccant bottle of ginger beer had no idea who would in the end consume it. All they knew was that someone would. You may adopt the formula *Certum est qui certum reddi potest*. The unidentifiability in advance of the ultimate consumer and victim did not, by displacing the notion of proximity or in any other way, protect them from liability. I am therefore of opinion that this argument fails.

Singular consequences would follow if the principle laid down in *Donoghue's* case (*supra*) were applied to negligent misrepresentation in every case in which the representee were proximate to the representor. The case had been instanced by Professor Winfield and referred to by Lord Justice Denning of a marine hydrographer who carelessly omits to indicate on his map the existence of a reef. The captain of a liner, in reliance on the map and having no opportunity of checking it by reference to any other map, steers her on the unsuspected rocks, and she becomes a total loss. Is the unfortunate cartographer to be liable to her owners in negligence for some millions of pounds damages? Yet what line can be drawn between him and the defendants in the present case? If it be said that there is no proximity between the cartographer and those for whose use his map is designed, the reply surely is that there is just as much as there was between the manufacturer of the peccant ginger beer bottle and its ultimate consumer.

In the present state of our law different rules still seem to apply to the negligent misstatement on the one hand and to the negligent circulation or repair of chattels on the other; and *Donoghue's* case (*supra*) does not seem to me to have abolished these differences. I am not concerned with defending the existing state of the law or contending that it is strictly logical—it clearly is not—but I am merely recording what I think it is. If this relegates me to the company of "timorous souls," I must face that consequence with such fortitude as I can command.

I am of opinion that the appeal should be dismissed.

Lord Justice Cohen.—The Judge dismissed the plaintiff's claim. He found "no fraud" and from this part of his judgment the plaintiff does not appeal. He also found that the only duty which the defendants owed to the plaintiff was to produce accounts which they honestly believed to be the draft accounts of the company. In other words, he found that they owed no duty of care to the plaintiff. From that part of his judgment the plaintiff appeals on two grounds.

He says, first, that, since to the knowledge of the defendants' employee, Mr. Fraser, the plaintiff was a prospective investor in the company and was asking for information about the accounts of the company to assist him in reaching a decision whether to make the investment, the defendants, in accordance with the principles laid down by Lord Atkin in *Donoghue* v. *Stevenson* (48 *The Times* L. R. 494; [1932] A.C. 562) owed a duty to the plaintiff, when giving him that information, to exercise care to see that it was accurate. Secondly, he says that since the information given to the plaintiff was inaccurate in material particulars owing to the negligence of the defendants' employee Mr. Fraser, the defendants are liable in damages. Alternatively, the plaintiff alleges that as he became a shareholder in the company and the defendants were the auditors of the company, they owed a duty to him as shareholder to give him the accurate information which they should have given him when he was a prospective investor. This duty, he says, was broken and accordingly he is entitled to damages.

So far as the second ground is concerned, I entirely agree with the Judge that no damage flowed from the breach of such duty as is owed by the defendants as auditors to the plaintiff as a shareholder. The £2,000 had been irretrievably invested before the relationship had become operative. I would add that I doubt whether the defendants' alleged duty as auditors extends to cover information given to the plaintiff before he became a shareholder.

The first ground presents more difficulty, but in spite of Mr. Lawson's able and lucid argument I have come to the conclusion that we are bound by authority to hold that the Judge came to the right conclusion.

Mr. Foster submitted, first, that Mr. Fraser was not acting within the scope of his employment in giving to the plaintiff information as to the accounts and therefore the defendants could not be liable for his negligence in the preparation thereof. So far as this point is concerned, I have nothing to add to the reasons given by my brethren for thinking that it cannot be sustained. Secondly, he said that the principle of *Donoghue* v. *Stevenson* (*supra*) had never been applied to a case of negligent misstatement. A defendant could only be liable for negligent misstatement where there was a contractual nexus or a fiduciary relationship between him and the plaintiff. In the absence of such a relationship the decision in *Derry* v. *Peek* ((1889) 5 *The Times* L. R. 625; 14 App. Cas. 337), as interpreted in *Nocton* v. *Ashburton* (30 *The Times* L. R. 602; [1914] A.C. 932) is, Mr. Foster said, authority that no liability in negligence exists. This argument is, I think, well founded.

In *Donoghue* v. *Stevenson* (*supra*) as in all the other cases to which our attention was called, the breach of duty alleged has been one which has resulted in damages to the person of the plaintiff: see *Hazeldine* v. *C. A. Daw and Son, Limited* (58 *The Times* L. R. 1; [1941] 2 K. B. 343); *Denny* v. *Supplies and Transport Company, Limited* (66 *The Times* L. R. (Pt. 1) 1168; [1950] 2 K. B. 374). In *Old Gate Estates* v. *Toplis and Harding and Russell* ((1939) 161 L. T. Rep. 227) Mr. Justice Wrottesley refused to apply the principle of *Donoghue* v. *Stevenson* (*supra*) to a case where a company had paid too much for a property owing to an over-valuation by the defendants, who had been instructed by the promoters to value it for the purpose of the promotion. The company, which was the plaintiff, was not formed at the time of the valuation. Mr. Justice Wrottesley, rejecting an argument based on *Donoghue* v. *Stevenson* (*supra*) and (161 L. T. Rep., at p. 229): "The conception which runs through all these cases, both in those applications of the principle and in *Donoghue* v. *Stevenson* (*supra*) itself, is that something was negligently created or put into circulation which was dangerous either to life or limb"—those are, I think, the very words of Lord Atkin himself and the other learned Lords who delivered opinions, or the opinions of a majority, in *Donoghue* v. *Stevenson* (*supra*)—"or else that something carelessly handled, made, or mended, which would become dangerous to life or limb or health. It is as true to-day as it was in 1893, when *Le Lievre* v. *Gould* (9 *The Times* L. R. 243; [1893] 1 Q. B. 491) was decided, that, to use the words of Lord Justice Bowen ([1893] 1 Q. B., at p. 502): 'It is idle to refer to cases which were decided under totally different aspects, and upon totally different considerations of the law. Take, for example, the case of an owner of a chattel, such as a horse, a gun, or a carriage, or any other instrument, which is in itself of such a character that, if it be used carelessly, it may injure some third person who is near to it; then it is as plain as daylight that the owner of that chattel, who is responsible for its management, is bound to be careful how he uses it. Exactly in the same way with regard to the owner of premises. If the owner of premises knows that his premises are in a dangerous condition, and that people are coming there to work on them by his own permission and invitation, of course he must take reasonable care that those premises do not injure those who are coming there. . . . How has it any application to the present case? [that was, of a certificate given by an architect.] Only, I suppose, on the suggestion that a man is responsible for what he states in a certificate to any person to whom he may have reason to suppose that the certificate may be shown. But the law of England does not go to that extent: it does not consider that what a man writes on paper is like a gun or other dangerous instrument, and, unless he intended to deceive, the law does not, in the absence of contract, hold him responsible for drawing his certificate carelessly.' "—I think that that is as true to-day as it was when it was said by Lord Justice Bowen. —"There is nothing in my opinion, in *Donoghue* v. *Stevenson* (*supra*) which makes that bad law. The exceptions laid down by *Donoghue* v. *Stevenson* (*supra*)"—the exceptions to the rule that a man is obliged to be careful only to those to whom he owes a duty by contract—"are, as I understand the decision, confined to negligence which results in danger to life, danger to limb, or danger to health, and, the present case not being one of those exceptions, the plaintiffs have, in my opinion, no cause of action on the analogy of that case." Mr. Foster submitted that those observations constituted a correct statement of the law at any rate if the words "or property" were added after the words "or danger to health."

The question of liability for negligent misstatement was also considered by Mr. Justice Devlin in *Heskell* v. *Continental Express Limited* ([1950] 1 All E.R. 1033), a case where, through carelessness, a bill of lading had been issued for goods which had not been shipped. Mr. Justice Devlin said (at p. 1041): "In my judgment, therefore, the plaintiff has not established any contractual relationship with Strick giving rise to any particular duty owing to him. In putting forward the wider proposition that Strick owed a duty to the public not carelessly to circulate a document of title knowing it would be used as such, counsel for the plaintiff acknowledged the difficulty he encountered because of *Le Lievre* v. *Gould* (*supra*) and other similar decisions which make it plain that negligent misstatement can never give rise to a cause of action." Read literally, this statement is too wide, since negligent misstatement can give rise to a cause of action not only where there is a contractual relationship, but also where there is a fiduciary relationship: see *Nocton* v. *Ashburton* (*supra*). But with this limitation the statement is, in my opinion, correct.

So far as I am aware, there is only one reported case involving negligent misstatement which supports the plaintiff's claim. That is the decision of Mr. Justice Chitty in *Cann* v. *Willson* ((1882) 4 *The Times* L. R. 588; 39 Ch. D. 39). In that case (I am reading from the headnote in the Law Reports): "An intending mortgagor, at the request of the solicitors of an intending mortgagee, applied to a firm of valuers for a valuation of the property proposed to be mortgaged. A valuation at the sum of £3,000 was sent in by the valuers direct to the mortgagee's solicitors, and the mortgage was subsequently carried out. Default having been made in payment by the mortgagor, and a loss having resulted to the mortgagee, he commenced an action against the valuers for damages for the loss sustained through their negligence, misrepresentation, and breach of duty. The Court being satisfied on the evidence that the defendants knew at the time the valuation was made that it was for the purpose of an advance, and that the valuation as made was in fact no valuation at all:—Held, that, under the circumstances, the defendants were liable on two grounds: (1) that they (independently of contract) owed a duty to the plaintiff which they had failed to discharge; (2) that they had made reckless statements on which the plaintiff had acted."

If the first ground of decision was good law, it would support Mr. Lawson's argument; but this Court considered the case in *Le Lievre* v. *Gould* (*supra*), and Lord Esher, M. R., Lord Justice Bowen and Lord Justice A. L. Smith all agreed that *Cann* v. *Wilson* (*supra*) must be treated as overruled by *Derry* v. *Peek* (*supra*). The facts in *Le Lievre* v. *Gould* (*supra*) differed somewhat from those in the present case, but I do not think the Court thought the differences material, for Lord Esher stated the problem with which the Court was then faced in the following terms ([1893] 1 Q. B., at p. 496): "Then it is said that, even if there was no contract between the plaintiff Dennes and the defendant, nevertheless the defendant is liable to the plaintiffs for having given certificates which contained untrue statements; for it is said, the defendant owed a duty to the plaintiffs to exercise care in giving the certificates, because he knew that the plaintiffs would or might act upon them by advancing money to Lovering."

Lord Esher in *Le Lievre* v. *Gould* (*supra*) then proceeded to consider the problem. He treated *Heaven* v. *Pender* ((1883) 11 Q. B. D. 503), which was the foundation of *Donoghue* v. *Stevenson* (*supra*), as good law, saying (9 *The Times* L. R. at p. 244; [1893] 1 Q. B., at p. 497): "If one man is near to another, or is near to the property of another, a duty lies upon him not to do that which may cause a personal injury to that other, or may injure his property. For instance, if a man is driving along a road, it is his duty not to do that which may injure another person whom he meets on the road, or to his horse or his carriage." He then considered *Cann* v. *Willson* (*supra*) and said it was not good law, and finally came to the conclusion that the action failed, saying, in the last two or three lines of his judgment: "Such negligence, in the absence of contract with the plaintiffs, can give no right of action at law or in equity. All the grounds urged on behalf of the plaintiffs fail, and the appeal must be dismissed." Lord Justice Bowen and Lord Justice A. L. Smith gave judgment to the same effect. I need not, I think, refer to any passages in their judgments, because I have referred to the material passage in Lord Justice Bowen's judgment which Mr. Justice Wrottesley cited in *Old Gate Estates* v. *Toplis and Harding and Russell* (*supra*).

The principle of that decision seems to me directly in point in the present case. It is binding on us unless it can be said to be inconsistent with some other decision of this Court or of the House of Lords. I am unable to find any such decision. Mr. Lawson asked us to say that it is inconsistent with the principle laid down by Lord Atkin in *Donoghue* v. *Stevenson* (*supra*). It is to be observed that in *Donoghue* v. *Stevenson* (*supra*) Lord Atkin himself cited with approval some passages from the judgments of Lord Esher and Lord Justice A. L. Smith in *Le Lievre* v. *Gould* (*supra*), and I am unable to believe that if he had thought the *ratio decidendi* in that case was wrong he would have cited those passages without making it clear that he was not approving the decision. I think, therefore, that, although the passages (48 *The Times* L. R., at p. 499; [1932] A.C., at pp. 580-1) in Lord Atkin's speech are couched in such general terms that they might possibly cover the case of negligent misstatement, that question was not present to Lord Atkin's mind or intended to be covered by his statement.

Mr. Lawson further submitted that *Derry* v. *Peek* (*supra*) was purely a case of fraud and did not touch the question of negligent misstatement. It is true that the cause of action in *Derry* v. *Peek* (*supra*) was one of fraud, but it is, I think, implicit in the speeches that their Lordships would have reached the same conclusion had there been an alternative plea of negligence. I am fortified in this conclusion by the observations of two of their Lordships in *Nocton* v. *Ashburton* (*supra*). Lord Haldane, L. C., said ([1914] A.C., at p. 947): "The discussion of the case by the noble and learned Lords who took part in the decision appears to me to exclude the hypothesis that they considered any other question to be before them that what was the necessary foundation of an ordinary action for deceit." He is examining the decision in *Derry* v. *Peek* (*supra*). "They must indeed be taken to have thought that the facts proved as to the relationship of the parties in *Derry* v. *Peek* (*supra*) were not enough to establish any special duty arising out of that relationship other than the general duty of honesty."

Again, Lord Shaw in *Nocton* v. *Ashburton* ([1914] A.C., at p. 971) cited with approval the following passage from the judgment of Lord Justice Bowen in *Low* v. *Bouverie* (7 *The Times* L. R. 582; [1891] 3 Ch. 82, at p. 105): " '*Derry* v. *Peek* (*supra*) decides . . . that in cases such as those of which that case was an instance, there is no duty enforceable at law to be careful in the representation which is made. Negligent misrepresentation does not certainly amount to deceit, and negligent misrepresentation can only amount to a cause of action if there exist a duty to be careful—not to give information except after careful inquiry. In *Derry* v. *Peek* (*supra*) the House of Lords considered that the circumstances raised no such duty. It is hardly necessary to point out that, if the duty is assumed to exist, there must be a remedy for its non-performance, and that therefore the doctrine that negligent misrepresentation affords no cause of action is confined to cases in which there is no duty, such as the law recognizes, to be careful.' "

Derry v. *Peek* (*supra*) was a case where the action was founded on an allegation of a false statement in a prospectus, and I find it difficult to imagine a case where the proximity test laid down by Lord Atkin in *Donoghue* v. *Stevenson* (*supra*) would more clearly be satisfied if the principle of that case is applicable to negligent misstatement. Mr. Lawson submitted that there was a distinction between *Derry* v. *Peek* (*supra*) and the present case in that a prospectus is issued to the world at large, whereas Mr. Fraser's statements were addressed to the plaintiff in particular. This seems to me to be a distinction without a difference in principle.

For these reasons I think the decision in *Le Lievre* v. *Gould* (*supra*) is still good law and is conclusive of the present case. I might perhaps add that the conclusion which I have reached appears to accord with the views of the textbook writers. The learned editor of Salmond on the Law of Torts expresses the view that with certain exceptions not material to the present case, "A false statement is not actionable as a tort unless it is wilfully false. Mere negligence in the making of false statements is not actionable either as deceit or as any other kind of tort" (10th ed., p. 580). He regards the rule as anomalous. Winfield's Textbook of the Law of Tort (4th ed., pp. 386 and 387) expresses his dislike of it in more forcible language, be he recognizes that decisions of this Court are definitely against the existence of any action in tort for nelgigent statement. He thinks that it is open to the House of Lords to take the contrary view. On this point I need express no opinion.

Before parting with the textbook writers, I ought perhaps to mention that Mr. Charlesworth, in his book on the Law of Negligence (2nd ed., p. 16) suggests an explanation of the alleged anomaly in the rule. He states: "The duty to take care is ultimately based on the possible consequences which will occur if care is not taken. What the consequences may be of any particular act or omission is often a very difficult problem involving inquiry into questions of causation. This inquiry is difficult enough in cases where physical damage is concerned in which the cause, whether it be defective vehicles or machinery or lack of care and skill in management, can usually be accurately traced. To regard the issue of a certificate, an opinion, or a report as carrying the same duty of care as the delivery of a defective chattel would be to introduce a most disturbing factor into the mutual intercourse of society." I do not find this explanation entirely satisfactory, but I am unable to suggest a better one. Be that as it may, I am satisfied that on the authorities, as they stand, we have no alternative but to dismiss this appeal.

Since writing this judgment my attention has been directed by Professor Goodhart to a case in the New York Reports where a similar point was considered. The case is *Ultramares Corporation* v. *Touche* ((1931) 255 N. Y. Rep. 170; 174 N. E. Rep. 441). It has the merit that the decision of the Court was given by Mr. Justice Cardozo. In that case the accountants had certified the annual report of a company which, in order to finance its operations, required extensive credit and borrowed large sums from banks and other lenders.

The facts are stated quite shortly and sufficiently for my present purpose (at pp. 173 and 442 of the respective reports): "In January, 1924, the defendants, a firm of public accountants, were employed by Fred Stern and Co., Inc., to prepare and certify a balance-sheet exhibiting the condition of its business as of December 31, 1923. They had been employed at the end of each of the three years preceding to render a like service. Fred Stern and Co., Inc., which was in substance Stern himself, was engaged in the importation and sale of rubber. To finance its operations, it required extensive credit and borrowed large sums of money from banks and other lenders. All this was known to the defendants. The defendants knew also that in the usual course of business the balance-sheet when certified would be exhibited by the Stern company to banks, creditors, stockholders, purchasers or sellers, according to the needs of the occasion, as the basis of financial dealings. Accordingly, when the balance-sheet was made up, the defendants supplied the Stern company with 32 copies certified with serial numbers as counterpart originals. Nothing was said as to the persons to whom these counterparts would be shown or the extent or number of the transactions in which they would be used. In particular there was no mention of the plaintiff, a corporation doing business chiefly as a factor, which till then had never made advances to the Stern company, though it had sold merchandise in small amounts. The range of the transactions in which a certificate of audit might be expected to play a part was as indefinite and wide as the possibilities of the business that was mirrored in the summary."

The Court held that mere negligence did not make the defendants liable to the plaintiff, who had made advances on the strength of the certified accounts, though they in fact found that there was evidence of negligence by the defendants in making their report. Mr. Justice Cardozo said (at pp. 179 and 444): "We are brought to the question of duty, its origin and measure. The defendants owed to their employer a duty imposed by law to make their certificate without fraud, and a duty growing out of contract to make it with the care and caution proper to their calling. Fraud includes the pretence of knowledge when knowledge there is none. To creditors and investors to whom the employer exhibited the certificate, the defendants owed a like duty to make it without fraud, since there was notice in the circumstances of its making that the employer did not intend to keep it to himself." I pause there to say that there follow citations, but I do not propose to burden this judgment with the citations of the Judge except where they are of English cases. Mr. Justice Cardozo continued:

"A different question develops when we ask whether they owed a duty to these to make it without negligence. If liability for negligence exists, a thoughtless slip or blunder, the failure to detect a theft or forgery beneath the cover of deceptive entries, may expose accountants to a liability in an indeterminate amount for an indeterminate time to an indeterminate class. The hazards of a business conducted on these terms are so extreme as to enkindle doubt whether a flaw may not exist in the implication of a duty that exposes to these consequences. We put aside for the moment any statement in the certificate which involves the representation of a fact as true to the knowledge of the auditors. If such a statement was made, whether believed to be true or not, the defendants are liable for deceit in the event that it was false. The plaintiff does not need the invention of novel doctrine to help it out in such conditions. The case was submitted to the jury and the verdict was returned upon the theory that, even in the absence of a misstatement of fact, there is a liability also for erroneous opinion. The expression of an opinion is to be subject to a warranty implied by law. What, then, is the warranty, as yet unformulated, to be? Is it merely that the opinion is honestly conceived and that the preliminary inquiry has been honestly pursued, that a halt has not been made without a genuine belief that the search has been reasonably adequate to bring disclosure of the truth? Or does it go farther and involve the assumption of a liability for any blunder or inattention that could fairly be spoken of as negligence if the controversy were one between accountant and employer for breach of a contract to render services for pay?

"The assault upon the citadel of privity is proceeding in these days apace. How far the inroads shall extend is now a favourite subject of juridical discussion. . . . In the field of the law of contract there has been a gradual widening of the doctrine of *Lawrence* v. *Fox* (20 N. Y. 268) until to-day the beneficiary of a promise, clearly designated as such, is seldom left without a remedy. . . . Even in that field, however, the remedy is narrower where the beneficiaries of the promise are indeterminate or general. Something more must then appear than an intention that the promise shall redound to the benefit of the public or to that of a class of indefinite extension. The promise must be such as to 'bespeak the assumption of a duty to make reparation directly to the individual members of the public, if the benefit is lost'. . . . In the field of the law of torts a manufacturer who is negligent in the manufacture of a chattel in circumstances pointing to an unreasonable risk of serious bodily harm to those using it thereafter may be liable for negligence, though privity is lacking between manufacturer and user. . . . A force or instrument of harm having been launched with potentialities of danger manifest to the eye of prudence, the one who launches it is under a duty to keep it within bounds. . . . Even so, the question is still open whether the potentialities of danger that will charge with liability are confined to harm to the person, or include injury to property. . . . In either view, however, what is released or set in motion is a physical force. We are now asked to say that a like liability attaches to the circulation of a thought or a release of the explosive power resident in words."

The Judge then considered three cases which were said to support the plaintiff's action, and continued (at pp. 185 and 447): "From the foregoing analysis the conclusion is, we think, inevitable that nothing in our previous decisions commits us to a holding of liability for negligence in the circumstances of the case at hand, and that such liability, if recognized, will be an extension of the principle of those decisions to different conditions even if more or less analogous. The question then is whether such an extension shall be made. The extension, if made, will so expand the field of liability for negligent speech as to make it nearly, if not quite, coterminous with that of liability for fraud. Again and again, in decisions of this Court, the bounds of this latter liability have been set up, with futility the fate of every endeavour to dislodge them. *Scienter* has been declared to be an indispensable element except where the representation has been put forward as true of one's own knowledge . . . or in circumstances where the expression of opinion was a dishonourable pretense. . . . Even an opinion, especially an opinion by an expert, may be found to be fraudulent if the grounds supporting it are so flimsy as to lead to the conclusion that there was no genuine belief back of it. Farther than that this Court has never gone. Directors of corporations have been acquitted of liability for deceit though they have been lax in investigation and negligent in speech. . . . This has not meant, to be sure, that negligence may not be evidence from which a trier of the facts may draw an inference of fraud . . . but merely that if that inference is rejected, or, in the light of all the circumstances, is found to be unreasonable, negligence alone is not a substitute for fraud. Many also are the cases that have distinguished between the wilful or reckless representation essential to the maintenance at law of an action for deceit, and the misrepresentation, negligent or innocent, that will lay a sufficient basis for rescission in equity. . . . If this action is well conceived, all these principles and distinctions, so nicely wrought and formulated, have been a waste of time and effort. They have even been a snare, entrapping litigants and lawyers into an abandonment of the true remedy lying ready to the call. The suitors thrown out of Court because they proved negligence, and nothing else, in an action for deceit, might have ridden to triumphant victory if they had proved the self-same facts, but had given the wrong another label, and all this in a State where forms of action have been abolished. So to hold is near to saying that we have been paltering with justice. A word of caution or suggestion would have set the erring suitor right. Many pages of opinion were written by Judges the most eminent, yet the word was never spoken. We may not speak it now."

The final passage which I wish to read (at pp. 188 and 448) is this: "Liability for negligence if adjudged in this case will extend to many callings other than an auditor's. Lawyers who certify their opinion as to the validity of municipal or corporate bonds with knowledge that the opinion will be brought to the notice of the public, will become liable to the investors, if they have overlooked a statute or a decision, to the same extent as if the controversy were one between client and adviser. Title companies insuring titles to a tract of land, with knowledge that at an approaching auction the fact that they have insured will be stated to the bidders, will become liable to purchasers who may wish the benefit of a policy without payment of a premium.

"These illustrations may seem to be extreme, but they go little, if any, farther than we are invited to go now. Negligence, moreover, will have one standard when viewed in relation to the employer, and another and at times a stricter standard when viewed in relation to the public. Explanations that might seem plausible, omissions that might be reasonable, if the duty is confined to the employer, conducting a business that presumably at least is not a fraud upon his creditors, might wear another aspect if an independent duty to be suspicious even of one's principal is owing to investors. 'Everyone making a promise having the quality of a contract will be under a duty to the promisee by virtue of the promise, but under another duty, apart from contract, to an indefinite number of potential beneficiaries when performance has begun. The assumption of one relation will mean the involuntary assumption of a series of new relations, inescapably hooked together'. . . . 'The law does not spread its protection so far'. . . . Our holding does not emancipate accountants from the consequences of fraud. It does not relieve them if their audit has been so negligent as to justify a finding that they had no genuine belief in its adequacy, for this again is fraud. It does no more than say that, if less than this is proved, if there has been neither reckless misstatement nor insincere profession of an opinion, but only honest blunder, the ensuing liability for negligence is one that is bounded by the contract, and is to be enforced between the parties by whom the contract has been made. We doubt whether the average business man receiving a certificate without paying for it, and receiving it merely as one among a multitude of possible investors, would look for anything more."

I am glad, therefore, to find that the conclusion which I have reached on the basis of the English authorities seems to accord with the opinion of so eminent a student of the common law as Mr. Justice Cardozo.

I would only add that, despite the observations of Lord Justice Denning, I do not think that the conclusion which I have reached will encourage accountants to fall short of the high standard of conduct which the institutes to which they belong have laid down for their members.

In the result the appeal will be dismissed.

DURO SPORTSWEAR, INC. v. COGEN

Supreme Court of New York, Special Term, 1954. 131 N. Y. LAW JOURNAL 7.

WASSERVOGEL, Referee. Plaintiffs seek to recover from defendants the sum of $20,000 as damages allegedly resulting from malpractice by the defendant Cogen, a certified public accountant, and the fraudulent representations by all defendants as to the financial condition of the plaintiff corporation as of December, 1950.

Prior to January 6, 1951, plaintiff Schwartz and defendant Louis Leff owned the entire capital stock of the plaintiff corporation, the shares of which were registered in the names of their respective wives. On or about January 6, 1951, plaintiffs and the defendants Leff entered into a written agreement which provided, among other things that: (1) Schwartz would acquire all of the capital stock of the corporation; (2) Schwartz would loan $10,000 to the corporation without interest; (3) defendant Louis Leff would be relieved of certain liabilities then due and owing by him and would remain as an employee of the corporation at a fixed salary plus 25 per cent of its net profits; and (4) defendant Louis Leff would remain liable for one-half of the deficit of the corporation as it then existed. The defendant Cogen, a son-in-law of the defendants Leff, was employed to audit the books of account of the plaintiff corporation and to present to the parties a statement of its financial condition in order to determine the amount of deficit, in accordance with the terms of the above-mentioned agreement.

The record shows that when the agreement was entered into by the parties, the defendant Cogen, at the request of the individual plaintiff, certified as correct a statement of the financial condition of the corporation which fixed its deficit at $3,458.84. Subsequent thereto, however, and in or about March 1951, Cogen delivered to Schwartz a "Statement of Adjustments" which indicated that the deficit of the corporation was increased to $5,534.84. It is plaintiffs' claim that Cogen and the other defendants knowingly caused the deficit of the plaintiff corporation to be understated by approximately $12,000 in order to induce the individual plaintiff to acquire all of the stock of the corporation and to relieve the defendant Louis Leff of certain liabilities, as set forth in the agreement entered into on January 6, 1951.

The documentary evidence and credible testimony adduced upon the trial clearly established that Schwartz consented to acquire the stock of the corporation at a time when defendant Cogen advised him that its deficit was not in excess of $3,600, whereas, in fact, the deficit was greater than $9,000. The difference between the amount indicated in Cogen's original financial statement and the actual deficit consists, for the most part, of a series of bills which were not entered on the books of the corporation as of December 26, 1950, the closing date of the financial statement prepared by Cogen, but which were purportedly entered subsequent thereto. Plaintiffs, however, have failed to prove that defendants, or any of them, willfully, deliberately, or fraudulently caused these bills to be omitted from either the original books of account or the financial statement prepared by Cogen. Contrary to plaintiffs' contention, it appears most unlikely that defendants could have fraudulently concealed any substantial bill which had to be paid by the corporation, inasmuch as the record shows that Schwartz was in charge of the office, made the purchases, paid the bills, made entries in the original books of account, kept a diary of due dates of bills, and, thus, had an independent source of knowledge of the finances of the corporation. The mere fact that plaintiff established that the defendant Louis Leff had failed to approve certain bills which were not entered in the corporate books of account prior to Cogen's audit thereof is insufficient to establish plaintiffs' claim of fraud, particularly in view of the evidence which shows that it was the practice of Schwartz and other employees of plaintiff corporation to delay the posting and entry of such bills for at least several weeks after they were received. In the absence of other proof, therefore, it necessarily follows that plaintiffs' second cause of action against all of the defendants, which is predicated upon allegations of fraud, must be dismissed upon the merits.

However, although there is not sufficient evidence to substantiate fraudulent intent on the part of any of the defendants, Cogen's unqualified certification of the financial statement and his method of preparing same is sufficient to sustain plaintiffs' claim that at the very least he is guilty of malpractice. It cannot be disputed that at the time the certified statement was delivered to plaintiffs, it did not accurately reflect the true financial condition of the corporation. Cogen's testimony that he took into consideration "all bills then available," is inconsistent with his certification, which was absolute and not qualified in any manner. There is sufficient evidence to establish that Cogen failed to fully investigate the probability that the original books of account did not reflect outstanding bills due as of the date of his financial statement, although such bills had been received by the corporation but had not been entered or posted by either the individual plaintiff, the defendant Louis Leff, or any employee of the plaintiff corporation. Cogen, however, was associated with the plaintiff corporation for a considerable length of time prior to his preparation of the financial statement. He, therefore, was fully familiar with the customary delay in posting and entering bills in the books of account. Despite his knowledge of this practice, he nevertheless failed to take it into consideration and qualify his certification accordingly. His apparent refusal to realize the effect of an absolute certification and his evident reckless disregard of the consequences of such action, in the opinion of the court, is sufficient to constitute malpractice.

Moreover, it further appears that defendant Cogen, in April, 1951, made a journal entry wherein he added $10,000 to the corporation's surplus account by crediting "Surplus" and debiting "Accountants Payable—Chic Style," a dress contracting business wholly owned by the individual plaintiff, his son and wife. It was Cogen's contention upon the trial that his authority for such entry was the January 6, 1951, agreement executed by the individual plaintiff and the defendants Leff. The record, however, establishes that Cogen did not post the $10,000 charge against the Chic Style account in the "Accounts Payable" ledger of the plaintiff corporation, as good accounting practice required. Likewise the journal entry made by Cogen does not in any manner reflect a loan as contemplated by the parties at the time of the execution of their agreement. Nowhere in this agreement is there any provision which justifies the journal entry as made by Cogen, which, in effect, reflects a complete forgiveness of the money due and owing Chic Style by the corporation. If this journal entry had been correctly made and in accordance with the provisions of the January, 1951, agreement, the total liabilities of the corporation would not have decreased by $10,000, which was the effect of Cogen's act. The individual plaintiff had merely agreed to make a loan to the corporation and a proper $10,000 loan entry would not have had the effect upon the capital, surplus, or deficit of the corporation as indicated in the financial statement prepared by Cogen. It clearly appears, therefore, that the defendant Cogen, as a certified public accountant, improperly recorded the intention of the parties in the books of account and, at the very least, must be deemed negligent in the preparation of the financial statement relied upon by the parties prior to the actual execution of the agreement on January 6, 1951. Plaintiffs' claim for damages is obviously based upon the opinion of the Court of Appeals in the case of *Ultramares Corporation* v. *Touche* (255 N. Y., 170). In view of the holding by this court, as above noted, that plaintiffs have failed to establish fraud on the part of any of the defendants, the *Ultramares* case is not applicable. In the cited case, the Court of Appeals, in substance, held that in the absence of fraud, an accountant's liability for negligence "is one that is bounded by * * * contract, and is to be enforced between the parties by whom the contract has been made" (supra, p. 189). In the instant action, there is no privity of contract between Cogen and Schwartz. The record is clear that Cogen was employed only by the plaintiff-corporation and not by Schwartz. The mere fact that he gratuitously prepared personal income tax returns for Schwartz and his family is not sufficient basis for concluding that an employer-employee relationship existed between them within the intendment of the *Ultramares* case. Likewise, the fact that Cogen was employed by Schwartz to audit the books of Chic Style Company does not impose a contractual obligation upon Cogen with respect to Schwartz to use care and diligence in the preparation of his accounting statements for plaintiff-corporation. Plaintiff corporation and Chic Style Company are two separate entities with no legal relationship. There is no claim in this action that Cogen was negligent insofar as his work for Chic Style Company was concerned. The fact that he was an employee of this company as well as the plaintiff-corporation is not material to the issues before the court.

Although the corporation, as Cogen's employer, was joined in the action as a party-plaintiff, the claim for damages in its behalf, in effect, was abandoned by counsel in the briefs submitted to the court after trial. In any event, there is nothing in the record which shows that the corporation suffered any loss as a result of Cogen's negligence or malpractice which would enable it to recover damages under the *Ultramares* case.

In a subsequent case, however, the Court of Appeals made it clear that under certain circumstances accountants may be held liable to third parties even where there is lacking deliberate or active fraud (*State Street Trust Co.* v. *Ernst,* 278 N. Y., 104, 112). In order for Schwartz to recover damages, it would be necessary for the court to find that Cogen was guilty of gross negligence rather than mere faulty judgment. In the opinion of the court, the relevant facts of the instant action clearly require such finding.

Cogen's heedlessness and wanton disregard of the consequences of his incorrect financial statements take the place of a deliberate intention to defraud. Even under the principles set forth in the *Ultramares* case, "negligence or blindness, even when not equivalent to fraud, is none the less evidence to sustain the inference of fraud. At least this is so if the negligence is gross" (supra, p. 190). As already stated, this court has found that there is not sufficient evidence to warrant a specific finding of fraud. Nevertheless, the proof establishes that Cogen was derelict in his duty to thoroughly investigate the status of the corporate books of account prior to the preparation of his initial financial statement, and more particularly in view of the fact that he had personal knowledge of the practice of the corporation's bookkeepers to delay the entering and posting of such bills in these books of account. His unqualified certification and his failure to note the possibility of such unentered bills in the financial statements are matters which have not been explained to the satisfaction of the court. As a licensed certified public accountant, Cogen must be deemed to be aware of the reliance which normally is attached to an absolute certification of a financial report. Moreover, it cannot be denied that Cogen knew about specific unentered bills on or before March 25, 1951, at which time he delivered a supplemental financial statement to Schwartz. His repeated failure to include such bills in this statement is inexcusable, as is the fact that he incorrectly reflected Schwartz' loan of $10,000 to the corporation in the journal book of account. Thus, the record is replete with the foregoing evidence and other proof, both oral and documentary, showing Cogen's "refusal to see the obvious * * * and his failure to investigate the doubtful," which are sufficient to impose liability upon him for damage suffered by Schwartz (*State Street Trust Co.,* supra).

Contrary to defendant's contention, the mere fact that the damage to Schwartz cannot be measured with absolute mathematical certainty, is not sufficient to preclude his recovery herein. Where it is certain that damages have been caused by a wrong and the only uncertainty is as to the precise amount, there can rarely be good reason for refusing any damages whatever for the wrong on account of such uncertainty (*Wakeman* v. *Wheeler & Wilson Mfg. Co.,* 101 N. Y. 205; *Nat. Concert & Artists Corp.* v. *Murray,* 281 App. Div., 230, 233; *Alexander's Department Stores, Inc.,* v. *Ohrbach's Inc.,* 269 App. Div., 321, 328–29). A wrongdoer may not escape liability simply because the ordinary standards for measuring damages are not available. In any event, there is sufficient evidence in this record from which the court can reasonably evaluate the loss to Schwartz. Credible and disinterested expert testimony establishes that the actual deficit of the corporation as of January 6, 1951, was $9,448.68. Prior to the execution of the agreement entered into on the same date, Schwartz, as one-half owner of the stock of the corporation, was liable for one-half of such deficit, to wit, $4,724.34. As a result of the agreement, Schwartz consented to acquire the corporation with a deficit of $3,458.84, as reported to him by Cogen. This amount, subtracted from the remaining one-half of the actual deficit which Schwartz was obligated to take over on January 6, 1951, to wit, $4,724.34, leaves a balance of $1,265.50 above the amount of the deficit Schwartz had agreed to assume in reliance upon Cogen's financial statement. This amount, therefore, represents the damage to Schwartz.

Contrary to plaintiffs' contention, there is no merit to the claim that Schwartz was additionally damaged to the extent of $10,000, which amount allegedly represents moneys advanced by him to the corporation in reliance upon Cogen's reports. This sum of $10,000 is part of the liabilities set forth in the financial statements here involved and is already taken into consideration in reaching the foregoing deficit of the corporation as above set forth. Furthermore, nothing in the record warrants the conclusion that Schwartz agreed to advance additional capital to the corporation in sole reliance upon Cogen's financial statements. The credible testimony adduced upon the trial shows that Schwartz had agreed to make such loans prior to the preparation of any report by Cogen. Concededly, the financial statement submitted to Schwartz in January, 1951, did not reflect the true condition of the corporation.

Nevertheless, Schwartz had already committed himself to make certain advances to the corporation and was cognizant of its insolvency, although he was not aware of the exact amount of the deficit. His own testimony indicates that it was because of known past losses that he was compelled to make loans to the corporation. Plaintiffs have failed to establish that Schwartz was induced to lend an additional $10,000 in reliance upon Cogen's financial statements and thereby incur any loss other than that already considered by the court in fixing the damage he sustained.

Judgment is rendered in favor of plaintiff Schwartz against defendant Cogen on the first cause of action for the sum of $1,265.50, with interest thereon from January 6, 1951. Judgment is rendered in favor of defendants dismissing the second cause of action upon the merits. The above constitutes the decision of the court as required by the applicable provisions of the Civil Practice Act. The defendant Cogen may have a thirty day stay of execution.

SECTION 4

LIABILITY TO THIRD PARTIES BY STATUTE

SHONTS v. HIRLIMAN *

District Court of the United States, S. D. California, 1939. 28 F. Supp. 478.

The plaintiffs, who were purchasers of stock in Condor Pictures, Incorporated, brought three actions against certain officers of the corporation and Webster, Atz & Company, the auditors, to recover damages, the price paid for the stock, under the provisions of the Securities Act of 1933, section 11, 15 U.S.C.A. § 77k, establishing civil liability against certain persons for falsity in the registration statement. The cases were consolidated for trial. The falsity relied on related to misrepresentations and omissions concerning a lease by the Condor Pictures, Incorporated, and Western Service Studios, and, more particularly, the failure to set forth in the amendments to the registration statement, dated January 23, 1937, and February 1, 1937, that Condor Pictures, Incorporated, was obligated under the lease to use the studio a minimum of one hundred days a year at a total rental of thirty-five thousand dollars. The form in which the alleged false statements appeared on the respective dates in the second and third amendments was:

The second amendment to Registration Statement, paragraph No. 3 read:

"The issuer is fully equipped to carry out its present program and business. It owns no substantial physical properties or studios but carries on its production program at the present by rental of the use of studio and equipment at RKO Pathe Studio, Culver City, California. This policy will be continued by the issuer until such time as it becomes advantageous to purchase or build its own studio. At the present time this does not appear advisable as there are fully equipped operating studios available for rental one of which the issuer is now leasing and using and which is more than ample for the present requirements. There are sufficient space, equipment and facilities to meet issuer's requirements even should the present production program be doubled. The issuer's leasing arrangement with the studio provides the issuer with all necessary equipment for the production volume above stated in addition to all necessary offices for production staff.

"It is not necessary for the issuer to make any substantial investment in equipment because the studio lease provides the issuer with the essentials.

"The affiliate of the issuer, The Van Beuren Corporation, does not

* This case is discussed at p. 48 *supra*.

own any physical property or equipment of material account, neither does it require the ownership of such property or equipment for the present or proposed program. The properties and studio or location and equipment used by said Company are likewise leased. The volume that may be produced with properties and equipment so leased is more than double the present program."

The third amendment read:

"The issuer is fully equipped to carry out its present program and business. It owns no substantial physical properties or studios but carries on its production program at the present by rental of the use of studio and equipment at the Western Service Studios, Hollywood, California. This policy will be continued by the issuer until such time as it becomes advantageous to purchase or build its own studio. At the present time this does not appear advisable as there are fully equipped operating studios available for rental one of which the issuer is now leasing and using and which is more than ample for the present requirements. There are sufficient space, equipment and facilities to meet issuer's requirements even should the present production program be doubled. The issuer's leasing arrangement with the studio provides the issuer with all necessary equipment for the production volume above stated in addition to all necessary offices for production staff.

"The Western Service Studios are rented to the registrant by Grand National Films, Inc., the present lessee, for a period of approximately one (1) year from the date of this registration statement with options to renew granted solely to the registrant for a further nine (9) year period terminable only by the registrant at the end of any year during the first four (4) years of the 9-year period but not terminable during the succeeding five (5) year period if the registrant exercises its option to renew at the commencement of said 5-year period. The rental basis is at the rate of $350 per shooting day with no payments for any days on which there is no shooting. "It is not necessary for the issuer to make any substantial investment in equipment because the studio lease provides the issuer with the essentials.

"The affiliate of the issuer, The Van Beuren Corporation, does not own any physical property or equipment of material account, neither does it require the ownership of such property or equipment for the present or proposed program. The properties and studio or location and equipment used by said Corporation are likewise leased. The volume that may be produced with properties and equipment so leased is more than double the present program."

Paragraph No. 46 read:

"The registrant has entered into a rental agreement with Grand National Films, Inc., the present lessee of the Western Service Studios in Hollywood, California, whereby space, facilities and equipment to meet the requirements of the registrant's production program, even should it be doubled, together with all necessary offices for production staff are rented to the registrant. The studio is a fully equipped operating studio and the amount of space varies and is made available according to the stage and settings required.

"The Western Service Studios are rented to the registrant by Grand

National Films, Inc. for a period of approximately 1 year from the date of this registration statement with options to renew granted solely to the registrant for a further 9-year period terminable only by the registrant at the end of any year during the first 4 years of the 9-year period but not terminable during the succeeding 5-year period. The rental basis is at the rate of $350 per shooting day with no payments for any days on which there is no shooting. A copy of this agreement is to be filed as a post effective amendment to the registration statement."

The evidence showed that a formal lease was not entered into until March 9, 1937. However, a telegram signed by the President of Western Service Studios, dated January 31, 1937, committed the company to a rental arrangement to be followed by a formal leasing. This telegram, however, did not refer to a minimum guarantee. On May 11, 1937, the Securities Exchange Commission issued a stop order by reason of the alleged misrepresentations in the registration statement. The auditors, in their certificate dated January 19, 1937, did not set up the obligation to pay a minimum rental of $35,000 as a contingent liability. The defendants stipulated, without conceding the materiality of the matter, that the stock had no market value. The plaintiffs did not offer any evidence as to the actual value of the stock at the time the actions were instituted. At the conclusion of the plaintiffs' case, the defendants moved to dismiss the complaints upon the ground that no damage had been shown and that the actions were barred by Section 13 of the Securities Act of 1933, 15 U.S.C.A. § 77m.

Yankwich, District Judge (after stating facts as above). The problems presented by these motions must be solved by an analysis of the statute or by reference to similar statutes or claims of similar character, because, owing to the newness of the Securities Act of 1933, there are no cases determining them.

The Congress of the United States, for the first time in its history, undertook in 1933, to pass a statute similar to the state Corporate Securities statutes, commonly known as "blue sky laws". They take their name from their object, which is to prevent promoters of corporate securities from selling "the blue sky" to investors, or at least, from promising it to them. Most of these statutes are regulatory only. They regulate the securities which may or may not be issued or sold in a state and set up agencies for the granting of permits to issue or sell securities. They do not, as a rule, create any special claim of a civil nature for falsity in the application for a permit. The person who feels defrauded, by any misrepresentation relating to the stock, must resort to the law action of deceit or to the equity suit of rescission.

This Act, however, creates a civil liability of a specific character. It provides that if any part of the registration statement contains an untrue statement of material facts or omits to state material facts, the person who acquires the security, without knowledge of the untruth or omission, may sue either at law or in equity, the person who signed the registration statement, the officers or directors of the corporation which applied for the registration, and the accountants or others who certified to the registration statement or prepared it. 15 U.S.C.A. § 77k.

The measure of damages is not the one which usually obtains in fraud, —the difference between the value of the thing bought and what it would have been if it had been as represented.

I refer, for illustration of the latter rule, to *Hines* v. *Brode*, 1914, 168

Cal. 507, 143 P. 729, and to a later case, in which I was of counsel for the defendant, *Palladine* v. *Imperial Valley Farms Lands Association,* 1924, 65 Cal. App. 727, 225 P. 291. I quote from *Hines* v. *Brode, supra* [168 Cal. 507, 143 P. 730]: "The price paid may be considered only as evidence of value. Therefore, in a proper case, a wronged plaintiff may assert, as here, and, if possible, show, that the actual value of the property was only $100, and that its value, if the property had been as represented, was $4,000. He may also show and recover for the depreciation in the value of the improvements which he may have placed upon the property—a depreciation resulting from the fact that the actual value was not the represented value; and he may also recover for any other legitimate expenditures he may have made." This rule was abolished in California by the Amendment of 1935 to Section 3343 of the Civil Code (St. 1935, p. 1612).

If we study the Securities Act of 1933, and especially Section 11, which creates a right of action which would not otherwise exist, we find that the Congress did not adopt this rule, but *made the measure of recovery that which had always obtained* in actions for fraud in the courts of the United States. Thus, the Supreme Court in *Smith* v. *Bolles,* 1889, 132 U. S. 125, 129, 130, 10 S. Ct. 39, 40, 33 L. Ed. 279:

"The measure of damages was not the difference between the contract price and the reasonable market value if the property had been as represented to be, even if the stock had been worth the price paid for it; nor, if the stock were worthless, could the plaintiff have recovered the value it would have had if the property had been equal to the representations. What the plaintiff might have gained is not the question, but what he had lost by being deceived into the purchase. The suit was not brought for breach of contract. The gist of the action was that the plaintiff was fraudulently induced by the defendant to purchase stock upon the faith of certain false and fraudulent representations, and so as to the other persons on whose claims the plaintiff sought to recover. If the jury believed from the evidence that the defendant was guilty of the fraudulent and false representations alleged, and that the purchase of stock had been made in reliance thereon, then the defendant was liable to respond in such damages as naturally and proximately resulted from the fraud. He was bound to make good the loss sustained,—such as the moneys the plaintiff had paid out and interest, and any other outlay legitimately attributable to defendant's fraudulent conduct; but this liability did not include the expected fruits of an unrealized speculation. The reasonable market value, if the property had been as represented, afforded, therefore, no proper element of recovery.

"Nor had the contract price the bearing given to it by the court. What the plaintiff paid for the stock was properly put in evidence, not as the basis of the application of the rule in relation to the difference between the contract price and the market or actual value, but as establishing the loss he had sustained in that particular. *If the stock had a value in fact, that would necessarily be applied in reduction of the damages.* 'The damage to be recovered must always be *the natural and proximate consequence of the act complained of,'* says Mr. Greenleaf (volume 2, § 256); and 'the test is,' adds Chief Justice Beasley in *Crater* v. *Binninger,* 33 N.J.L. [4 Vroom] 513 [518, 97 Am. Dec. 737], 'that those results are proximate which the wrong-doer, from his position, must have contemplated as the probable consequence of his fraud or breach of contract.'

In that case the plaintiff had been induced by the deceit of the defendant to enter into an oil speculation, and the defendant was held responsible for the moneys put into the scheme by the plaintiff in the ordinary course of the business, which moneys were lost, less the value of the interest which the plaintiff retained in the property held by those associated in the speculation." (Italics added.)

And see, *Sigafus* v. *Porter,* 1900, 179 U. S. 116, 21 S. Ct. 34, 45 L. Ed. 113; *Tooker* v. *Alston,* 1907, 8 Cir., 159 F. 599, 16 L. R. A., N. S., 818; *Towle* v. *Maxwell Motor Sales Corp.,* 8 Cir., 1928, 26 F. 2d 209.

The Act, in section 11, subdivision (e), provides that the recovery shall be of such damages as shall represent the difference between the amount paid for the security and " (1) the value thereof as of the time such suit was brought, or (2) the price at which such security shall have been disposed of in the market before suit, or (3) the price at which such security shall have been disposed of after suit but before judgment if such damages shall be less than the damages representing the difference between the amount paid for the security (not exceeding the price at which the security was offered to the public) and the value thereof as of the time such suit was brought." 15 U. S. C.A. § 77k (e).

It is evident that the Congress intended to make the action, notwithstanding its origin in fraud, *purely compensatory.* And so, it provided for the recovery of the price paid. It anticipated three possible contingencies: (1) Where there has been no sale of the stock; (2) where there has been a sale of the stock before the action was brought or (3) a sale after the action was brought.

Where there has been no sale of the stock, the recovery is for the difference between the value of the stock when purchased, and its value as of the time suit is brought. Where there has been a sale, the recovery is for the difference between the price received by the seller and the price he paid.

Before disposing of this question and the question of limitation, I comment briefly on the evidence in the record as it relates to the elements of the action created by the statute.

I am satisfied that the omission from the statement of the minimum requirements in the leases, which obligated Condor Pictures, Inc., to shoot at least 100 days a year, is material. It is not of any great significance that the lease was not actually entered into until later. For that reason, I am of the view that there is no falsity in the statement that they had certain rental arrangements with a particular company. I think the oral negotiations and the telegram of January 1, 1937, showed a commitment which the parties themselves considered binding, and which was to be later embodied in a more formal instrument. The effect of these conclusions is this: No misstatement or omission appears in the registration statement until after the last certificate of Webster, Atz & Co., dated January 19, 1937. Prior to January 31, 1937, there were merely discussions of rental, and no definite undertaking by either side or guarantee of a minimum, which was binding on the company. The failure of the certificate of Webster, Atz & Co. to set up the rental undertaking and the minimum guarantee of $35,000 as a contingent liability, is not the omission of anything which existed then. The rental arrangement was not called to their attention. There was no entry on the books at their disposal, from which, by further inquiry, they might have discovered that there was such an undertaking. Absent these, they cannot be charged with a misrepresentation which was made later—long after their certification.

In sum, we cannot, as to Webster, Atz & Co., take the subsequent omissions and retroject them to the date of January 19, 1937, so as to "tie" them to a certificate, which they made on the basis of facts as they then existed and which showed no rental arrangement of any kind.

We return to the element of damages. It is stipulated that, at the time the actions were begun, the stock had no "market value." But *it is not conceded* that it had *no intrinsic value.* In the view I take, this value is of utmost importance. The object of the statute is not to penalize promoters or auditors for the full value of the stock, merely because the stock—which may be that of a new corporation—might not have a "market value." The object of the Congress was to compensate a person for the depreciation in the value—*the actual value* of his security.

Mark you, the object of this section is compensatory. No penalties are intended. The object is not to recover the *full value* of the stock, *under all circumstances.* The plaintiffs are not required, as a condition precedent to recovery, to surrender for cancellation to the defendants or to the court, the stock, or even to tender it back. They retain it. If, as counsel claim, they may retain the stock and then recover its full value by showing that there is no market for it at a particular time, then we have this situation: A person might recover the full value of the stock, retain his position as a stockholder in the corporation, exercise his full rights as such, and then, at some future time, when the stock had acquired a "market value," reap the full benefit of his investment, after he has already been repaid it. This would be a penalty, inconsistent with the compensatory nature of the Act.

The finding of insolvency in the reorganization proceedings is not proof that the stock was valueless. A petition for reorganization was filed on November 29, 1937. Under Section 77B of the old Bankruptcy Act, 11 U. S. C. A. § 207, and Chapter 10 of the Chandler Act, a petition for reorganization may be filed either if a corporation is insolvent, or if it is unable to pay its debts as they mature. 11 U. S. C. A., Ch. 10, § 530 (1). Insolvency here is interpreted as it is defined in clause (19) of Section 1 of the new Bankruptcy Act, namely: A condition existing when the aggregate of a debtor's property, exclusive of any property which he may have concealed, transferred or removed with intent to defraud, is not, at a fair valuation, sufficient in amount to pay his debts. 11 U. S. C. A., Ch. 1, § 1 (19).

A corporation may seek the benefit of corporate reorganization, *without being insolvent.* The only object of determining insolvency is to dispense with the need for the assent of a majority of the stockholders to the plan of reorganization. That was the rule under 77B and is the rule under the present Act, subdivision 8 of Section 216, which provides that protection for stockholders shall not be required after the Judge determines that the debtor is insolvent. 11 U.S.C.A. § 616 (8).

A reorganization differs from an ordinary proceeding in bankruptcy, whether upon a voluntary or involuntary petition. In an involuntary petition in bankruptcy, it is usually alleged that the defendant is insolvent and has committed certain acts of bankruptcy. 11 U. S. C. A., Ch. 3, § 21. If, later on, the issue is tried, the finding of insolvency reverts to the date of the filing of the petition. 11 U. S. C. A., Ch. 1, § 1 (13). For that is the issue presented by the pleadings. I think that this is the principle which counsel had in mind in urging that the finding of insolvency in the reorganization proceedings of Condor Pictures, Inc., on the 30th of December, 1938, reverted back to the filing of the petition. When a petition for reorganization is filed, by either the debtor or some of its creditors, the object is to subject at once the property to the equity powers of the court. And the court is not called upon, in approving the petition, to determine whether the debtor is solvent or insolvent. When, in the course of the proceedings, it becomes necessary to determine the voting rights of the stockholders, the court may make a finding of insolvency. This finding is merely for the purpose of reorganization. For if reorganization fails, either through the failure of the plan formulated and approved by the court, to receive the assent of the requisite number of creditors or because the court is satisfied that no reorganization is possible, the court has the choice of liquidating or of dismissing. If the court liquidates, then its finding of insolvency becomes effective, and liquidation is ordered through a trustee. 11 U. S. C. A. §§ 636–638.

I refer to these matters in order to point out how provisional all acts done in the course of a reorganization proceeding may be until there is actually a reorganization or liquidation.

Now, to get back to the specific order. The minute order of Judge Ralph E. Jenney says specifically: "This matter coming on for hearing on (8) motion of Ben Pivar, et al, creditors to dismiss the proceedings numbered 31,013-C, Bankruptcy, the court finds the corporation insolvent in both the bankruptcy and the equity sense *at this time."*

Judge Jenney did not order liquidation. Had he ordered liquidation, it might be argued that we are in bankruptcy and ought to consider it as though an adjudication had been made upon an involuntary petition, and that it refers back to the date of the petition. But, he did not do so. He continued the efforts at reorganization. His only object in making the finding was to say to the reorganizers: "You may proceed to formulate a plan, and if that plan is approved by me, it will be confirmed when you secure the assent of two-thirds of the creditors. You do not need the assent of a majority of the stockholders."

We cannot retroject into the past this finding, which says that insolvency exists *"at this time,"* so as (in the language of the street) "to pin" insolvency on the corporation as of November 29, 1937.

The documentary evidence offered to show insolvency is insufficient. We have an auditor's summary of the books of the company, which shows an operating loss, during a certain period of time. But an operating loss is not the equivalent of insolvency, either in the sense of inability to meet debts—which, of course, would not help us here—or in the sense that the assets, at a fair valuation, are less than the liabilities.

I am of the view, therefore, that the evidence does not show insolvency, so as to warrant the court in concluding that, on the date when these suits were instituted, between March and October, 1937, the stock was of no value, so as to entitle the plaintiffs to recover without proof of value.

I realize that there may be difficulties in proving value. But this type of legislation is novel. We know the opposition encountered when such legislation is sought to be enacted. And, no doubt, because of this opposition, on the part of persons whose affairs had not been, heretofore, regulated by federal law,—an opposition which, indubitably, expressed itself in the Congress—a compromise had to be reached and the law made less harsh.

Counsel themselves have adverted to the fact that recovery was greater under the original enactment. This indicates that, ultimately, the counsel of those prevailed who thought that liability should *not be* penal in nature, but merely compensatory, limited to the actual loss suffered. And as there can be no claim unless there is loss, the requirement that the plaintiff prove loss by showing depreciation in the value of his security, merely makes him prove what any person who has an action purely compensatory, must prove in a court of law. There is no such proof of loss here.

We now pass to another matter—the effect of the one-year limitation contained in Section 13, which reads: "No action shall be maintained to enforce any liability created under section 11 [77k] or section 12 [77*l*] (2) unless brought within one year after the discovery of the untrue statement or the omission, or after such discovery should have been made by the exercise of reasonable diligence, or, if the action is to enforce a liability created under section 12 [77*l*] (1), unless brought within one year after the violation upon which it is based. In no event shall any such action be brought to enforce a liability created under section 11 [77k] or Section 12 [77*l*] (1) more than three years after the security was bona fide offered to the public, or under section 12 [77*l*] (2) more than three years after the sale." 15 U. S. C. A. § 77 (m).

Statutes of limitation are statutes of repose. They are based upon the thought that the law should aid the diligent, and not him who sleeps on his rights. *United States* v. *Oregon Lumber Co.,* 1922, 260 U. S. 290, 299, 300, 43 S. Ct. 100, 67 L. Ed. 261. They do not wipe out the debt. They merely destroy the remedy. So much so that the due process clause is not violated if a limitation is changed. See *Canadian Northern R. Co.* v. *Eggen,* 1920, 252 U. S. 553, 559, 40 S. Ct. 402, 64 L. Ed. 713.

In interpreting limitations, the general rule is that the statute begins to run from the time the right of action accrues. And the right of action accrues when an act, amounting to either a breach of contract or a breach or violation of duty takes place, regardless of concealment or discovery. The extent to which courts have gone in applying this principle to statutes of limitation is illustrated by *Staples* v. *Zoph,* 1935, 9 Cal. App.2d 369, 49 P.2d 1131, which arose before me while a Judge of the Superior Court of California. A woman sent an anonymous letter to another person reflecting on the character of the plaintiff—also a woman. The plaintiff did not discover the identity of the sender until after the expiration of one year, which is the California statutory limitation in actions for libel. The plaintiff alleged that fact in an endeavor to take the case out of the statute. I held that there were no exceptions to the rule which starts the running of statutes of limitations from the accrual of the right of action, except in the case of fraud, and that the fraudulent concealment of the identity of the defendant did not extend the period of limitation.

On appeal, the District Court of Appeals, Second District, affirmed the judgment, stating: "Concealment of the identity of the party liable cannot be deemed the same as concealment of a cause of action. * * * This rule does not operate unjustly to plaintiff, since at any time within one year after accrual of her cause of action she could have filed suit naming a fictitious defendant." As stated, the only exception to this rule is that obtaining in fraud cases. In California, an action for relief, upon the ground of fraud or mistake, must be brought within three years. But the cause of action is not deemed to have accrued until the discovery by the aggrieved party of the facts constituting the fraud or mistake. California Code of Civil Procedure, § 338.

While the wording of this section is different from the limitation in Section 13 of the Securities Act of 1933, the meaning of both sections is the same. They both mean that the action *must be brought within one year after discovery.* More, the statute under discussion goes further. Instead of merely speaking of discovery, it gives recognition to imputed discovery, i. e., discovery which should have been made by the exercise of reasonable diligence.

I think that, ultimately, the courts would have interpreted the statute in like manner. For that has been the general rule. See, *Foster* v. *Mansfield, Coldwater, etc. Ry.*, 1892, 146 U. S. 88, 13 S. Ct. 28, 36 L. Ed. 899; *Johnston* v. *Standard Mining Co.*, 1893, 148 U. S. 360, 370, 13 S. Ct. 585, 37 L. Ed. 480; *Victor Oil Co.* v. *Drum*, 1920, 184 Cal. 226, 193 P. 243; *Bancroft* v. *Woodward*, 1920, 183 Cal. 99, 190 P. 445; *Consolidated, etc., Co.* v. *Scarborough, infra.* When we deal with the statute of limitations as applied to fraud, *discovery becomes a part of the cause of action.*

In *Lady Washington Consolidated Co.* v. *Wood*, 1896, 113 Cal. 482, 45 P. 809, 810, the court says: "The right of a plaintiff to invoke the aid of a court of equity for relief against fraud, after the expiration of three years from the time when the fraud was committed, is an exception to the general statute on that subject, and cannot be asserted unless the plaintiff brings himself within the terms of the exception. It must appear that he did not discover the facts constituing the fraud until within three years prior to commencing the action. This is an element of the plaintiff's right of action, and must be affirmatively pleaded by him in order to authorize the court to entertain his complaint."

This case has been followed consistently. In *Original Mining & Milling Company* v. *Casad*, 1930, 210 Cal. 71, 290 P. 456, the court gives the allegations which the complaint *must* contain in order to show discovery. They are: (1) When the fraud was discovered; (2) the circumstances under which it was discovered; (3) facts to show that plaintiff is not at fault in failing to discover the fraud sooner, and that the plaintiff has no actual or presumptive knowledge of facts sufficient to put him on inquiry. Among the latest California cases on the subject is *Consolidated Reservoir & Power Co.* v. *Scarborough*, 1932, 216 Cal. 698, 16 P.2d 268, where the older cases are reviewed and approved. These cases express a general rule, which has the sanction of the Supreme Court of the United States.

In *Wood* v. *Carpenter*, 1879, 101 U. S. 135, 140, 25 L. Ed. 807, the court, in interpreting the Indiana statute relating to limitations of actions in fraud, laid down a similar rule: "In this class of cases the plaintiff is held to stringent rules of pleading and evidence, *'and especially must there be distinct averments as to the time when the fraud, mistake, concealment, or misrepresentation was discovered, and what the discovery is, so that the court may clearly see whether, by ordinary diligence, the discovery might not have been before made.'* [Citing case.] 'This is necessary to enable the defendant to meet the fraud and the time of its discovery.' * * * *A general allegation of ignorance at one time and of knowledge at another are of no effect. If the plaintiff made any particular discovery, it should be stated when it was made, what it was, how it was made, and why it was not made sooner.*" (Italics added.)

The opinion concludes:

"There must be reasonable diligence; and the means of knowledge are the same thing in effect as knowledge itself.

"The circumstances of the discovery must be fully stated and proved, and the delay which has occurred must be shown to be consistent with the requisite diligence." (Italics added.)

And see, *Arkansas Natural Gas Co.* v. *Sartor,* 1935, 5 Cir., 78 F.2d 924; *United States* v. *Christopher,* 1934, 10 Cir., 71 F.2d 764.

As the basis of the right to recover under the Securities Act is fraud, and the limitation is made dependent upon discovery, these principles should be applied to it.

The rule which allows discovery to be the starting point of limitation is made for the benefit of the person who claims to be injured by the fraud of another. It works to the disadvantage of the person charged with the fraud. If we apply it to stockholders seeking redress under the civil liability sections of the Security Act, no hardship or injustice results. Stockholders are in a position to inquire, and to detect fraud on the part of the officers of a corporation, *in matters of record,* as they have access to its books and records.

The maximum time provision in Section 13, to the effect that, in no event, shall an action be brought more than three years after the security was offered to the public, does not extend the limitation period. This provision means that if discovery is not made within three years, no action lies, *under any circumstances.* Otherwise put, if more than three years have elapsed since the offer of the security, the discovery of defendant's fraud comes too late. The object of this clause is merely to set the maximum period during which a person might be held liable, *under any circumstances,* by reason of any false statements in the registration statement. It does not dispense with the requirement that any person who brings an action within the three year period, must do so also within one year after the discovery of the falsity of the statement or the omission.

There is no proof as to the date of discovery, although the complaints contain allegations of discovery in May, 1938. Nor were facts stated in the complaint or proved at the trial explaining why discovery was not made sooner. Unless I hold that such proof is unnecessary, the actions are clearly barred. For the reasons stated, I cannot so hold.

It follows that the motions to dismiss should be granted as to all the defendants. It is so ordered. The causes are also dismissed as to defendants named but not served.

SECTION 5

WORKING PAPERS

IPSWICH MILLS v. DILLON *

Supreme Judicial Court of Massachusetts, 1927. 260 Mass. 453, 157 N. E. 604.

Suit in equity by the Ipswich Mills against William Dillon and another, to require defendants to turn over to plaintiff papers and documents in their possession. On reservation and report. Decree to be entered for plaintiff in accordance with opinion.

CARROLL, J. The question involved in this suit in equity is the ownership of certain papers. The plaintiff is a manufacturer of hosiery. The defendants are accountants, father and son, who have been partners since January 1, 1921. In 1912 or 1913 the father, and later the firm, were employed by the plaintiff as accountants to make an annual audit, to prepare tax returns, and to perform services on matters of bookkeeping, cost accounting and statements for banks. This employment continued until December, 1925. In 1922 or 1923 the defendants were employed to conduct a federal tax case before the Bureau of Internal Revenue as attorneys in fact for the plaintiff. While a federal revenue agent was making an examination of the plaintiff's returns for the years 1922, 1923, 1924, he was sent by the plaintiff to the defendants to examine certain papers in their possession relating to the plaintiff's affairs, more particularly the defendants' "work sheets" relating to the revaluation of the plant assets and to certain adjusted inventories developed in their work on the tax case. The defendants refused the revenue agent access to these papers. On January 6, 1926, the plaintiff demanded of the defendants "all papers in your possession belonging to Ipswich Mills." No papers were delivered and this suit was instituted.

All the papers involved which were in the defendants' possession were produced by them at the trial. They were examined by the parties, grouped, initialed and impounded, awaiting the final decision of the case. Group A consisted of papers that originated in the plaintiff's office or in the office of its selling agents, or of some one associated with them, including papers relating to the 1917 federal tax return of the plaintiff. The defendants conceded that the plaintiff is the owner of these papers in group A, and entitled to possession of them. Group B included copy of the amended federal tax return of the plaintiff for the year 1918, and certain papers (not work sheets) relating thereto. In group C there were copies of the plaintiff's tentative and amended tax return for 1919 with work sheets and correspondence in connection therewith. In group D were papers and work sheets of the revaluation of the plaintiff's plant assets. The papers in group E were the defendants' work sheets of their July, 1922, report. Group F included papers, reports, returns, copies,

* This case is discussed at p. 54 f. *supra*.

work sheets, data, correspondence and memoranda respecting the tax case, together with some letters originating in the plaintiff's office.

It was found by the trial judge that work sheets meant papers on which original compilations, computations and analyses are made by accountants, which later are gathered together in a summary form and the figures rendered in a schedule, exhibit, report or return upon which the accountant is working. The judge ruled that the plaintiff was the owner of the papers in groups B, C, D and E, and entitled to the immediate possession of them, the defendants being entitled to take and preserve such photostatic copies as they desired. With reference to the papers initialed F, the judge ruled that the parties were jointly interested in these particular papers, with the right in the plaintiff to take them temporarily from the defendant. An order for a decree was made. The case was then reported to this court.

Concerning the papers marked B, which consist of "copy of amended federal tax return of the plaintiff for 1918 and certain papers (not work sheets) relating thereto," the judge found:

> "The defendants were under employ as accountants—auditing, checking up and verifying, and making a research for the original costs of the plaintiff's plant assets then in use and applying depreciation figures decided upon by the directors with respect to the different classes of property. It was work of a character requiring accounting skill and experience, and good judgment in reaching sound and dependable conclusions where original entries were obscure or vouchers missing. It was fully paid for by the plaintiff."

We assume that the original tax return was delivered to the plaintiff and the copy of this return retained by the defendants. The defendants were not the agents or servants of the plaintiff, they were independent contractors. In the making of the documents and papers and in collecting the information involved in them, the defendants were independent accountants engaged in their own occupation. See *Pearl* v. *West End Street Railway,* 176 Mass. 177, 179, 57 N. E. 339, 49 L. R. A. 826, 79 Am. St. Rep. 302; *Leverone* v. *Arancio,* 179 Mass. 439, 443, 61 N. E. 45. They had the right to make and retain copies of the tax return. It might be necessary to have possession of the copies if the accuracy of their work was questioned. There was nothing in the contract of employment which required the defendants to surrender this copy and in the absence of such an agreement they could not be compelled to surrender it.

The other papers relating to the federal tax return of 1918, mentioned in group B, we understand are office copies of letters sent by the defendants. The defendants could retain copies of these letters as well as copies of the schedules which are indicated by the evidence as being a part of the "papers * * * relating thereto." This copy of the return and the papers relating thereto may have contained information of importance to the plaintiff. The right of the plaintiff to restrain its publication is not before us. Even if it be assumed that the defendants could be enjoined from the publication of the contents of these papers, the title to them was in the defendants.

Group C consisted of (1) carbon copies of letters from the defendants to the plaintiff; (2) original letters from the plaintiff to the defendants; (3) original letters to the defendants from the plaintiff's attorneys; and (4) carbon copies of letters from the defendants to the collector of internal revenue.

The carbon copies of the defendants' letters to the plaintiff were the property of the defendants. The plaintiff did not own these copies and was not entitled to their possession. The contract of employment did not require the defendants to furnish these copies to the plaintiff.

The original letters from the plaintiff to the defendants belonged to the defendants. They were the recipients, and therefore owned them. It was decided in *Baker* v. *Libbie,* 210 Mass. 599, 606, 97 N. E. 109, 37 L. R. A. (N. S.) 944, Ann. Cas. 1912D, 551, after an exhaustive review of the authorities, that as a general rule the publication of letters may be restrained by the author, but in the absence of some special arrangement the recipient of the letter is the owner. "The author parts with the physical and material elements which are conveyed by and in the envelope. These are given to the receiver. The paper upon which the letter is written belongs to the receiver. *Oliver* v. *Oliver,* 11 C. B. (N. S.) 139; *Grigsby* v. *Breckinridge,* 2 Bush (65 Ky.) 480, 486, 92 Am. Dec. 509; *Pope* v. *Curl,* 2 Atk. 341; *Werckmeister* v. *American Lithographic Co.* (C. C.) 142 F. 827, 830. A duty of preservation would impose an unreasonable burden in most instances. It is obvious that no such obligation rests upon the receiver, and he may destroy or keep at pleasure." The same principle is applicable to the letters sent from the plaintiff's attorneys to the defendants. As the defendants were the receivers of these letters, they were the property of the defendants.

The carbon copies of the defendants' letters to the collector of internal revenue did not belong to the plaintiff. Whatever right it may have to examine these copies, or take copies of them, which point we are not called upon to decide, the defendants' copies did not belong to the plaintiff; they were owned by the defendants. The fact that the copies of these letters concern the plaintiff is not a sufficient reason for depriving the defendants of their property. In writing the letters the defendants were not the plaintiff's servants.

In group C there are copies of federal tax returns. These, as we understand from the record, were the defendants' office copies. The record shows that copies of all returns and schedules prepared by the defendants for the plaintiff were sent to the plaintiff. Even if the plaintiff has a right to require further copies, a question not involved in this suit, it has no right to demand of the defendants the surrender of these office copies. They were the property of the defendants.

The work sheets, as defined by the trial judge, were the defendants' property. They were made by them while engaged in their own business. The paper on which the computations were made belonged to them. They were not employed to make these sheets. The sheets were merely the means by which the work for which the defendants were employed might be accomplished. The title to the work sheets remained in the defendants after the computations were made. In the absence of an agreement that these sheets were to belong to the plaintiff, or were to be held for it, they were owned by the defendants. It may be that these papers contained information confidential in its nature and of importance to the plaintiff; but the defendants did not receive this information as the plaintiff's servants. It has been held that plans prepared by an architect employed for that purpose belong to the one for whom they are made. *Walsh* v. *St. Louis Exposition & Music Hall Association,* 101 Mo. 534, 535, 14 S. W. 722; *Gibbon* v. *Pease* [1905], 1 K. B. 810. See *Kutts* v. *Pelby,* 20 Pick. 65, 66. But it has never been decided so far as we know that the preliminary plans and sketches of an architect belong to the person by whom the architect is employed, see in this connection *Rutan*

v. *Coolidge,* 241 Mass. 584, 136 N. E. 257; nor has it been held so far as we are aware that the preliminary sketches and drawings of an artist employed to paint a portrait belong to the sitter; or that memoranda made by a physician of his examination of a patient, or the notes and records of a lawyer, his preliminary drafts of legal documents or his minutes of testimony, belong respectively to the patient or client. See *Anonymous Case,* 31 Me. 590; *In re Wheatcroft,* 6 Ch. Div. 97. As to property rights in a negative where a photograph is taken for pay in the usual course, see *Boucas* v. *Cooke* [1903], 2 K. B. 227, 238; *Pollard* v. *Photographic Co.,* 40 Ch. Div. 345. The interest of the plaintiff in the information collected and copied by the defendants and the confidential nature of this information do not give title to the plaintiff of the defendants' working papers. They were made by the defendants solely for their own assistance in preparing the tax returns.

With reference to group F, the letters addressed to the defendants, copies of letters written by the defendants, copies of returns furnished to the plaintiff, and work sheets relating to the tax case, are the sole property of the defendants, and this true of the papers and reports collected by the defendants in the preparation of the tax case. The plaintiff is not jointly interested with the defendants in these documents. We do not understand that any of these reports, papers and returns were property of the plaintiff which had been placed in the defendants' custody by the plaintiff or merely delivered to the defendants. If there are any papers belonging to the plaintiff which were lent to the defendants, the plaintiff is entitled to them; but as we construe the record, the papers referred to in group F were gathered and collected by the defendants in the course of their business, and were not papers of the plaintiff placed by it in the defendants' possession.

On the record of the evidence disclosed in this case the defendants were under no legal obligation to surrender their working sheets or other papers to the plaintiff. The testimony of Leonard and Dillon does not prove that the defendants gave the plaintiff any right or title in them. It is apparent that at one time papers in the possession of the defendants, including their working papers, were turned over to the plaintiff, for which receipts were given by the plaintiff to the defendants. These papers were again returned to the defendants. The plaintiff contends that by this transaction the plaintiff's rights of property and possession of all these papers were settled. Dillon testified that these papers were merely lent to the plaintiff. An investigation of the letters and receipts, and an examination of the record, do not satisfy us that the defendants in placing these documents in the possession of the plaintiff intended to part with their title and property in them.

It follows that the papers in group A belong to the plaintiff. The other papers and documents belong to the defendants. A decree is to be entered for the plaintiff, directing that the plaintiff is the owner and entitled to immediate possession of the documents described in group A

Ordered accordingly.

Estate of WILLIAM H. DENNIS *

Surrogate's Court of New York County, 1936. 95 N. Y. LAW JOURNAL 827.

This was a proceeding for an accounting in which numerous objections

* This case is discussed at p. 56 *supra*.

by creditors were first disposed of. The Court then continued:

The executrix of the estate and the beneficiary named in clause FOURTH of deceased's will ask for a construction of it. Its text is:

FOURTH: I give and bequeath all of my office files and records to Amelia Dale, residing at 147 West 55 Street, Borough of Manhattan, New York, N. Y.

Deceased was an accountant by profession. In his office files no doubt are papers which represent work done by him for clients and such papers contain no doubt information given to deceased in confidence. In respect of such working papers and data of a confidential nature it is the duty and obligation of the executrix to return to the clients of deceased such copies of papers or other data as they furnish to deceased, or if that cannot be done to destroy such papers. The executrix should likewise destroy the work sheets of deceased relating to such confidential work. Before taking the irrevocable step of destruction of any record, the executrix must assure herself that there is no basis for claims against the estate which would require the preservation of the papers for the protection of the estate. In so far as the office files and records are non-confidential they will pass under this provision of the will. Though the accounting has shown that such items have no value they are nevertheless tangible things which are capable of manual delivery and so the executrix should make them available to the legatee so that the latter may take them at her own cost. If possession of them is not sought by the legatee within a reasonable time after notice that they are available, such articles may be destroyed by the executrix.

In re FRYE *

Supreme Court of Ohio, 1951. 155 Ohio St. 345, 98 N. E. 2d 798.

Syllabus by the Court

1. In the absence of a privilege created by constitution or statute not to disclose available information, a witness may not refuse to testify to pertinent facts in a judicial proceeding merely because such testimony comprehends a communication or report from himself as agent to his principal or as independent contractor to his employer, no matter how confidential may be the character of the communication itself or the relationship between the parties thereto.

2. A witness possessing knowledge of facts material to the vindication of the rights of another may be compelled by judicial process to appear and as to such facts give evidence or produce documents and papers within his possession and control in behalf of such other, notwithstanding the evidence thus coerced may involve the private papers of the witness.

3. A witness who is not a party to a legal proceeding has no right, upon the taking of his deposition in such proceeding, to refuse to answer any question upon the advice of his counsel merely because such counsel believes that the testimony sought is irrelevant, incompetent or immaterial.

4. Section 55 (f) (1), Title 26 U. S. C. A., a part of the Internal Revenue Act, which provides, among other things, that "it shall be unlawful * * * for any person to print or publish in any manner whatever not provided

---

* This case is discussed at p. 57 ff. *supra*.

by law any income return, or any part thereof or source of income, profits, losses, or expenditures appearing in any income return," does not inhibit the disclosure by a witness as evidence in a proper judicial inquiry of the operative financial data relating to the business of a taxpayer, even though such data comprehends the elemental facts and information from which his income tax return is necessarily made up.

In November 1948 Raymond J. Saile instituted an action against Meridian Plastics, Inc., hereinafter called Meridian, in the Common Pleas Court of Guernsey County, which action is still pending. Saile was a sales agent employed by the defendant. In the first cause of action set out in his petition he alleges that a certain amount of money is due him as commissions earned under a contract with Meridian to be computed on a percentage basis on all sales of merchandise made by Meridian to distributors established by him and on all sales made by him directly to retail outlets. In the second cause of action he alleges there is due him from Meridian on a *quantum meruit* basis a certain amount of money.

Saile in the prosecution of that action served a subpoena *duces tecum* on Marion A. Frye, a resident of Lorain county, a certified public accountant and auditor for Meridian, to appear before a notary public in Cuyahoga county for the purpose of giving testimony. She is not a party to that action.

The material part of the subpoena reads as follows: "Please bring with you all records or copies of records in your possession relating to the financial condition or operation of Meridian Plastics, Inc., from the date of its organization to the present day; including copies of all * * * tax returns, state or federal * * *."

Upon receiving notice of the taking of Frye's deposition and before it was taken, counsel for Meridian filed a motion for an injunction, as follows: "Now comes the defendant and moves the court that the plaintiff or his attorneys be enjoined from taking the deposition of Marian A. Frye which deposition is scheduled for hearing on the 16th day of December, 1948, at 10 a. m. * * *."

That motion was overruled, whereupon Meridian perfected an appeal to the Court of Appeals for Guernsey county, and that court, in January 1949, affirmed the judgment of the Common Pleas Court.

In a written opinion, that court, in part, said: "It would be impossible for this court in advance to know what questions would be asked or what answers might be given by said witness. We do not know whether they would be incompetent or irrelevant. This court cannot speculate on these matters, and in the final analysis the competency or relevancy of the testimony must be determined by the trial judge."

No appeal was taken from the judgment of the Court of Appeals, and the time for such appeal has expired.

On February 7, 1949, Saile, pursuant to the subpoena theretofore served, proceeded to take the deposition of Frye, he and Meridian each being represented by counsel. Frye was not represented generally by counsel. She testified, without objection, that she had been Meridian's auditor since its organization; and that she had present the papers called for by the subpoena and had her work sheets covering the account of Saile as to commissions owing to him from Meridian for the years 1946, 1947. She submitted them to be marked as exhibits in connection with her testimony. In all, 30 exhibits, consisting of examination reports on the books of the company, financial statements and commission statements, were identified by the witness.

The taking of the deposition was adjourned until February 14, 1949, for the purpose of having photostats made, when Frye appeared with her own counsel who objected to the introduction in evidence as a part of the deposition Frye's personal work sheets or photostatic replicas thereof.

On that date, on examination of Frye by her own counsel, she testified that she was not an officer or employee of Meridian, but did work for it as an independent contractor in the capacity of auditor; that she had no records which belonged to Meridian; that the records which she had previously identified were her own personal records; and that when she made up the tax returns for the company she gave it the originals and copies for its files and the company did the filing.

Counsel for Frye then stated that he refused to permit either the original work sheets or the photostatic copies to be made a part of the deposition. Upon Frye's refusal to surrender the exhibits which had previously been identified by her, she was placed under technical arrest and technically committed to jail by the sheriff of Cuyahoga county.

A petition for a writ of habeas corpus for the release of Frye was filed in the Common Pleas Court of Cuyahoga County. The issues were made up by the submission of an agreed statement of facts by counsel for Saile and Frye.

The stipulation covered a copy of the petition in the Saile action, a copy of a motion for injunction, the appeal proceedings in the Court of Appeals for Guernsey County, a copy of the opinion of the Court of Appeals, a copy of the journal entry of the Court of Appeals affirming the judgment of the Common Pleas Court, a copy of the transcript of the deposition, in which Frye substantiated the fact that plaintiff's exhibits 1 through 30 were her work sheets and copies of her reports made as auditor of Meridian, a copy of the articles of commitment of Frye by the notary public and a statement that the taking of the deposition, the subpoena of the witness, the attendance of the witness and the taking of her testimony were all in conformance to law.

Frye was discharged from custody by the Common Pleas Court of Cuyahoga County. Upon appeal to the Court of Appeals, the judgment of the Common Pleas Court was affirmed without opinion, one judge dissenting. The cause is now in this court by reason of the allowance of a motion to certify the record.

HART, Judge. The general rule is that a witness, especially when not a party to the controversy, may be required to testify upon any subject concerning which judicial inquiry is made and upon which he possesses specific personal information. To this general rule, there are certain well recognized exceptions. A witness may always claim as privileged that which tends to incriminate him. Article V, Amendments, U. S. Constitution, and Section 10, Article I, Constitution of Ohio.

Also, under Section 11494, General Code, a witness who stands in either of several relationships named in the statute shall not testify, with certain exceptions, because the subject matter under the statute is privileged. See, generally, In re *Martin, Jr.*, 141 Ohio St. 87, 47 N. E. 2d 388; In re *Hyde*, 149 Ohio St. 407, 79 N. E. 2d 224; In re *Keough*, 151 Ohio St. 307, 85 N. E. 2d 550; *Weis* v. *Weis*, 147 Ohio St. 416, 72 N. E. 2d 245, 169 A. L. R. 668.

Frye seeks to broaden the area of these privileges. In the first place, she claims that the papers and documents sought to be introduced in evidence through her are her own personal property—work sheets and memoranda made by her, not as an employee but as an independent contractor in her private and confidential employment as a public accountant, from the private books and papers of her employer made at large expense to the latter; and that she should not be required to disclose this confidential information and to part with her property for attachment to an official court document.

In support of her position she relies on the case of *Ipswich Mills* v. *Dillon,* 260 Mass. 453, 157 N. E. 604, 53 A. L. R. 792. In that case, a corporation, to gain possession of certain documents, brought a suit in equity against certified public accountants who had been theretofore employed by it to make annual audits, prepare tax returns and statements for banks and to conduct a federal tax case before the Bureau of Internal Revenue. It appeared that there had been no special agreement between the parties as to the ownership of the documents. All the papers involved which were in the possession of the accountants were voluntarily produced by them at the trial, were examined by all the parties and were submitted to the trial court as evidence in the case. The court held that the public accountants were not the agents or servants of the corporation but were independent contractors and as such owned and had a right to retain their work sheets and copies made by them of papers and documents of the corporation used in its business. In that case the papers were not under subpoena in the hands of the accountants to produce them in court. Doubtless they were subject to subpoena but this question was in no way before the court. The sole question determined was the ownership of the papers. Doubtless in a proper case a court will protect the owner of papers and documents so far as their custody is concerned by requiring the party calling for them for evidential purposes to make photostatic or other proper copies of the same so that the owner may retain the originals. Such an offer was made to Frye by the plaintiff in the instant case but the offer was rejected.

A further claim is made by Frye that the papers and documents sought to be introduced in evidence are not the best evidence and are therefore incompetent. The answer to this claim is that it is not the function of the witness to pass upon the relevancy or competency of evidence to be offered in any court action. That is the function of the trial court.

This question was decided by this court in In re *Martin, Jr., supra* [141 Ohio St. 87, 47 N. E. 2d 389], wherein this court held: "A witness who is not a party has no legal right upon the taking of his deposition to refuse to answer any question, upon the advice of his attorney, merely because the attorney believes that the testimony sought is irrelevant, incompetent or immaterial." See, also, In re *Hyde, supra.*

Furthermore, it is impossible, before the time of the trial of a case in which the deposition is taken, to determine what is the "best evidence," as such determination depends upon other circumstances surrounding the case appearing at the time of trial.

As a further reason for Frye's refusal to again produce documents to be attached to her deposition, notwithstanding she had already produced and identified them, and notwithstanding they had already been introduced in evidence, she claims that by so producing them she may incriminate herself and possibly subject herself to a federal criminal prosecution, and to a possible revocation of her license as a certified public accountant. She predicates her claim in this respect on the provisions of Section 55 (f) (1), Title 26, U. S. C. A., the pertinent parts of which are as follows: "It shall be unlawful * * * for any person to print or publish in any manner whatever not provided by law any income return, or any part thereof or source of income, profits, losses, or expenditures appearing in any income return * * *."

This claim is necessarily based upon the assumption that the documents sought to be produced through the witness are federal tax returns or copies of the same. The deposition itself does not support this assumption. No income tax returns or copies of tax returns were offered in evidence. She testified on this subject only that she had made up tentative tax returns and had sent them to Meridian for it to execute and forward to the proper revenue collector. The record does not show any violation or proposed violation of the statute.

Furthermore, there is no infraction of the statute involved in this proceeding. The latter part of the statute above quoted prohibits any person from printing or publishing *tax returns* or sources of income, profit, losses or expenditures *appearing in any income return*, in any manner "not provided by law." This statute does not and could not legally inhibit the disclosure, as evidence in a proper judicial inquiry or where required by law, of the operative financial data relating to the business of a taxpayer, even though such data comprehends the elemental facts and information from which his income tax return is necessarily made up. The law could never sanction such a sweeping prohibition of disclosure of the essential facts of the business world. It must be evident that the statute in question has no such purpose or intent.

This statute, penal in nature, must be strictly construed in favor of a witness called upon to testify concerning business transactions affecting a taxpayer. The court in the case of *United States* v. *Baltimore Post Co.*, D. C., 2 F.2d 761, 764, in construing this specific statute said: "To 'publish' is to make public; to make known to people in general. In the statute, it does not cover the private communication by one person to another. It is not synonymous with 'communicate,' as it may be in the law of libel or slander. Other provisions of the law make this clear."

Frye could not be guilty of any criminal intent and therefore is not amenable to the statute, under the circumstances here presented. She is called upon to make certain disclosures under the compulsion of court process. In so doing she is protected from criminal prosecution. 12 Ohio Jurisprudence, 69, Section 23.

Finally, assuming there was no self-incrimination involved, there has been a complete waiver of any privilege on the part of Frye, if she ever had one, from testifying in the Saile action. She has already testified freely and without objection to all phases of the subject matter disclosed by the books of Meridian relating to the issues involved in the Saile action. In connection with her testimony she has identified all the exhibits sought to be attached to her deposition. It is now too late to refuse to allow them to be made a part of her deposition in regular course, especially since Saile is willing to reimburse her for any expense in producing copies of the exhibits to be used in lieu of the originals. *Burke* v. *State*, 104 Ohio St. 220, 229, 135 N. E. 644; 42 Ohio Jurisprudence, 66, Section 52.

In the absence of a privilege created by constitution or statute not to disclose available information, a witness may not refuse to testify to pertinent facts in a judicial proceeding merely because such testimony comprehends a communication or report from himself as agent to his principal or as independent contractor to his employer, no matter how confidential may be the character of the communication itself or the relationship between the parties thereto. See *Robertson* v. *Com.,* 181 Va. 520, 25 S. E. 2d 352, 146 A. L. R. 966. And where one possesses knowledge of facts which are pertinent to a judicial inquiry, he may be required to testify or to produce papers and documents as to such facts.

In discussing this subject, 58 American Jurisprudence, 40, Section 32, states the rule as follows: "It is a general rule that a witness possessing knowledge of facts material to the vindication of the rights of another may be compelled by judicial process to appear and give evidence in behalf of that other party, notwithstanding the evidence thus coerced may uncover the witness's private business. This rule is also generally held applicable when the information sought is contained in books and papers. Accordingly, it has been held that it is no ground for the refusal of a witness to produce books and papers, when required by lawful authority, that they are private. The duty of witnesses to disclose the details of their private business for the benefit of third persons when required in the administration of justice, is one devolving on them as members of a civilized community." See *McMann* v. *Securities and Exchange Commission,* 2 Cir., 87 F.2d 377, 109 A. L. R. 1445.

Since a commissioner or notary public is not invested with the ultimate authority to pass upon the relevancy, competency or materiality of testimony taken before him on deposition, Ex parte *Bevan,* 126 Ohio St. 126, 184 N. E. 393, he may order the witness to answer any question, even though objection is made thereto, subject only to the exclusion of the testimony by the court when offered at the trial. A witness refuses to answer any question at the risk of commitment for contempt, even though an answer would infringe any personal privilege or right granted by the Constitution or statutes of the state. If committed for contempt, the witness is entitled in a habeas corpus proceeding to have the relevancy and competency of the matters inquired about in taking his deposition determined by the court. In re *Martin, Jr., supra.*

It must be recognized that this is cumbersome procedure with which to determine the rights and privileges of a witness whose deposition is being taken before a commissioner appointed by a court or before a notary public. In cases where the nature and subject matter of the testimony sought by deposition can be anticipated in advance of the taking of the deposition, a witness may protect himself from the enforced disclosure of a privileged or harmful subject matter by an appeal to a court of equity where equitable principles may be applied in determining the specific rights of a witness.

An attempt to follow this method of procedure was made in the Saile action, so far as the rights of Meridian were concerned, but the courts denied the remedy because the injunctive relief sought was either too broad or lacked merit, or both.

The judgment of the Court of Appeals is reversed and the cause is remanded to the Common Pleas Court for proceedings according to law, consistent with this opinion.

Judgment reversed.

SECTION 6

PRIVILEGED COMMUNICATIONS

In re FISHER *

District Court of the United States, S. D. New York, 1931. 51 F. 2d 424.

In Bankruptcy. In the matter of A. Edward Fisher, bankrupt. William Bernstein, being called to testify, refused to answer certain questions upon the basis of privilege arising from the attorney-client relationship with bankrupt.

KNOX, District Judge. It appears that the witness William Bernstein acted as bankrupt's accountant for a number of years, and, after his admission to the bar, also acted as bankrupt's attorney. Upon the basis of the privilege arising from the attorney-client relationship, he has refused to answer questions relating to bankrupt's books and to produce in evidence monthly account sheets made by accountants in his employ in course of auditing bankrupt's books.

There is no privilege with regard to communications made to accountants. The information given to the witness and to the accountants in his employ for the purpose of making financial statements and doing other work characteristically performed by accountants is not privileged, despite the fact that the witness may also have rendered legal advice on the basis of such data. See Matter of *Robinson,* 140 App. Div. 329, 125 N. Y. S. 193, where it was held that an attorney for a corporation, who was one of its directors, could not refuse to disclose information about corporate affairs by claiming his professional privilege.

Furthermore, the privilege accorded to an attorney is the privilege of the client and not of the attorney. *Baumann* v. *Steingester,* 213 N. Y. 328, 107 N. E. 578, Ann. Cas. 1916C, 1071. For this reason the attorney cannot claim privilege where the client has already disclosed the substance of the communication. *Baumann* v. *Steingester, supra.* Nor can he claim privilege where the communication was made with the understanding that it was to be imparted to third parties. *Rosseau* v. *Bleau,* 131 N. Y. 177, 30 N. E. 52, 27 Am. St. Rep. 578.

In the case at bar it appears that the bankrupt has already testified with respect to the matters contained in his books and records. And the income tax returns and financial statements drawn up from the communications made by bankrupt to the witness were obviously intended to be communicated to others.

For these reasons, the witness should be directed to testify with regard to the bankrupt's books and to produce in evidence the monthly work sheets made by the accountants.

---

* This case is discussed at p. 61 f. *supra.*

HIMMELFARB v. UNITED STATES *

Court of Appeals of the United States for the Ninth Circuit, 1949.
175 F. 2d 924, cert. denied, 338 U. S. 860.

STEPHENS, Circuit Judge. Sam Ormont and Phillip Himmelfarb were, on January 22, 1947, jointly charged by a federal grand jury with four counts under Section 145 (b) of the Internal Revenue Code, 26 U. S. C. A. § 145 (b). Count one charged that Ormont and Himmelfarb attempted to defeat and evade federal income tax owed by Ormont for the calendar year 1944 by filing a false tax return understating Ormont's net income and income tax for that year. Count two contained similar charges against both in connection with Himmelfarb's return for income and income tax for 1944. Counts three and four contained similar charges against Ormont as to his returns for the years 1942 and 1943. Individual returns were filed by Himmelfarb and Ormont at the proper times as to income received in the conduct of the Acme Meat Co. An information return was subsequently filed by them for "Miscellaneous Enterprises," asserted by them to be a joint venture, for the fiscal year beginning May 1, 1944, and ending April 30, 1945, in the sum of $71,388.84 with no deductions or other information stated and disclosing an equal division between them of income.

There is much in this opinion which applies to the cases of both defendants-appellants. There is considerable in the opinion which applies solely to either one or the other of the defendants-appellants. Generally speaking it will be obvious what portions appertain to either or both. Where it has seemed useful we have plainly stated the defendant-appellant concerned.

Motion for dismissal of the indictment was denied and a motion for a bill of particulars was denied in part and granted in part. Pleas of not guilty to each of the counts were entered. The court dismissed counts two, three and four as to Ormont and count one as to Himmelfarb. A jury trial was had, and Ormont was found guilty upon count one and Himmelfarb guilty on count two. Motions for acquittal and for a new trial were denied and each has separately appealed.

The evidence discloses that Sam Ormont owned and operated a wholesale meat business under the fictitious name of Acme Meat Co. in Vernon, California, and employed Phillip Himmelfarb who, prior to May 1, 1944, had been a government licensed meat wholesaler and packer. After this latter date the two operated the business in partnership until (at least) April 30, 1945. The books of the Acme Meat Co. were kept on a calendar year basis. Shortly before the filing of the joint return, heretofore mentioned, investigations were made concerning the income tax returns of both appellants for the years 1942 to 1944 inclusive. According to the evidence, income from sales of meat, made within ceiling prices under OPA, were reported on invoices and recorded in the company books and appellants' returns for 1944 were based on these figures. It is indicated that "bonus" or "overceiling" payments of additional cash sums paid by customers of Acme Meat Co. were received but not reported on the books nor were they reported for income tax purposes for the year 1944; as to all of which both appellants were well aware.

Further, there is testimony that income from certain sales was shown on

* This case is discussed at p. 62 *supra*.

invoices which were not transmitted to the appellants' bookkeeper and therefore were never entered nor included in the books from which the income returns were made. These unreported invoices or lists were kept in a desk drawer at the plant. There is also indication of some falsity in keeping of records which goes to the general intent of appellants to misrepresent their income.

Evidence is in the record of a partnership return declaring additional income of some $71,000.00, claimed to have come from the so-called "Miscellaneous Enterprises," bank records and bank documents pertaining to each appellant, records of business dealings, invoices, canceled checks, transcripts of portions of the records of the Acme Meat Co. and bond records.

There is testimony that Ormont made admissions to Internal Revenue Agents which were adverse to his interest and which were recorded at the time made in an affidavit signed by Ormont, and that Ormont later retrieved the affidavit by subterfuge and destroyed it. There is also testimony to the effect that the appellants operated a partnership and divided profits therefrom equally; that the $71,000.00 claimed to have come from "Miscellaneous Enterprises" came from so-called "bonuses" received in the Acme Meat Co. business and not recorded in the company's books. However, there is evidence that a private record thereof was kept by Ormont in a small memorandum book claimed to have been seen by government witness Bircher, Special Agent for the Bureau of Internal Revenue. He stated that he saw a page in the back of the book on which an amount a little in excess of $35,000.00 was itemized, something in excess of $11,000.00 being recorded as having been earned from secret and unrecorded charges or bonuses from May 1, 1944, to January 5, 1945, and the balance or some $23,000.00 being recorded as earned from such sources from January 5, 1945 to April 30, 1945.

* * * *

Objections are entered to any and all testimony offered by the government witness, William S. Malin, an accountant employed by appellants' attorney, Mr. Mirman, who acted for Mr. Ormont and Mr. Himmelfarb jointly. It is claimed that such testimony is within the rule of privilege and inadmissible. Testimony concerned a list of bonds and other exhibits and the mailing thereof. It is argued that communications between a client and his attorney and the latter's agents include all persons acting as such, and are privileged, citing Wigmore on Evidence, Vol. 8, 3rd Ed., p. 584. The record is not clear as to the source of the information recorded by Malin in the various exhibits offered through him by the Government. He testified that Mirman contacted him by telephone on May 21, 1945, requesting an appointment to discuss income tax matters of Mirman's clients, Ormont and Himmelfarb, that he first met Ormont on May 21, 1945, at his office in the company of Mirman, that there was another meeting on May 22, 1945, at Mirman's house, at which both Ormont and Himmelfarb were present. Certainly, not all of the data was supplied Malin at those meetings. We consider it unnecessary to determine whether the factual basis for the preparation of the written exhibits had its source in information, books, or documents, given or showed to Malin by either or both of the accused, or disclosed at the above meetings, or given by Ormont or Himmelfarb to Mirman who, out of the presence of either or both of the accused, informed or showed them to Malin. Privileged communications are not recognized as between a client and his accountant. Of course, communications from a client to his attorney are generally privileged. Assuming that Malin was Mirman's agent (it appears that Mirman engaged Malin) and that disclosures were made at the meetings to Mirman and overheard by Malin, were such communications privileged? Where the presence of a third person is indispensable in order for the communication to be made to the attorney, the policy of the privilege will protect the client, that is, his presence is required in order to "secure the client's subjective freedom of consultation." 8 Wigmore on Evidence (3rd Ed.), § 2311, p. 602. Malin's presence was not indispensable in the sense that the presence of an attorney's secretary may be. It was a convenience which, unfortunately for the accused, served to remove the privileged character of whatever communications were made. Of course, communications made by the client to such a third party in the presence of the attorney are not within the privilege. On the other hand, if the data was obtained through voluntary and indirect disclosures by the attorney of matters received in confidence from his clients, admission in evidence of what was disclosed would violate the privilege as much as would the attorney's voluntary disclosures on the stand. However, granting that such voluntary extrajudicial disclosures by the attorney are generally inadmissible, we feel that special circumstances may show that the client impliedly authorized the attorney to make disclosures to the third person. See 8 Wigmore on Evidence (3rd Ed.), § 2325, p. 628. If such authority is found, the problem is no different than where the communication is made to the attorney in the presence of a third person who is not indispensably necessary to the communication. Here, Ormont and Himmelfarb were aware of Malin's employment and even participated in one or more meetings with Malin and Mirman relative to their income taxes. Some of the exhibits offered indeed were signed by the accused at Malin's request. It is reasonable to conclude that whatever disclosures were made by Mirman to Malin were authorized by the accused.

* * * *

[Judgments affirmed.]

GARIEPY v. UNITED STATES *

Court of Appeals of the United States for the Sixth Circuit, 1951. 189 F. 2d 459.

[Gariepy was convicted in the District Court of attempting to defeat and evade income taxes by filing false and fraudulent returns, and he appealed. This opinion is by Circuit Judge SIMONS.]

* * * *

The accountant's testimony was not privileged. There is no evidence to show that the accountant, at the time he received and relayed the information to the investigators, was in the employ of counsel for the appellant, but even if so there is respectable authority that denies him the privilege status. *Himmelfarb* v. *United States,* 9 Cir., 175 F.2d 924; 8 Wigmore on Evidence, 3rd Ed. § 2325.

* * * *

[Judgment affirmed.]

*** This case is discussed at p. 63 *supra*.**

UNITED STATES v. STOEHR *

District Court of the United States, M. D. Pennsylvania, 1951. 100 F. Supp. 143, aff'd, 196 F.2d 276, cert. denied, 344 U. S. 826.

MURPHY, District Judge. Defendant, found guilty by verdict of a jury of three violations of § 145 (b), Internal Revenue Code, 26 U. S. C. A. § 145 (b), moves for a judgment of acquittal and in the alternative for a new trial. Defendant was charged with having wilfully and knowingly attempted to defeat and evade a large part of his income taxes due and owing to the United States of America for 1943, 1944 and 1945 by filing and causing to be filed a false and fraudulent income tax return for each year wherein he knowingly understated his net income and the amount of tax due thereon.

Defendant, as sole owner and proprietor, operated a retail household furnishing store at Scranton, Pennsylvania, under the name of Robert E. Stoehr, trading as Stoehr and Fister. Edith Passetti as bookkeeper was in charge of the books of original entry. August W. Tross, defendant's office manager, did all the posting, was in charge of the general ledger cards, and prepared defendant's financial statements. Donald C. Griffiths, a certified public accountant prepared defendant's income tax returns. He never made an audit of or examined defendant's book of account but relied solely on information prepared by Tross and submitted by defendant or at his direction.

* * * *

In each of the three years after the true net income for the year was ascertained, two sets of financial statements were prepared, one set true for the eyes of defendant and Tross only, the other set false to be submitted to Griffiths for preparation of defendant's income tax return. At defendant's request and direction and with his knowledge, in order to reduce apparent net income and the amount of income taxes defendant would have to pay, false entries were made whereby a portion of inventory was dropped, purchase and expenses overstated, sales understated. Likewise defendant's living expenses, the purchase of $110,000 in United States government bonds, and the payment of $32,847.57 personal life insurance premiums, were disguised on defendant's records—personal expenses charged as business expenses, life insurance premiums charged as furniture, carpet and drapery purchases. Bonds were not listed as an asset or as a reduction in capital account. None of the foregoing was shown on the statements furnished to Griffiths.

* * * *

March 15, 1946, defendant sold the business. In early 1947 Griffiths made repeated requests for a balance sheet and reconciliation of capital account in order to prepare defendant's income tax return for 1946. When the information was not forthcoming, a return was prepared without the basic information and filed with a certificate that no audit of defendant's books of account was made.

In order to get the facts involved, a meeting was arranged with defendant and Tross. After much insistence he finally learned from papers then submitted that the figures furnished him for 1944 were false. When he confronted the defendant with this fact and asked if the same was

* See footnote 101 *supra*.

true as to the other years, defendant broke down and admitted that the statements furnished Griffiths had been falsified to reduce defendant's income taxes; that while he did not know the amounts, he knew what it meant, felt very bad about it, and offered to pay Griffiths any price, any fee, if he would keep the matter quiet.

On the witness stand defendant admitted that he signed the returns, caused them to be filed and paid the tax stated to be due thereon; that the 1943 return was false; that in 1943 and 1945, sales and purchases were incorrectly stated; that they obviously varied from those shown in a private personal record prepared by Tross for defendant's eyes only and kept in his possession; that the three years in question he paid far less taxes than were due; that Peterson, his accountant, advised him that for the three years there were taxes owed and unpaid of $278,000.

He insisted that he never examined more than the front page of the return; never compared the figures thereon with those in his possession, or checked the calculations made. Despite his many years experience and his close attention to details of his business he testified that he was not aware of what profits he made. He stated—and all the evidence is to the same effect—that Griffiths was in no manner responsible for the variance between defendant's records and his returns. He denied making any requests or giving any directions to Tross to falsify his records on his behalf, insisted he never had any knowledge that such things were done.

As to the accuracy of his books and records he relied on Tross. As to the correctness and accuracy of his returns he relied on Tross and Griffiths.

When Griffiths was unable to obtain the facts in connection with defendant's returns, prepared and filed by him and attested as having been correct, he reported the matter to the Group Chief of the Internal Revenue Office at Scranton, Pennsylvania, on April 23, 1947, advising that the defendant and Tross had admitted to him that the information furnished to him to prepare defendant's returns was falsified, and that he no longer represented the defendant. An investigation was commenced immediately. Defendant was indicted March 1, 1950.

* * * *

Placed in their proper context, the lack of merit in defendant's complaints will be amply demonstrated. See *Gariepy* v. *United States,* 6 Cir., 1951, 189 F.2d 459, at page 464. Tross testified that without his working papers then in defendant's possession he could not state the amount of taxes defendant wanted to pay in 1943, 1944 and 1945, or identify restored items. Defense counsel handed the witness a large "batch of papers," apparently not in their regular order. See *United States* v. *Michener, supra,* 152 F.2d at page 885. Included were defendant's private copies, papers of Stoehr & Fister, of the three corporations and of defendant's business from 1939 to 1946. Upon the court's insistence they were marked and identified as defendant's Exhibits 3 to 23 inclusive. The witness, asked by defense counsel to examine and describe each paper, was in the act of doing so (see R. p. 290-291) when defense counsel inadvertently or otherwise prodded him with a "Go ahead." The witness asked not to be hurried; the court advised he would not be. The net result was that Tross testified that the papers contained the true and false income for each year but that the amount of taxes as such was never reduced to writing.

* * * *

We see no error (15F) in permitting defendant to be questioned and to state that he always thought Griffiths had a high reputation for integrity.

* * * *

There was obviously no attempt on defendant's part over the years to make a voluntary disclosure. Defense counsel sought to introduce evidence as to the Treasury Department's policy in regard thereto (R. pp. 1151, 1179, 1182, 1690); to cross examine Griffiths as to his knowledge thereof, and as to why, after he had been deceived by the defendant, he did not advise him as to such policy and afford him an opportunity to make a voluntary disclosure before he reported the matter to the Internal Revenue Department.[1] Did defendant already know the policy? Would he make a voluntary disclosure? Would he disclose that he had committed fraud? Would the Commissioner, notwithstanding, recommend prosecution? In the absence of a statute the right to immunity is only an equitable one. See *United States* v. *Levy, supra,* 153 F.2d at page 997, and see opinions of Attorneys General, Vol. 38 (1934-1937) p. 94; Mertens Op. Cit. *supra,* § 55.32, footnote 88. Defendant did not file an amended return or pay his taxes up to the time of trial. The answers to these questions are pure speculation; they presented collateral matters. See *Ferreria* v. *Wilson Borough,* 344 Pa. 567, 570-573, 26 A.2d 342. The answers thereto would not in our judgment in any way impeach the credibility of Griffiths, nor were the questions competent to show bias on his part. For these reasons they were excluded (5, 6) and we declined to include any reference thereto in our charge (14.49, 52).

[Defendant's motion for a new trial denied.]

Petition of BORDEN CO. *

District Court of the United States, N. D. Illinois, 1948. 75 F. Supp. 857.

BARNES, District Judge. The petition of The Borden Company to quash a subpoena *duces tecum* issued out of the office of the clerk of this court and commanding that company to produce before a grand jury of this court on December 12, 1947, certain contracts, agreements, reports, studies, memoranda, notes and other documents, came on to be heard and was heard on Tuesday, December 30, 1947.

* * * *

It is contended that the reports made by public accountants for The Borden Company, called for by the subpoena *duces tecum* in question, are privileged. Section 51, Chapter 110½, Illinois Revised Statutes 1947, provides:

"A public accountant shall not be required by any court to divulge information or evidence which has been obtained by him in his confidential capacity as a public accountant."

It is doubtful whether the privilege granted by this section to a public

---

[1] Himmelfarb v. United States, supra, 175 F.2d at page 939. "Privileged communications are not recognized as between a client and his accountant." And see United States v. Hiss, 2 Cir., 1950, 185 F.2d 822, at page 832.

* This case is discussed at p. 66 *supra*.

accountant extends to his written report after he has released it, but it is unnecessary for the court to decide whether the privilege created by the section does extend to the report after its release for the reason that Rule 26 of the Federal Rules of Criminal Procedure, 18 U. S. C. A. following section 687, provides:

"The admissibility of evidence and the competency and privileges of witnesses shall be governed, except when an act of Congress or these rules otherwise provide, by the principles of the common law as they may be interpreted by the courts of the United States in the light of reason and experience."

At common law the reports of public accountants are not privileged. No act of Congress and no one of the Federal Rules of Criminal Procedure provides otherwise. Accordingly, the court concludes that the reports of public accountants are not privileged.

* * * *

[Petition denied.]

FALSONE v. UNITED STATES *

Court of Appeals of the United States for the Fifth Circuit, 1953.
205 F.2d 734, cert. denied, 74 Sup. Ct. 103.

Rives, Circuit Judge. An Internal Revenue Agent, acting under authority of 26 U. S. C. A. 3614 (a),[1] served appellant, a certified public accountant, with summons to appear before him and testify in the matter of the tax liability of Salvatore Italiano and his wife, Maria, for the years 1947 to 1951, inclusive, and to bring with him the following books and papers:

"All books, papers, records or memoranda in your files relating to: (1) Individual income tax returns of Salvatore Italiano and Maria Italiano for the years 1940 to 1946, inclusive. (2) Corporation income tax returns of Anthony Distributors, Inc., for 1940 to 1951, inclusive."

In response to the summons, appellant appeared at the agent's office but refused to produce the books, papers, records and memoranda called for in the summons or to testify regarding said documents.

The United States then filed in the District Court a petition to enforce the summons under 26 U. S. C. A. 3633 (a).[2] Upon an *ex parte* hearing,

---

* This case is discussed at p. 66 *supra*.

1 "Sec. 3614. *Examination of books and witnesses*

"(a) *To determine liability of the taxpayer*. The Commissioner for the purpose of ascertaining the correctness of any return or for the purpose of making a return where none has been made, is authorized, by any officer or employee of the Bureau of Internal Revenue, including the field service, designated by him for that purpose, to examine any books, papers, records or memoranda bearing upon the matters required to be included in the return, and may require the attendance of the person rendering the return or of any officer or employee of such person, or the attendance of any other person having knowledge in the premises, and may take his testimony with reference to the matter required by law to be included in such return, with power to administer oaths to such person or persons." See 26 U. S. C. A. 3615 for Collector's similar authority to summon witnesses and require the production of books of account.

2 "Sec. 3633. *Jurisdiction of district courts*

"(a) *To enforce summons*. If any person is summoned under the internal revenue laws to appear, to testify, or to produce books, papers, or other data, the District Court the District Court entered an order directing the appellant to obey the summons and to retain all of said documents in his possession for compliance with the summons or such other disposition as the court might direct.

A motion to vacate that order and to quash the summons of the Internal Revenue Agent was filed by the appellant. After a hearing, the District Court denied that motion and ordered the appellant to appear before another special agent of the Bureau of Internal Revenue, to produce the documents requested, and to give testimony pursuant to the summons. From that order this appeal is prosecuted.

Although the appellee has not moved to dismiss the appeal, it is nevertheless incumbent upon this Court to ascertain whether the order of the District Court is final and appealable, and, hence, whether this Court has jurisdiction. The question is not without difficulty; it has apparently been answered in the affirmative by the Eighth Circuit [3] and by the Ninth Circuit,[4] while a closely related question, the summons having been issued by the Collector under 26 U. S. C. A. 3615, has been answered in the negative by the Seventh Circuit.[5] In a similar proceeding, an appeal from an order entered earlier than the reported opinion in *Torras* v. *Strandley,* (Dist. Ct. Ga.) 103 F. Supp. 737, the present writer has heretofore denied supersedeas, because he was then of the opinion that the order of the District Court was not final.

It is settled that an order of the District Court denying a motion to quash a subpoena *duces tecum* requiring one to appear with papers and testify before a grand jury is not a final and appealable decision. *Cobbledick* v. *United States,* 309 U. S. 323. The power granted to the Commissioner of Internal Revenue by 26 U. S. C. A. 3614 is inquisitorial in character and has been compared to the power vested in Federal grand juries. *Bolich* v. *Rubel* (2nd Cir), 67 F. 2d 894, 895; *Brownson* v. *United States* (8th Cir.), 32 F.2d 844, 848. An important difference, however, is that, while the reports of grand juries are made to the court, the results of tax investigations are reported to the Commissioner and it is for him to determine what action, if any, is required under the law in view of the facts revealed.

Judge Learned Hand has indicated that the distinction to be observed is between orders which are merely interlocutory steps in judicial proceedings and are not appealable and court orders ancillary to an administrative proceeding and final because they complete the court's action. *Capital Company* v. *Fox* (2nd. Cir.), 85 F.2d 97, 99. Professor Moore seems to follow the same distinction. Moore's Commentary on the United States Judicial Code (1949), pages 501, 502.[6] In *Cobbledick* v. *United States, supra,* at p. 330, the Supreme Court recognized the difference

of the United States for the district in which such person resides shall have jurisdiction by appropriate process to compel such attendance, testimony, or production of books, papers, or other data."

See 26 U. S. C. A. 3615 (e) for enforcement of Collector's summons.

3 Brownson v. United States (8th Cir.), 32 F.2d 844.

4 Martin v. Chandis Securities Co. (9th Cir.), 128 F.2d 731.

5 Jarecki v. Whetstone (7th Cir.), 192 F.2d 121.

6 That distinction might explain cases where the administrative agency was proceeding under other statutes, such as Oklahoma Press Publishing Co. v. Walling, 327 U.S. 186; Endicott Johnson Corp., et al., v. Perkins, 317 U.S. 501; N.L.R.B. v. Anchor Rome Mills (5th Cir.), 197 F.2d 447. Compare the enforcement of agency subpoenas under the Administrative Procedure Act, 5 U. S. C. A. 1005 (c).

between a proceeding "self-contained, so far as the judiciary is concerned" where the District Court's direction to testify "is the end of a proceeding begun against the witness" and controversies "arising out of court proceedings unrelated to any administrative agency."

In *First National Bank of Mobile* v. *United States,* 267, U. S. 576, the Supreme Court affirmed an order of the District Court [*United States* v. *First National Bank of Mobile* (Dist. Ct. Ala.), 295 Fed. 1942] requiring an employee of a bank to appear before an Internal Revenue Agent and to testify and produce books and records as to the transactions of one of the bank's depositors; and, as the Eighth Circuit has aptly commented, "The affirmance of the order necessarily involved a holding that the order was appealable." *Brownson* v. *United States, supra,* at p. 846. We hold, therefore, that the order in the present case was final and that this court has jurisdiction.

The pleadings which frame the issues for our decision consist of the petition to enforce the summons and the motion to vacate the *ex parte* order and to quash the summons. Attached to the petition was an affidavit of the agent stating that, in his official capacity at the direction of the Commissioner of Internal Revenue, he was investigating the tax returns of Salvatore Italiano and his wife, Maria, for the years 1947 through 1951 for alleged evasion of income tax; that his investigation had revealed that from the years 1942 through 1951 the taxpayers reported income of approximately $303,000.00, while their expenditures during that period had been in the approximate amount of $466,000.00; that it is necessary to make a determination of their income by means of the so-called net worth-expenditures method,[7] and in order to determine net worth as of January 1, 1947, it is necessary to reconstruct the financial history of the taxpayers in prior years; that the official records of the Bureau of Internal Revenue disclosed that at times during the period 1942 through 1951 Salvatore Italiano, as General Manager of Anthony Distributors, Inc., engaged in the purchase and sale of beverages over the O. P. A. Ceiling Prices to his personal benefit.

Appellant's sworn motion and affidavit denying the District Court's right to issue the order enforcing the summons is based essentially on the following facts and circumstances therein stated:

1. The appellant, Frank J. Falsone, is a certified public accountant of the State of Florida and enrolled to practice before the Treasury Department; and Salvatore Italiano, Maria Italiano and Anthony Distributors, Inc., are "clients" of his whom he represents in Federal tax matters.

2. That the books, papers, records and memoranda in appellant's files ordered produced by the District Court are of two classifications: (a) Those which are the personal and private books, papers, records and memoranda of his clients entrusted to him for the purpose of enabling him to prepare their tax returns; and the return of these has now been demanded by the clients. (b) Those which are the work papers and work products of the appellant based on information given to the appellant by his clients.

3. Concerning the information and documents for some of the years requested: (a) The statute of limitations has run. (b) The returns have

---

[7] See United States v. Johnson, 319 U.S. 503, 517; Kenney v. Commissioner (5th Cir.), 111 F.2d 374; Pollock v. United States, No. 14,126 (5th Cir.), M/s, Decided Feb. 27, 1953; Montgomery v. United States, No. 14,115 (5th Cir.), M/s, Decided April 17, 1953.

once been audited and fully examined by the Internal Revenue Bureau and the taxpayers have paid all taxes found to be due by said examinations and audits.

In considering appellant's contentions based on privilege, we make two preliminary assumptions in favor of the appellant: (1) That the conduct of investigations under this statute is subject to the same testimonial privileges as judicial proceedings.[8] (2) That since the "client" is not a party, the agent or accountant may claim the privilege in his behalf.[9]

The taxpayer is required to keep records, 26 U. S. C. A. 54 (a) and the Commissioner, for the purpose of ascertaining the correctness of any return, is authorized by any officer or employee of the Bureau to examine the taxpayer's books and records and to require the attendance of the person rendering the return and the taking of his testimony, 26 U. S. C. A. 3614. (Footnote 1, *supra.*) Statutes granting such authorities have been held constitutional as against the contentions that they provide for unreasonable searches and seizures and compel the taxpayer to be a witness against himself. Ann. 103 A. L. R. 523; 47 Am. Jur., Searches and Seizures, Sec. 62; 51 Am. Jur., Taxation, Sec. 671; see also *Bolich* v. *Rubel, supra; Shushan* v. *United States* (5th Cir.), 117 F. 2d. 110, 117; *Nicola* v. *United States* (3rd Cir.)., 72 F. 2d 780, 784; *Stillman* v. *United States* (9th Cir.) 177 F. 2d 607, 617; *cf. United States* v. *Murdock,* 284 U.S. 141; *Shapiro* v. *United States,* 335 U. S. 1, 32.

The books and papers of a taxpayer, even though received by an attorney for purposes of consultation, cannot be regarded as privileged communications. (Footnote 9, *supra.*) *Grant* v. *United States,* 227 U.S. 74, 79; 58 Am. Jur., Witnesses, Sec. 501. According to the last cited text, "The reason is obvious; the administration of justice could easily be defeated if a party and his counsel could, by transferring from the one to the other important papers required as evidence in a cause, thereby prevent the court from compelling the production of important papers on a trial." Or, as more succinctly stated, "If documents are not privileged while in the hands of a party, he does not make them privileged by merely handing them to his counsel." *Edison Electric Light Co.* v. *U. S. Electric Lighting Co.* (Cir. Ct., N. Y.), 44 Fed. 294, 297; 45 Id. 55. It seems clear, therefore, that, even if we should consider the relation between a taxpayer and his certified public accountant as confidential as that between client and attorney, the accountant would, nevertheless, be required to produce the books and records of the taxpayer.

---

[8] In McMann v. Securities & Exchange Commission (2nd Cir.), 87 F.2d 377, Judge Learned Hand said: "Therefore, although we assume, as we do, that the conduct of investigations under these statutes is subject to the same testimonial privileges as judicial proceedings, it will not serve McMann; he must erect a new privilege 'ad hoc.'"

[9] "Furthermore, the privilege not being the attorney's but the client's, the *attorney* is not justified (when the client is a party to the cause) in refusing to obey a ruling (though erroneous) against the privilege; the client is the one to protect himself by appellate proceedings . . ." 8 Wigmore on Evidence (3rd ed.), Sec. 2321, p. 626.

See also 58 Am. Jur., Witnesses, Secs. 519, 520, id. Secs. 48 and 49; Rogers v. United States, 340 U. S. 367, 370.

"It follows, then, that *when the client himself would be privileged* from production of the document, either as a party at common law, or as a third person claiming title, or as exempt from self-crimination, the attorney having possession of the document is not bound to produce; and such has invariably been the ruling. On the other hand, if the *client would be compellable* to produce, either by motion or by subpoena or by bill of discovery, then the attorney is equally compellable, if the document is in his custody, to produce under the appropriate procedure." 8 Wigmore on Evidence (3rd ed.), Sec. 2307, pp. 592-593.

The only other documents claimed to be in possession of the appellant and concerning which he might be required to testify are his work papers and notes. The terms of the subpoena are broad enough to require the production of such work papers and notes and, if it should appear to this court that the subpoena is too broadly drawn, it may be modified accordingly. *N. L. R. B.* v. *Anchor Rome Mills, Inc.* (5th Cir.), 197 F. 2d 447, 449; *Jackson Packing Co., et al.* v. *N. L. R. B.* (5th Cir.), Ms. No. 14,446, decided May 29, 1953. The motion avers:

"That the remaining books, papers, records and memoranda in the Respondent's files are work papers and work products of the Respondent based upon information given to Respondent by the above-named clients and as such are privileged communications and Respondent is not legally empowered or authorized to divulge such information."

Further, the terms of the subpoena are broad enough to authorize examination of the witness as to any matter, whether referred to in the books and memoranda or not, relevant to the tax liability of Salvator and Maria Italiano for the years 1947 to 1951, inclusive.

Appellant concedes, as he must, that at common law no privilege was attached to communications from "client" to accountant. If such a privilege exists, it can only arise from some Federal or state statute. Apellant's insistence is based upon both. He contends: (1) that the attorney-client privilege extends to certified public accountants who, like appellant, are enrolled before the Treasury Department; and (2) that the State of Florida, by specific statute, has made privileged all communications between certified public accountants and their clients.

Professor Wigmore has stated the conditions necessary to the establishment of a privilege,[10] and has further cautioned us as follows:

"For more than three centuries it has now been recognized as a fundamental maxim that the public (in the words sanctioned by Lord Hardwicke) has a right to every man's evidence. When we come to examine the various claims of exemption, we start with the primary assumption that there is a general duty to give what testimony one is capable of giving, and that any exemptions which may exist are distinctly exceptional being so many derogations from a positive general rule. . . .

". . . The investigation of truth and the enforcement of testimonial duty demand the restriction, not the expansion, of these privileges. They should be recognized only within the narrowest limits required by principle. Every step beyond these limits helps to provide, without any real

---

[10] "Looking back upon the principle of Privilege, as an exception to the general liability of every person to give testimony upon all facts inquired of in a court of justice, and keeping in view that preponderance of extrinsic policy which alone can justify the recognition of any such exception (ante, Secs. 2192, 2197), four fundamental conditions may be predicated as necessary to the establishment of a privilege against the disclosure of communications between persons standing in a given relation:

"(1) The communications must originate in a *confidence* that they will not be disclosed;

"(2) The element of *confidentiality must be essential* to the full and satisfactory maintenance of the relation between the parties;

"(3) The *relation* must be one which in the opinion of the community must be sedulously *fostered;* and

"(4) The *injury* that would inure to the relation by the disclosure of the communications must be *greater than the benefit* thereby gained for the correct disposal of litigation.

"These four conditions being present, a privilege should be recognized; and not otherwise." 8 Wigmore on Evidence (3rd ed.), Sec. 2285, p. 531.

necessity, an obstacle to the administration of justice." (8 Wigmore on Evidence (3rd ed.), Sec. 2192, pp. 64, 67.)

On the other hand, Professor Wigmore has suggested that logically the reasons justifying a privilege for communications between clients and their attorneys practicing before a court of justice apply also to communications between clients and their agents practicing before an administrative tribunal, if its regulations treat the persons who appear before it representing parties in interest as a licensed body having the responsibility of attorneys, and subject to professional discipline. (8 Wigmore on Evidence (3rd ed.), Sec. 2300 (a), pp. 583, 584.) He states, however, that judicial precedent in this field is scanty, and such rulings as he cites hold the relationship of client and agent not to be within the privilege.[11]

The Treasury Department has promulgated, pursuant to Section 3, Act of July 7, 1884, 23 Stat. 258,[12] certain rules and regulations governing recognition of attorneys and agents representing persons before the Treasury Department. This Circular 230 as revised December 9, 1951, known as Part 10 of Sub-Title A of Title 31 of the Code of Federal Regulations, governs the admission of attorneys and agents and the conduct of such attorneys and agents before the Bureau of Internal Revenue and for "disbarment" proceedings.[13]

---

[11] Professor Wigmore's footnote to the text that, "Naturally, judicial precedent in this field is scanty" reads:

"The only rulings discovered to date are the following: McKercher v. Vancouver-Iowa Shingle Co., [1929] 4 D. L. R. 231, Br. C. (a patent agent is not within the privilege); 1892, Brunger v. Smith, C. C. Mass., 49 Fed. 124 (patent interference proceeding; an agent practicing before the Commissioner of Patents was held not privileged to withhold information obtained from his client; the reasons offered in his argument are convincing, but the opinion is curt and gives no attention to the reasoning)." The decisions later than that footnote are likewise against the extention of the privilege. See United States v. United Shoe Machinery Corporation, 89 F. Supp. 357, 360; Kent Jewelry Corp., et al., v. Kiefer, 113 N. Y. S. 2nd 12, 18.

[12] The pertinent part of 23 Stat. 258 reads as follows:

"Provided, that the Secretary of the Treasury may prescribe rules and regulations governing the recognition of agents, attorneys, or other persons representing claimants before his Department, and may require of such person, agents and attorneys, before being recognized as representatives of claimants, that they shall show that they are of good character and in good repute, possessed of the necessary qualifications to enable them to render such claimants valuable service, and otherwise competent to advise and assist such claimants in the presentation of their cases. And such Secretary may after due notice and opportunity for hearing suspend, and disbar from further practice before his Department any such person, agent, or attorney shown to be incompetent, disreputable, or who refuses to comply with the said rules and regulations, or who shall with intent to defraud, in any manner willfully and knowingly deceive, mislead, or threaten any claimant or prospective claimant, by word, circular, letter, or by advertisement." This provision is brought forward as 5 U. S. C. A. 261.

[13] Part 10.2, Sec. (f), provides the following:

"An agent enrolled before the Treasury Department shall have the same rights, powers, and privileges and be subject to the same duties as an enrolled attorney: PROVIDED, That an enrolled agent shall not have the privilege of drafting or preparing any written instrument by which title to real or personal property may be conveyed or transferred for the purpose of affecting Federal taxes nor shall such enrolled agent advise a client as to the legal sufficiency of such an instrument or its legal effect upon the Federal taxes of such client; AND PROVIDED FURTHER, That nothing in these regulations in this part shall be construed as authorizing persons not members of the bar to practice law."

In Section 10.3 Title 1 Code of Federal Regulations qualifications for enrollment are set forth, and in part say:

"(a)(1) Persons of the following classes who are found, upon consideration of their

The rules and regulations of the Treasury Department grant to enrolled agents the same "rights, powers, and privileges . . . . as an enrolled attorney" in order to provide for the effective discharge of the duties of such agents. There is no provision that a client's communications to an enrolled agent are privileged, and after all, the privilege, if any, belongs to the client and not to the agent. (See Footnote 9, *supra.*) If, however, the rules and regulations could be construed as so providing, then, it seems to us that they would be in conflict with the statute, 26 U. S. C. A. 3614 (a), (Footnote 1, *supra*), and that the statute must prevail.

Section 473.15, Florida Statutes 1951 (F. S. A. Sec. 473.15 formerly St. 1927 c. 12290, Sec. 17, Comp. G. L. 1927 Sec. 3933) provides as follows:

"All communications between certified public accountants and public accountants and the person for whom such certified public accountant or public accountant shall have made any audit or other investigation in a professional capacity, and all information obtained by certified public accountants and public accountants in their professional capacity concerning the business and affairs of clients shall be deemed privileged communications in all of the courts of this state, and no such certified public accountant or public accountant shall be permitted to testify with respect to any of said matters, except with the consent in writing of such client or his legal representative."

Appellant insists that this is a civil case, and, as such, subject to the Federal Rules of Civil Procedure, citing Rules 1, 81 (a) (3); *McCrone* v. *United States,* 307 U. S. 61; and, further, that under those rules the competency and privilege of witnesses is governed by state laws. Rule 43 (a), 5 Moore's Federal Practice (2nd ed.), Secs. 43.06, 43.07, pp. 1330-1333. Both insistences might be conceded and it still would not follow that the privilege provided by the Florida statute would be applicable to appellant's testimony before the Internal Revenue agent under 26 U. S. C. A. 3614. Appellant has failed to observe the important distinction between the administrative proceeding under that section and the court action to enforce the summons under 26 U. S. C. A. 3633 (a). Rule 81 (a) (3) makes the Rules of Civil Procedure applicable to "proceedings to compel the giving of testimony or production of documents in accordance with a subpoena issued by an officer or agency of the United States. . . ." That means that the rules are applicable to the court action to enforce the summons under 26 U. S. C. A. 3633 (a). To contend that the proceeding itself before the Commissioner or the Internal Revenue agent is also a civil case subject to the Rules of Civil Procedure, and particularly to Rule 43 (a) as to the admissibility of evidence, would be going too far. For, speaking generally, the system of rules of evidence in force for trials by jury or even in courts of equity is not applicable, either by historical precedent, or by sound practical policy, to inquiries of fact determinable by ad-

---

applications, to possess the qualifications required by the regulations in this part may be admitted to practice before the Treasury Department as attorneys or agents respectively:

"(i) Attorneys at law who have been admitted to practice before the courts of any State or Territory, or the District of Columbia, and who are lawfully engaged in the active practice of their profession.

"(ii) Certified public accountants who have duly qualified to practice as certified public accountants in their own names, under the laws and regulations of any State or Territory, or the District of Columbia, and who are lawfully engaged in active practice as certified public accountants."

ministrative tribunals or officers.[14] That is generally true as to Federal administrative officials [1 Wigmore on Evidence (3rd ed.), Sec. 4c, p. 44] and is more specifically applicable to disputes arising between taxpayers and the Federal Government under the Internal Revenue Laws [1 Wigmore on Evidence (3rd ed.), Sec. 4c, sub-div. 14, pp. 58, *et seq.;* see also 26 U. S. C. A. 1111, Rule 31; Sec. 3614, Sec. 3632; *Whitlow* v. *Commissioner* (8th Cir.), 82 F. 2d 569, 571]. Clearly, in the part of Rule 81 (a) (3) quoted, *supra,* when construed in connection with Rule 43 (a), it was not intended to make so radical a change in administrative procedure as to require that such agencies be restricted by the rigid rules of evidence.[15]

We have heretofore noted that the power granted to the Commissioner by 26 U. S. C. A. 3614 is inquisitorial in character and is similar to the power vested in Federal grand juries. As said by the Eight Circuit in *Brownson* v. *United States, supra,* at p. 848, ". . . the statutes involved . . . should receive a like liberal construction in view of the like important ends sought by the Government." Or as stated in *United States* v. *Murdock,* 284 U. S. 141, 149, "Investigation for Federal purposes may not be prevented by matters depending upon state law." See also *Doll* v. *Commissioner* (8th Cir.), 149 F. 2d 239. Or in the language of this Court, "These statutes, enacted to effectuate a Constitutional power, are the supreme law of the land. If they are in conflict with state law, constitutional or statutory, the latter must yield." *Shambaugh* v. *Scofield* (5th Cir.), 132 F. 2d 345, 346.

The appellant next insists that Section 3631, Internal Revenue Code,[16] prohibits unnecessary investigations and is a limitation on the power of the Bureau and of the Commissioner and not merely a personal right available to the taxpayer, citing *Martin* v. *Chandis Securities Co., supra,* and *First National Bank of Mobile* v. *United States* (5th Cir.), 160 F. 2d 532, 535. That much might be conceded, but it does not appear that the investigation in aid of which this summons issued was unnecessary. True, the statute of limitations has run against the returns for some of the earlier years, but in order to determine tax liability under the net worth-expenditures method (see Footnote 7, *supra*), the Commissioner is required to establish a sound starting point and may well have to reconstruct the financial history of the taxpayers in prior years. It is not claimed that there has been any examination of the taxpayers' returns for the years 1949, 1950 and 1951.

We find no error in the record, and the judgment or order of the District Court is therefore affirmed.

---

14 Federal Trade Comm'n v. Cement Institute, 333 U. S. 683, 705, 706; Opp Cotton Mills v. Administrator, 312 U. S. 126, 155; Consolidated Edison Co. v. Labor Board, 305 U. S. 197, 229, 230; Interstate Commerce Comm'n v. Baird, 194 U. S. 25, 44; Southern Stevedoring Co. v. Voris (5th Cir.), 190 F.2d 275, 277; Woolley v. United States (9th Cir.), 97 F.2d 258, 262; 42 Am. Jur., Public Administrative Law, Sec. 129, p. 461; 1 Wigmore on Evidence 3rd ed.), Sec. 4a, p. 25.

15 In the Notes of the Advisory Committee on Rules as to 81(a)(3) appears the following: ". . . the provision allows full recognition of the fact that the rigid application of the rules in the proceedings themselves may conflict with the summary determination desired. . . ."

16 26 U. S. C. A. Sec. 3631, reads as follows:

"No taxpayer shall be subject to unnecessary examinations or investigations, and only one inspection of a taxpayer's books of account shall be made for each taxable year unless the taxpayer requests otherwise or unless the Commissioner, after investigation, notifies the taxpayer in writing that an additional inspection is necessary."

HOPKINS v. THE PEOPLE *

Supreme Court of Colorado, 1931. 89 Colo. 296, 1 P.2d 937.

[Defendant was convicted of embezzlement. On this appeal he contends, inter alia, that it was error to admit the testimony of a certified public accountant who had been employed by the county to examine the court records of the estate for which the defendant was administrator.]

* * * *

3. Complaint is made to the admission and refusal to admit certain evidence. One Lindsay, a certified public accountant, was called by the people to testify to certain facts learned by him in the examination of the record in the Miers Fisher estate in the county court. The county court record was long and very much involved, and the evidence of Lindsay assisted the jury materially in determining certain facts which the district attorney considered important and which the trial court held to be proper evidence. It affirmatively appears from this record that Lindsay was employed by the county or county court, and that he had no business or professional connection with defendant. The testimony of Lindsay was objected to by defendant because of the provisions of section 1, par. 6, page 644, chapter 185, Session Laws of Colorado 1929, which provides that a certified public accountant shall not, under certain circumstances without the consent of his client, be examined as a witness. The employment of Lindsay was not by defendant, and, in the absence of proof that defendant was Lindsay's client, the statute has no application whatever to the facts in this case.

* * * *

[Judgment affirmed.]

* This case is discussed at p. 68 *supra*.